THE BANKERS
OF PUTEOLI

Finance, Trade and Industry
in the Roman World

THE BANKERS OF PUTEOLI

Finance, Trade and Industry
in the Roman World

DAVID JONES

TEMPUS

For Sylvia

Front cover: A banker and his clerk reconcile their ledgers (*Original in National Museum, Belgra*de).

Frontispiece: An idealised *villa maritima* on the Bay of Naples (*Wall painting from the Stabiae, in the National Archaeological Museum, Naples*).

First published 2006

Tempus Publishing Limited
The Mill, Brimscombe Port,
Stroud, Gloucestershire, GL5 2QG
www.tempus-publishing.com

© David Jones, 2006

The right of David Jones to be identified as the Author of this work has been asserted in accordance with the Copyrights, Designs and Patents Act 1988.

All rights reserved. No part of this book may be reprinted or reproduced or utilised in any form or by any electronic, mechanical or other means, now known or hereafter invented, including photocopying and recording, or in any information storage or retrieval system, without the permission in writing from the Publishers.

British Library Cataloguing in Publication Data.
A catalogue record for this book is available from the British Library.

ISBN 0 7524 3594 9

Typesetting and origination by Tempus Publishing Limited
Printed in Great Britain

CONTENTS

List of Abbreviations		6
Preface		7
INTRODUCTION: THE MURECINE ARCHIVE		11
PART I: BANKING AND COMMERCE IN PUTEOLI		21
I	A Port and its People	23
II	The Bank of the Sulpicii	47
III	The Business of the Sulpicii	64
IV	Sales at Auction	79
V	Grain Dealers	92
VI	The Merchant, the Agent and the Shipper	103
VII	Well-to-do Women	118
VIII	Slaves	133
IX	Disputes	144
PART II: LOOKING BEYOND THE SULPICII		163
X	Financing Trade and Industry	165
XI	Maritime Finance	175
XII	Public Works	187
XIII	The Companies of Tax Collectors	203
XIV	The Family Firm	218
EPILOGUE		244
APPENDICES		247
I	Freeborn Persons in the Archive	247
II	Freedmen Formally Identified in the Archive	248
III	Puteoli's Other Bankers	249
IV	More Family Firms	249
V	Money and Credit	251
VI	Moving Cash	252
VII	Interest Rates	253
VIII	Elite Financiers	254
IX	Rome's Imports of Grain	255
X	Horace Odes 1.4	255
Notes		257
Bibliography		274
Index		282

LIST OF ABBREVIATIONS

CIL	*Corpus Inscriptionum Latinarum*
D.	*Digesta Iustiniani*, revised trans. ed. Watson A. (1998)
Eph. Ep.	*Ephemeris Epigraphica*
FIRA	*Fontes Iuris Romani AnteIustiniani*, ed. Riccobono S. et al. (1940-43)
Gai. *Inst.*	Gaius, *Institutionum Commentarii Quattuor*, ed. and trans. Zulueta, F. de (1946).
IG	*Inscriptiones Graecae*
ILS	*Inscriptiones Latinae Selectae*
NAM inv.	Inventory number, National Archaeological Museum, Naples
T.	Tablet from the archive of L. Caecilius Iucundus, CIL 4, Suppl. 1, ed. Zangemeister, K. (1898)
Tab. Vindol. 2	Tablet from *The Vindolanda Writing Tablets (Tabulae Vindolandenses II)*, edd. Bowman A. and Thomas J., (1994)
TPSulp.	Tablet from the Murecine archive of the Sulpicii, *Tabulae Pompeianae Sulpiciorum*, ed. Camodeca, G. (1999)

PREFACE

In 1999 the Italian scholar Giuseppe Camodeca published *Tabulae Pompeianae Sulpiciorum*, the Latin text and critical edition of an archive belonging to the Sulpicii, a group of Roman bankers who carried on their business at the port of Puteoli (the modern Pozzuoli), some eight miles west of Naples (*1*).

The archive was first discovered in 1959, in a Roman building in the Agro Murecine just outside the ancient city of Pompeii, during the construction of the *autostrada* between Pompeii and Salerno.

The first part of this book consists of an exploration of the Murecine archive, which contains over a hundred wax writing tablets concerned with commercial life in the early Roman Empire. We enter the forum at Puteoli, where we see people buying and selling goods at auction, lending and borrowing money and appearing before magistrates in legal disputes. We meet grain dealers, merchants, shippers and their agents, well-to-do women and foreigners resident in the port. And of course we meet the bankers themselves, in particular Gaius Sulpicius Faustus and Gaius Sulpicius Cinnamus. Faustus and Cinnamus, like most of the people with whom they did business, were freedmen, that is to say, ex-slaves.

The Sulpicii, it emerges, provided working capital for small business enterprises and bridging finance for private individuals. This was a local bank, typical no doubt of similar enterprises in other Italian towns.

A conundrum remains. The late Republic and early Empire saw a surge in production and trading activity, fuelled by the spoils of imperial conquest. During this period wealth was poured into mines, quarries and timber yards, into public and private building projects, into shipbuilding and ships, into pottery, textile and metal manufacture and into overseas commerce. Yet the ancient sources frequently indicate that the landowning elite (senators, equestrians and municipal notables), who held the major share of Rome's wealth, shunned any investment in commerce. The conundrum is this: if neither bankers nor the landed gentry invested in trade and industry, how was all this activity financed?

In the second part of this book I attempt to answer this conundrum. I go beyond the Sulpicii and look at the financing of three major sectors of the Roman economy – large-scale shipping ventures, public works projects and partnerships set up to collect the state's taxes. I also investigate commercial and industrial enterprises that lasted for more than one generation, the 'family firms' of the Roman world. My intention is to see if the conundrum proves to be nothing more than a smokescreen created by the Roman elite themselves, behind which men of power and prestige pursued extensive business interests.

It will be obvious that I do not subscribe to the view that pre-modern economies were 'primitive', and so cannot be legitimately discussed in terms that we commonly use today.[1] The Roman state developed a body of law during the expansionary years of the late Republic that enabled businessmen to enter into contracts which were legally enforceable. These rules were firmly based in the realities of Roman life: they were created by the Roman elite and accommodated the wish of the elite to engage, directly or through agents, in trade for profit. Documents in the Murecine archive cover a wide range of commercial transactions which are governed by contract law; these transactions – buying and selling, lending and borrowing, leasing and hiring – are not specifically 'modern'; they are the means by which people in many societies in many periods have found it effective to conduct their business dealings.

SOURCES

No manuals on finance – accounting, banking or commerce - have survived from the Roman world, and it is doubtful whether any were written. This is in sharp distinction to the survival of treatises dealing with agriculture and farm management, architecture and land surveying. If finance is to be a subject for serious discussion, Cicero said, it is best left to the professionals:[2]

> ...concerning the acquisition and placing of money and its use, certain excellent fellows, whose place of business is near the temple of Janus, converse more eloquently than any philosophers of any school.

In those instances when ancient writers are concerned with commercial matters the discussion usually revolves around issues of morality or status. For example, in a celebrated passage in the *De Officiis*, Cicero asserts that small-scale trade is vulgar and likely to involve the trader in temptations and lies.[3] Similarly Livy commented on the *lex Claudia* of 219-218 BC (which restricted the trading activities of senators and their sons), 'every form of profit-seeking was thought unsuitable for senators' (*quaestus omnis patribus indecorus visus*).[4]

While investment in property or in moneylending is discussed in the correspondence of Cicero, Seneca and Pliny, trade and manufacturing are rarely mentioned in the literary record. For the financing and organisation of Roman commerce we need to turn to the legal, epigraphic and archaeological sources. *The Institutes of Gaius*, dating from the mid-second century AD, provides an elementary introduction to Roman law and procedure. Issues arising in connection with legal contracts are covered in considerable detail in *The Digest of Justinian*, a major source of information on Roman law: contracts of partnership (*societas*), loan (*mutuum*), lease/hire (*locatio conductio*) and purchase/sale (*emptio venditio*) are of particular relevance. It is impossible, however, to use the legal sources to judge the frequency with which a particular business procedure was followed.[5] Summaries of legal questions and disputes reveal issues that interested jurists – but they do not tell us how significant these issues were in everyday life. Nor is it always easy to judge whether a particular case is real or imaginary. Nevertheless I have assumed as a guiding principle that cases described in the Digest provide basic information about Roman business practice.

Such documentary evidence as there is for Roman commerce is haphazard and fragmentary: there are no Roman business statistics and no sets of company records. What we do have from Roman Italy are a few collections of writing tablets, in particular an archive from Pompeii (see Chapter 4), which contains receipts for payments made by the financier Lucius Caecilius Jucundus, and, since 1999, a definitive version of the archive of the Sulpicii. The papyrus record from Graeco-Roman Egypt is a vast and potentially rich source which lies beyond the scope of this book; I have, however, drawn on this material for a few examples which bear directly on my discussion.[6]

The epigraphic record is revealing in that it includes publicly-displayed contracts and regulations, while funerary monuments can provide the names and the status of people who produced and traded goods and commodities. Furthermore it can be rewarding to trace the activities of individual manufacturing and trading enterprises in the archaeological record. For instance, through analysis of stamps on finished products and on finds of moulds and rejects near kiln sites, it is possible to make reasonable inferences about how pottery businesses were organised and how widely the products of particular manufacturers were distributed. But a note of warning is required. Because of their indestructibility, clay artefacts provide the principal evidence for the existence of individual business enterprises. This presents a distorted picture of the Roman economy: the largest part of the non-agricultural workforce may well have been employed in the textile industry, of which relatively few traces have survived.

ACKNOWLEDGEMENTS

The texts and commentary in *Tabulae Pompeianae Sulpiciorum* provide an unrivalled source of information about Roman ways of doing business and have been the essential foundation for my study of the Bank of the Sulpicii and its customers. I am also grateful to Professor Camodeca for allowing me to reproduce illustrations of several tablets from the archive.

The diagram of a diptych writing tablet in the Introduction is reproduced by permission of the Roman Society. The photograph of the letter from Octavius to Candidus in Chapter 10 was taken by Alison Rutherford and is reproduced by permission of the Vindolanda Trust. The wall paintings from Pompeii and the bust of L. Caecilius Felix are reproduced by permission of the National Archaeological Museum in Naples. The drawings of Roman sculptured reliefs, wall paintings and buildings, the reconstruction drawing of the harbour at Puteoli and the map of The Bay of Naples are all by Merida Woodford, as is the rendering of the engraved scene on the late Roman flask from Puteoli. Merida Woodford holds the copyright to these drawings and asserts her moral rights as illustrator.

I owe a debt of gratitude to many people. Tony Birley, Dominic Rathbone, Jeremy Paterson, Philip Perkins, Paul Davies and Jenny Morris have all encouraged me to develop my interest in Roman finance and commerce. I have also benefited from guidance on specialist topics – from Ulrike Gall (auctions), Charlotte Luckhurst (legal procedure), Gordon Newman (IT support), Dinah Prentice (textiles), Martin Stather (translation of German material), Gregory Stevens Cox (pre-modern shipping) and Peter Tagart (present-day freight business). Peter Kemmis Betty, Fran Gannon, Tom Sunley and Laura Perehinec at Tempus Publishing have provided invaluable support. To all, my thanks.

Italic figures in brackets within the text refer to illustrations.

INTRODUCTION: THE MURECINE ARCHIVE

The archive of the Sulpicii, bankers of Puteoli, was discovered at Pompeii, in the Agro Murecine, 500 yards to the south of the Stabiae Gate of the city. The building in which the cache of documents was housed has been variously described as a private villa, the offices of a commercial company or a trade guild or even as an inn.[1] Decipherable dates are preserved in 78 out of the 127 documents; the bulk of the dated documents, however, come from the years AD 35-55.[2] Where legible, the place of writing is Puteoli – except for two documents written at Capua and one at Volturnum.[3] Just over 200 people, bearing some 100 'family' names (*nomina gentilicia*), are attested.[4]

TABLETS

The documents that make up the archive are written on wooden tablets. The Romans applied the term tablets (*tabulae*) to any flat substance used for writing. Official notices might be inscribed on large tablets of stone or metal, for public display; but in Italy and the western provinces, commercial and legal documents, ledgers, and private correspondence were commonly written on tablets of wood that could be easily handled. Another term given to the smaller-sized tablets is *pugillares*, (thought to be derived from *pugillus*, literally a 'fistful').[5]

Two references to a senatorial decree of Nero's time, which appears to give statutory authority to what was already current practice, indicate the form that a commercial or legal document was required to take:[6]

> A measure was brought in against forgery. Every signed tablet was to be perforated in three places with a cord (*linum*) passed through the holes (*foramina*)....

> The senate decreed that those tablets which contain the written record of a public or a private contract should, when witnesses have been summoned, be sealed as follows: when perforated at the edge of the margin at the middle part they should be bound together with a threefold thread, and seals of wax should be set on the thread, so that

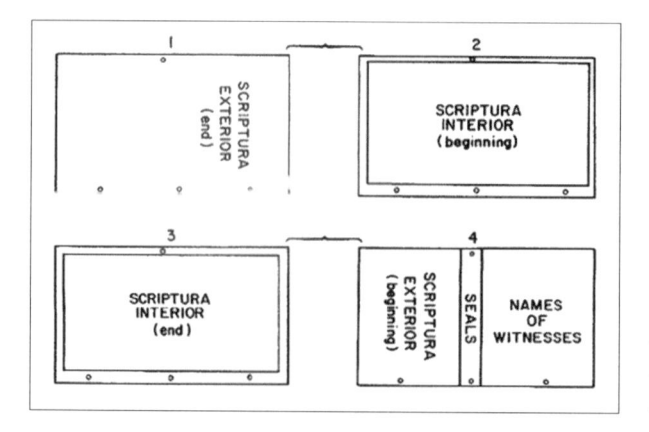

This diagram indicates the form of a typical diptych.

the interior text (*scriptura interior*) should preserve the integrity (*fides*) of the writing by means of the exterior text (*scriptura exterior*). Tablets produced in any other way shall not be considered to have legal effect.

The documents in the archive conform broadly to these rules. Each document consists of a set of wooden tablets joined together by threads passed through holes in the edges and acting as hinges. A set of two tablets attached to each other is known as a diptych (i.e. 'two-folded', from the Greek *diptychos*), and similarly three tablets folded together form a triptych. A diptych produces a document of four pages and a triptych six pages. The largest group of documents in the archive, 60 out of 127, are in the form of triptychs. A second group of 28 documents (and possibly another six) are in the form of diptychs. The format of the remaining documents has not yet been determined.

The procedure for producing a legal or commercial document was as follows. On the pages where the substantive text (as opposed to its title and witness signatures) was to appear, the wood would be hollowed out in the centre and filled with wax. A metal pen (*stilus* or *graphium*), tapering to a point at one end and flattened to form an eraser at the other, would be used to write in the wax; texts that have survived are usually preserved in the form of scratch marks in the underlying wood where the stylus has penetrated the original (and long-vanished) layer of wax.[7] On pages where there was no embedded wax, any required text would be written on the wood in ink (*atramentum*).

In diptychs, the *scriptura interior*, the substantive text, was incised in wax on pages 2 and 3. The *scriptura exterior*, the public copy, was written crossways in ink on the left part of page 4, to continue if necessary on page 1. The right-hand part of page 4 was reserved for the names of the witnesses (*signatores*); these were recorded in the genitive case, written in ink and positioned alongside their seals which occupied a central column running down the page.

The *scriptura interior* of triptychs was also inscribed in wax on pages 2 and 3; in triptychs, however, the *scriptura exterior* was inscribed on page 5. Again the names of the witnesses were written in ink on page 4 and aligned with their respective wax seals. But in triptychs the seals were housed in a groove (*sulcus*); this allowed the tablet containing pages 3 and 4 to fit snugly against the third tablet containing pages 5 and 6.

Both types of tablet might carry a brief note of the contents (*index*). This might be written in ink on an external page or even incised in the wood. The index could be used for quick identification once the tablets had been filed in an archive.

When the document had been written and signed, the tablets were bound together by a cord going through the holes in their edges; this cord was then tied round them and its ends were secured by the seals of the witnesses. The document now contained two texts: one was sealed up so as to prevent any alteration, while the other was left open, so that it might be read by any interested party.

I should make it clear that the so-called 'stylus tablets' described above are very different from the late first-century 'leaf tablets' discovered at the Roman fort of Vindolanda, a mile or so south of Hadrian's Wall.[7] Some stylus tablets have been found at Vindolanda, but the great majority of documents from this site are of postcard size, written with pen and ink on thin sheets of smooth, fine-grained wood. In the northern provinces of the Roman empire leaf tablets were presumably cheaper than papyrus, which would have to be imported from Egypt, or stylus tablets, which required a more complex manufacturing process.[8]

Dating

Documents in the Murecine archive were dated in the standard Roman way. The year was indicated by the names of the consuls (in the ablative case). Under the Republic the consulship had been held from 1 January to 31 December; from 5 BC, however, Augustus doubled the number of consuls each year by replacing the traditional pair of 'ordinary' consuls (who continued to open the year) with two 'suffects' on 1 July. The number of suffects later came to be increased and the terms of holders of both types of consulships became proportionately shorter.

Within each of the twelve months of the calendar year introduced by Julius Caesar, three fixed points were recognised: the Kalends (1st of the month), Nones (5th of the month but 7th in March, May, July and October) and Ides (eight days after the Nones and thus either the 13th or the 15th of the month). In a leap year the date 24 February was repeated. Days were counted retrospectively (and inclusively) from these fixed points.

How this system was used in practice can be seen in TPSulp. 45. On page 2, in the *scriptura interior*, the date is given as follows:

C Caesare Germanico Augusto
Ti Claudio Nerone Germanico cos
VI non Iulias.

The first piece of dating information given by this tablet is that the consuls for this part of the year in question were the emperor Gaius ('Caligula') and the future emperor Claudius. This dates the tablet to AD 37. Secondly, the tablet tells us that the day of the transaction was the sixth day before the Nones of July. In July the Nones fell on the 7th. Counting back from the Nones, inclusively (i.e. the Nones was the first day to be counted), the sixth day was the 2 July. The tablet can thus be precisely dated to 2 July AD 37.

(A brief note on nomenclature: 'C' was used by the Romans in written texts as the standard abbreviation for the name Gaius and likewise 'Cn' for Gnaeus. In English versions of Latin texts I use Gaius and Gnaeus.)[9]

CONTRACTS

The Romans made a distinction between the actual transaction or contract, which was concluded verbally, and the written document in which the act was recorded. The jurist Gaius makes the point succinctly:[10]

> An agreement for a mortgage not in writing, if proved, will be effective. The point of writing is to prove the transaction more easily, but the transaction, if proved, is valid without it, like an undocumented marriage.

From the late Republic onwards, however, Romans made frequent use of written documents to record financial and commercial transactions, since with the expansion of commerce it became increasingly convenient to have a documentary record of what had been agreed verbally between contracting parties.

The greater number of the documents in the archive, some 80 in all, were drawn up in the objective, third person form – for example, 'he said that he had received (*dixit se accepisse*)'; these documents were known as testimonies (*testationes*) and seem to have depended for their validity on the form of words that was used. The formula of the *testatio* is used in certain procedural documents: promises to appear in court (*vadimonia*), questions put in a preliminary court hearing (*interrogationes in iure*), agreements to submit to arbitration (*compromissa*), fixing a date (*intertium*) for the full trial, and testifying on oath (*iusiurandum*). In business dealings the *testatio* is used for the loan documents known as *nomina arcaria* and for various formalities connected with sale at auction.

Just over 40 documents employ the formula of the hand-written 'chirograph'. This means that they were drawn up in the subjective, first person form – for example, 'I have written that I have received (*scripsi me accepisse*)'. Chirographs are used in certain procedural agreements such as the settling of a dispute (*finiendae controversiae*) and the appointment of a judge (*de iudice addicendo*). In commercial documents chirographs are used to record loans (*mutua*), receipts (*apochae*), contracts of hire (*locationes*) and contracts of mandate (*mandata*).

Contracts that could be recorded in the form of chirographs were devised as Roman traders followed the legions throughout the Mediterranean; fresh business opportunities were constantly arising and it was frequently necessary to enter into agreements with new, previously unknown counterparties. Such contracts could be concluded between a wide range of people – man, woman, slave or free, citizen or resident alien (*peregrinus*). The new contracts did not depend for their validity on specific formulae but were concluded and became binding upon the parties by agreement and through good faith (*bona fides*). Over the years praetors – the state's chief law officers – introduced through their annual 'edicts' legal remedies for aggrieved parties who had entered into good faith contracts. (The Praetor's Edict was the formal source of much private law.)[11]

The term *fides* is a portmanteau word which may be conveniently translated as trust between two parties to a relationship. The term implied privileges and responsibilities on both sides. It might be used in both public and private life – in relations between nations, between master and slave, patron and ex-slave, patron and freeborn client, friend and friend, and, in the present context, in relations between business counterparties.

Cicero explores the concept of good faith in his treatise *On Duties*:[12]

> For how weighty are the words, 'That I be not deceived and defrauded through you and my confidence in you (*propter te fidemve tuam*)'. How precious are these [words], 'As between honest people there ought to be honest dealing and no deception'! But who are 'honest people', and what is 'honest dealing' – these are serious questions. It was Quintus Scaevola, the *pontifex maximus*, who used to attach the greatest importance to all questions of arbitration to which the formula 'as good faith requires' was appended; and he held that the expression 'good faith' had a very extensive application, for it was employed in trusteeships and partnerships, in trusts and commissions, in buying and selling, in hiring and letting – in a word, in all the transactions on which the social relations of daily life depend; in these he said, it required a judge of great ability to decide the extent of each individual's obligation to the other, especially when counter-claims were admissible in most cases.

Stipulations

In some chirographs there is a reference to a stipulation (*stipulatio*) that has been made between the two parties. The stipulation was the oldest form of Roman contract: it consisted of formal question and answer which had to form one continuous transaction and correspond exactly, to remove all ambiguity. The jurist Gaius gives examples for use in various circumstances. He begins with *sponsio*, the ancient form of promise which was reserved for Roman citizens; the other forms, belonging to the 'law of nations' (*ius gentium*), were valid between all men, Romans and non-Romans (*peregrini*) alike:[13]

> *1) Question:* Do you solemnly promise that you will convey [a sum of money on a certain date, a rate of interest, a specific item of merchandise or property]? (*Dari spondes?*).
> *Answer:* I solemnly promise that I will convey (*Spondeo*).

2) Question: Will you convey? (*Dabis?*).
Answer: I will convey (*Dabo*).

3) Question: Do you promise? (*Promittis?*).
Answer: I promise (*Promitto*).

4) Question: Do you promise on your honour? (*Fidepromittis?*).
Answer: I promise on my honour (*Fidepromitto*).

5) Question: Do you guarantee on your honour? (*Fideiubes?*).
Answer: I guarantee on my honour (*Fideiubeo*).

6) Question: Will you do? (*Facies?*).
Answer: I will do (*Faciam*).

Varro provides a down-to-earth example of a stipulation, which he describes as the ancient form of words (*antiqua formula*). Two farmers have reached agreement on the sale of a flock of sheep:[14]

> The purchaser: 'They are sold at such a price?'
> The seller: 'They are.'
>
> The money then changes hands.
>
> The purchaser: 'You guarantee that the sheep in question are perfectly sound, up to the standard of a flock which is perfectly sound, excepting those blind of one eye, deaf or with bellies bare of wool; that they do not come from a diseased flock and that title may legally pass – that all this may be properly done?' Even after all this has been agreed, the flock does not change hands unless the money has been counted....

Parties would enter into a stipulation to add precision to good faith contracts. For instance the contract for a loan of money (*mutuum*) covered the delivery of the money from the lender to the borrower but it made no provision for the date of repayment or for the rate of interest. These important details would be added by stipulation:[15]

> ...interest is not owed on money which is lent unless this is reduced to a stipulation.

We can see the sequence of events in a case cited by the jurist Paul:[16]

> Two men formed a partnership to teach grammar, and agreed that they would share between them any profit that they might make. They set down in a formal agreement of partnership the terms they wished to be observed, and then made a stipulation as

follows: 'Do you promise that the things written down above will be duly given and done, and that nothing will be done against the terms? Do you promise to give me [HS] 20,000 if the things so stipulated are not given and done?'

In this transaction the two principals first reached a *verbal* contract of partnership. They then set down *in writing* the general terms of their contract; and they added, through *verbal stipulation*, a condition fixing the penalty payable if either party broke the terms of the contract. The principals will very likely have added to their written contract of partnership a clause stating that stipulation on a penalty for breaking the contract had been made between them.

AUTHORS AND WITNESSES

Authors and witnesses did not sign documents with written signatures but used personal seals incorporated in signet rings. The Romans traced this practice back to remote antiquity: [17]

> The ancients (*veteres*) used to carry a ring with them, not for ornament but for the sake of sealing. For this reason it was not allowed to own more than one, nor for anyone to have one who was not a free man; the faith (*fides*) which is contained in a little seal (*signaculum*) is fitting only for [free] men. Therefore slaves used not to have the right to wear a ring (*ius anulorum*).

The importance of a man's signet ring is emphasised by Cicero in a letter to his brother Quintus: [18]

> Your signet ring should not be the instrument of another man's purposes, but the witness of your own (*non minister alienae voluntatis, sed testis tuae*).

The Roman practice of using seals was in contrast to that in other societies. The elder Pliny noted in the mid-first century: [19]

> The greater part of the races of mankind, and even of the people who live under our empire, possess no rings at all; the east and Egypt do not seal documents even now, but are content with only writing.

The seal of the person who has drawn up a chirograph would be placed on page 3, at the foot of the *scriptura interior*. TPSulp. 46 seems to carry the seals both of the slave who drew up the deed and of his illiterate master; in TPSulp. 78 three seals were considered necessary: one belonging to the borrower who wrote in Greek, one belonging to his surety who spoke in Latin but was illiterate, one belonging to the man who actually wrote the text on the surety's behalf.

Time-honoured procedures such as the conveyance of property (*mancipatio*) and making wills required the presence of witnesses to assert that the correct procedures had been observed. Witnessing was an ancient privilege: being deprived of the capacity to bear witness, or having your will witnessed, being declared *intestabilis*, was a recognised form of punishment.[20]

It was not strictly necessary, however, to have witnesses to validate the more informal 'good faith' contracts that were a feature of commercial life in the late Republic and early Empire. The reason that witnesses were asked to sign such documents seems to have been precautionary: in the event of disputes, they could be summoned to give verbal evidence to the effect that the transaction had actually taken place.

'Oral evidence is often and necessarily given and should be sought particularly from those who are reliable,' said the jurist Arcadius Charisius.[21] And what constituted reliability? Callistratus set out some criteria:[22]

> One must first enquire into their status. Are they decurions [i.e. members of the council of former magistrates] or plebeians? Do they lead an honest and blameless life, or has there been some mark of disgrace? Are they well-off or needy, so that they may readily act for gain? Are they enemies of those against whom they give evidence or friends of those for whom they give it? Evidence can be admitted if it is free from suspicion, because of the witness (an honest man) or the motive (not gain, favour or enmity).

It is doubtful whether these criteria were strictly followed. The elder Pliny commented, disapprovingly, that everyone in his day had signature rings, 'it is the custom of the common mob (*consuetudo volgi*)'.[23] Furthermore it is clear from the Murecine archive that all sorts of people in Roman Italy – free men and women, freed persons and slaves – did indeed possess signet rings and used them to seal documents as witnesses. Nevertheless the nuances of social hierarchy were preserved, since signatories to documents in the archive were usually ranked in order, with freedmen and slaves signing below free persons.[24]

Where traces of witness lists have survived, the highest number of signatories is eleven (TPSulp. 34) – in this transaction all the witnesses, except possibly the first man to sign, are freedmen.[25] The principal who draws up a chirograph usually, but not always, signs as a witness in the first and last position. Witnesses might be supplied by both parties to a financial transaction.[26]

It is not clear why particular people, other than the protagonists, were prepared to take part as witnesses in these proceedings – or indeed how they were chosen. Perhaps witnesses lived near to the house or office (*taberna*) where the Sulpicii conducted their business. In this case they may have considered attendance on such occasions to be part of their regular social round. Some witnesses will have been business associates of the Sulpicii or of the principals in a transaction (2).[27]

It is likely that sealed commercial documents – in contrast to wills and private letters – were rarely opened for inspection. The summary on the 'exterior' page was there to provide an account of what the document contained and with their seals the witnesses had deployed their *fides* to guarantee that this summary was an accurate reflection of the 'interior' page. It was no light thing to break the seals on a legal document: to commit such an act of intrusion would be to cast doubt on the *fides* of the witnesses. In Roman courts judges may well have been reluctant to permit a course of action that would question the very basis of everyday business practice.[28]

STATUS OF THE PARTICIPANTS

In formal documents a freeborn man or woman (*ingenuus/a*) would use 'filiation' – the inclusion in their name of their father's personal name (*praenomen*) in the genitive case followed by *filius/a* (usually abbreviated to *f*) – to indicate that they possessed freeborn status. Similarly a freedman or freedwoman (*libertus/a*) might include the *praenomen* of their former master in the genitive followed by *libertus* (usually abbreviated to *l*) to indicate their status as an ex-slave; when the former master was an emperor the *praenomen* would be replaced by a term in the genitive indicating the imperial title, such as *Augusti* or *Caesaris*.

I can find only six Roman citizens and five aliens (*peregrini/ae*) in the archive who indicate through filiation that they are freeborn (Appendix 1). Similarly very few freedmen provide a formal indication of their status (Appendix 2). This leaves open the status of the great majority of people in the archive, who bear the three names (*tria nomina*) of a Roman citizen but give no indication of their origin. A large number were undoubtedly freedmen who chose to conceal their servile origin by omitting the indicator of status from their names. This subterfuge was certainly adopted in epitaphs throughout the Roman world where the deceased bears the three names, but where neither the designation *f* nor the designation *l* appears – nevertheless mention of a former master (*patronus*), a fellow slave (*conservus*) or a fellow freedman (*collibertus*) will reveal that a particular epitaph does in fact belong to a freedman.[29] We may conclude with confidence that the majority of people in the archive, including the Sulpicii themselves, were ex-slaves. In first century Puteoli, it emerges, freedmen played a major role in everyday commercial life.

PART I

Banking and Commerce in Puteoli

I

A PORT AND ITS PEOPLE

In the summer of AD 14 the emperor Augustus visited his villa on the island of Capri. As the emperor's ship sailed past Puteoli news of his presence spread through the harbour:[1]

> The passengers (*vectores*) and crew of a recently arrived Alexandrian ship put on white robes and garlands, burned incense, wished him good fortune and praised him. They said that they owed their lives to him and their liberty to sail the seas; through him they enjoyed their freedom and their prosperity. This so pleased Augustus that he gave each member of his staff forty gold pieces, making them swear on oath to spend the coins only on Alexandrian goods (*merces Alexandrinae*).

The Alexandrian ship was most likely to have been a grain freighter; the 'passengers' will have been supercargoes (itinerant merchants travelling with their goods). Passengers and crew regarded Augustus as their benefactor because he had cleared the seas of pirates and ensured that Egyptian grain would reach Italy on a regular basis; trade could now flourish as never before between Alexandria and Puteoli, the principal port of entry for Rome.[2]

Puteoli could trace its history back to the late sixth century BC, when Greek settlers had founded the city of Dicaearchia on the promontory of Rione Terra. The promontory juts out into the Bay of Naples from a crescent of volcanic hills; the harbour below and to the west of the promontory proved to be valuable to the Romans in the wars against Hannibal. In 194 BC, the senate sent a colony of 300 settlers to the city.[3] The government in Rome kept a close eye on its affairs; in the first century BC the dictator Sulla settled a dispute between opposing factions in Puteoli and drafted fresh laws to regulate the colony's administration.[4] By the time of Augustus Puteoli was a major entrepôt and packet port for goods and passengers travelling between the Tyrrhenian coast of Italy and the ports of the eastern Mediterranean.

Puteoli was also a manufacturing centre serving the prosperous region of Campania. Most manufacture would have taken place in the houses of individual artisans, or in small workshops (*tabernae* or *officinae*) attached to shops where the products were sold.[5] Occasionally we catch glimpses of production on a larger scale, as in Diodorus Siculus' account of the manufacture of finished metal goods.[6]

> [Pieces of sponge iron smelted in Elba] are bought by traders in exchange [for money or goods] and are then shipped to Puteoli or the other trading stations, where there are people who purchase these cargoes. With the aid of a great number of metal workers, whom they have assembled, they then work the metal further and manufacture iron objects of every description. Some of these are worked into the shape of armour, and others are cleverly fabricated into shapes that are suitable for two-pronged forks and sickles and other tools; and these are then transported by traders to every region....

Glass manufacture also constituted a local industry of some importance; Vitruvius records that Vestorius, a local businessman, had introduced to Puteoli from Alexandria a method of manufacturing blue glass.[7] In the late Roman Empire glass flasks from Puteoli, engraved with local scenes, were produced for sale to tourists (3).[8]

A significant source of revenue for some local landowners will have been the extraction and sale of Puteolan cement (*pulvis Puteolana*), commonly known as Pozzolana. Produced from the local volcanic dust, this was an essential component of the concrete of Roman Italy:[9]

> There is also a kind of powder, which from natural causes produces amazing results. It is found in the neighbourhood of Baiae and in the country belonging to the towns about Mt Vesuvius. When mixed with lime and rubble, this substance lends strength to buildings, and when piers made of it are built in the sea they set hard under the water.

The city authorities of Puteoli put the local building material to good use:[10]

> The city has become a great trading port (*emporium*), since it has harbours that have been constructed by the hand of man – this has been made possible by the natural qualities of the sand...by mixing the sand-ash with the lime, they can extend jetties out into the sea and make the open shores curve into the form of bays, so that the largest merchant ships can moor there safely.

The majority of vessels operating from Puteoli were small, that is to say carrying no more than 15,000 *modii* which amounted to a burden of some 100 tons. (The *modius* was the standard Roman measure of volume for dry goods. As a rule of thumb I take 150 modii to be the equivalent of one ton.) These ships were captained by their owners, men like Lichas the sea captain in Petronius' novel, *Satyricon*.[11] Some shipowners would operate on a cabotage basis, tramping from port to port, buying and selling cargoes as they went. Others would travel on regular routes carrying cargoes of tools, pottery, glass, foodstuffs and Campanian wine.[12]

On the import side of the trading balance, before the annexation of Egypt brought with it a great increase in the grain trade, the principal commodity that passed through the port of Puteoli consisted of slaves. Even before the despatch of the first colonists, the Roman statesman Scipio Africanus had set up a customs post at the port to collect the sales tax on imported slaves (*portoria venalicium*).[13] By the mid-second century BC traders from Campania had established bases at the Aegean island of Delos, the centre of the Mediterranean slave trade.[14] It was said that following Rome's conquest of Corinth in 146 BC Delos could handle over 10,000 slaves in a single day.[15] Many slave ships arriving in Italy from the eastern Mediterranean put into Puteoli, where their human cargoes were sold in the city's slave market. Puteolans were so deeply involved in the trade that the city was described by the poet Lucilius as a lesser Delos (*Delus minor*).[16]

A steady flow of luxury goods – silk cloth, perfumes, spices and dyestuffs – also passed through the port. In the late Republic, for instance, we hear of ships belonging to the wealthy equestrian Rabirius Postumus putting into Puteoli with cargoes of papyrus, linen and glass.[17] Demand for luxury items came from the wealthy elite in Rome – members of the senate and the equestrian order and, from the time of Augustus onward, the imperial court; but there must have been demand, too, from the gentry and their families in the municipalities of Italy not least in Campania, in cities such as Pompeii, Herculaneum, Capua, Nola and, of course, in Puteoli itself. Numerically the elite of Rome and the municipalities represented a tiny fraction of the empire's population, but this elite commanded substantial purchasing power.[18]

Another source of traffic through the port of Puteoli was the importation of construction materials (typically marble from Greece) which were much in demand for building programmes in the capital, and for municipal and private building projects elsewhere in Italy. A great obelisk that Augustus brought to Rome from Egypt was unloaded at Puteoli and the specially constructed ship that carried it was put on show as an exhibit in the harbour, where it remained until it caught fire and was destroyed.[19]

Mention should also be made of the enterprising Alexandrian traders who travelled up the Nile in river craft to Coptus. From here they crossed the eastern desert to the ports of Myos Hormos or Berenice on the Red Sea and embarked to India.[20] They brought back to Alexandria, often for onward shipment to Italy, gems, spices, silks and ivory, which were largely paid for in precious metals. As contemporaries noted, exports from Alexandria exceeded imports. 'Anyone can tell this if he stands in either Alexandria or Dicaearchia (Puteoli), watching the merchantmen as they arrive and depart and compares the weight of the loads going in each direction,' noted Strabo.[21] In two passages the elder Pliny offers an estimate of the adverse balance of payments:[22]

> In no year does India absorb less than HS50 million of our empire's wealth, sending merchandise to be sold in our markets at a hundred times its original cost.

> At the lowest reckoning India, China and the Arabian peninsula drain our empire of HS100 million every year: that is what our luxuries and womenfolk cost us.

THE GRAIN TRADE

By the first century AD Rome depended for its wheat largely on grain imported from its overseas provinces, in particular from Egypt and Africa.[23] Augustus had set up a department in Rome to coordinate these imports. An early prefect of the grain supply (*praefectus annonae*) was Pompeius Paulinus, to whom his son-in-law Seneca wrote, 'You keep the accounts of the whole world' (*tu quidem orbis terrarum rationes administras*).[24] It is difficult to imagine a more demanding task, since a long and complex supply chain extended from farmers in overseas provinces to warehouses in Rome. Wheat was acquired in several ways: as tax (*tributum*) levied on provincial landowners and their tenants; as rents collected from tenants of public or imperial estates; and through purchases in local markets by government officials or by private traders (*negotiatores*).[25] Furthermore, the Roman state possessed no merchant marine; consequently the department of the *annona* had to rely on grain ships owned by wealthy investors or independent shippers who bid for contracts to carry the government's supplies. The Roman people, commented Tacitus acidly, now cultivated Africa and Egypt rather than Italy, and committed their very lives 'to ships and all their risks'.[26]

The headquarters of the department of the *annona* were in Rome, located hard by one of the city's dockside markets, the Forum Boarium. We know from epigraphic evidence, mainly from the second century, that the *annona* maintained branch offices at Ostia and at Puteoli.[27] At Ostia the manager of the grain supply (*procurator ad annonam*), on an annual salary of HS60,000, is attested.[28] His office employed a paymaster (*praepositus mensae nummulariae fisci frumentarii Ostiensis*).[29] This official's duties will have been to make payments from public funds to those who were working in the grain trade on the government's behalf: shipmasters, dock and harbour workers, merchants and warehouse owners. At Puteoli the staff included a pay clerk who had worked both at Ostia and at Puteoli (*dispensator a fruminto Puteolis et Ostis*) and an imperial freedman who was deputy head of records (*Augusti libertus proximus commentariorum annonae*).[30]

The arrival at Puteoli of the first grain cargoes of the season was a major event. In a letter to a friend, Seneca describes the scene:[31]

> Today, without warning, the Alexandrian *tabellariae* came into view. These are the ships which they always send on ahead to give the news that the fleet (*classis*) is on its way. This is a very welcome sight for the Campanians; the whole population of Puteoli settles down on the quayside and tries to spot the Alexandrian ships by the type of rigging. They can do it, too, even though the whole bay is full of ships, because only the grain fleet is allowed to use the sail called the *siparum*, and all the ships hoist it high on their masts…
>
> Within the strait between Capri and the headland … other ships are ordered to use only an ordinary sail, so that the *siparum* is a sure sign of an Alexandrian. Everyone was in a rush to get down to the shore, and it was a great satisfaction to me to take my time and not to be in a hurry to get the letters from my staff which I was expecting, and to know from them what was the state of my affairs (*status rerum mearum*).

The arrival of the grain ships meant paid work for a great army of boatmen and dockworkers. The rich epigraphic record from Ostia, and from the nearby dock complex of Portus (see below), provides a glimpse of the labour force that was employed at a major Roman port. Among those attested are lightermen (*lenuncularii*), divers (*urinatores*), porters (*saccarii*), warehousemen (*horrearii*), corn measurers (*mensores frumentarii*) and shipbuilders and repairers (*fabri navales*). At one time the guild of shipbuilders (*corpus fabrum navalium*) at Ostia had nearly one hundred members.[32]

A tombstone from Ravenna provides us with a glimpse of work in progress at a small shipyard.[33] Two freedmen, Publius Longidienus Rufio and Publius Longidienus Philadespotus, are commemorating their patron, the *faber navalis* Publius Longidienus. The lower part of the monument represents a ship being built; it is almost complete and is propped up on the slipway. In the foreground a man in a short tunic is cutting with an adze into a curved beam of wood, perhaps getting the ship ready for launching. Above and to the right of the ship is written on a tablet, *P. Longidienus P.f. ad onus properat* ('Publius Longidienus, son of Publius, hastens to complete his task'). The two freedmen presumably worked alongside their patron as his assistants; this is suggested by the placing of their images, which share the front face of the tombstone with their patron and the ship which he is building.[34]

The arrival of the grain fleet also brought business for all sorts of people not directly connected with the multiple trades of the harbour. Puteoli's grain dealers (*frumentarii*) would be haggling with travelling merchants (*mercatores*) over the price of the new season's stocks. Shippers (*navicularii*) and businessmen with overseas interests (*negotiatores*) would be checking incoming consignments and entering into fresh contracts for outgoing cargoes.[35] For bankers (*argentarii*) there were loans to be called in and new financing to arrange. And there would be brisk trade for Puteoli's shops, bars and brothels.

Reading between the lines of Seneca's letter it is possible to piece together some information about the organisation of the grain fleet. The Alexandrian freighters sailed in convoy; the shipmasters followed various predetermined orders (for instance, on how to signal their arrival); and regulations governed the conduct of other ships using the harbour. The department of the *annona* evidently exercised some control over the fleet and over the port of Puteoli, even though the Alexandrian freighters and other merchant vessels using the harbour were owned and operated by independent shippers. An insight into the control that was eventually to be exercised by the *annona* comes from a letter dated to the second or third century, when Ostia/Portus had become the Italian terminus for the Alexandrian fleet. The writer (probably a shipmaster) had travelled with one of the grain ships:[36]

> Irenaeus to Apollinarius, his dearest brother, many greetings...I wish you to know that I reached land on the 6th of the month Epeiph and we unloaded [our cargo] on the 18th. I went up to Rome on the 25th...we are every day expecting our discharge; up until today no one in the grain fleet has been cleared...

On this occasion twelve days had elapsed between the arrival of Irenaeus' ship and the unloading of the cargo (or perhaps before unloading was fully completed); furthermore the master had to wait a good many more days before the paperwork was completed and the ship could set out on the return journey to Alexandria.

The operations of the grain fleet were determined by the sailing season. This stretched from late May to early September; but in some years of exceptionally mild weather it might begin in early March and end in early November. During the sailing season the wind in the eastern Mediterranean blows mainly from the north or the north-west. This meant that square-rigged ships sailing from Italy to Egypt could make good time with the wind behind them: Pliny records a journey from Puteoli to Alexandria, a distance of 1,000 nautical miles, which was accomplished, in light winds, in eight-and-a-half days.[37] Similarly the emperor Gaius advised the Jewish prince Herod Agrippa not to travel home by the tiring, coast-hugging route from Brindisi to Syria but to make a direct crossing to Alexandria; the Alexandrian sea captains, said the emperor, drove their ships like charioteers. So Agrippa went down by road from Rome to Puteoli. Here he saw some ships from Alexandria lying at anchor and ready to sail; they must have discharged their loads of grain and taken on board their return cargoes. Agrippa and his retinue embarked on one of these vessels and reached the coast of Egypt, 'a few days later'.[38]

However when fully laden the grain freighters would have to sail from Alexandria to Italy against the northerly winds. This forced them to take one of two circuitous routes: the northern route via the southern coast of Turkey to Malta and then to the straits of Messina, or the southern route via the north African coast. In each case the distance was some 1,400 nautical miles and the voyage from Alexandria to the Bay of Naples could take at least a month and sometimes two. If Seneca's account of the arrival of the first cargoes of the year may be dated to early June, the fleet would most probably have set out on its journey to Italy in April.

The apostle Paul's journey to Rome in 62 provides a dramatic account of a voyage on the northern route made late in the year. At Myra (on the southern coast of Turkey) he boarded a grain freighter, carrying 276 crew and passengers. The captain (*kubernetes*) and the shipper (*naukleros*) decided to put in for the winter at a small harbour. When a favourable wind sprang up they changed their minds and made for a better harbour. It was an unfortunate decision: they were caught by a north-east gale and ran before it for two weeks. To save the ship the crew had to jettison the cargo of grain. Eventually they fetched up at Malta, where Paul waited for three months, that is until the following spring; he then boarded another Alexandrian grain ship, the Castor and Pollux, which had spent the entire winter at Malta and was now ready to complete the voyage to Puteoli.[39]

THE RIVAL CLAIMS OF PUTEOLI AND OSTIA

In this account of the development and growth of Puteoli it has been taken very much for granted that the city was the natural port of entry for Egyptian grain destined for Rome. But a puzzling question has to be answered. Why was Puteoli, 140 miles by road from Rome, chosen for this pivotal role, when the port of Ostia, at the mouth of the Tiber, was just 15 miles from the capital?

A useful starting point is that there were evidently sound commercial reasons for shippers to favour Puteoli. The city was the principal port for goods leaving, as well as entering, Campania – one of the most productive regions of Roman Italy. Shippers unloading cargoes of grain in the Campanian port could expect to pick up cargoes here for the return journey.[40] Ostia, by contrast, could not play the same role. It was not so easy to find outgoing cargoes; the port at the mouth of the Tiber served principally as the gateway leading into Rome – and the capital was a great consumer city rather than a major producer of goods that could find markets overseas.

But there was also a very practical reason for the development of Puteoli as a grain port – the size of the Alexandrian freighters. The investigation of shipwrecks, mostly from the last century of the Republic, indicates that Roman shippers certainly used vessels capable of carrying loads of more than 400 tons.[41] Many, perhaps most, of the Alexandrian grain freighters will have been in this category. Vessels of this size needed to discharge their cargoes in a secure deepwater anchorage.

Ostia did not provide such an anchorage. True, Dionysius of Halicarnassus, writing at the close of the first century BC, reported that there were no sand banks at the mouth of the Tiber and ships with oars could be rowed up to Rome; he added that merchant ships with sails might also be rowed or towed up to Rome – but only if their cargo capacity was no greater than 3,000 *amphorae*, i.e. 9,000 *modii*, which would be some 60 tons burden.[42] This in itself would have ruled out the Alexandrian freighters. At this period the bulk of Rome's imports of grain seems to have come from North Africa (e.g. modern Tunisia) rather than from Egypt.[43] The journey times on this route were much shorter – two and a half days from Utica near Carthage to Rome on one celebrated occasion – and the ships were presumably much smaller than the Alexandrian freighters and made more frequent sailings.[44]

A few years later, according to Strabo, the position at Ostia was if anything even less satisfactory:[45]

> Ostia is harbourless on account of the silting which is caused by the Tiber.... Although it is dangerous for the merchant ships to anchor far out in the surf, the prospect of profit prevails. Many lighters take off the cargoes and bring back others in exchange. This makes it possible for the ships to sail away quickly before they enter the river, or else, after having partly unloaded their cargoes, they sail in to the Tiber and run inland as far as Rome.

It appears, then, that while there might be return cargoes to be picked up at Ostia, although at some physical risk, there were still no adequate deepwater moorings for the Alexandrian grain ships at the mouth of the Tiber. (When Strabo describes partly unloaded vessels that make their way up the river to Rome, he can hardly be describing the Alexandrian freighters.) Puteoli by contrast offered a sheltered deepwater harbour where the Alexandrian freighters could discharge their cargoes of grain – and pick up return cargoes of Campanian goods (*4*).

But how were cargoes of grain unloaded at Puteoli to reach Rome? Grain was regularly carried by pack animals.[46] At a speed of perhaps eight miles a day the journey by land was slow and expensive and could result in doubling the price of grain by the time it reached Rome.[47] The answer was to transship the corn from the Alexandrian freighters at Puteoli into smaller coastal vessels which would sail up the coast to Ostia. Further transshipment to Tiber river craft might then be required for the last few miles of the journey to the capital.

In effect there were two grain fleets. One was the *classis* proper, composed of the large Alexandrian freighters which made the long sea voyage to Puteoli and when possible travelled in convoy; this is not to say that the entire fleet sailed at the same time – it was probably organised into squadrons which set off from Alexandria at different times during the sailing season. Although the business of getting wheat supplies to Rome was in private hands the owners or captains of the grain freighters did cooperate with each other and accepted a measure of operational control imposed by the department of the *annona*. This may even have been written into their contracts. The second fleet was made up of coastal vessels which shuttled between Puteoli and Ostia on round trips which took the better part of a week; here it is difficult to see how any degree of organisation could have been introduced.

Successive measures offering incentives for investment in grain ships indicate that the authorities made a distinction between on the one hand grain-carrying ships of 10,000 *modii* (65 tons burden) and on the other larger carriers that carried a minimum load of 50,000 *modii* (320 tons). The emperor Claudius sought to encourage merchants to make 'dangerous' (i.e. winter) journeys by promising full compensation for any loss incurred through storms.[48]

> He devised every possible means to import supplies [to the capital], even during the winter months. He insured merchants (*negotiatores*) against the loss of their ships in storms, thus guaranteeing them a profit, and he offered privileges (*commoda*) to those who built merchant ships (*naves mercaturae*): citizens were exempted from the Papian-Poppaean Law [penalising bachelors and the childless to encourage marriage and parenthood]; Latins [mainly ex-slaves freed informally and enjoying a limited form of citizenship] received full citizenship; and women were granted the privileges of those who had borne four children [which in particular meant release from the tutelage of a guardian].

Additional details are supplied by the jurist Gaius:[49]

would enable grain from Egypt to be transshipped at Puteoli into canal craft rather than into coasting vessels. The canal barges could then make the journey from Puteoli to the heart of Rome. This would avoid the dangers of piracy and shipwreck on the run along the Tyrrhenian coast; but it would be quicker and cheaper than the journey by land. It is not known how Nero's proposal to transport cargoes of grain by inland waterway was viewed in Puteoli; it may be assumed that feelings were mixed. The new system would take away business from shippers and merchants plying the coastal route to Ostia, but it would open up opportunities for the operators of canal barges. Work on the canal was begun in 64, the year when Claudius' new harbour at Portus was completed. But Nero's grand project was soon abandoned. A project that did reach completion at this time, however, was the construction of the *opus pilarum*, the breakwater or mole that became one of the most famous features of Puteoli and of which traces have survived to this day.[56]

It was left to Trajan to add to the Claudian harbour near Ostia a completely sheltered octagonal basin, lined with quays and warehouses; from this inland harbour another canal was dug to provide a connection to the Tiber. As a result of these developments the Alexandrian fleet, or a significant proportion of it, seems to have begun in the second century AD to make regular use of Portus.

The transshipment of grain at Ostia is depicted in the wall-painting of a river vessel, the Isis Giminiana, now in the Vatican Museum. Standing on a cabin in the stern is Farnaces, the ship's master. He is holding the handle of the starboard steering oar. To the right of Farnaces stands a grain measurer (*mensor frumentarius*), probably a supervisor. Abascantus, another measurer, is checking the quantity of grain (*res*) which is being poured into a measuring bucket, presumably of one *modius* capacity, by the first of four porters. The second porter is holding up his hand over another *modius* bucket, on which is written 'I have finished my work' (*feci*). The last two porters are carrying sacks of grain up the gangplank from the quay. Because this is a river boat, the mast does not carry sails but is placed near the prow to take the tow rope. There is a puzzle here. We are shown the grain arriving on the Isis Giminiana in sacks; are all these sack-loads now going to be poured into the hold for the short trip up the Tiber to the warehouses in Rome? It beggars belief that porters at Rome would be required to bag up the grain in fresh sacks to get it ashore and into the warehouses. The answer must be that the grain measurers at Ostia were employed by the *annona* to take a sample (perhaps every tenth sack) of the loads that were put aboard the Tiber river boats, to check for weight and quality. The choice of this scene for depiction (on an Ostian tomb) indicates the importance of the role played by the grain measurers. Similar checking and inspection, mutatis mutandis, of incoming cargoes will have been an everyday occurrence at the port of Puteoli (5).

In the final analysis too much may be made of competition between Puteoli and Ostia. At one level the authorities took a calculated decision to invest in improved harbour facilities at Ostia/Portus; this would enable them to exercise greater control over the capital's supply of grain. Nevertheless it may well have suited successive

who do business in Alexandria, Asia and Syria, (*mercatores qui in Alexandr[iai] Asiai Syriai negotiantur*)'.[63] When Tiberius launched a programme of financial aid for Asian cities destroyed in the earthquake of AD 17, the *augustales* of Puteoli dedicated a statue to him as a formal thank-offering.[64]

To serve the needs of the expanding city, a new system of local government was introduced. The urban area of Puteoli was divided into districts (*regiones*) - which were in turn divided into wards (*vici*), modelled on the local administrative units of Rome.[65] The names of some of the new urban units, known from later inscriptions, commemorate the names of families who were dominant in the Augustan period. Among the districts and wards in the main part of the town were the *regio arae Lucullianae*, the *regio Hortensiana* and the *regio vici Vestoriani et Calpurniani*. The *vicus Spurinus* lay on the road to Capua, while the *vicus Annianus* and the *vicus Lartidianus* were situated along the coastal strip leading to Lake Lucrinus. Other ward names reflect the business of the tradesmen who worked in the locality, such as the perfume merchants of the *vicus turarius* and the glass makers of the *clivus vitriarius*. A community of merchants and traders who originated from Tyana in Cappadocia had settled in the *vicus Tyanianus*. Tyana itself was an inland city; but it was a staging post on the road which led from the interior of Anatolia to the ports of Cilicia, most notably to Tarsus.

Under Augustus, too, was commenced the Serino aqueduct, the Aqua Augusta, which brought fresh water to the cities of the coast from the falls of Acquaro, six miles south-east of Abellinum, and extended at its greatest length for some 60 miles. A fourth century inscription lists, in order of importance, the cities the aqueduct then served: Puteoli, Neapolis, Nola, Atella, Cumae, Acerrae, Baiae and Misenum, where it cumulated in the great collection tank known as the Piscina Mirabilis. (Before the eruption of Vesuvius in 79 the aqueduct had served Pompeii.)[66] The emperor's close interest in the affairs of the city was recognised through the grant of a new title, 'colony of Julius Augustus at Puteoli' (*colonia Iulia Augusta Puteolis*). Spurred on by this mark of imperial favour the aristocratic families of Puteoli contributed their own funds to the city's regeneration. Recent excavations on the Rione Terra have revealed statues, mosaics and reliefs that reflect a surge of public and private building in the Augustan and Julio-Claudian era.[66] L. Calpurnius even employed on the restoration of the Capitolium one of the most distinguished architect/builders of the day, the freedman L. Cocceius Auctus, who had worked for Agrippa on the Portus Julius project.[67]

Other wealthy Puteolan families financed public buildings in and around the harbour. A new forum, the *forum Augusti*, was constructed on a terraced site. Here the Annii provided a hall, the *basilica Augusti Anniana*, as a meeting place for the municipal council of magistrates and ex-magistrates (*ordo decurionum*).[68] The Sextii contributed a covered promenade, the *porticus Augusti Sextiana*. Other examples of private munificence include colonnaded vestibules (*chalcidica*) provided by the Octavii, Caesonii, the Hordeonii and the Suettii and altars to Augustus provided by the Hordeonii and the Suettii.[69]

One of the Granii was in office in 78 BC when the dictator Sulla drafted a constitution for the town.⁷⁷ A certain Publius Granius was among the witnesses at the show trial in Rome in 70 BC, where Cicero was prosecuting Gaius Verres, the ex-governor of Sicily, on charges of corruption; this Granius was evidently engaged in trade with Sicily:⁷⁸

> The merchants (*mercatores*) [of Puteoli], wealthy and honourable men, have come in great numbers for this trial. They tell us that their partners (*socii*), their freedmen or their fellow freedmen were plundered or thrown into prison; some were beheaded.... When I call for the evidence of Publius Granius, so that he can tell how his own freedmen were beheaded by you [Verres], and claim back his ship and cargo from you, you shall prove him a liar if you can.

Later in the century A. Granius Puteolanus, who had become a member of the equestrian order in Rome, lost his life fighting on Caesar's side in the civil war between Caesar and Pompey.⁷⁹ In AD 35 L. Granius Probus was a senior magistrate (*duumvir*) and acted as judge in a case involving the Sulpicii.⁸⁰ And at the end of the second century Granii were still prominent in the city.⁸¹

The interests and activities of another Puteolan family will serve to reinforce the impression of elite wealth and influence enduring over several generations. Standing as a witness alongside Publius Granius at the trial of Verres in 70 BC was M. Annius who had business interests in Sicily.⁸² In July AD 6 another Annius with trading connections comes into view – this time, in Egypt's Eastern Desert. Here Lysas, slave of Publius Annius Plocamus, cut two graffiti, in Greek and Latin, into the rock of a cave on the Berenice road where he had taken shelter.⁸³ Lysas was presumably travelling on business for the Annii. Members of the family are recorded again in Claudius' reign, when an unnamed freedman of Annius Plocamus, on a voyage round Arabia, was blown off course to Sri Lanka; Pliny noted that Annius Plocamus himself held the contract to collect the taxes of the Red Sea (*qui Maris Rubri vectigal a fisco redemerat*).⁸⁴ The Annii, as noted above, financed the building of a basilica in the Augustan forum. Like the Granii, Annii were still prominent in Puteoli in the late second century.⁸⁵

Surviving charters – notably from Bantia, Tarentum and Heraclea – and inscriptions and graffiti preserved at nearby Pompeii indicate that local administration in Italian municipalities such as Puteoli was usually modelled on that of Rome.⁸⁶ There would be, for instance, a sequence of public offices (*cursus honorum*) for which elections were held annually: electoral graffiti from Pompeii reveal vigorous election campaigns, in which groups of traders and individuals record their support for candidates.⁸⁷

The most junior magistrates were the quaestors, whose responsibilities were principally financial. Above them were the aediles, whose responsibilities included the upkeep of streets and public buildings, the regulation of markets and the organising of public games and shows. At the apex of the hierarchy were the two chief magistrates (*duumviri*). Among their various duties, the chief magistrates were required to preside

It is not surprising that disputes should arise from time to time amidst Puteoli's large and heterogeneous population. During the period covered by the Murecine archive there is one report of serious disorder; but this was not, as might have been expected, between Romans and incomers or even between slaves and free citizens – but between the wealthy men who sat on the town council and the rest of the citizen body. The trouble flared up in Nero's reign. Tacitus reports the incident:[92]

> In this year [58] Puteoli sent two rival delegations to the senate [in Rome], one from the town council (*ordo*), the other from the citizens (*plebs*). The council complained of public disorder (*vis multitudinis*), the people complained of the greed shown by the magistrates and leading citizens. There had been riots (*seditio*) with stone throwing and threats of arson. Gaius Cassius [Longinus] was appointed to prevent armed warfare from breaking out and to find a solution. But the measures he took were so severe that the people could not tolerate him; at his own request the assignment was transferred to the Scribonius brothers, who were allocated a cohort of the [emperor Nero's] Praetorian Guard. The guard struck terror into the populace; a few of the rioters were executed; and peace returned to the city.

The sequel to this outburst and its harsh repression was the plantation in 60 of a batch of veteran soldiers and the granting to Puteoli of the honorific title of Colonia Claudia Neronensis. Omitting to mention that Puteoli was in fact already a colony, named after Augustus, Tacitus reported that Puteoli 'was given the status of a Roman settlement and named after Nero'; he also brackets Puteoli with other cities to which colonies of veterans were despatched at this time.[93] The disorder at Puteoli in 58 may have been part of wider unrest in Campania. Only a year later a riot, which ended in bloodshed, occurred in the amphitheatre at Pompeii between the people of Pompeii and the nearby colony of Nuceria.[94]

VISITORS

Large numbers of senators and Roman knights, members of Rome's elite in other words, owned property on the Bay of Naples.[95] From the letters of Cicero, it seems that everyone who was anyone aspired to build their own luxurious villa, complete with fishponds, swimming pools and seaside moorings, on the shores of the Bay, a veritable 'bowl of delights' (*cratera illum delicatum*).[96]

The resort par excellence was Baiae, a city of hot sulphur baths, 'catering for the ailments of the sick and the pleasures of the sound'.[97] In one of his most blistering speeches, Cicero attacks the wealthy Clodia as a Roman matron with the morals of a prostitute; to make his point it is enough for him simply to mention the city in the list of Clodia's self-indulgent practices – 'orgies, flirtations, Baiae, beach parties, dinner parties, musical entertainments, concerts and boating parties'.[98]

– and see to it that they pay interest on any funds which they claim they are keeping on deposit. When Cluvius died he made Cicero co-heir to his estate, along with Julius Caesar and T. Hordionius. The villa by the shore that Cicero describes as his Puteolanum was part of his inheritance from Cluvius.

Another Puteolan businessman with whom Cicero was on good terms was Gaius Vestorius.[110] After Cicero had been to dinner with Vestorius on one occasion, he told Atticus that Vestorius was as incapable of taking part in philosophical discussion as he was expert in keeping his accounts (*hominem remotum a dialecticis, in arithmeticis satis exercitatum*).[111] Cicero may have derided Vestorius for being no intellectual; but he was only too happy to use his business skills. Vestorius performed a signal service for Cicero by sorting out some rental property (*tabernae*) in Puteoli that formed part of the legacy from Cluvius. Vestorius put the buildings into habitable condition, found tenants and produced rental profits of HS80,000, increasing to HS100,000 a year.[112] This is the same Vestorius who introduced the manufacture of blue glass to Puteoli.

Campania remained a popular holiday haven for the Roman aristocracy under the early emperors. Augustus and his successor Tiberius favoured the island of Capri; but Augustus also owned properties along the north shores of the Bay of Naples, including villas at Baiae and Pausilypon flanking the territory of Puteoli on the west and east respectively.

Although the imperial estates in the district passed on Augustus' death to Tiberius, Rome's second emperor seems to have paid little special attention to Puteoli and its immediate neighbourhood. His successor Gaius, however, was devoted to the region. He was remembered in particular for one spectacle, the re-enactment of a Roman triumph on a bridge of boats linking Baiae with Puteoli. Suetonius provides a graphic description:[113]

> He collected all the merchant ships he could and anchored them in two lines, close together, the whole way from Baiae to the mole [presumably an earlier structure than the Neronian breakwater] at Puteoli, a distance of just over three miles. He then had boards placed across the ships and earth heaped on the planks. This made a kind of Appian Way, across which he rode back and forward for two days. On the first day he wore an oak-leaved crown, sword and buckler and a cloak of cloth-of-gold and rode on a finely decorated charger. On the second he appeared in charioteer's costume, driving a team of two famous horses, with young Darius, a [royal] hostage taken from the Parthians, triumphantly displayed in the chariot beside him. Behind came the entire Praetorian Guard and a number of his friends riding in Gallic carriages.

Cassius Dio adds further details. As night fell, the participants continued their feasting and fires were lit on the surrounding hills. The emperor ordered people to be hurled into the water and the swimmers were attacked by boats equipped with beaks: 'the majority, though drunk, managed to save themselves'.[114]

Nero's vacations in and around Baiae were characterised, according to Tacitus and Suetonius, by criminal and licentious behaviour.[117] As already noted, Nero's grand plan to link Puteoli to Rome by canal was never completed.

It is possible to catch glimpses of other visitors to Puteoli during the early imperial period. The apostle Paul has already been mentioned. Another visitor was Gaius Licinius Mucianus, principal ally of Vespasian in his successful bid for power in 69 and also a part-time author and adviser to the emperor. Mucianus reported that he had once seen terrified elephants walking backwards down the gangplank from ship to shore at Puteoli; no doubt they were being transported to Rome to take part in the games.[118] Lastly, it would be a pity not to mention the seer Apollonius of Tyana, famed for healing the sick and raising the dead, who was the subject of a fantastical biography written in the early third century by Philostratus. Apollonius was en route from Greece to Rome to face the emperor Domitian, who suspected that Apollonius was plotting against him.[119] He was welcomed in Puteoli by the Cynic philosopher Demetrius; the two sages retired to the garden of the villa which had once belonged to Cicero, to discuss philosophy. On their return to the city, Demetrius pointed out the great crowd of merchant ships anchored in the bay and suggested that Apollonius should embark on one of them to escape the fury of the emperor. But Apollonius refused and sailed that day for Rome – where he was imprisoned and subsequently stood trial before the emperor. At his trial Apollonius made a long speech in his own defence and then, by supernatural means, succeeded in travelling from Rome back to Puteoli in the course of a single afternoon![120]

FREEDMEN

In Puteoli, as elsewhere in the Roman world, freedmen were barred from holding magistracies (quaestor, aedile and duumvir) and therefore from membership of the *ordo* – although a successful freedman might be granted the outward trappings of membership, the *ornamenta duumviralia*.[121] (The son of a freedman on the other hand might be elected to the town council, even at a young age).[122]

Neverthless freedmen were not entirely excluded from participation in public life. They might be enrolled among the *augustales*, an order set up by the emperor Augustus which was largely, although not entirely, composed of ex-slaves; a member might be known as *sevir*, *sevir augustalis*, *augustalis*, or even *sevir et augustalis*.[123] *Augustales* ranked below members of the *ordo* but above the mass of free people (*plebs*);

in some communities they displayed the symbols of a magistrate – a special toga and the accompaniment of attendants (*lictores*) carrying bundles of rods (*fasces*) – and they had access to privileged seats in the theatre. The *augustale*s may be regarded as a secular order, their relationship to the *ordo decurionum* parallelling in the municipalities the position that *equites* occupied vis-à-vis the senate at Rome.

Membership of the order is often an indication of success in business, in as much as *augustales* required sufficient wealth to pay an entry fee, contribute to public feasts and make other benefactions. A second century inscription on a statue base from Misenum, across the bay from Puteoli, commemorates the *augustalis* Q. Cominius Abascantus and his wife Nymphidia Monime and spells out their benefactions to the town in minute detail:[124]

> For Quintus Cominius Abascantus, honoured with insignia of decurional rank (*ornamentis decurionalibus honoratus*), lifetime curator of the *augustales*. He placed two statues – of the Genius of the Town and of the Protectress of the Fleet (*classis tutela*) – in the forum (and) on the occasion of their dedication gave HS20 to the individual decurions, HS12 to the *augustales* formally enrolled in the association, HS8 to the *augustales* who were not enrolled in the association, HS6 to freeborn citizens formally enrolled in professional *collegia*, (and) HS4 to the townspeople. In addition, he gave HS110,000 to the decurions, so that they and the people could drink honeyed wine on 17 December, his birthday, and likewise (gave) HS20,000 to the associated *augustales*, so that from the interest on these amounts there would be an annual division, based on the formula that he established, on the aforesaid day. And over and above this, he generously gave HS10,000 for procuring wine for these same *augustales*. Nymphidia Monime (had this statue erected) to Abascantus, best of husbands; at its dedication she gave HS8 and a banquet to each of the *augustales* enrolled in the association.

Abascantus emerges as an *augustalis* of considerable wealth who had been awarded the honorary status of decurion. Indeed, the total of the capital sums he provided for his various foundations comfortably exceeded the minimum property qualification for membership of the municipal *ordo*. Abascantus was probably a *negotiator* who had made his fortune by supplying goods and services to the fleet based at Misenum, as evidenced by his dedication of a statue to the Protectress of the Fleet.

In a vivid passage elsewhere D'Arms evokes the public life of the *augustales* of Ostia in the second century. This passage, which I have slightly adapted, will serve to describe the activities of the *augustales* of Puteoli in the first century:[125]

> In their headquarters there was space for the members to banquet, to sacrifice, to undertake acts of corporate munificence. There was opportunity, also, to exchange shipping information derived from various ports, to share news of market rates and property values, to learn of current developments among the builders, lightermen, ferry operators, ship builders and ship repairers and to sift and synthesize these reports through common discussion in a common meeting place.

circle.[126] Extant fragments describe the adventures of Encolpius and his boyfriend, the slave Giton; some of these adventures, including the heroes' attendance at an extravagant dinner party given by Trimalchio (the *Cena Trimalchionis*), take part in a Campanian seaport (there are references to Baiae, to Capua and to Cumae). Working from clues in the novel, it is possible to build a strong case for Puteoli as the mise-en-scène of this episode. The city is described at one point as a Greek city (*Graeca urbs*). Nevertheless it possesses a forum, bars (*popinae*), apartment blocks (*insulae*), and an amphitheatre where gladiatorial contests are staged by candidates for office; all these are typical features of an Italian *civitas*. There is even a fire brigade (*vigiles*); as already noted, Puteoli had been sent a detachment of *vigiles* by Claudius. Encolpius loses his way on two occasions, which suggests that the city is quite large; furthermore the harbour can accommodate sea-going vessels. Lastly, several characters in the *Satyricon* refer to the city as a *colonia*.

Trimalchio

Like many of the guests at his dinner party, Trimalchio was a freed slave. As a boy he had learned to keep accounts (*ratiocinari didicisset*) for his master and had been promoted to act as steward (*dispensator*).[127] He was freed in his master's will and made co-heir, with the emperor, of the family estate; Trimalchio's share was 'a senator's portion' (*patrimonium laticlavium*), i.e. a fortune worth HS1 million the minimum census qualification for a senator.[128] Trimalchio's story continues:

> I became passionate about business (*concupivi negotiari*)...I built five ships, got a cargo of wine – which was worth its weight in gold at the time – and sent them to Rome...every one was wrecked...Neptune swallowed up HS30 million in one day...I built some more bigger, better and luckier ships...I got another cargo – wine, bacon, beans, perfumes and slaves. Fortunata [Trimalchio's wife, also an ex-slave] did a noble thing at this time: she sold all her jewellery and clothes and put a hundred gold pieces into my hand. This was the yeast for my fortune (*peculii mei fermentum*)...I made a clear HS10 million on one voyage. Straightaway I paid off the mortgages on all the estates which had belonged to my patron. I built a house and bought slaves and cattle; whatever I touched grew like a honeycomb. When I found that I was wealthier than the whole of my native land (*tota patria mea*) I threw in my hand; I retired from day-to-day business (*sustuli me de negotiatione*) and I began to lend money to [or through] freedmen (*coepi libertos faenerare*).

The details of Trimalchio's imagined business career provide a portrait, exaggerated but nonetheless informative, of a Campanian businessman. He uses his inheritance to build five ships; they were probably coastal vessels, the 65-tonners that would sail as far as Ostia and then be towed up the Tiber to Rome. He loads them with wine, one of

Campania's major exports. Trimalchio then loses all his ships and all his cargo on his first voyage. Obviously he did not accompany his small fleet; he must have employed a business agent as well as sea captains. Undaunted he builds bigger and better ships. Aided by a contribution of HS10,000 from his wife (a surprisingly modest sum to which he assigns great symbolic value) he puts together another cargo, presumably also destined for Rome. Again he loads his ships with wine; but this time he includes bacon and beans (which sound typically Campanian), perfumes (which he may have bought from a Puteolan importer with interests in the east) and slaves (which he must surely have acquired at Puteoli's great slave market.) Trimalchio makes HS10 million on this one venture and uses the proceeds to buy up the estates of his late patron. He next devotes himself to the life of the rich landlord; his income is doubtless made up of rents, sales of livestock and produce, and earnings from estate-based enterprises. He engaged in some slave-dealing as well. But when he found that he was seriously rich, he took less and less interest in direct business ventures and invested his money in enterprises run by freedmen.

The epitaph which Trimalchio chose for his tomb declares that that he was a *sevir* – an official in the local order of *augustales*:[129]

> Here lies Gaius Pompeius Trimalchio Maecenatianus. He was made a *sevir* in his absence. He might have served as an attendant to any magistrate in Rome, but he was not inclined to do so. Dutiful, courageous, loyal, he grew from very little and left HS30 million. He never listened to a philosopher. Fare well, Trimalchio, and fare thee well, passer-by.

He also told his guests that he would be setting all his slaves free in his will and added that he would be leaving property to some of them:

> I am leaving a farm (*fundus*) and his mistress (*contubernalis*) to Philargyrus, and to Cario I am leaving an apartment block (*insula*) and his manumission tax (*vicesima*) and his bed and bedding.

'Don't look down on Trimalchio's freedman friends,' says one of Trimalchio's guests to Encolpius.[130] He continues:

> They're very juicy (*valde sucosi sunt*). You see that one lying at the end of the lowest couch. Today he has HS800,000. He grew from nothing (*de nihilo crevit*). A little time ago he was carrying loads of wood on his back. People say – I know nothing but I've heard – that he pulled off a goblin's cap and found a treasure. I don't envy anyone if God gives them something. But he still bears the mark of his master's slap [part of the formal ritual of freeing a slave] and has a high opinion of himself. He has put up a notice next to his house, 'Gaius Pompeius Diogenes is letting his apartment from the 1st July because he has bought a house' (*C. Pompeius Diogenes ex kalendis Iuliis cenaculum locat; ipse enim domum emit*).

There is no better man alive. But it is those rascally freedmen of his who have made off with everything. You know how it is: you're in partnership, things go off the boil and the moment business takes a turn for the worse your friends vanish. He ran such a good business, and now you see him like this. He was an undertaker (*libitinarius*). He used to dine like a king: boars served in their skins, fancy cakes, gamebirds...cooks, bakers. More wine was spilt under his table than anyone else would have in their cellar. He was not a man, he was a dream (*phantasia*)! When his business was failing and he was afraid that his creditors would think that he was going bankrupt, he put up some goods for auction with the notice, 'Gaius Julius Proculus will offer for sale some articles for which he has no further use' (*C. Iulius Proculus auctionem faciet rerum supervacuarum*).

Another guest is Echion, a clothes dealer (*centonarius*), who invites a fellow guest to come down to his country place (*villa*) and see his little estate (*casulae*).[131] His son is studying Latin and Greek and he has bought the boy some law books (*libra rubricata*). Echion tells his neighbour:

> I want him to know something of the law, so that he can manage the family property. Law is what brings in the bread. He has dipped into literature quite enough. If he shies away from the law I am going to have him taught a trade (*artificium*), as a barber (*tonstrinus*), an auctioneer (*praeco*) or at least an advocate (*causidicus*) – only death can take away a man's trade. So every day I go on at him, 'Primigenius, believe me, whatever you learn, you learn for yourself. Look at Philero the advocate: if he had not worked at his books, he wouldn't be able to keep the wolf from the door today. It's not so long ago that he that was a pedlar, carrying his goods round on his back. And now he puts up a good show, even against Norbanus. Education is a treasure and a trade is with you for life.'

And then there is Hermeros who told his fellow guests that he was a king's son who had sold himself into slavery:[132]

> I preferred to be a Roman citizen than a provincial paying taxes... I owe no one a brass penny...I have never been taken to court...no one has ever said to me in public, 'Pay me what you owe me.' I have bought a little property and collected some plate (*glebulas emi, lamellulas paravi*)... I have to feed twenty bellies and a dog... I purchased my fellow slave's freedom so that no one could wash their hands in her lap...I paid 1000 denarii for my own freedom; I was made a *sevir* and paid no entrance fee...I hope that when I die I shall have nothing to be ashamed of.

And so the talk ebbs and flows through Trimalchio's dining room.

Image and reality

Through these caricatures Petronius introduces us to the world of Puteoli's freedmen, ex-slaves who have made money in business. To a man and woman the Roman aristocracy, Petronius' readers, were slave owners; most of them at some time will have set free some of their own slaves. They must have recognised, with a shudder of distaste, an affectionate smile or even a gale of laughter, the nouveau riche businessmen at Trimalchio's dinner party. Trimalchio himself had been granted his freedom in his master's will and had been left a good-sized fortune; Diogenes had been set free while his master was still alive. We are not told how Proculus achieved his freedom; but he went into business as an undertaker, set his own slaves free and formed a partnership with them; but things went wrong and Proculus' freedmen ran off with the funds. Hermeros, who had long ago sold himself into slavery, eventually purchased his freedom for a substantial sum of money. It is not entirely clear whether Echion, the clothes dealer, was a freedman or a freeborn citizen (*ingenuus*) but with his concern that his son should get a 'professional' education he fits very well into Trimalchio's circle.[133] This is a group of self-made men who have worked hard, who like spending money and who are proud of their achievements. We shall meet their real-life counterparts in the transactions from the Murecine archive which form the subject of the following chapters (Chapters 2-9).

THE BANK OF THE SULPICII

The banking firm run in Puteoli by the Sulpicii was in business to our certain knowledge for very nearly 35 years, from March in AD 26 to February AD 61 – that is to say it lasted from the middle of the reign of Tiberius, Rome's second emperor, throughout the reigns of Gaius (Caligula) and Claudius and was still operating during the reign of Nero. Quite possibly the business may have started earlier and lasted longer.

The Sulpicii were professional bankers, who made their living from banking. And they were freedmen. They moved in a very different world from wealthy freeborn financiers such as Cicero's friend Atticus (see Appendix 8).

Professional bankers in the Roman world may be conveniently grouped into four specialist occupations:[1]

★ The *argentarius* was a banker who took deposits from customers, made loans and offered money transfer services. *Argentarii* were frequently to be found at auction sales, where they advanced credit to buyers.

★ The *coactor* was a debt-collector, who collected the purchase money from buyers at auctions.

★ The *coactor argentarius* was a banker who combined three functions – taking deposits, advancing loans and collecting debts at auctions.

★ The *nummularius* was a moneychanger, who assayed coins (verified their weight, quality and type) and handled exchange between gold, silver and base metal currencies circulating in different parts of the Roman world.

This categorisation is useful in that it reflects the variety of Roman banking activities. The term *argentarius*, however, is the most widely employed in the legal and epigraphic record and for simplicity I shall use it as the generic term for a banker. (One caveat is necessary: *faber argentarius* is the occupational description of a craftsman who worked in silver; from the context it is usually clear which trade is meant.) *Argentarii* were men – women were barred from conducting banking operations – who took in deposits and made loans as their specialist occupation; they usually charged their clients a fee or commission (*merces*) and some of their operations were regulated by law.[2] In Cicero's Rome bankers were to be found at the Temple of Janus in the Forum.[3] Under the Empire they congregated on the Velabrum, near the city's docks and markets, where the Arch of the Bankers (*Arcus Argentariorum*) can be seen to this day.

In the eyes of the elite, bankers who dealt with the public at large were considered to be tradesmen. Augustus' enemies, says Suetonius, sneered at the emperor's grandfather Gaius Octavius, describing him as a banker (*argentarius*) and as a moneychanger (*nummularius, mensarius*).[4] And when Suetonius wanted to emphasise the emperor Vespasian's humble origins, he pointed out that Vespasian's grandfather, Titus Flavius Petro, had specialised in providing finance at auction sales (*coactor argentarius*).[5] At the other end of the social scale, Horace gives us a glimpse of what it was like to endure the condescension of the elite. Horace's father was a freedman (*libertinus pater*) who took his son from southern Italy to give him a good education in Rome.[6] Horace feels it necessary to point out that his father:

> ...did not act out of fear that someone at some time might blame him were I to pursue a modest income as an auctioneer (*praeco*), or as he was himself, a collecting banker (*coactor*) – and I would not have reproached him...

Many generations later, when the scholiast Porphyrio commented on this passage he explained that the profession of banker was 'a lowly and disgraceful way of making money' (*humile et turpissimum genus quaestus*).[7]

It was quite common for slaves to operate banking businesses. A slave could open a bank, with or without his master's knowledge:[8]

> Where a slave sets up as a banker (*argentariam faciat*) (for he can) - if he does this with his master's consent...if he acted without his master's knowledge....

We hear of a slave who had been appointed by his master 'to make loans and accept pledges as security for these loans'; the slave in question exceeded the terms of his appointment and ran several businesses on the side, collecting debts owed to grain merchants and renting out warehouses.[9] An early Pope, the ex-slave Callistus, was reputed to have started out in business as a banker. According to his opponents he embezzled the deposits that were placed with him 'on behalf of widows and other Christians'.[10]

It was just as common for an ex-slave, a freedman such as Horace's father, to be a professional banker. It was not always quite clear who really did own the business. The jurist Scaevola discusses a case involving Lucius Titius (the name was used by Roman lawyers much as American lawyers today use 'John Doe') who had appointed Terminalis, a freedman, to run his banking business (*mensa nummularia*). Terminalis

bank simply for safe keeping; this type of deposit was non-interest bearing. Other types of deposit earned interest. The distinction is made by Ulpian in a passage where he states that depositors holding non-interest bearing deposits would receive preference in the case of a banker's insolvency:[14]

> When bankers become insolvent, it is customary for account of the depositors to be taken first, that is, of those who had money on deposit, not money at interest with the bankers, either invested in conjunction with the bankers, or left with them to make use of *(quotiens foro cedunt nummularii, solet primo loco ratio haberi depositariorum, hoc est eorum qui depositas pecunias habuerunt, non quas faenore apud nummularios vel cum nummulariis vel per ipsos exercebant).*

The significance of this passage is Ulpian's analysis of the way in which interest-bearing funds (*quas [pecunias] faenore apud nummularios*) could be put to work. Some depositors invested (*exercebant*) their funds at interest in conjunction with the bankers (*cum nummulariis*), i.e. the banker would recommend investment opportunities, which meant in practice finding suitable borrowers. There were other depositors, however, whose funds were invested through the bankers themselves (*vel per ipsos*), i.e. the bankers would make loans at their own risk.

This last category puts Roman deposit bankers in a line of descent that stems back to Greek bankers of the fourth century BC. It had long been recognised in the Greek world that lending clients' deposits at their own risk was the principal activity of bankers. Demosthenes, for instance, had described a bank as 'a business operation (*ergasia*) that produces risk-laden revenues (*prosodous epikindunous*) from other people's money'.[15] The passage from Ulpian indicates that this concept was recognised in the Roman world: bankers provided a financial market where the funds of depositors were channelled to borrowers. This was true financial intermediation: there was no need for lenders and borrowers to come into contact with, or even to know, one another. In the course of his trade the Roman banker would need to deploy the basic skills of banking in any age: borrowing cheap and lending dear, matching the inflow of deposits against the outflow of loans and finding creditworthy borrowers.

The bank account
Bankers were required to keep records of the accounts held with them by their customers; this requirement was laid down in the Praetor's Edict, the source of much private law:[16]

> Let those who operate a banking business produce accounts in matters relating to their business, with the day and consul [i.e. the date of each transaction] added (*argentariae mensae exercitores rationem, quae ad se pertinet, edent adiecto die et consule*).

entered in the same ledger in date order. Among outgoings, for instance, might be payments for purchases of equipment and loans to debtors and among receipts might be income from sales of finished products and interest on loans. Not only were different types of transaction lumped together, but there was no formal distinction, through entries in separate columns, between 'payments in' or 'payments out'.

In the case of a banker and his client the bank account was kept in the same way – that is to say, entries were made in narrative rather than in tabular form. But while the bank account was narrower in its scope, since it dealt only with money in and money out, it had a more wide-reaching function: it provided a legal record of the transactions effected between banker and customer. Two unusually large-sized tablets in the archive of the Sulpicii (TPSulp. 94, 95) appear to be fragments of the firm's account book (*codex rationum*); they record, from the point of view of the banker, the payment of funds (more on these two tablets in Chapter 3).

A banker can be seen checking his accounts on a relief from Serbia: a clerk is reading from a papyrus roll to his master, who sits with a writing tablet in his hands at a table on which lies a bag of coins. The papyrus presumably contains the *adversaria*; the writing tablet will be the *codex accepti et expensi*. This seems to be the monument of a banker who wished himself to be depicted carrying out his professional activity. His clerk is reading out the running record of transactions; the banker is reconciling these entries with the entries in his cash book (6).[23]

Money transfer

A client who held money on non-interest bearing deposit with his bank could withdraw funds on demand. The jurist Papinian outlines a case where the recipient of a deposit writes to the depositor to tell him that the 100 coins have safely arrived. 'These coins I will pay to you on demand when you wish and where you wish,' the banker adds.[24] The last words of the promise imply a very useful service: moving funds about the Roman world could be a complex logistical exercise (see Appendix 6). When instructed, bankers would also pay out funds to third parties from their customers' accounts. In a case discussed by Scaevola, Lucius Titius had instructed (*mandaverat*) his banker to pay 300 [coins] to his patron from funds that the banker held on his account (*ex ratione mensae*).[25]

An episode in Polybius illustrates how bankers handled money transfers on their clients' behalf. Scipio Aemilianus had instructed his banker to pay the money to two senators. The two payees went in person to the bank. The banker then wrote out a notification of funds transfer (*diagraphe*) to each of them. The banker needed to create this document so that each senator could countersign it and thus indicate that he had received the funds due to him. The signed transfer notes could then be given by the banker to Scipio, as proof that the banker had discharged the obligation on Scipio's behalf.[26]

When a creditor and a debtor held their accounts at the same bank it would not have been necessary to move coins about at all; the transfer of funds between

> I am wondering whether Marcus' allowance can be paid in Athens, or whether he must take it with him and I should be glad if you would give the whole thing your consideration, both as to method and as to time.

Three days later Cicero wrote:[30]

> I shall do as you suggest about Marcus, leaving the time to his own choice; please see that a letter of credit is drawn for the sum needed.

The arrangement made for Cicero's son at university indicates the type of arrangement that might be set up for the use of an agent who was on commercial business overseas. The example is particularly apposite because young Marcus Cicero, as a son in power (*in potestate*) stood in the same legal relationship to Cicero, his paterfamilias, as would a slave acting as agent for his master on commercial business.

A *permutatio* was, however, only of use if the two financiers involved knew and trusted each other. Furthermore, the *permutatio* does not seem to have been negotiable; the only people who could draw on the funds underpinning the *permutatio* were the account holder or someone specifically authorised to act on the account holder's behalf.

THE SULPICII

And now we may turn to the Bank of the Sulpicii. Three people emerge from the Murecine archive as the leading figures in the firm.

Gaius Sulpicius Faustus is the first of the Sulpicii to appear in the archive, on 18 March 26 (TPSulp. 42). His last appearance is on 6 May 52 (TPSulp. 40). In three tablets (TPSulp. 22,42,66) he is described as Faustus major (presumably to distinguish him from another, younger, Gaius Sulpicius Faustus, about whom nothing is known).

Gaius Sulpicius Cinnamus is the most frequently mentioned of the three protagonists, with references in almost 50 documents. He is revealed as Faustus' freedman in two tablets (TPSulp. 72,74), where he refers to Faustus as 'my patron' (*patronus meus*). Cinnamus first appears in the archive on 20 March 42 (TPSulp. 62) and makes his final appearance on 9 March 56 (TPSulp. 105).

Gaius Sulpicius Onirus is present in just five documents, four of them (TPSulp. 90-93) dated to February 61. Perhaps it was Onirus who took this selection of tablets from the firm's archive in Puteoli to the building outside Pompeii, where they were discovered in 1959. Were the Sulpicii setting up a branch office? Was the bank relocating from Puteoli to Pompeii? Such questions can only be a subject for speculation.

It is tempting to assume that two of the protagonists (Faustus and Onirus) were brothers, the sons of a freedman who commemorated his family on a tombstone reported to have been found in nearby Cumae. In this inscription, Gaius Sulpicius

actuarius (keeper of the records), and *actor* (manager). These occupations can be found in funerary inscriptions – for example M. Licinius Eutychus, former steward (*qui dispensavit*) to Volusius Torquatus, Onesimus, *dispensator* to Caepio Hispo, Aprilis, *arcarius fidelissimus* of Annidus Severus, and Cerdo, *actor fidelissimus* of M. Caesonius Spectatus.[35]

The prime function of the steward was to keep his master's accounts and to handle his cash receipts and expenditure. 'The farm manager knows about agriculture, but the steward knows about bookkeeping (*vilicus naturam agri novit, dispensator litteras scit*).'[36] The importance placed on good bookkeeping can be seen in Roman wills. Antonius Silvanus says: 'As for my slave Cronio, after my death, if he has handled everything properly and handed it over to my above-named heir or business manager (procurator) then I wish him to be free and I wish that the 5 per cent [manumission] tax be paid from my property.'[37] (I treat 'procurator' as an English term.)

The slave who managed his master's loan book (*servus kalendario praepositus*) carried particular financial responsibilities.[38] The term *kalendarium* reflects the fact that in loan deeds it was common for the Kalends, the first of the month, to be specified as the date from which a loan would run, while interest and capital repayments might be due on a subsequent Kalends. The *kalendarium* was the record of interest-bearing loans (*mutua*) in which a paterfamilias recorded funds paid out (*expensa*) to (*nomina*) and payments received (*accepta*). Presumably the entries for loans also included the terms agreed on interest (*usurae*) and repayment of capital (*sors*). Arrears of tenants' rents (*reliqua*) were entered in the *kalendarium* as *expensa* and their payments as accepta. When Trimalchio's accountant (*actuarius*) reads out the *nomina vilicorum* (literally, 'debts of the bailiffs') he is listing money owed by tenants but not yet collected.[39]

The *accepta* also included sums paid into the kalendarium by the *dominus*, for investing in loans.[40] At regular intervals the loans clerk had to prepare and submit his accounts (*reddere rationes*) for the *dominus* to approve and sign off.[41] Things did not always go smoothly: Scaevola discusses the responsibility of the *actor* whose assistants (*adiutores*) had failed to enter in the *kalendarium* sums of money that had been collected.[42]

At some point a steward or loans clerk might be appointed as the manager (*institor*) of a specific business directly owned by his master.[43] For instance the jurist Paul discusses a case where a certain Titianus Primus appointed a slave to lend money and accept securities (*mutuis pecuniis dandis et pignoribus accipiendis*).[44] An *institor* was granted a formal notice of appointment (*lex praepositionis*) that set out (for the benefit of interested parties) the terms under which he would do business.[45] *Institor* is a legal definition rather than a job title: it is explained by the jurists Paul and Ulpian:[46]

> An *institor* is someone who is appointed to manage a shop or other establishment for the purpose of buying and selling, or even just to conduct business, with no fixed place specified.
>
> A man is called an *institor* because he is in charge of carrying on business. It does not matter very much whether he is appointed to run a shop or any other sort of business.

Alternatively an able slave might be encouraged to carry out business transactions on his master's behalf using a special fund known as the *peculium*. This was a fund made available to certain slaves (and to the adult children of the paterfamilias) which was at their disposal for handling expenses and receipts, but which remained the property of the paterfamilias.[47] The *peculium* of a run-of-the-mill slave would be largely made up of wages and tips; a slave who was too old or infirm to continue in their former occupation might use it to purchase their freedom. The *peculium* of a highly regarded slave could be built into a sizeable fund - containing cash, real estate and even other slaves - which he could manage as he saw fit.[48]

Both *institores* who held specific appointments and slaves who operated on a less closely defined basis through their *peculium* could be found running banks:[49]

> A person will be liable [in any future lawsuit] on account of a slave whom he appoints [as an *institor*] to run a bank....

> If a slave sets up as a banker with his *peculium*, the master is liable [in any future lawsuit] under the action on the *peculium*....

The crucial step in the career of an able slave was the grant of freedom. A slave could be set free through a formal ceremony of manumission or through his master's will. Under legislation passed by Augustus certain limits were placed on the eligibility of slaves for manumission – most notably a requirement that they should have reached the age of thirty; but in practice these rules seem to have been frequently ignored. When a slave received his freedom the relationship changed from that of master and slave to one of patron and client; the ex-slave was now a citizen but he owed obligations of dutifulness (*pietas*) to his patron or to his patron's heir.[50] Different masters had different motives for freeing able slaves – but a frequent reason was undoubtedly a wish to capitalise on their business acumen. A slave who had acted as a manager for his master would have demonstrated his ability to handle staff, enter into contracts and pursue commercial opportunities; after manumission, the former slave could continue in the same business. The difference was that, energised by manumission, the 'independent' freedman might be expected to produce even greater profits.[51] Whether through an equity holding, or through the return on loans, the patron – or his heir in the case of a freedman manumitted *ex testamento* – would hope to profit from the earnings of an expanding business.

Furthermore the return on the family's investment in a capable ex-slave was boosted in certain circumstances by legal provisions governing the disposal of a freedman's estate. Under time-honoured Roman law a patron, or his children in the male line, would succeed to the estate of a freedman who died intestate and left no children or wife to inherit. This law was later changed to provide additional benefits to the slave-owning class: a patron could succeed against certain 'automatic' heirs (e.g. adopted children and wife) of a freedman who died intestate; and even if there was a will the patron could claim a half share of the freedman's estate. Legislation introduced under Augustus provided further financial privileges for slave owners: when a freedman worth at least HS100,000 died, will or no will, the patron could claim a share even against biological children: if the freedman left one child, half the estate went to the patron (as it did if there were no children); it took three children to exclude his claim entirely.[52]

When we see the Roman authorities passing measures designed to secure for patrons a sizeable share in their former slaves' estates we may infer that the elite expected talented ex-slaves to prosper. The same expectation underlies measures offering full citizen rights to 'Junian Latins'; these were freedmen whose masters had not complied fully with the regulations governing manumission, such as the requirement that a slave had to be at least 30 years old. We saw in Chapter 1 that Claudius offered full citizen rights to Junian Latins who built grain ships. Further measures rewarding entrepreneurial freedmen were introduced by later emperors. The jurist Gaius provides a summary:[53]

> By an edict of Claudius, Latins obtain full citizen rights if they have built a sea-going ship with a capacity of not less than 10,000 *modii* of corn, and that ship, or its replacement, has been used to bring corn to Rome over a period of six years.
>
> Furthermore, it was enacted by Nero that a Latin who owned property worth HS200,000 or more and built a house in the city of Rome on which he spent not less than half his wealth, could obtain full citizen rights.
>
> Finally, Trajan enacted that if a Latin kept a mill going in the city over a period of three years, grinding not less than 100 *modii* of grain daily, he could acquire full citizen rights.

It was evidently a widespread perception that talented freedmen had it in them to be successful businessmen – in such diverse spheres as shipbuilding and shipping, property development and grain milling. The literary representation of freedmen – as vulgar, ambitious and energetic – reflects this impression. For instance, Juvenal's pushy freedman tells anyone who will listen that his five shops bring in HS400,000 a year – a sum equal to the capital that a freeborn citizen (*ingenuus*) had to register with the censors to qualify as an equestrian.[54] Similarly, once the freedman Trimalchio's career was fully launched, everything he set his hand to 'grew like a honeycomb'.[55] Belief in the business abilities of freedmen was further reinforced by many ex-slaves in their epitaphs. The Roman elite boasted on their tombstones of their birth and of the civic honours, open only to the freeborn, that they had received in life. Successful, that is wealthy, freedmen were unable to make comparable boasts; instead they claimed

commonly due from freedman to patron; the most time-consuming of these obligations was to carry out an agreed number of days of work (*operae*).[63]

It was through the mechanism of manumission, I believe, accompanied by a grant of capital from his former master, that a freedman from the household of a wealthy Gaius Sulpicius became a banker in Puteoli. Further details may be added. Let us suppose that the bank's first owner/manager was the Faustus major of the Murecine archive. During his years in servitude Faustus had shown himself to be literate and numerate and been appointed to be loans clerk (*servus kalendario praepositus*) for the household (*domus*). While holding this position he had demonstrated his ability to manage staff, keep accurate books, prepare the necessary loan documentation and chase up debts. After a few years Gaius Sulpicius decided to manumit Faustus, on the understanding that he would go into business as an *argentarius*; he would run a deposit-taking bank which would deal with the public at large and operate at arm's length from the general business of the *domus*. (The broad outline of this model would be the same if Faustus had been manumitted *ex testamento* and reached a similar agreement with the heir of his former master.)

The new business would need start-up capital. Faustus had taken the opportunity to build up a sizeable *peculium* as loans clerk, since this position had allowed him considerable opportunity for trading on his own account. Gaius Sulpicius allowed him to take these funds with him into the business.

As part of the terms on which he was granted his freedom, Faustus entered into a contract of partnership with his former master, now his patron. Under their contract, the *peculium* was declared to be the risk capital of the business, owned in agreed proportions by patron and freedman. Gaius Sulpicius may also have indicated to Faustus that he would from time to time provide further capital in the form of loans, on which Faustus would pay interest. Faustus was to manage the business as he saw fit; but he would be required to pay dividends on the capital in the business as and when profits were earned. After a few years Faustus bought out his former master's share in the partnership and became sole proprietor.

The narrative of our model eventually shades into the narrative of the enterprise documented in the Murecine archive, when the real-life Faustus major first appears on 18 March 26 (TPSulp. 42). Two competing accounts of the firm's organisation during the years covered by the archive are plausible. The first account is built around two tablets dating to 47 and 51 (TPSulp. 72, 74). These tablets record transactions in which Cinnamus collects funds that are due to the bank and issues receipts on behalf of Faustus, his former master (*patronus*). This indicates that Cinnamus is acting as business manager (procurator) for Faustus; when a borrower paid back a debt to his creditor's procurator, the debt was regarded as settled. It was common for a slave to be set free in order to become his former master's procurator and this is evidently how the Bank of the Sulpicii operated: in TPSulp. 87 (dated to 51) Gaius Sulpicius Eutychus, another ex-slave, describes himself as the procurator of Cinnamus.

From these tablets it may be inferred that Cinnamus, who had been Faustus' slave,

When read carefully this document suggests that Cinnamus provided on his own account HS80,000, the major part of this loan of HS130,000, since only HS50,000 was due to be repaid to Faustus. Here it looks very much as if Faustus and Cinnamus were acting as banking partners (*socii argentarii*). They had each provided funds, in differing amounts to a single borrower.

I find this alternative account of the firm's organisation the more convincing. Faustus, the founder, is to be regarded as the senior figure during the early years documented in the archive. At some point before the end of the year 47, he freed his slave Cinnamus and appointed him as general manager (procurator). The two men went into partnership. Faustus seems to have left the business, through retirement or death, in about 52; by this time Cinnamus in his turn had freed one of his slaves, Eutychus, to act as his general manager. Cinnamus may have gone into partnership with Eutychus and subsequently Onirus may have become a partner in his turn. Roman law made specific provision for bankers acting in partnership. A treatise on rhetoric from the late Republic states:[64]

> A client who has deposited money with a banker can, by virtue of usage rather than of strict law (*sine lege aeque ac si legitimum sit usitatum est*), reclaim it from a partner of that banker.

Furthermore the jurist Paul said that a pact made with either of two bankers, provided that they are partners, applies to both.[65] This was an exemption from the general rule that partners were separately responsible for contracts that each had entered into. Without such an exemption, it would have been difficult if not impossible for a deposit-taking bank to be operated by a partnership: people would be unwilling to hand over funds to a banker who was in partnership if they could not later withdraw them from another partner in the business. An agreement preserved on a wax tablet from Dacia dated to AD 167 will serve, mutatis mutandis, to provide an indication of how the partnership between Faustus and Cinnamus might have been structured:[66]

> Between Cassius Frontinus and Julius Alexander a moneylending partnership (*societas danistariae*) from last December 23, in the consulship of Pudens and Polio, to April 12 next was agreed to on the following terms - that [the partners] would be obliged to accept in equal shares whatever return came from the capital (*ab re natum*) in this partnership, whether profit or loss occurred. To this partnership Julius Alexander contributed 500 denarii in cash and money out on loan credit (*in fructo*) and Secundus, slave and business manager (*servus actor*) of Cassius Palumbus, contributed 267 *denarii* on behalf of Frontinus....
>
> In this partnership, if either partner is apprehended in the commission of malicious fraud, he shall be obliged to pay the other 1 denarius for each *as*, and 20 *denarii* for each *denarius*...And when the period of the contract is complete, they shall each recover the

and Julius Alexander gave his promise (*spopondit*). Two sets of tablets concerning this agreement have been signed and sealed. Likewise, 50 *denarii* are due to Cossa, which he shall be entitled to recover from the above-mentioned partners.

This deed was enacted at Deusara on March 28 in the consulship of Verus (for the third time) and Quadratus.

This partnership agreement was made on December 23, but not written down, signed and sealed until March 28 (i.e. three months later), with less than a month to run before it was due to expire (on April 12). The legal contract was constituted by the oral agreement, in the form of stipulation. The later written agreement provided evidence that a contract had been entered into.

We should note that the contributions made by each partner did not have to be equal or of the same kind. In the Dacian agreement Julius Alexander contributed, as his share, 500 *denarii* made up of ready cash and money out on loan. Cassius Frontinus contributed a smaller amount, just 267 *denarii*. His contribution was paid in cash by Secundus, slave and business manager of Cassius Palumbus; presumably Palumbus provided these funds in settlement of a debt he owed to Frontinus. Despite any inequality in contribution to the partnership, any profit or loss was to be equally shared. An existing obligation to a third party, Cossa, was to be the joint responsibility of the partners. Julius Alexander was already an established money lender in Dacia; a loan for 60 *denarii*, payable on demand, is recorded in a tablet dated five years earlier.[67] The partnership with Frontinus was presumably made to provide extra funds for some anticipated lending opportunity; there is no mention in the document of taking deposits. Frontinus seems to be the senior partner, since it is he who stipulated and Alexander who responded.

The partnership between Faustus and Cinnamus will have differed in two important aspects from the partnership between the Dacian bankers. As will emerge shortly, the loans made by the Sulpicii were based on funds deposited with them by customers, whereas the bank in Dacia apparently made its loans only from capital provided by the two proprietors.

Furthermore, the Dacian partnership was for a finite (and relatively short) period, whereas the arrangement between Faustus and Cinnamus was, if not open-ended, at least intended to last for several years. Presumably on each occasion that a partner died, or simply retired from the business, a new partnership agreement was drawn up to take account of the change in ownership.

III

THE BUSINESS OF THE SULPICII

As the empire expanded, Roman traders followed the legions throughout the Mediterranean world; in the mid-first century BC Cicero claimed that in Narbonese Gaul, 'not a penny changes hands without the transaction being recorded in the books of Roman citizens' (*nummus in Gallia nullus sine civium Romanorum tabulis commovetur*).[1] The boom in trade brought prosperity to the ports of Roman Italy. And where people are busy making money there is a heightened demand for working capital – funds to buy raw materials and to pay wages. Part of the business of the Sulpicii was to provide short-term bridging finance to people selling goods at auction; but they also supplied businessmen with working capital.

Before detailed analysis of the way that the Sulpicii ran their business, some brief observations. The Sulpicii took care to cultivate the good will of their depositors: not only did they look after people's money but they provided services – money transfers and investment opportunities – for which no doubt the depositors were charged appropriate fees. This made good commercial sense. Deposits are the lifeblood of a bank and its depositors are a bank's most valued customers.

When it came to borrowing, there was less need to become so closely involved in customers' affairs. There were always plenty of people who needed cash, and in a community where everyone knew everyone else it was easy enough to know a borrower's credit standing. Roman lenders rarely felt it necessary to enquire closely about the purpose of a loan; it did not matter very much whether a loan was to fund personal consumption or to supply working capital for a business. But the Romans were realists and recognised that even the best-intentioned borrower might renege on a deal. Borrowers were required to provide security in the form of pledged assets or guarantees from third parties of good standing. Further assurance was provided by stipulation, the contractual procedure (outlined in the Introduction) by which borrowers or their agents would give, face to face, a solemn promise to fulfil closely defined obligations such as the date of repayment of a loan and the rate of interest that would be paid. In the last resort there were the courts, where a claimant could sue a defaulting borrower for the payment of a loan by means of an action for the recovery of a specific sum of money. (We shall see the Sulpicii in court in Chapter 9.)

account details were held. If this is the case then I suggest, *pace* Camodeca, that these transactions were not loans but draw-downs by the two slaves from funds held by the Sulpicii which belonged to their respective masters. As in the case of TPSulp. 69, we may be looking at cash held in Puteoli to pay for incoming cargoes.

TPSulp. 100 is a very fragmentary tablet in which Faustus appears to promise by stipulation to pay back a loan of an unknown amount. Again this indicates a loan made to the banker, that is to say a deposit.

The Murecine archive contains several instances (TPSulp. 48, 49, 105) of mandates given by individuals, whom I consider to be depositors, to the Sulpicii to make payments on their behalf.

The first of these three tablets, TPSulp. 48, illustrates the range of services that a depositor expected to be provided by the Sulpicii. This is a complex document which may be conveniently divided into two parts. First the mandate itself (my Paragraph 1); second, a stipulation (my Paragraph 2) under which Prudens accepted terms laid down by Cinnamus:

TPSulp. 48
January/June 48

I, Gaius Julius Prudens, have written:

[1] I have requested and instructed Gaius Sulpicius Cinnamus (*me rogasse C. Sulpicium Cinnamum eique mandasse*) that however much money he [Cinnamus] or Eros or[----]us or Titianus or Martialis, his slaves, or Gaius Sulpicius Faustus (or anyone else under the order, request or instruction of any of them) has given, lent or promised or pledged or stood surety for, or for any other reason has undertaken an obligation, [Cinnamus and his staff should pay that money] once or many times (*semel saepiusve*) to my freedman Suavis or my slave Hyginus, or to anyone else under their order.

[2] And whatever the sum that will thus be given or lent or whatever the sum for which an obligation for whatever reason – as provided for above – shall have been undertaken, that so much money be paid. And Gaius Sulpicius Cinnamus stipulated and I, Gaius Julius Prudens, have pledged that fraud (*dolus malus*) is and shall be absent from this matter and this promise, on the part of me and my heir and all those who are parties to this matter. And in as much as fraud is not absent and will not be absent, that a proportionate amount of money be paid, and that this be rightly paid and done.

Through this mandate Prudens gives authority to conduct business on his behalf, to Cinnamus, to Cinnamus' staff (the slaves Eros, Titianus, Martialis and one other whose name is illegible) and to Gaius Sulpicius Faustus, Cinnamus' patron (and, I believe, partner). The bankers are to provide funds and enter into obligations when required to do so by Prudens' staff. In effect it provides a framework within which Prudens

on deposit at the bank. Prudens would earn the interest on the loans and he would assume the risk. For the Sulpicii, 'depositor loans' of this nature would generate various transfers of funds in and out of Prudens' account and doubtless the bankers would have charged him a fee for these services. Here is a concrete example of the practice mentioned by the jurist Ulpian (see Chapter 2) whereby depositors invested their funds at interest 'in conjunction with bankers'. In a word the bankers would recommend investment opportunities, which in practice meant finding suitable borrowers.

Consequently we should not be surprised that the Murecine archive contains not only records of loans made by the bankers but also records of loans made by third parties. (Under the broad heading of loans I include not only loan contracts (*mutua*) that have survived in the archive but also loans already made, the existence of which may be inferred from surviving records of repayments and other transactions.) Third party lenders who held funds on deposit with the Sulpicii were the bank's clients, in the modern sense of the term. Placing loans on their behalf was risk-free, fee-earning business which would be recognisable to a present-day investment banker.

From the point of view of the borrower, it probably did not matter very much whether a loan came from a depositor or from a banker. However a comparison between depositor loans and the loans made by the Sulpicii can provide an insight into the operations of the bank. For the purposes of this comparison, only depositor loans where the sums involved and the names of both lender and borrower are known will come under consideration; similarly in the case of loans made by the Sulpicii only those transactions will be analysed where the names of the borrowers and the sums involved are known. In both groups, where the named lender or borrower is acting as manager or agent I show, on first appearance, the name of their principal in brackets.

I have identified ten depositor loans:

TABLE 1: DEPOSITOR LOANS

TPSulp.	Date	Lender	Borrower	Amount (HS)
51	18 or 28 Jun 37	Hesychus (Evenus Primianus)	Eunus	10,000
52	2 Jul 37	Hesychus	Eunus	3,000
55	3 Mar 49	Numenius	Ampliatus	5,000
60	20 Mar 43	Titinia Anthracis	Euplia	1,600
67	29 Aug 38	Hesychus (Emp. Gaius) +	Eunus	1,130
68	15 Sep 39	Hesychus	Eunus	1,250

I have received a loan of HS 5,000 from Sextus Granius Numenius and owe him this sum. Sextus Granius Numenius has stipulated that the above mentioned HS 5,000 shall be duly paid back in good coin and I, Publius Vergilius Ampliatus, have promised [to repay this sum].

...I have given to Sextus Granius Numenius as security (*pignus*) silver of a weight of more or less 10 [---] lb. This silver has been stamped by me with my signature...This is on account of the HS 5,000 which I have received from him as a loan on this day through the agreement drawn up in my handwriting (*per chirographum meum*).

Numenius looks very much as if he was an entrepreneurial businessman, short of funds on one occasion, flush with cash on another.

This leaves us with two more transactions, in both cases involving women debtors. TPSulp. 71 is a receipt (for repayment of a loan) given by Amarantus to Pyramus, slave of Caesia Priscilla, who also borrows from the Sulpicii (see below). The fragmentary TPSulp. 99 shows Marcia Fausta agreeing to repay a debt in three instalments to Fortunatus; I assume that this agreement was made when the loan was taken out. We have no indication of the purpose of these loans. (The origins and significance of wealth held by women will be discussed in Chapter 7.)

The second set of transactions consists of loans made by the Sulpicii on their own account and at their own risk. As stated above, only those transactions where I have been able to identify both the name of the borrower and the amount lent will be considered. This has meant excluding several loans: TPSulp. 59, a fragmentary tablet that records a loan of HS 4,000 made by Faustus to an unknown borrower; TPSulp. 65, another fragmentary tablet in which Cinnamus pays out a loan of HS 1,510 to an unknown recipient; TPSulp. 74, which is a receipt issued by Cinnamus to a slave jointly-owned by a certain Fortunatus and another (unknown) borrower for repayment of HS 130,000, the largest single transaction recorded in the archive (a loan which was provided jointly by Faustus and Cinnamus); and TPSulp. 77, which is connected with a loan of an unknown amount made by Cinnamus to Gaius Caesius Quartio (which will be discussed in Chapter 4). This leaves fifteen loans granted by the Sulpicii where I have identified both the value of the loan and the name of the borrower. Again the name of the principal, where appropriate, is given in brackets:

TABLE 2: LOANS MADE BY THE SULPICII

TPSulp.	Date	Lender	Borrower	Amount (HS)
31*	Jun/Oct 52	Cinnamus	Saturninus	18,000
50	9 Nov 35	Faustus	Antonius Maximus	2,000
53	13 Mar 40	Faustus	Jucundus	20,000

Publius Urvinus Zosimus (TPSulp. 57) borrows HS2,000 on top of a previous loan of HS12,000.

Pyramus (TPSulp. 58) is the slave of Caesia Priscilla. He also borrows funds from the depositor Amarantus (see TPSulp. 71 above). In this particular transaction Pyramus borrows HS4,000 from Faustus – in addition to a previous loan of HS20,000 which has been booked to the account (*ratio*) of his mistress.

Euplia (TPSulp. 61, 62) is a freeborn Greek woman, a member of Puteoli's community of resident aliens (*peregrini/ae*). In these two loans she borrows HS500 and HS1,000. As we have already seen, she also borrows funds from Titinia Anthracis, a depositor (TPSulp. 60).

Magia Pulchra (TPSulp. 63) is freeborn. She borrows the relatively large sum of HS30,000 from Cinnamus (or possibly Faustus).

Marcus Caecilius Maximus (TPSulp. 66) owes Faustus HS3,000. There is a mention, in this fragmentary tablet, of profit (*quaestus*) and possibly of copper or bronze (*aerugo*). Camodeca suggests that he may be a moneychanger (*nummularius*).

Alcimus (TPSulp. 72) is the slave of a certain Gaius Eprius Valgus. He repays part of a loan, presumably on his master's behalf, to Cinnamus. The part-repayment in question is HS30,000 (in instalments of HS28,000 and HS2,000) out of a total debt contracted with Faustus of HS50,000.(*9*).

Marcus Egnatius Suavis (TPSulp. 85) has defaulted on a loan of HS26,000 from Cinnamus. (More on Suavis in Chapter 4.)

THE LOANS COMPARED

What distinctions, if any, can be drawn between depositor loans and loans granted directly by the Sulpicii? A fruitful way of approaching this question is to analyse the principal features of the two sets of loans: their value, term, security required and their 'seasonality' (the time of year when they were granted).

Value
Both depositors and the Sulpicii themselves make small value loans. Depositors are recorded lending HS1,130 (TPSulp. 67), HS1,250 (TPSulp. 68) and HS1,600 (TPSulp. 60); the bankers make loans of HS500 (TPSulp. 61), HS1,000 (TPSulp. 56, 62) and HS2,000 (TPSulp. 50, 57).

However, the highest loan made by any depositor – the HS10,000 lent by Hesychus

Security

I can find no marked difference between the two sets of loans in the requirements set by borrowers for security.

TABLE 4: SECURITY TAKEN FOR LOANS

TPSulp.	Lender	Status	Borrower	Amount (HS)	Security
51	Hesychus	Depositor	Eunus	10,000	Foodstuffs
52	Hesychus	Depositor	Eunus	3,000	Foodstuffs
53*	Faustus	Banker	Jucundus	20,000	Grain
54**	Cinnamus	Banker	Philippus	20,000	Surety (Gaius Avilius Cinnamus)
55	Numenius	Depositor	Ampliatus	5,000	Silver
57	Cinnamus	Banker	Zosimus	2,000	Surety (Lucius Annius Felix)
60	Titinia Anthracis	Depositor	Euplia	1,600	Surety (Epichares)
61	Cinnamus	Banker	Euplia	500	Surety (Epichares)
62	Cinnamus	Banker	Euplia	1,000	Surety (Epichares)
78	Primus	Depositor	Menelaus	4,000	Surety (Marcus Barbatius Celer)
85	Cinnamus	Banker	Suavis	26,000	Six slaves
99	Fortunatus	Depositor	Marcia Fausta	2,000 minimum	Surety (...Onesimus)

★ The security required is indicated in TPSulp. 79.
★★ Avilius Cinnamus also appears as a surety for Philippus in TPSulp. 109.

Seven of these loans were backed by personal sureties and five with pledges of assets in the form of commodities, silver or slaves. In addition Agathemer, who was very likely a cloth trader, pledges (TPSulp. 83) Laconian purple cloth for his loan of an unknown amount from Cinnamus (see Chapter 4). When physical assets were pledged they would be put up for auction in the event of the borrower defaulting. Sureties, on the other hand, could be sued for the amount of an outstanding debt.

In two other cases security was provided by oath. In TPSulp. 63 Magia Pulchra has a guarantor (whose name has disappeared); she also swears to repay her large loan (of HS30,000) from Cinnamus or Faustus with an oath 'by Jupiter and the Divinity (*numen*) of the Deified Augustus'. In TPSulp. 68 the grain merchant Eunus guarantees repayment of a loan of HS1,250 from Hesychus with an oath 'by Jupiter Best and Greatest and by the Divinity of the Deified Augustus and by the Genius of Gaius

TPSulp.	Lender	Status	Borrower	Amount (HS)	Month
99	Fortunatus	Depositor	Marcia Fausta	2,000 minimum	February
Most frequent month					March (5 loans out of 17)

Again there is no marked difference between the two groups of lenders. There is, however, a bias in this admittedly small sample towards increased lending activity in the spring. Five loans were made in March – to which we might add one on the last day of February (TPSulp. 99) – and two in April. This was a time of year when domestic stocks of food laid in for the winter were running low and when the price of supplies stored in granaries would be rising. People would be running short of cash – and the squeeze would be felt in the business community as well as by private individuals. March was also the beginning of the sailing season, a time when boat builders and ships' chandlers would require working capital.

It is noticeable that in none of these transactions (with the exception of a penal rate specified in TPSulp. 68, which will be discussed in Chapter 5) is interest mentioned. Yet the interest on a loan and the length of time that the funds were available to the borrower were of crucial importance: together these conditions determined the return on the lenders' funds. The reason for the omission of such vital conditions must be the form of the standard contract governing a loan of money, the contract of *mutuum*. Under this contract the borrower was simply required to restore the equivalent value of the sum borrowed. As already noted, the subsidiary – but financially important – clauses setting out the length of the loan and rate of interest were attached by a separate stipulation.

However, if there were stipulations as to interest and term of loan it seems extraordinary that no record of these subsidiary conditions has survived. Camodeca has put forward an ingenious explanation. He sugggests, if I understand him correctly, that a rate of interest and the term for the loan may have been agreed in an informal pact between lender and borrower, where the borrower would undertake to pay back an agreed sum every month (which would include both capital and interest). Any default would immediately result in a demand for the repayment of the whole sum. The point of this would be to hide *usurae ultra modum*, a rate of interest above the officially approved maximum of 12 per cent a year. Lenders and borrowers would then be operating solely on verbal agreements and on trust (*fides*).[3]

WORKING CAPITAL AND BRIDGING FINANCE

We may conclude that the core business of the Sulpicii consisted in the provision of short-term loans. They provided working capital for small business enterprises and

by freedmen and slaves. The obverse of this is that when finance was required for overseas trading ventures or for public contracts it was supplied directly by wealthy private individuals. These issues will be explored in Part II. In the remaining chapters of Part I, however, we shall look in detail at the everyday business of the Sulpicii. We shall attend auction sales; we shall meet their customers – grain dealers, merchants and shippers and well-to-do women; we shall look at the role played by slaves in the business life of Puteoli; and we shall follow the Sulpicii and their customers into the law courts.

(TPSulp. 88) and textiles (TPSulp. 83-84). Auction sales are also documented in another set of tablets from the Bay of Naples, the archive of the Pompeian banker L. Caecilius Jucundus.[4]

ARRANGING THE AUCTION

Someone with goods to sell at auction was known as the master (or mistress) of the sale (*dominus/domina auctionis*). The vendor would approach a banker and ask him to handle the sale; a contract would be drawn up, the *promissio auctionatoris*. The archive contains a fragmentary example of this promise:

TPSulp. 81
20 June 45

I, Aulus Castricius [---]s, have written:

I have promised [to pay] to Gaius Sulpicius Faustus however much money resulting from the auction of [the goods pledged by] Publius Servilius Narcissus will come [from the buyer], as a result of the stipulation asked [of the buyer] by me or my staff, after the banker's fee (*merces*) has been deducted....

This contract covers a sale where Gaius Sulpicius Faustus is the vendor. Faustus has evidently lent money to a certain Publius Servilius Narcissus; Narcissus has failed to pay back the loan and Faustus wants to sell at auction the goods that Narcissus has given him as security. Although Faustus is himself an *argentarius* he gets Aulus Castricius, another banker, to manage the auction.

As already noted, *argentarii* might extend credit to buyers in the form of medium-term loans on which they charged interest. This is what is indicated here when Castricius says that he will pay over the proceeds of an auction (less the banker's fee) to the vendor Gaius Sulpicius Faustus – 'as a result of the stipulation asked [of the buyer] by me or my staff'. This is a shorthand way of saying that Castricius is prepared to provide a credit, at interest, to the buyer for a period longer than the usual few days.

When the vendor and the banker handling the auction had made their contract, the vendor would post a bill of sale (*libellus*) in a public place. This notice stated that a sale of goods belonging to the vendor would take place in the forum on a future market day; the notice had to be displayed for thirty consecutive days.[5] The vendor seems to have been required to make a declaration (*testatio*) at regular intervals from the day when the advertisement (*proscriptio*) first appeared, to the effect that the actual bill of sale was still on public display. Declarations by the Sulpicii (TPSulp. 90-93), following a notice of sale posted on 4 February 61, are preserved in the archive. These declarations refer to the sale at auction of a single slave, the 'Woman Fortunata'.

TPSulp. 90
16 February 61

At Puteoli in the Sextian Portico of Augustus there has been fixed to a column a notice in which was written what appears below:

'The [slave] woman Fortunata, whom Marcia Aucta was said to have handed over as security on payment of a single sesterce to Gaius Sulpicius Onirus, will come up for sale under the auctioneer (*sub praecone*) on 5 March next at Puteoli in front of the Chalcidicum of Caesonius, for ready cash (*pecunia praesenti*). The [slave given as] security in this matter was first advertised for sale on 4 February 61.'

This bill of sale told passers-by that the slave Fortunata was to be sold in the forum by Gaius Sulpicius Onirus, a member of the banking firm of the Sulpicii. They would see that Fortunata had been pledged by Marcia Aucta as security (*fiducia*) for a loan and that, since Marcia Aucta had failed to meet her obligation, Fortunata was being sold off by Onirus. Prospective purchasers could be assured that Onirus had legal title to the slave, since when she first made the pledge Marcia Aucta had formally transferred ownership to him using a time-honoured legal procedure, the handing over of lands, slaves or cattle for a single sesterce (*mancipatio nummo uno*).

A document recording the temporary transfer of ownership of two slaves as security from debtor to lender, using a slightly different procedure, has survived in the Tablets of Poppaea Note from Pompeii.[6] The freedwoman Poppaea Note borrowed money from Dicidia Margaris; Poppaea Note 'sold' the two slaves to Dicidia Margaris for HS1,450, the amount of the loan. If the loan was repaid by the due date, the slaves would be returned to Poppaea Note – if not, then Dicidia Margaris would be free to sell the slaves 'at Pompeii in the forum publicly in the daytime'. Any surplus over and above the outstanding debt would be returned to the original borrower:

> If these slaves in question are sold for a lesser sum, [the balance, once the price has been deducted from the initial sum,] will be owed to myself or to my heir. [But if] these slaves in question are sold [for a higher sum, the surplus will be returned to you or to your] heir [...]

THE SALE

An auction sale would be conducted by a public herald (*praeco*). A late commentator on Horace described the market in Rome where olives were sold at auction. He was explaining Horace's allusion to his father's occupation as a collecting banker (*coactor*):[7]

> By heralds (*praecones*) were meant those who stood by the spear [indicating the site of the auction] and called out the prices that were bid. Collectors (*coactores*) were the employees (*mercennarii*) of those who held the bank (*argentarium*); the bankers (*argentarii*) are those who hold the total (*summa*) of the items that are sold. We call a banker (*argentarius*) the man who holds the whole quantity of the olives (*summa olivarum*); from him the men who do business in the forum (*forani*) get their olives. The collector (*coactor*) is the man who demands money from those who stand around in the forum (*circumforani*). Another way of putting it is this: the collectors (*coactores*) are what the bankers (*argentarii*) are called who collect money in the auction; these men are the collectors (*collectarii*).

This rather confusing account describes bankers and their staff as they go about their work in the wholesale market where olives are being auctioned. Each individual banker (*argentarius*) holds the stocks of olives that are being auctioned by the vendors for whom he is working; at the conclusion of the sale he will hand over the various lots to the successful bidders. The herald (*praeco*) shouts out the prices that are bid. Collectors (*coactores*) are employed by the bankers; they collect the purchase money from the successful bidders. The scene comes to life in Rome on the monument of the *argentarius* L. Calpurnius Daphnus from the Macellum Magnum, the market on the Caelian Hill. On his funeral stele Daphnus is flanked by porters carrying fish. He is shouting 'Bring your fish for sale' (*da piscen [sic]*).[8]

At the sale the bankers would enter the names of the buyers and the prices paid for each item in their books. The elder Seneca commented on the prodigious memory of the Republican orator Hortensius:[9]

> ...[he] sat through a whole day at an auction and then recited all the items, all the prices and all the buyers in their correct order, with the bankers (*argentarii*) checking [in their books] to see that he made no mistake.

Similarly Cicero gives us a glimpse of bankers at work in a small Italian town, where an inquiry was being carried out into a burglary:[10]

> It was noticed that the bottom of the strong-box had been cut out, and there was a good deal of speculation about how this could have been done. Then one of Sassia's friends remembered having attended an auction sale recently where he had seen a small circular saw with an indented handle and teeth round the edge. This could have been the instrument used to cut round the base of the safe. Inquiries were made from the bankers (*coactores*) and it was found that the saw had been bought by Strato....

any dispute, witnesses would not usually be required to give verbal evidence that a particular transaction had taken place; the presence of their signatures and seals were sufficient.[14]

DEFAULTING BORROWERS

Several tablets in the archive show Gaius Sulpicius Cinnamus arranging for goods pledged to him as security to be sold, following default on the part of the borrower. It seems unlikely, in the light of TPSulp. 81 (above) that Cinnamus proposed to conduct the auctions himself.

One defaulting borrower is a certain Lucius Marius Agathemer. The relevant documents are TPSulp. 83 and 84:

TPSulp. 83
6 September 51

At Puteoli in the Sextian Portico of Augustus, there has been fixed to a column a notice in which was written what appears below:

'The residue/remnants of Laconian purple (*purpuras laconicas reliquas*), which Lucius Marius Agathemer is said to have given as security (*pignus*) to Gaius Sulpicius Cinnamus, will come up for sale on 9 September next.'

TPSulp. 84
6 (or 7) September 51

At Puteoli in the Sextian Portico of Augustus, there has been fixed to a column a notice in which was written what appears below:

'The residue/remnants of Laconian purple, (*purpuras laconicas reliquas*) which Lucius Marius Agathemer is said to have given as security (*pignus*) to Gaius Sulpicius Cinnamus, will come up for sale on 9 September next.'

The first declaration (TPSulp. 83) indicates that an auction of Laconian purple textiles was to take place in three days' time, that is on 9 September. (The original advertisement had presumably been posted 27 days earlier to give the due notice.) The second record (TPSulp. 84) differs only in one respect from the first: the name of one of the consuls (whose term of office was used for dating the year) turns out to have been given incorrectly in TPSulp. 83; this is put right in the second tablet. In legal documents it was necessary for the name of the consuls (a crucial element in recording the date) to be correctly given.

a business, since the very materials that were needed for sale or manufacture were no longer available to the debtor. Agathemer failed to pay the loan by the due date; to recoup the money owing to him Cinnamus decided to sell the material at auction.

Three tablets in the archive (TPSulp. 85-87) refer to a sale of pledged goods forfeited when Marcus Egnatius Suavis defaulted on a loan of HS26,000 made to him by Cinnamus. The first tablet records the amount of the loan and gives details of the security provided by Suavis:

TPSulp. 85
5 October 51

At Puteoli in the forum in the Sextian Portico of Augustus, a notice has been fixed to a column, in which was written what is written here below:

'The man Felix, the man Carus, the man Januarius, the woman Primigenia, the woman Primigenia Junior, the boy Ampliatus, slaves that Marcus Egnatius Suavis was said to have given to Gaius Sulpicius Cinnamus as security (*fiducia*), on payment of a single sesterce, for a loan of HS26,000, will come up for sale on 14 October next at Puteoli in the forum in front of the Chalcidicum of Caesonius at the third hour.

The pledged goods were first advertised for sale on 15 September.'

The notice states that a sale is to take place on 14 October. Up for auction will be six slaves, all identified by name, whom Suavis was said to have given to Cinnamus as security for a loan of HS26,000. As with the loan taken out by Marcia Aucta (TPSulp. 90, see above) Suavis had formally transferred ownership to the lender using the ancient legal procedure, the handing over of lands, slaves or cattle for a single sesterce (*mancipatio nummo uno*).

In this case, however, complications arose, as will be seen from the next tablet in the series:

TPSulp. 86
23 October 51

At Puteoli in the forum in the Sextian Portico of Augustus, a notice has been fixed to a column, in which was written what is written here below:

'The guarantors and creditors of Marcus Egnatius Suavis of the colony of Puteoli, who has no extant heir....'

It emerges from this document that Suavis had died, apparently before the auction, which was scheduled for 14 October, could take place. By 23 October it had been

by the jurist Gaius:[4]

> The estates of deceased persons are sold when it is established that they have left no heirs...Where the estate that is being sold...is that of a deceased person, it is advertised for 15 days. After that the praetor orders the creditors to meet and appoint one of their number as manager (*magister*), that is, the one to carry out the sale...

From the mention of guarantors and creditors it looks very much as if the whole of Suavis' estate was to be sold up, for the benefit of all those to whom he owed money. On the face of it, this put Cinnamus in a difficult position. He had already initiated proceedings to sell the six slaves that had been pledged to him as security for his loan. Was he now to contribute these slaves to a common pool of assets which would be sold for the benefit of all Suavis' creditors?

The fragmentary text of TPSulp. 87 continues the story. I give the broad gist:

> TPSulp. 87
> 30 October 51
>
> At Puteoli in the forum in front of the Chalcidicum of Caesonius, Gaius Sulpicius Eutychus, who said that he was the procurator of Gaius Sulpicius Cinnamus, testified that he had handed over to the herald (*praeco*) the man Felix and the man Carus and the man Januarius and the woman Primigenia and the woman Primigenia Junior and the boy Ampliatus - slaves whom Marcus Egnatius Suavis is said to have given to Gaius Sulpicius Cinnamus as security, on payment of a single sesterce, for a loan of HS26,000. And that the sale had been put off until the next market day (*nundinae*).

The sale of Suavis' estate has now been postponed until the next market day. Cinnamus, who was evidently engaged elsewhere, has instructed Eutychus, his manager (procurator), to hand over the six slaves to the herald who acted as auctioneer. (Presumably the expenses of feeding and maintaining the slaves would eventually be met out of Suavis' estate.) It rather looks as if the six slaves were being lumped in with the rest of Suavis' property and Cinnamus would have to take his share of the proceeds alongside the other creditors.

Another defaulting borrower was Gaius Caesius Quartio:

> TPSulp. 77
> 12 January 48
> I, Gaius Caesius Quartio, have written:

I have received from Gaius Sulpicius Cinnamus HS4,300 from the proceeds of an auction of slaves; this sum I have received directly (*protinus*) from Publius Acilius Primus.

What seems to have happened is this. Quartio had guaranteed a loan from Cinnamus by pledging slaves as security. When Quartio defaulted, Cinnamus as usual arranged for the slaves to be auctioned by another *argentarius*. At the auction sale the amount paid by the purchaser Primus produced a surplus of HS4,300 over and above the amount of the debt owed to Cinnamus. Under the usual procedure the entire proceeds of the sale should have come to Cinnamus who would then have handed the surplus to Quartio. But in this case the purchaser paid the surplus direct to Quartio. To keep the record straight Quartio has given a receipt for the HS4,300 to Cinnamus but he has made it clear that he has received the funds directly from the purchaser. The outcome is the same. Quartio has repaid his debt to Cinnamus and has some cash in hand.

THE BUSINESS OF LUCIUS CAECILIUS JUCUNDUS

An archive of 153 tablets recording the transactions of the Pompeian banker and businessman Lucius Caecilius Jucundus throws further light on the conduct of Roman auctions. Discovered at Pompeii in July 1875, these tablets had been stored after the earthquake of AD 62 in a wooden chest in House 26 in Insula 1 of Region V. The business of Jucundus has been the subject of a major study by Andreau.[25]

Jucundus' house, decorated with wall paintings, is described by Andreau as 'comfortable and spacious'; it was presumably his place of work. The house suffered much damage as a result of the earthquake in AD 62, but it was then restored. The tablets form an archive, stretching over a quarter of a century, of receipts given to Jucundus (or, in one case, his predecessor) for payments made by the firm. The archive must represent only a fraction of the transactions carried out by the business during this period. The earliest tablet (T. 1) is dated to the year 15, when the transaction involved the banker Lucius Caecilius Felix. I assume that L. Caecilius Felix is the middle-aged man who is depicted in a bronze portrait bust set on a short marble column ('herm') found in the atrium of the House of Caecilius Iucundus; bronze genitalia set lower down in the column indicate the potency of money, the banker's stock in trade. The herm, dated to the Augustan period, bears the inscription 'To the Genius of our Lucius. His freedman Felix set this up'. This is a portrait, I suggest, of the proprietor of the banking firm in the early years of the first century and the bust was dedicated to him by his freedman, also called Felix. At some point the succession passed to Lucius Caecilius Jucundus: the second tablet in the archive (T2), and the first to carry his name, is dated to 27. The bulk of the tablets are dated to the years 54 to 58. The latest tablet in the collection (T. 151) dates from the month of January 62, shortly before the earthquake of that year (*11*).

that the principals may be engaged in commerce. In T. 5 Gaius Julius Onesimus sells boxwood (*buxaria*), which might be used for the manufacture of furniture or flutes, for HS1,985; Jucundus granted the purchaser credit for two months and five days. In T. 100 Ptolemy, son of Masyllus, of Alexandria, sells linen for an unknown sum. It seems likely that Ptolemy was a native of Alexandria, now resident in Pompeii, who was engaged in the textile trade between his home port and Campania.

THE IMPORTANCE OF AUCTION SALES

Auction sales constituted a significant part of a banker's business. *Argentarii* could earn commission from vendors for collecting the funds due to them; and they could also earn interest from lending funds to buyers. To modern eyes, this dual role – acting on behalf both of buyers and of vendors – might seem to present a conflict of interest, but this does not seem to have been an issue in Roman business circles.

Seen in a wider perspective, auction sales provided an important contribution to overall economic activity in the Roman world. This is because they provided a mechanism that enabled someone who lent money against security in the form of real estate or goods to stand a good chance of recouping their funds, in the event of default by the borrower. This safety net encouraged the lending of money by wealthy individuals as well as by bankers. Auction sales also provided public authorities with a safety net when they let contracts. The treasury in Rome (*aerarium*), and municipal councils elsewhere, required guarantees in the form of real estate that contracts for building works would be completed satisfactorily and on time. If a contract went sour, estates pledged by the guarantors could be sold at auction. Auction sales were a significant factor in the velocity of circulation, the rate at which money circulated through the Roman economy.

A puzzling question remains to be answered. Why did Roman bankers keep receipts from auction sales which had occurred several decades earlier?

It is tempting to see legal and commercial significance in this practice. First, the receipts provided written evidence that the money due from goods being sold at auction had actually been paid over, less the banker's commission, to the vendor. They could be produced in case of a dispute. They were also available for production to government officials for the purpose of accounting for the auction sales tax – which was collected by *argentarii*. But was no time limit set for keeping business records?

Second, the receipts could be used to demonstrate the firm's financial standing and probity. Jucundus undertook public contracts in Pompeii for such services as the collection of the pasture tax and he was paying banker for the partnership which collected the market tax. He depended on the continuing approval and good-will of the municipal authorities, and through his records he was able to show that his clients included members of Pompeii's elite. For instance Gnaeus Alleius Nigidius Maius was a vendor at an auction (T. 16) in 55, at a time when he was, or was about to become,

had interests in real estate – shops and apartments. He paid for public games, he was a priest of the imperial cult (*flamen Caesaris Augusti*) and was hailed as 'leader of the colony' (*princeps coloniae*).[26]

Equally important, perhaps more so, the tablets showed which citizens were prepared to go to Jucundus' house and witness his financial transactions. As Jongman has demonstrated, the witnesses were overwhelmingly drawn from the main occupants of the 600 or so large houses of Pompeii: thus in T. 77, Maius appears as first witness.[27] These receipts comprised a list of prestigious associates, which could be used to promote Jucundus' business interests.

It is quite possible, however, that the tablets were kept for a more mundane reason. Wax tablets were an expensive item and could be reused. The various caches of tablets found at sites in Campania and elsewhere may have been collections of writing material due to be erased and re-waxed for future use – in modern terminology, recycled.

V

GRAIN DEALERS

A substantial portion of the Egyptian wheat that arrived at Puteoli was shipped onwards to Rome. Here it was stored in warehouses on the quays by the Tiber, some of which were owned by the state, others by wealthy families.[1] A proportion of this grain was allocated to the imperial household, to government servants and to military units based in the city. Another call on these supplies was for the regular free distributions of grain (*frumentationes*) that were made to certain categories of citizens. Nevertheless most of Rome's million-strong population had to buy its wheat on the open market. 'The people of Rome were accustomed to buy their food on a daily basis,' commented Tacitus, describing the sense of crisis which swept the city in the winter of 69/70, when the arrival of the grain fleet had been delayed.[2]

In Rome and other cities a complex supply chain linked warehouses (*horrea*), retail grain traders (*mercatores frumentarii*), bakers (*pistores*) and food shops (*tabernae*). Several tablets in the Murecine archive are concerned with the operations of two grain traders based in Puteoli, Gaius Novius Eunus and Lucius Marius Jucundus. We have no information on their core business – perhaps they supplied local bakers and the general public; perhaps they had links to grain traders in Rome. What the archive does reveal, however, is that both Eunus and Jucundus speculated in grain, required ready finance and turned to the Sulpicii for the necessary funds.

THE FINANCIAL DEALINGS OF GAIUS NOVIUS EUNUS

In June 37 the freedman Gaius Novius Eunus took out out a loan of HS10,000.

> TPSulp. 51
> 18 (or 28) June 37
>
> I, Gaius Novius Eunus, have written:

Augustus (*ab Eueno Ti(berii) Cessaris Augusti liberto Primiano*); in Primianus' absence this loan was made to me by his slave Hesychus.

And I owe to him HS10,000 which I will return to him when he demands it. And the above mentioned HS10,000 Hesychus, the slave of Evenus Primianus, freedman of Tiberius Caesar Augustus, has stipulated is to be duly paid back to him in good coin; I Gaius Novius Eunus have promised that I shall do so.

And for this HS10,000 I have given to him by way of pledge (*pignus*) or earnest (*arabo*) approximately (*plus minus*) 7,000 modii of Alexandrian wheat and approximately 4,000 modii of chick peas, spelt, *monocopus* and lentils contained in 200 sacks. All of these items are in my possession and deposited in the publicly-owned Bassian warehouses in Puteoli. I declare that these items are at my risk (*periculo meo*), whatever the cause of any loss (*ab omni vi*).

[Witnessed]

Gaius Novius Eunus
Quintus Falernus [---]
Gaius Sulpicius Faustus
Gaius [---] [---]
[-] [---] Helvi[---]
Gaius Novius Eunus

In this loan transaction, recorded by Eunus in 'vulgar Latin', the lender is Hesychus, slave of Evenus Primianus, whom Eunus describes as Evenus Primianus, freedman of Tiberius Caesar Augustus. (Elsewhere (TPSulp. 45) he is rather more conventionally described as Tiberius Julius Evenus, imperial freedman (*Ti. Iulius Augusti libertus Evenus*).) We may infer from his name that Evenus had once been the slave of a certain Primus and had passed into the ownership of the emperor Tiberius, who had subsequently freed him. In the year 37 when these transactions take place, Tiberius has died and Evenus has passed as an imperial freedman (*Augusti libertus*) into the household of Tiberius' successor the emperor Gaius ('Caligula').

I believe that the emphasis put by Hesychus in this document on the absence of Evenus indicates that Hesychus was on this occasion acting as his master's business manager (*institor*) (see Chapter 2). Evidently Evenus holds an account with the Sulpicii and Hesychus is authorised to draw funds from this account; the transaction has been arranged by the banker Gaius Sulpicius Faustus, who acts as one of the witnesses.

The sum of money that Eunus is borrowing is HS10,000. The loan is repayable on demand and Eunus has pledged as security various foodstuffs – 7,000 *modii* of Alexandrian wheat and 200 sacks (containing 4,000 *modii* in all) of chickpeas, spelt, lentils and an unidentifiable commodity known as *monocopus*. These items, which

Eunus specifically declares to be in his possession (*penus* [sic] *me*) are stored in one of Puteoli's publicly-owned warehouse complexes, the *horrea Bassiana*.

At this point we should note that the value of the security pledged by Eunus – the sacks of wheat, spelt and other foodstuffs – is considerably higher than the HS10,000 that he has borrowed against it. Camodeca suggests that the price of a modius of wheat at the dockside in Puteoli would probably be HS3.[3] At this price the pledged wheat alone would be worth at the very least HS21,000, more than twice the amount that Eunus is borrowing.

This loan is soon followed by another:

> TPSulp. 52
> 2 July 37
>
> I, Gaius Novius Eunus, have written:
>
> I have received a loan from Hesychus, the slave of Evenus Primianus, freedman of Tiberius Caesar Augustus.
>
> And I owe him HS3,000, in addition to the other HS10,000 which in my other deed [it is recorded that] I owe him.
>
> And the above mentioned HS3,000 Hesychus, the slave of Evenus Primianus, freedman of Tiberius Caesar Augustus, has stipulated is to be duly paid back to him in good coin; I, Gaius Novius Eunus, have promised that I shall do so.
>
> And for all this sum I have given to him as a pledge (*pignus*) 7,000 *modii* of Alexandrian wheat, which is stored on the middle level of the publicly-owned Bassian warehouses (*in horreis Bassianis… medis* [sic]) in Puteoli in Bunker No. 12, and the 200 sacks of lentils, chick peas, *monocopus* and spelt, making 4,000 *modii*, which are stored in the same warehouse.
>
> I declare that all these items are at my risk, whatever the cause of any loss.
>
> [Witnessed]
>
> Gaius Novius Eunus
> Aulus Mevius Julius, son of Aulus, of the tribe Falerna.
> Cypaerus
> [------]
> Gaius Novius Eunus

this he decides to become the legally-recognised tenant of the space where they are stored. There is no need for the goods to be moved. Hesychus can simply take over the lease but he wants it to be made quite clear what space he is renting and what is stored there. This is why in the second loan document (TPSulp. 52) Eunus has been required to spell out the exact location of the stocks of Alexandrian wheat, the really valuable item. The lease document (TPSulp. 45) also contains this information and in addition specifies the location of the other pledged commodities held in the warehouse. For all this space Hesychus is to pay a rental of just HS1 per month. Now we know from another lease document from the Murecine archive (TPSulp. 46 below) that in the year 40 a bunker in another Puteolan warehouse, holding at least 13,000 modii, was leased at HS100 a month. Hesychus is evidently being charged a purely nominal rent.

Two questions arise about these transactions in June and July 37. First, if Eunus needed HS13,000 urgently, why did he not sell part of the foodstuffs (which were worth considerably more than HS13,000) that he already had in store? Second, why was the warehouse space leased to Hesychus at a nominal rent?

Our starting point must be that Eunus is speculating in grain.[4] These transactions have to be seen against the background of fluctuating wheat prices at Puteoli. In a typical year, prices fell when the new season's shipments reached Puteoli in early June but began to rise later in the year, as stocks diminished. Eunus wants to borrow cash on two occasions in June and July so that he can buy stocks of the new season's grain (which is now beginning to arrive from Alexandria.) He plans to make a profit by selling these stocks later in the year. From the profits, he calculates, he can pay back Hesychus, redeem his pledged grain (and the other foodstuffs) and sell these items, too, into a market where prices are rising.

In these speculative operations Eunus receives considerable assistance from Cypaerus, manager of the public warehouse and, it emerges, former master of Eunus. We know about the relationship between Cypaerus and Eunus because in the list of witnesses to the lease document TPSulp. 45 Eunus signs himself (in the genitive used by witnesses) as 'Gaius Novius Eunus, freedman of Cypaerus' (*C. Novii Cypaeri liberti Euni*). We can now see that Cypaerus was much in evidence on 2 July 37. He gets his slave Diognetus to draw up the lease of warehouse space to Hesychus, he witnesses the lease document, and he stands as witness to the loan contract (TPSulp. 52) taken out by Eunus on the same day. Furthermore Cypaerus granted a particular favour to Eunus, his former slave, by charging a nominal rent to Hesychus, Eunus' creditor. He might have let Hesychus rent the space for nothing, but I expect that Hesychus insisted on paying some rent, so that he retained the right to sue the warehouse in certain circumstances. Cypaerus evidently took a keen interest in the affairs of his freedman Eunus. On the assumption that former masters often invested in businesses run by their freedmen, Cypaerus is likely to have held a partnership stake in Eunus' grain trading business.

The archive contains two more documents recording loans made to Eunus by Hesychus, in 38 and 39. Hesychus is now known as Hesychus Evenianus, slave of

Deified Augustus and by the Genius of Gaius Caesar Augustus. And if I do not pay back this money on the due date, I will not only be held guilty of perjury but I will be obliged to pay as a penalty HS20 a day.

And the above mentioned HS1,250 Hesychus, slave of Gaius Caesar Augustus, has stipulated is to be duly paid back in good coin; I Gaius Novius Eunus have promised that I shall do so.

[Witnessed]

Gaius Novius Eunus
Gaius Julius Myrtilus
Gaius Marcius Diogenes
Gaius Publilius Theodorus
Gaius Novius Eunus

This loan agreement, the last of Eunus' transactions that has come down to us, states that the sum owed (HS1,250) constitutes the balance of Eunus' outstanding debt to Hesychus. Eunus' business is evidently not prospering and Hesychus has been having difficulty in getting his money back. Hesychus now fixes a final date, 1 November next, for repayment in full and he introduces tough terms. If Eunus defaults he will be liable to pay a penal rate of interest – HS20 a day, which on a debt of HS1,250 amounts to nearly 50 per cent a month! Eunus has also been made to swear by Jupiter, by the Divinity of Augustus and by the Genius of Caligula, that he will repay the outstanding debt on the due date. If he defaults, he will be guilty of perjury and, according to the jurist Ulpian, liable to a flogging.[5]

In neither of these two documents is there any suggestion, as there was in TPSulp. 51, that Hesychus is acting on instructions from his master (who is now the emperor). This is hardly surprising when such small amounts are in question. It looks, therefore, as if Hesychus is trading on his own account, through his *peculium* (see Chapter 2).

These last two documents also reveal the role that Sulpicius Faustus the banker played in these transactions. Until now Faustus' only overt involvement was to act in 37 as one of the witnesses for the loan of HS10,000 (TPSulp. 51). But in these later transactions Eunus promises to make repayments either to Hesychus or to Faustus. Faustus is acting as receiving banker for Hesychus; this indicates that Hesychus himself now has a deposit account with the bank.

The sequence of events can be reconstructed. In the summer of 37 Gaius Novius Eunus undertook some speculative deals in the grain market. He turned to the Sulpicii for finance. The bankers suggested that Eunus should borrow funds from the slave Hesychus, business manager for his master the imperial freedman Evenus Primianus (who held an account with the bank). To make the loan package as attractive as pos-

manager, for Hesychus to lease storage space at a nominal rent for the commodities pledged as security. On at least two subsequent occasions Eunus took out further loans from Hesychus – who had now become the slave of the emperor, was trading through his *peculium* and held an account with the Sulpicii. Eunus ran into financial trouble in 39 and Hesychus took a tough line with him over repayment of his outstanding debt.

THE FINANCIAL DEALINGS OF LUCIUS MARIUS JUCUNDUS

On 13 March in the year 40, the freedman L. Marius Jucundus took out a loan from the banker Gaius Sulpicius Faustus:

TPSulp. 53
13 March 40

I, Lucius Marius Jucundus, freedman of Dida, have written:

I have received from and owe to Gaius Sulpicius Faustus HS20,000 which I have received as a loan in cash. And the above mentioned HS20,000 Gaius Sulpicius Faustus has stipulated is to be duly paid back in good coin; and I, Lucius Marius Jucundus have promised that I shall do so.

[Witnessed]

Lucius Marius Jucundus
Marcus Marius(?) [--r---]
Gaius Julius Celer
[------]
Marcus Marius [---]
Publius Annius Felix

No term or security is mentioned in this document. It is worth noting, however, that among the witnesses to the transaction was the freedman P. Annius Felix; as already noted (Chapter 1) the Annii were a distinguished Puteolan family.

On the same day that the loan agreement was signed the lender, Sulpicius Faustus, took out a lease from another connection of the *gens Annia* – the warehouse manager Publius Annius Seleucus:

TPSulp. 46
13 March 40

I Nardus, slave of Publius Annius Seleucus, have written:

In the presence of and at the order of my master Seleucus (because he says that he does not know how to read and write) I have leased to Gaius Sulpicius Faustus Bunker No. 26 in the upper Barbatian warehouses of Domitia Lepida, in which are stored 13,000 modii of Alexandrian wheat (which my master will check with his slaves) for a rent of HS 100 a month.

[Witnessed]

Publius Annius Seleucus
Gnaeus Pollius Rufus, son of Gnaeus
Gaius Julius Felix
Nardus, slave of Publius Annius Seleucus
Publius Annius Seleucus

The salient points here are that Faustus the lender has taken out a lease on a bunker in a privately-owned warehouse where 13,000 *modii* of Alexandrian wheat have been stored. The rent of the bunker is HS 100 a month. Part of the arrangement is that Seleucus and his slaves will measure the precise amount of grain stored in the bunker.

Two days later, on 15 March, Jucundus signed another agreement with Faustus:

TPSulp. 79
15 March 40

I, Lucius Marius Jucundus, freedman of Dida, have written:

I have given to Gaius Sulpicius Faustus as security (*pignus*) the 13,000 *modii* of Alexandrian wheat which are stored in Bunker No. 26 in the upper Barbatian warehouses of Domitia Lepida on account of the [loan of] HS 20,000 for which I have given my signed obligation.

If on the 15 May next I have not repaid, settled or made satisfaction for the above mentioned HS 20,000, then it will be lawful for you [Faustus], as a condition of the pledge of security in this matter, to sell at auction (*sub praecone…vendere*) the wheat which is the subject of this transaction. If the sale fetches more [than the amount owed], you will return all the surplus funds to me or my heir; if it fetches less, then I will make up the difference to you or your heir. And all risk concerning the grain which is the subject of this transaction is to be assumed by me or my heir. I have agreed this with you and made a bargain (*pactus sum*).

as security if he, Jucundus, defaulted. But it is also made clear that any cash surplus arising from the sale would be returned to Jucundus or his heir (*13*).

VI

THE MERCHANT, THE AGENT AND THE SHIPPER

On 11 April 38, Primus, the slave of P. Attius Severus, made a loan of 1,000 *denarii* (HS4,000) to Menelaus, a native of Caria in Asia Minor:

TPSulp. 78
11 Apr 38

I, Menelaus, son of Irenaus, from Ceramos, have written:

I have received from Primus, slave of Publius Attius Severus, 1,000 denarii resulting from a duly signed maritime freight agreement (*ek naulotikes eksphragismenes*). I will repay willingly the loan that I have taken out according to the agreement that I have made with him. And I have set as a surety for the payment of the above-mentioned 1,000 *denarii*, Marcus Barbatius Celer.

I, Quintus Aelius Romanus, have written, at the request and instruction of Marcus Barbatius Celer and in his presence, because he says that he does not know how to read and write (*quod is litteras nesciret*) that he [Celer] guarantees the above-mentioned 1,000 *denarii* to Primus, slave of Publius Attius Severus, on behalf of Menelaus, son of Irenaus, from Ceramos – as has been written above.

This document is made up of two chirographs, the first of which is written in Greek. In the first chirograph Menelaus, a freeborn Greek from Caria, states that he has received 1,000 *denarii* (that is HS4,000), from Primus, slave of P. Attius Severus. This loan is connected in some way with a 'maritime agreement' (not reproduced in the loan document) that has already been concluded between the two participants. Use of the term *naulotike*, which is derived from the Greek *naulos* or *naulon* (Latin, *naulum*) meaning 'passage money', indicates that this prior agreement is a freight contract. Menelaus promises to repay the loan in accordance with this agreement. In the second chirograph, which is written in Latin, we are told that M. Barbatius Celer will stand surety for Menelaus. But because Celer is illiterate, the chirograph is written on his behalf, at his request and in his presence, by Quintus Aelius Romanus. Romanus also stands as witness to the transaction.

A raft of questions arises. Why was a loan being made by the slave Primus? Who was his master Severus? Who was the borrower Menelaus? Who were Celer and Romanus? What was the substance of the previous maritime freight agreement? And what is the purpose of the loan recorded in this document?

THE MERCHANT AND THE AGENT

The first point that emerges from this document is that the lender, Primus, is not a partner or employee of the Sulpicii. He is the slave of P. Attius Severus, a merchant. Primus is acting as Severus' commercial agent in Puteoli and the funds he is lending belong ultimately to his master. The reason why the loan in TPSulp. 78 belongs to the archive of the Sulpicii must be that Severus held cash balances on deposit with the banking firm. It was not unusual for deposits to be held in the name of a slave; TPSulp. 69, for instance, reveals that Phosphorus Lepidianus, slave of the emperor Claudius, has HS94,000 on short-term deposit with the bank.

As it happens, Severus is known to us from the archaeological record. He is attested in several inscriptions on *amphorae* found in Rome that had contained fish sauce (*garum*) exported to Italy from southern Spain.[1] The extent of trade between southern Spain and Italy is mentioned by Strabo who noted that the region of Turdetania produced grain, wine, olive oil, wax, honey, pitch, dye-stuffs, wool and woven fabrics as well as salt fish products. Strabo continues:[2]

> The abundance of the exports of Turdetania is indicated by the size and the number of the ships; for merchantmen of the greatest size sail from this country to Dicaearchia (Puteoli) and to Ostia, the seaport of Rome; and their number very nearly rivals that of the Libyan ships.

The agent of a merchant might be a slave, a freedman or a freeborn citizen. Agents might even own a share in the business: 100 years earlier the merchants of Puteoli, men of wealth and good reputation (*homines locupletes atque honesti*), complained bitterly of the mistreatment by Verres of their agents in Sicily, who were 'partners, freedmen and fellow-freedmen' (*socii, liberti, conliberti*).[3]

Not surprisingly, it was no light task for a Roman businessman to manage an enterprise that held extensive overseas interests:[4]

> Men often hope that that their assets are greater than they are. This frequently happens to people who carry on business overseas (*transmarinae negotiationes*) through slaves and freedmen or in regions where they are not living themselves; they are often ignorant of losses incurred over a long period and bestow the favour of freedom on their slaves, manumitting them without fraudulent intent.

The inference is that an agent might run an overseas business on his master's behalf for a considerable time (often years rather than months), and that the effective working of the system relied on trust (*fides*).

A shrewd merchant would take care to secure for his agent an introduction (*commendatio*) to well-placed overseas contacts.[5] Take for example Cicero's letter to Q. Cornificius, governor of Africa, on behalf of the equestrian L. Lamia. The relevant extract reads:[6]

> I would only ask you to believe that if you protect Lamia's interests (*negotia*) and assist his managers, freedmen and household (*procuratores, libertos, familiam*) as occasion may require, I shall be more beholden to you than if your generosity had to do with my own business (*rem familiarem meam*).

Roman law did not recognise that when an agent under contract conducted a transaction with a third party on behalf of his principal, rights and liabilities created by such a transaction could take effect between the principal and the third party without affecting the agent himself. Consequently when a Roman paterfamilias wished to enter into contracts at a distance, i.e. not face-to-face, he would employ a subordinate who had pre-existing legal obligations towards him to act as his agent. The subordinates who could most suitably be employed in commercial transactions were slaves, who were in his absolute power; when a slave entered into a contract any property and rights that he acquired automatically belonged to the paterfamilias.[7]

However, if a slave acting as agent was to carry out his duties effectively, counterparties needed assurance that when he gave a contractual undertaking they could sue for redress if they had a grievance. This raised a problem: a slave, being a non-person, could not be sued. To provide counterparties with suitable assurance, various legal remedies had been introduced during the period of Rome's commercial expansion.[8] One such remedy was the *actio de peculio et de in rem verso* (usually known simply as the *actio de peculio*). This was an action which an aggrieved creditor might bring against a paterfamilias; in this action the amount claimed was limited to the value of the slave's *peculium*, the fund he might use for trading (see Chapter 2), and also to the extent that the master's estate had profited from the transaction in question. The *actio de peculio* was available when the slave had entered a transaction without his master's knowledge; if the slave traded through his *peculium* with his master's knowledge, creditors could bring another action, the *actio tributoria*, which was less advantageous to the paterfamilias.

By making clever use of slaves and under-slaves trading through their *peculia* a paterfamilias might be able to distance himself from the day-to-day conduct (and therefore potential liabilities) of the business. Ulpian explains how this would work in practice:[9]

> If a ship is managed by a slave with the consent of a son-in-power (or by an under-slave with the consent of the slave) to whose *peculium* he belongs, the son [or slave] will be

liable in full, but the father or master, unless he consented, will be liable only up to the amount of the *peculium*.

Take the case of a paterfamilias who provides a slave with a substantial *peculium* that contains a ship. The ship-holding slave then, ostensibly on his own initiative, provides his slave, the *servus vicarius*, with a *peculium* that is large enough to fund the hire of a crew, the purchase of necessary stores and so on. The *servus vicarius* then sets up in a maritime business of some kind. Any liability that the under-slave incurs in the course of trading will be limited to the value of the *peculium* of the ship-holding slave. In other words, obligations incurred at a low level in the chain of business management need not be the responsibility of the paterfamilias; yet the paterfamilias would ultimately gain from all the profits earned by his slaves and *vicarii* since he was the legal owner of all the *peculia* involved.[10]

The two legal actions based on the *peculium* were crucial to the development of commerce. They provided limited liability to a principal carrying out trade through a slave acting as agent; at the same time they provided counterparties with assurance that they could enter into contracts with that agent and sue for redress, up to a certain limit, if things went wrong.[11]

Two other remedies, the *actio exercitoria* and the *actio institoria*, widened the range of people who might usefully act as agents. These remedies provided protection to counterparties dealing with a slave, a freedman or a free person who held an appointment to manage a particular business for his principal. Under both measures a principal would be fully liable for contractual obligations undertaken by his appointee.

The *actio exercitoria* applied when someone appointed by a paterfamilias to be in charge of a ship had entered into a contract. The *actio institoria*, with which this chapter is concerned, applied to agents with a specific appointment to manage a land-based enterprise:[12]

> Full liability attaches to the person who appoints another to lend money, to run a farm, to be a trader, to undertake public contracts, [or] to run a bank.

And it was clearly envisaged that this measure would be applicable to a merchant's agent based overseas:[13]

> If a shopkeeper sends his slave travelling to buy merchandise and consign it to him, the slave is to be treated as a business manager (*institor*).

The extent of the liability of a paterfamilias depended on how his business was constituted. If, on the one hand, he stayed at an arm's length from the business, and left it up to a slave to run affairs as the slave thought fit, then his liability was limited to the value of the slave's *peculium* and to any direct profits gained from the transaction. If, on the other hand, the paterfamilias took a direct interest in the business and appointed an agent to a set of specific duties, then he exposed himself to full liability under the *actio institoria* for contracts entered into by that agent, provided that these contracts did not go beyond the terms of the agent's appointment. One other point arises: if the appointed agent was not a slave or child in power but a free person, a creditor could sue the agent directly to recover sums due under contract, as an alternative to a suit against the paterfamilias under the *actio institoria*. Realistically, however, there was usually going to be more chance of recovering a debt from an employer, that is the paterfamilias, than from an employee.

It is possible to derive from these arcane legal points a general rule that was available to guide the Roman paterfamilias when he was planning an overseas venture. The rule may be formulated along the following lines. On the one hand, to leave it up to a slave to run a business through his *peculium* allowed the agent to operate very much as he thought fit, and therefore provided greater scope for enterprise; but because the principal's liability was limited, this tended to limit the value of transactions into which counterparties would enter. On the other hand, to appoint an agent to carry out a specific commercial operation might limit the scope of the business; but it opened up the possibility of conducting high value transactions. What the most common practice was is not known.

From the point of view of a counterparty it was of the greatest importance to discover both the status and the terms of appointment of an agent with whom he might wish to do business. Was the agent a slave dealing on his own initiative? In this case the principal's liability was limited and the counterparty would want the slave to demonstrate that he had sufficient funds in his *peculium* to underwrite the contract. But what if the agent was acting with a specific appointment as his principal's business manager (*institor*)? A counterparty would want to know that the agent was acting strictly within the terms of his appointment. The everyday tasks of an agent such as Primus would include finding locally-based counterparties of good credit standing with whom his principal could do business. He would also be required to manage the monetary balances that his principal held with local bankers. Furthermore his principal would expect him to be well-informed about economic and political conditions that would affect the business.

The importance of commercial intelligence emerges in Cicero's discussion of a topic that engaged Roman intellectuals. How justified was it to use privileged information for commercial gain? Cicero gives as a hypothetical example the case of an honest man (*vir bonus*) who had loaded at Alexandria a large amount of wheat on to a ship bound for Rhodes, where there was a famine. He knew, however, that other merchants (*mercatores*) from Alexandria would arrive with cargoes of wheat shortly after him. Should he reveal this information on his arrival at Rhodes, or keep silent so that he could command a higher price?[14] Cicero came to the conclusion that it was the duty of the merchant to disclose the information. I doubt if such scruples hindered the elder Cato, who praises the heroic (although reckless) qualities of the merchant in the preface to his treatise on agriculture:[15]

To make money by trade (*mercatura*) is sometimes more profitable [than agriculture] but can be very dangerous....The trader (*mercator*) I consider to be an energetic man (*strenuus*) who is keen on making money (*studiosus rei quaerendae*), but it is a dangerous occupation that can lead to disaster.

We may assume that an efficient agent would also take care to provide his principal with accurate information concerning the countries where he did business. Such information formed the mainstay of two manuals by anonymous authors – the first century 'Circumnavigation of the Red Sea' (*Periplus Maris Erythraei*), written for traders who sailed between Egypt and India, and the fourth century 'Account of the Whole World' (*Expositio Totius Mundi*), a commercial geography of the Mediterranean.

The most important part of the agent's business was to make the necessary arrangements for the handling of inward and outward cargoes on behalf of his principal. When a merchant vessel arrived in the port where he was stationed, the agent's first task was to discover whether its cargo included a consignment from his principal, since it was common practice for merchants to split consignments between different ships, to reduce risk in the event of shipwreck or piracy.[16] Once the agent at the port of delivery had located a consignment from his principal, he would need to make arrangements for its discharge and warehousing, negotiate sales with purchasers (if the consignee was not already specified) and make arrangements for his bank to handle payments. The agent of a particularly wealthy merchant might even extend credit to a prospective purchaser. If the agent was required to purchase and ship a consignment for the vessel's return journey, another set of financial and logistical arrangements would need to be made (*14*).

Trimalchio made his fortune as a merchant who first fitted out five vessels, loaded them with a cargo of wine and sent them to Rome. The story bears repetition:[17]

> Every [ship] was wrecked...Neptune swallowed up HS30 million in one day...I built some more bigger, better and luckier ships...I got another cargo – wine, bacon, beans, perfumes and slaves. Fortunata [Trimalchio's wife, also an ex-slave] did a noble thing at this time: she sold all her jewellery and clothes and put a hundred gold pieces into my hand. This was the yeast for my fortune (*peculii mei fermentum*)....I made a clear HS10 million on one voyage.

We should note that Petronius has not suggested that Trimalchio travelled with his cargoes; indeed if he had set out on the first voyage he would not have survived to tell his story. Nor is there any suggestion that he was present in person to negotiate the purchase of his cargoes at one end of the voyage or to sell them at the other. Petronius assumed that his audience would envisage, if they stopped to think about this at all, that Trimalchio had agents working on his behalf – agents who were capable of negotiating with vendors and purchasers and who could conclude contracts of purchase, sale and hire, give and receive guarantees, marshal the necessary funds, handle payments and deposit surplus balances with bankers.

Many items of trade – typically oil and wine and foodstuffs - were packed in *amphorae*, the all-purpose containers of the ancient world; to make identification easier the consigning merchant (*mercator* or *negotiator*) might mark the stopper (a cork bung sealed with *pozzolana*) with his name. From the great mound of broken jars in the Monte Testaccio at Rome scholars have been able to piece together details of additional trade-marks that were used to identify *amphorae* as they moved along the supply chain that connected producer, exporting merchant, shipper, agent, importer, wholesale merchant, retailer and consumer.[18]

Amphorae despatched by the trading enterprise of the Sexti Fadii from southern Spain to Italy in the mid-second century provide an example of the information available to merchants, agents and customs officials. As many as five different painted inscriptions (*tituli picti*) might be carried on the jars:[19]

(i) The weight of the empty container in pounds.

(ii) A full name (i.e. *the tria nomina*) in the genitive. I am inclined to believe that this represents the name of the shipper (*navicularius*).

(iii) The weight of the full vessel.

(iv) Information which seems to be provided for customs purposes, for example:[20]

R. Hispal. XX. CCXV.
Capitonis. aa. Car[---]
Imp. Comm. II et Vero

This may be interpreted as:

Received; Hispalis [the modern Seville];
Value HS20; Weight 215 lbs;
Estate of Capito; Export duty: 2 asses; Shipping clerk (Car---)
Consular date [AD 179].
(v) A figure that seems to be relevant for loading on the ship or for arrangement in storage facilities.

Two names of shippers for these particular *amphorae* can be identified with confidence, those of Sextus Fadius Anicetus and Sextus Fadius Musa. Since the contents of the jars (usually oil) were shipped to Rome from Baetica, it might be assumed that the business was based in Spain.[21] However an inscription from a statue base in Narbonne, dated by the consuls of AD 149, records that Sextus Fadius Pap. Secundus Musa, was patron of the guild of builders (*fabri subaediani*) in that city.[22] Fadius' membership of the tribe Papiria indicates that he was a Roman citizen and his cognomen Musa suggests he was of freedman stock. The inscription records that Musa had held all the official posts in the city (*omnibus honoribus in colonia Narbonensi functus*) and was senior priest of the imperial cult (*flamen primus Augusti*). It looks as if the Sexti Fadii were Narbonnese shippers who had a branch office in Hispalis where they handled oil produced in southern Spain for export to Rome.

The importance of the trade in oils from Spain and Gaul is underlined by the establishment of a customs house at Ostia (*statio Antonin(iana) XXXX Galliarum et Hispaniarum*) which handled incoming goods, subject to an import tax of one-fortieth (i.e. 2.5 per cent), from these provinces.[23] This is the same rate as that charged as export tax on the contents of the *amphorae* from the Spanish estate of Capito, which were valued at HS20 and paid tax at 2 asses.[24] Since Ostia was a port of arrival for cargoes despatched from Gaul and Spain, it is no surprise to discover that Sexti Fadii are attested at the port; they may be descended from freedmen stationed there as agents on behalf of the family firm.[25] To carry out their day-to-day business of collecting intelligence and to make arrangements for handling cargoes, agents in the major ports of the Mediterranean could contact the local offices of shippers, merchants and tradesmen. Such offices can be found in the so-called Piazzale delle Corporazioni behind the theatre at Ostia. The Piazzale is a large double colonnade contemporary with the construction (under Augustus) of the nearby theatre. In its present form 61 small rooms open off the colonnade. On the pavement in front of many of these rooms are mosaics which illustrate the occupation of the owners or lessees. A large proportion of these rooms are evidently connected with the grain trade; shippers doing business with Africa are conspicuous. Trades carried on in the port are also represented, including the tanners of Ostia and Portus (*corpus pellionum Ostiensium et Portensium*), rope-sellers (*stuppatores restiones*) and timber shippers (*navicularii lignarii*). These rooms are too small to hold stocks of goods and were doubtless designed to provide representatives of maritime trades and shipping lines with offices (*stationes*) where deals could be negotiated and orders placed. Similar offices will have existed at Puteoli. As we have seen (Chapter 1), overseas merchants maintained agencies at the port and made a direct contribution to the finances of the city: in the second century the Tyrian traders based in Puteoli wrote to their home city appealing for help towards paying their annual rent, which may have been as much as 25,000 *denarii* (HS100,000).[26] In response the city council of Tyre voted that the Tyrian agency at Rome, which had always paid the Puteolan agency's rent from its receipts, should continue to do so. However efficient the agent might be, communications to and from his principal were rarely smooth or predictable. News was hard to come by in Italy, let alone overseas: Cicero said that the people of Calabria might get news only two or three times a year.[27] Despatches sent from Rome to Athens could take from three weeks to six and a half weeks.[28] Furthermore from November to March or April, the Mediterranean was regarded as a 'closed sea' (*mare clausum*).[29]

In the absence of an official postal service that could be used by private citizens, anyone with business to transact would use members of their own, or their friends' households, as couriers (*tabellarii*) or they might even entrust letters to passing travellers. For instance, when he was en route to Italy in November 50 BC, Cicero wrote from Leucas to his freedman Tiro, who was in Patras:[30]

> See that Acastus [a servant] goes down to the waterfront every day. There will be plenty of people to whom you can safely give a letter and who will be glad to carry it to me. For my part I shall take advantage of every traveller to Patras.

THE SHIPPER

So much for Severus the merchant and Primus his agent – now for the borrower, the shipper Menelaus. He was a freeborn Greek-speaking native of Caria, a region of Asia Minor with a long tradition of shipbuilding and its associated trades.[31] We may surely assume that Menelaus was a member of the foreign community resident in Puteoli and held the legal status of *peregrinus*. His statement that he had previously signed a maritime freight agreement with Primus suggests that he was a shipper (*navicularius*). (At this point it is necessary to remove a source of ambiguity. In present-day commercial usage the term 'shipper' denotes the consignor of goods, while the enterprise that conveys the goods by sea, land or air is known as the 'carrier'. In the Roman context, however, it would be perverse not to use 'shipper' to translate the Latin *navicularius*, the man who carries goods by sea.)

We may suppose that Menelaus was a sea captain from Greece who had put into Puteoli on several occasions and had eventually decided to make his home there. He now seems to be operating a cargo boat in Italian coastal waters. His nearest counterpart in the *Satyricon* is the shipowner (*dominus navigii*) Lichas of Tarentum, a respectable man (*homo verecundissimus*) who has several estates (*fundi*) and some slaves employed in business (*familia negotians*).[32]

THE MARITIME FREIGHT AGREEMENT

The three protagonists – Severus the merchant, Primus his agent and Menelaus the shipper – are now in place. It is time to return to the original contract of maritime freight. What are likely to have been its terms?

The principal feature of the contract will have been agreement on the fee:[33]

> If there has been payment of a fee *(merces)*, there will be the action arising from letting or hiring (*locatio conductio*).

The contract of carriage by sea could take one of two forms. Menelaus may have been hired for a specific job, to convey goods or passengers (*locatio mercium vehendarum* or *locatio vectorum vehendorum*). Alternatively Primus might have taken a lease on part or all of the cargo space on the ship (*conductio loci in nave*). Although the business objective was the same in each case, the rights and duties of the parties were different under the two forms of contract, and the actions at law to which aggrieved parties were entitled were also different.[34] In either case, the shipper would only be liable for damage to or loss of the goods of passengers or merchants, if this was attributable to his own fraud (*dolus*) or incompetence (*culpa*).

In a contract where the merchant or his agent leased cargo space on the ship, either a flat rate or a pro rata fee will have been specified:[35]

> If you have hired a ship with a capacity of 2,000 jars and you put the jars on board, you owe the fee (*pretium*) for 2,000 jars....Indeed if the ship has been hired at a flat rate, the fee (*merces*) will be due for 2,000 jars. If the freight rate was fixed in relation to the number of jars loaded, the result is different, for you will only owe freight for the number of jars you put on board.

There will have been a clause or clauses in the contract specifying the latest date by which the cargo must reach its destination:[36]

> ...[a mariner (*nauta*) would not be liable] if his contract was to pay you a fixed penalty for failure to deliver your goods at the agreed destination before a certain day, provided that it was not his fault...Similar considerations underlie the rule when it is proved that the captain was unable to sail because he was ill, and the same must be said if his ship becomes unfit without any fault, deliberate or negligent, on his part.

The agreement will of course have identified the ship that was to carry Severus' cargo. A very mutilated tablet in the archive of the Sulpicii, TPSulp. 106, reveals the type of information that would be required:

> ...the ship *Notus*, belonging to...burden of approximately 18,000 *modii*...from Sidon with its emblem (*parasemum*)....

Whatever the specific terms agreed between Primus and Menelaus, the contract will have been underpinned by general conditions appropriate to carriage by sea. One of these conditions governed the liability of the carrier in case a cargo was lost due to force majeure:[37]

> If anything is lost through shipwreck or an attack by pirates, it is not unfair that a defence be given to the 'seaman' (*nauta*).

Similarly, in cases where a cargo had been jettisoned, a general rule was accepted by the courts, which was adopted from the maritime code of Rhodes:[38]

> The Rhodian law provides that if cargo has been jettisoned in order to lighten a ship, the sacrifice for the common good must be made good by common contribution... the owners who have lost the cargo for whose carriage they contracted may sue the captain (*magister*) on their contracts. Then, the captain may bring an action on his contracts of carriage against the others whose goods have been saved, so as to distribute the loss proportionally.

The effect of this rule was that when a captain threw goods overboard in a storm, to save his ship, the courts accepted that the loss was to be shared between all the consignors and the captain. If the captain was the appointee of an *exercitor*, then the usual rules governing the ultimate liability of his principal would apply.

Legal provision was also made for other eventualities, in particular for loss or damage due to transshipment. The jurist Labeo stated:[39]

> If you have chartered a ship for the carriage of your cargo and the captain needlessly transships the cargo to a less good vessel, knowing that you would disapprove, and your cargo goes down with the ship when carrying it, you have an action on the contract of hire against the original captain.... But not [comments the jurist Paul] if both ships go down on that voyage, in the absence of intentional or negligent fault on the part of the crew.

Similarly Ulpian asks:[40]

> If a shipper *(navicularius)* contracts to convey freight to Minturnae and then transfers the goods on to another ship because his own ship cannot get up Minturnae's river and the second ship then founders at the river's mouth, is the first shipper liable? Labeo says he is not liable if he is free from fault; but if he acted against the owner's will or at an improper time or if the transfer was to a less suitable ship, then there should be an action on the contract of hire.

These rules were particularly apposite for business conducted in Italian waters. As already noted (Chapter 1), cargoes destined for Rome might arrive in deep sea ports such as Puteoli, be transferred to coastal vessels for transportation to the mouth of the Tiber and then be transferred to river vessels for the last few miles of the journey. Since the primary agreement mentioned in TPSulp. 78 was a contract of freight transport, what then was the purpose of the loan that accompanied this contract? Several possible explanations present themselves.

A maritime loan?
A maritime loan (*fenus nauticum*) consisted of cash paid in advance to a merchant who needed to finance a voyage; the funds would be used principally for the purchase and carriage of a cargo overseas. This type of loan was sometimes described as 'travelling money' (*pecunia traiectitia*), because the funds often travelled with the shipper or mer-

chant.[41] But, it may be asked, why would Menelaus have needed a maritime loan? He did not need to purchase a cargo, since he was the shipper, who was carrying a cargo from Puteoli to Rome. If anyone might be in need of finance for this particular transaction it was Severus the merchant; yet so far from borrowing money, Severus was in a position to lend it. This was surely not a maritime loan.

An insurance premium?
Another possible explanation is that the loan was a form of insurance premium, paid by Primus on behalf of his master Severus to Menelaus, the shipper who was going to carry his goods. The pledge made by Menelaus to restore the sum of 1,000 *denarii* would only be activated if he failed to deliver the cargo to its destination.[42]

The principal objection to this explanation is the lack of evidence for private marine insurance in the Roman world.[43] When insurance is mentioned in the sources it is in the context of special arrangements made by the government in cases of emergency. For instance, when Rome needed supplies for the army in Spain during the war against Hannibal, the authorities agreed to insure the cargoes against attacks of the enemy and against loss due to storms; two of the nineteen traders involved subsequently put in false claims.[44] Again, when the emperor Claudius wanted to encourage merchants (*negotiatores*) to sail in the winter to carry wheat to Rome, he offered them 'guaranteed profits' by carrying any losses himself if they lost their ships in storms.[45] In both instances the inference must be that private insurance was not commonly available.

A freight charge?
An argument that the loan in TPSulp. 78 represents the freight charge paid in advance can be developed from a passage in the Digest:[46]

> When due to the loss of a ship the passage money (*vectura*) is reclaimed which he [the carrier] accepted as a loan (*pro mutua*), Antoninus Augustus (the emperor Caracalla) replied by rescript that it is not unreasonable for the emperor's procurator to reclaim passage money from him because he did not fulfil the duty to convey; this rule should hold for all persons alike.

This passage indicates that a freight charge might on occasion be paid in advance, in the form of a loan, and that a shipper who failed to carry the persons or goods for which he had contracted might be required to repay all or part of that charge. If, therefore, Menelaus failed to deliver the cargo he would be required to repay the 1,000 *denarii*; if he succeeded in conveying the cargo safely to its destination he could keep the money. Such a transaction may be described as a 'fictive loan'. The terms governing repayment would have been covered by a separate stipulation.

However, I am not convinced that the payment in TPSulp. 78 represented the freight charge. The sum involved, 1,000 *denarii* (HS4,000) is quite small and would hardly offer a realistic return to the shipper. It is on this last point that I base the argument in the next section.

Funds to pay customs duties?

I suggest that the 1,000 *denarii* was indeed a 'fictive' loan, but it was an advance of funds to Menelaus to provide him with cash to pay customs duty (*portorium*) on his arrival at Ostia. Under the Roman tax system customs dues were levied at many different points – at the frontiers of the empire, at the boundaries between provinces and at the larger ports. Goods carried within the empire might be required to pay duty each time that they were landed. A case discussed by the jurists concerned a merchant who hired a ship to sail 'for a fixed fee', from the province of Cyrene to Aquileia.[47] The ship was duly loaded with oil and grain but it was then held in the harbour in Cyrene for nine months and the cargo was confiscated; the *negotiator* had presumably not provided the ship's captain or his own agent with sufficient funds to pay the customs duties.

Livy records that customs duty (*portorium*) was collected at Puteoli in the second century BC.[48] The duty was bitterly resented and briefly abolished in Italy in the mid-first century BC, only to be re-imposed by Julius Caesar.[49] We know that under the empire duty was levied at Brindisi: the port is the setting for an anecdote recording fraud on the part of slave merchants seeking to avoid tolls.[50] And, very much to the point, as noted above there was a customs house at Ostia, which collected the 2.5 per cent import duty on goods from Gaul and Spain.

What light does this throw on the 'loan' made to Menelaus? Let us suppose that the 1,000 *denarii* (HS4,000) was earmarked for customs duties at Ostia; this would imply a cargo of *garum* worth 40,000 *denarii* or HS160,000. Is this a plausible figure for the value of such a cargo? Top-quality *garum* is cited in ancient literary sources as an item of great expense. Seneca and Manilius describe *garum* as expensive (*pretiosum*) and Martial suggests that *garum* made from mackerel would only be sent as a gift to a rich man. This type of evidence cannot be regarded as entirely reliable; the author may well be exaggerating in order to criticise the extravagance of contemporary tastes. Nevertheless the elder Pliny says that an *amphora* of *garum sociorum*, a particularly prized product, might fetch HS4,000.[51] This figure may serve as the starting-point for some back-of-the-envelope calculations.

The price of HS4,000 is presumably the retail price. Local importers and shopkeepers will have taken their cut along the way, amounting no doubt to a mark-up of 100 per cent – Pliny observed even higher mark-ups on goods reaching Rome from India.[52] So a single jar of best quality *garum* would be priced at HS2,000 at the dockside. At a rate of import duty of 2.5 per cent, the levy payable on a jar of *garum* at Ostia would be HS50. At this rate it only takes a cargo of 80 jars of high-quality *garum* to attract an import levy of HS4,000 – the amount lent by Primus to Menelaus. A cargo of 80 jars would certainly have been well within the capacity of the small coasting vessel that Menelaus operated on the run to Ostia: in the *lex Claudia* of 219-218 BC forbidding senators and senators' sons to own a sea-going ship (*maritima navis*), the capacity of such a vessel was defined as greater than 300 *amphorae*. If this particular consignment was of lower quality *garum*, then the price per jar would be lower and the number of jars shipped would be higher. In any event, the sum of 1,000 *denarii* seems to be of the right order of magnitude for paying customs duties of 2.5 per cent on a cargo of *garum*.

THE TRANSACTIONS OF 11 APRIL 38

A plausible version of events can now be reconstructed. A shipment of *garum* belonging to the merchant P. Attius Severus had just arrived in Puteoli from Spain. Since this was still early April, barely a month after the opening of the sailing season, this may have been one of the first inward cargoes of the year. Severus' cargo now had to be transshipped from the deep-sea freighter in which it had arrived to a coastal vessel for carriage up the Tyrrhenian coast to Ostia, for onward transit to Rome.

Severus' agent in Puteoli was Primus, one of his slaves. It was Primus' job to find a reliable shipper in Puteoli to transport the cargo to Ostia. This is where the Sulpicii came into the picture; they were the bankers with whom Attius Severus kept his balances and with whom Primus regularly did business on his master's behalf. The Sulpicii recommended as shipper another of their customers, Menelaus, a resident member of the 'peregrine' community in Puteoli; they also arranged the documentation for a freight transport contract. This agreement specified inter alia the type of contract (hire of cargo space or blanket commissioning of shipper to carry out the job), the type and quantity of goods to be carried, the name and capacity of the ship, the name of its captain, the fee (*merces*) and the latest date by which the cargo must reach its destination. The freight charge was paid to Menelaus in advance by Primus, drawing on cash balances that his master Severus held with the Sulpicii, by means of a 'fictive' loan: if Menelaus failed to meet his obligation, Primus could demand repayment.

Severus had also authorised his slave Primus to provide 1,000 denarii to Menelaus for paying the customs authorities at Ostia on arrival. Again Primus was able to draw on his master's account to provide cash to Menelaus; this formed a second 'fictive' loan and is the subject of the document TPSulp. 78. The terms governing repayment of each loan, in the event of Menelaus failing to deliver the goods to their destination or to pay the customs dues, will have been set out in separate stipulations. In the case of this second loan, if the funds were duly paid over to the customs authorities, then the debt would be cancelled; if not, then Menelaus would be bound to repay the loan.

And what of the other two people involved in this transaction, Celer and Romanus? As part of their services to their depositor Severus, the Sulpicii found someone of means to stand surety for Menelaus, Marcus Barbatius Celer. But there was a complication: Celer was illiterate. So yet another person needed to be found, who would write the chirograph on behalf of Celer. The Sulpicii produced another customer of theirs, Quintus Aelius Romanus, to write out the required statement. (Since he was on the spot, Romanus was also asked to sign the document as one of the witnesses.)

To conclude, the second loan contract – and the (now missing) first loan contract and the 'maritime freight agreement' – were held by the Sulpicii because they were Severus' bankers and had provided Primus with funds from cash balances that Severus had deposited in his name. But the Sulpicii did rather more than this. They drafted the maritime freight contract and both loan contracts, produced for Menelaus a guarantor (Celer) and found for Celer a literate proxy (Romanus).

It may even be that a letter of credit (*permutatio*) recording the 'loan' of funds for payment of customs duties was produced for Menelaus to present to bankers at Ostia, with whom the Sulpicii held an account. If this was the case, the 1,000 *denarii* did not have to be carried on Menelaus' ship. Menelaus would simply present the document to the bankers at Ostia and instruct them to pay over the necessary funds to the customs authorities. The appropriate amount would then be debited from the account held by the Sulpicii with their Ostian bankers.

VII

WELL-TO-DO WOMEN

Women play a significant part in the Murecine archive, acting as principals in a variety of transactions including the sale of goods at auction, and lending and borrowing money. Taken as a group the women who did business with or through the Sulpicii demonstrate a considerable degree of financial independence; but we shall find that in several ways they were excluded, or excluded themselves, from some of the formalities of everyday business transactions.

SOURCES OF WEALTH

How did well-to-do Roman women acquire their wealth? Principally through inheritance.[1] A father was expected to nominate his children as heirs and a will that took no account of children was invalid if they were not explicitly disinherited. If a father died intestate, his daughter ranked alongside her brothers among his automatic heirs (*sui heredes*). Children did not inherit automatically from a mother if she was intestate, but it was common for a mother to make bequests to her children.

During our period the most common form of marriage was the so-called 'free marriage' (*sine manu*). Under this arrangement a wife would remain under the authority of her father, if he was still alive – although since she lived in a separate household it is difficult to see how this authority could have been exercised in a very effective way. If a woman's father had died, she was legally independent (*sui iuris*) and entitled to own property. Property that a woman who was *sui iuris* brought into the marriage remained hers.

A wife had no legal claim to maintenance by her husband, but she would usually bring a dowry (*dos*) to her marriage. This became the property of her husband (or his father if he was still alive) as long as the marriage lasted. The dowry might be invested by the husband to generate income to maintain his wife or the couple might agree that the wife should use the dowry to maintain herself and her slaves. As a general rule gifts *inter vivos* between husband and wife were legally invalid; this ban seems to have been intended to preserve the property of their respective parental families. However a husband was permitted to give his wife modest gifts – wool to make clothes, an allowance from the interest on the dowry and cash to buy luxuries such as delicacies, perfume and provisions for her personal servants.

A dowry was recoverable on a husband's death; the idea was that it should be available for the maintenance of the widow or to help her secure another marriage. Sometimes a husband might leave the dowry to his wife as a legacy. If the marriage ended in divorce the wife (or her father if he was alive) could bring an action for recovery of the dowry. The husband could, however, claim and retain some of it under various heads, such as funds for continuing maintenance of their children and expenses incurred during the marriage.

Cicero's dealings with his wife Terentia illustrate the financial arrangements of an upper class marriage in the late Republic.[2] Terentia was said to have brought with her a dowry of HS400,000. She lived in her husband's house but continued to possess and manage her own funds, her own property and her own household of slaves and freedmen. Her dowry was used during the marriage to cover various expenses, including financial provision for the children, but was administered by her husband. When the marriage was terminated through divorce it was Cicero's responsibility to return Terentia's dowry, less certain expenses.

A widow was not an automatic heir to a man who died intestate. However, following legislation introduced by Augustus, wives who held the 'privilege accorded to those bearing children' (*ius liberorum*) – three children for freeborn women, four for freedwomen – could receive bequests from their husbands to the full value of the estate. (Wealthy and influential women might be awarded the privilege without having to bear the children.) Alternatively a man's heirs might be requested in a will to pay his widow an annuity during her lifetime. And a husband would often leave to his widow specific household goods (*supellex*) and provisions (*penus*); these would be items that she would have been able to use freely during the marriage.

The Augustan marriage legislation, intended as it was to encourage the birth of legitimate children, penalised wealthy unmarried and childless men and women. Unmarried persons in the top property class were prohibited from accepting inheritances or legacies and childless persons in the same class could accept only half. But there were exceptions to these rules and many unmarried and childless women may still have been able to benefit from inheritances or legacies.

As already noted, a woman of *sui iuris* status, married or unmarried, could be the owner of property and administer it herself, lend and borrow money and engage in buying, selling and leasing. She was, however, legally required to have a guardian whose authorisation was necessary for transactions which might have the effect of diminishing the property of her *familia*: these transactions included making a will, accepting an inheritance (since this might bring with it liabilities) and entering into certain contracts. If no guardian had been appointed in the will of her father, the guardian would be a male 'agnate', that is to say a brother or uncle or cousin on her father's side. However under Augustus' marriage legislation women were freed from *tutela* if they possessed the *ius liberorum*. The lack of any mention of a guardian in the property dealings of Cicero's wife Terentia suggests that, by the late Republic, in some upper-class families the role of the guardian was already a mere formality. In the second century the jurist Gaius commented:[3]

> But hardly any valid argument seems to exist in favour of women of full age being in a guardian's care (*tutela*). The argument which is commonly accepted, namely that they are very liable to be deceived owing to their instability of judgment (*levitas animi*) and that therefore they ought to be governed by the authority (*auctoritas*) of guardians, seems more specious than true. For women of full age conduct their own affairs (*sibi negotia tractant*), the interposition of their guardian's authority in certain cases being a mere matter of form; indeed often a guardian is compelled by the praetor to give authority even against his will.

A good many of the women whose transactions are documented in the Murecine archive were freedwomen. How did these ex-slaves amass their wealth? When a female slave (*ancilla*) was manumitted she entered into the guardianship (*tutela*) of her ex-master, now her patron. As in the case of a freeborn woman, the guardian of a freedwoman was supposed to protect her interests and guide her in administering her property. Guardianship of an ex-slave could be profitable: the entire estate of a freedwoman under his supervision went to the guardian on her death, unless he authorised her to bequeath it to other heirs. Marriages between patrons and freedwomen were relatively common and given formal recognition under Augustus' legislation. The minimum age at which a slave might be formally manumitted was set at thirty, but an exception was made when a female slave was freed before this age by her master for the purpose of marriage (*matrimonii causa*).[4] (However a senator who had married a freedwoman could only make her his lawful wife (*iusta uxor*) if he obtained a special dispensation from the emperor.) Marriages between patrons and freedwomen are often commemorated in freedwomen's epitaphs by such formulae as *vir et patronus*, *patronus et coniunx* and *patronus idem coniunx*. A widowed freedwoman would be in the same position vis-à-vis her late husband's estate as a freeborn woman.

Like their male counterparts, freedwomen were able to use their capital and connections to build business enterprises; in the occupational inscriptions of Rome, female ex-slaves are to be found engaged in such trades as purple-dyeing and the supply of incense. For instance, a set of inscriptions from the late Republic and early Empire reveals a group of freedmen and freedwomen, many of them connected with the elite family of the Veturii, who traded in purple cloth or dyestuffs at various establishments in Rome over several decades.[5] And when Claudius introduced measures to encourage the building of ships for the grain supply, among the incentives he specified was 'the privilege of four children'; he was surely pitching his appeal at wealthy freedwomen with business interests: possession of the *ius liberorum* released a freedwoman from guardianship and allowed her to make a will (15,30).

This brief outline of the sources of women's wealth may be concluded with a snapshot of a widow (quite possibly a young widow) who is trying to cope with her financial and legal affairs:[6]

A man left his wife her dowry and much more property besides, with a formal request (*fideicommissum*) that she manumit her slave Aquilinus before an official council (*consilium*). She says that she is not bound to do this, since the slave is her own property. The question is, is freedom due to him? Scaevola [the jurist] replied: if the wife wished to receive not only the dowry but the other bequests as well, she should be compelled on the basis of the formal request to manumit Aquilinus and once he was free, it would be for him to take action to secure legacies.

In this case the husband had left the dowry to his wife as a legacy. This meant that she did not have to go through the formal process of suing his heirs under the *actio rei uxoriae* but could claim immediate payment, less certain expenses, from his estate. The jurist's opinion was that she should manumit her slave in accordance with her husband's will; she would then be legally entitled to have the dowry and the other legacies made over to her. Mention of the council indicates that the manumission would be governed by the terms of the *lex Aelia Sentia* (another piece of Augustan legislation) which stated that for manumission to be valid the owner must be twenty or over or the slave must be thirty or over. The jurist evidently envisaged that once free her freedman would act for her in business and legal matters.

WOMEN BORROWERS

We have already met women in the Murecine archive acting as principals in financial dealings. Gavia Primigenia employed Cinnamus as her business agent (procurator) to make a loan to Gaius Iulius Atimetus (TPSulp. 105, discussed in Chapter 3); Patulcia Erotis employed the Sulpicii to handle an auction of goods on her behalf (TPSulp. 82, Chapter 4); and the aristocratic Domitia Lepida is the owner of a warehouse (TPSulp. 46 and 79, Chapter 5).

What of the women who borrowed money from the Sulpicii or from people who held deposits with the Sulpicii? In principle there seems to be no distinction drawn between men and women borrowers: as far as the lender was concerned, the prime consideration was that the borrower should provide security or produce a guarantor. However when loans were made to women the procedures were different from those followed when the borrower was a male. A guardian (*tutor*) was usually present; when this was the case we may assume that the woman principal was not able to claim the 'privilege of children' (*ius liberorum*). Furthermore women do not usually produce written chirographs, that is first-person statements of the type, 'I have written that I have received'. Instead a slave, a business manager (procurator) or a guardian would produce a third-person statement to the effect that the woman had received a sum of money. Nevertheless, as we shall see, women might be present in person when borrowing money.

The transactions of six women borrowers will serve to illustrate how loans to women might be handled:

1. Marcia Fausta

In the fragmentary document TPSulp. 99, dated to 28 February 44, Marcia Fausta takes out a loan from M. Octavius Fortunatus, a depositor with the Sulpicii.

The surviving text records in the third person that Marcia Fausta has promised (*spopondit*) with the agreement of her guardian (*tutore auctore*) – his name has disappeared – to repay the sum owed to Marcus Octavius Fortunatus in three instalments. The first instalment of HS800 is due on a date between 15 March and 15 April, the second, perhaps also of HS800, is due before the next Kalends of May, which is the date on which the payment of the third and last instalment is due.

The complete amount of the debt of Marcia to Fortunatus is unknown, but it is likely to have been greater than HS2,000.[7] If she fails to repay an instalment by the due date she will be liable to pay a monetary penalty. Marcia has obtained a guarantee from a surety (*fideiussor*), whose cognomen Onesimus suggests that he was a freedman or freedman-born, like Fausta herself and the lender Fortunatus. In summary, to arrange her financial affairs Marcia is dependent on two men: first there is her guardian, who has to authorise her borrowing, which tells us that she did not enjoy the 'privilege of children' (*ius liberorum*); second there is her surety, Onesimus. Nevertheless, as Marcia's promise indicates, she was certainly present when this transaction took place.

2. Lollia Saturnina

Lollia Saturnina is the principal in absentia behind three transactions, TPSulp. 54, TPSulp. 109 and TPSulp. 73.

> TPSulp. 54
> 3 October 45.
>
> I, Marcus Lollius Philippus, have written:
>
> I have received a loan of HS20,000 from Gaius Sulpicius Cinnamus and owe him this sum. And the above mentioned HS20,000 Gaius Sulpicius Cinnamus has stipulated is to be duly paid back to him in good coin; I, Marcus Lollius Philippus, have promised that I shall do so.
>
> And on the same date, I, Gaius Avilius Cinnamus, at the request of Gaius Sulpicius Cinnamus, have written: the above-mentioned HS20,000, I have guaranteed (*fide iussi*) to Gaius Sulpicius Cinnamus at my risk (*periculo meo*) on behalf of Marcus Lollius Philippus. Also I profess and have sworn by Jupiter and by the Genius of the Deified Augustus that this year I have made no guarantee to anyone else for this same person.

This document contains two chirographs. In the first Lollius Philippus acknowledges a loan of HS20,000 granted to him by Cinnamus. The second chirograph is a statement of guarantee provided for Lollius Philippus by Gaius Avilius Cinnamus. Avilius Cinnamus (not to be confused with the banker Sulpicius Cinnamus) makes a point of stating on oath that he has not made a guarantee this year to anyone else for Philippus; he presumably intends to show that he is observing the terms of the *lex Cornelia*. In fact Avilius Cinnamus is being over-scrupulous; the *lex Cornelia*, as recorded by the jurist Gaius, precluded the same person standing as surety 'for the same debtor to the same creditor (not 'to any creditor'), in the same year for a larger amount than HS20,000'.[8]

We next meet Lollius Philippus making a partial repayment of a loan to Sulpicius Cinnamus and again the loan has been backed by a pledge from Avilius Cinnamus. Quite possibly this is the same loan that was mentioned in TPSulp. 54:

TPSulp. 109
45 ?

[I Gaius Sulpicius Cinnamus, have written:
I have received from M. Lollius Philippus ...sesterces in partial payment of ...sesterces] owed to me by him. The total sum Gaius Avilius Cinnamus guaranteed (*fide iussit*) on behalf of M. Lollius Philippus.

In the third document, which records another loan repayment, it emerges that Lollius Philippus is connected with the household of a certain Lollia Saturnina:

TPSulp. 73
21 August 48

I, Gaius Sulpicius Cinammus, have written:

I have received from Gnostus, slave of Lollia Saturnina, on behalf of Marcus Lollius Philippus, the sum of....

Lollia Saturnina's husband D. Valerius Asiaticus had owned a villa at Baiae; he had held the consulship but was condemned to death in 47.[9] Lollius Philippus is presumably Lollia Saturnina's freedman, acting as her business agent (*procurator*) and taking out loans from the Sulpicii on Lollia's behalf. In the loan which is the subject of TPSulp. 73 Lollia has arranged for her slave Gnostus, doubtless her cashier (*servus dispensator*), to handle the repayment. Here is an example of a wealthy woman taking out loans from bankers, but having the actual business transactions handled by members of her staff.

3. Caesia Priscilla

Two transactions involving the freedwoman Caesia Priscilla are recorded in the archive (TPSulp. 58 and 71). Caesia, like Lollia Saturnina, conducts her business through her staff. In the first (undated) document Caesia's slave Pyramus takes out a loan on his mistress' behalf:

> TPSulp. 58
>
> ...In addition to the HS20,000 [of debt] listed in the account (*ratio*) of my mistress Priscilla, Gaius Sulpicius Faustus has asked (*fide rogavit*) that the sum of HS4,000 above-mentioned shall be duly paid back in good coin and I, Pyramus, slave of Caesia Priscilla, have promised (*fide promisi*) to repay this sum.
>
> [Witnessed]
>
> Pyramus, slave of Caesia Priscilla
> Decimus Caesius Lucrio
> Marcus Valerius Euphemus
> Aulus [F?]utius Alexander
> Pyramus, slave of Caesia Priscilla

This fragmentary text is part of a chirograph written by Caesia's slave Pyramus. Caesia appears to be an established borrower from the Sulpicii, since the HS4,000 of this loan follows a loan of HS20,000 already booked to her account. From his name it looks as if Decimus Caesius Lucrio, who stands second in the list of witnesses, is her patron and guardian and has authorised the transaction. But it is Pyramus, Caesia's slave, who makes the promise (using the legal formula known as *fidepromissio*) to repay the loan.

In TPSulp 71 it emerges that Caesia is paying back a loan of HS3,000 from another lender:

> TPSulp 71
> 23 March 46
>
> I, Gaius Iulius Amarantus, have written:
>
> I have received from Pyramus, slave of Caesia Priscilla, HS3,000 in accordance with a letter...

Pyramus is again acting on Caesia's behalf. This time he is paying back a loan that has been provided by Amarantus, a depositor with the Sulpicii. In both transactions

Caesia is legally responsible for repayment; she has authorised Pyramus as her business manager (*institor*) to carry out these transactions on her behalf.

Our remaining three women borrowers took out 'cash-box loans' (*nomina arcaria*). Under this procedure the loan document consists of an entry (*nomen*) in the lender's ledger to the effect that a certain sum has been paid out 'in the house from the cash-box' (*domo ex arca* or *ex risco*), in response to a request from the borrower.

4. Euplia

The freeborn Greek woman Euplia appears in three tablets recording cash-box loans: in two of them she borrows funds from the Sulpicii and in one she receives a loan from another woman, Titinia Anthracis. Each of the three loans was eventually paid off, as indicated by addition of the word 'PAID' (*SOLUTUM*) to each respective *scriptura interior*.

The first transaction in this series was on 20 March 42, when Euplia borrowed HS1,000 from Sulpicius Cinnamus. (In my version of each loan I have drawn on Camodeca's reconstruction to list the details of the entry very much as they must have appeared in the lender's ledger.)

TPSulp. 62
20 March 42

ACCOUNTS (*TABELLAE*) OF GAIUS SULPICIUS KINNAMUS

Payments (*Expensos*).

To Euplia, daughter of Theodorus – HS1,000.

A citizen of Melos, she has the authority of her guardian (*tutore auctore*), Epichares, son of Aphrodisius, a citizen of Athens.

She asked for, and received in cash (*numeratos*)

In the house from the cash-box (*domo ex arca*)

Received (*Acceptos*)

Provided by the cash box (*arcae*) – HS1,000.

The above-mentioned HS1,000, in response to a question put by Gaius Sulpicius Cinnamus (*interrogante C. Sulpicio Kinnamo*), Epichares, son of Aphrodisius, a citizen of Athens, has guaranteed (*fide iussit*) to Gaius Sulpicius Cinnamus on behalf of Euplia, daughter of Theodorus, a citizen of Melos.

Exactly a year later, Euplia used the same procedure to borrow HS1,600 from a woman, Titinia Anthracis:

TPSulp. 60
20 March 43

ACCOUNTS (*TABELLAE*) of TITINIA ANTHRACIS

Paid to Euplia, daughter of Theodorus, a citizen of Melos, [HS1,600], with the authority of her guardian Epichares, son of Aphrodisius, a citizen of Athens.

She asked for and received in cash in the house from the cash-box, HS1,600

The above-mentioned HS1,600, in response to a question put by Titinia Anthracis, Epichares, son of Aphrodisius, a citizen of Athens, has guaranteed (*fide iussit*) to Titinia Anthracis on behalf of Euplia, daughter of Theodorus, a citizen of Melos.

Four months later Euplia borrowed a further HS500, this time from Sulpicius Cinnamus again:

TPSulp. 61
20 July 43

[ACCOUNTS (*TABELLAE*) OF GAIUS SULPICIUS CINNAMUS

Paid to Euplia, daughter of Theodorus, a citizen of Melos, HS500, with the authority of her guardian Epichares, son of Aphrodisius, a citizen of Athens.

She asked for and received in cash in the house from the cash-box HS500.

The above-mentioned HS500, in response to a question put by Gaius Sulpicius Cinnamus, Epichares, son of Aphrodisius, a citizen of Athens, has guaranteed (*fide iussit*) to Gaius Sulpicius Cinnamus on behalf of Euplia, daughter of Theodorus, a citizen of Melos.

Now this money is owed over and above the other sums which Euplia and Epichares owe to the same Gaius Sulpicius Cinnamus and to Titinia Anthracis.

This series of loans provides a glimpse of the financial affairs of foreign residents (*peregrini/ae*) in the port of Puteoli. In each transaction, Epichares, an Athenian who was Euplia's guardian, not only authorised her borrowing but stood surety for the debt. Epichares may have been husband or son of Euplia: as the jurist Gaius noted:[10]

among foreign residents women are ...in a sort of guardianship (*tutela*); a law of the Bithynians, for example, ordains that if a woman enters into any transaction, it must be authorised by her husband or full-grown son.

No rate of interest or date of repayment is stated in any of these three loans. Presumably they were underpinned by stipulations in which Euplia made the necessary promises to the respective lenders.

We have no means of knowing the purpose of these loans, which are for relatively small amounts. However the second and third loans in this series (TPSulp. 60, 61) illustrate the services that the Sulpicii might provide for their depositors. Titinia Anthracis evidently keeps funds on deposit with the bank and Cinnamus has recommended Euplia to her as a suitable borrower. In TPSulp. 60 Titinia Anthracis makes a loan to Euplia and extracts a guarantee of repayment from Euplia's guardian. But we learn from TPSulp. 61, when Euplia receives a cash-box loan from Cinnamus, that Titinia is now using Cinnamus to act as her receiving banker: 'this money is owed over and above the other sums which Euplia and Epichares owe to the same Gaius Sulpicius Cinnamus and to Titinia Anthracis'. It looks as if Titinia has been finding it difficult to obtain repayment from Euplia and so she has enlisted Cinnamus' support.

5. *Magia Pulchra*

Our next cash-box borrower is the freeborn Magia Pulchra:

TPSulp. 63
September–October 45

ACCOUNTS (*TABELLAE*) OF GAIUS [SULPICIUS CINNAMUS (or FAUSTUS)]

Paid to Magia Pulchra, daughter of Lucius.

She asked for and received HS30,000 in cash in the house from the cash-box.

Repayment of funds due on 1 May next.

If on 1 May next, to me or my heir, the above-mentioned HS30,000 has not been paid, by evil practice (*dolo malo*) on the part of either of you, and you have not come to an agreement with my heir or given satisfaction to me, Gaius Sulpicius Cinnamus [or Faustus] has stipulated that double the sum of money is to be duly repaid. Magia Pulchra, daughter of Lucius, has answered to this stipulation and made an oath by Jupiter and the Divinity (*numen*) of the Deified Augustus.
The same (*idem*) [guarantor's name] answered to this stipulation (*spopondit*).

This loan, for HS30,000, is one of the larger loans in the archive. The borrower's full name, 'Magia Pulchra, daughter of Lucius', tells us that she was of free birth (*ingenua*). Magia appears to be acting without the authorisation of a tutor and presumably has been freed from this requirement through possessing the *ius liberorum*. She has a guarantor, whose name has been lost.

This loan has been made by either Cinnamus or Faustus. The identity of the lender is immaterial in this context; for convenience I shall assume that it was Cinnamus. Cinnamus stipulates that Magia Pulchra is to pay back the loan on 1 May next. If she fails to pay by the due date she promises to pay a penalty, which will be double the amount owed. It is also stated in the third person that Magia Pulchra has taken an oath that she will repay the debt. She has sworn by Jupiter and by the Divinity of the Deified Augustus.

A third party, *idem*, whose name has disappeared, also answered to this stipulation. He must have been a guarantor who stood as personal surety for the loan. As already noted, under the terms of the *lex Cornelia*, the same person could not stand as surety for the same debtor to the same creditor in the same year for a larger loan than HS20,000. So at best only two-thirds of Magia's total loan of HS30,000 was guaranteed by her surety. This explains why Cinnamus imposed such tough terms. And they were tough: as we saw in the last of the loans granted by Hesychus to the grain dealer Eunus (TPSulp. 68), anyone who defaulted on a loan backed by an oath on the *numen* of the emperor would be guilty of perjury and liable to a flogging.

But as far as procedure goes, one point is very clear. Magia Pulchra was present when the loan was granted.

6. Faecia Prima

The last cash-box loan made to a woman is taken out by Faecia Prima. The document (TPSulp. 64) is in very fragmentary form. It does not reveal the amount borrowed but it does contain the names of nine witnesses:

TPSulp. 64
2 February 53

[ACCOUNTS (TABELLAE) OF TITINIA BASILIS]

Paid to Faecia Prima...HS... with the authority of her guardian [Numerius Castricius Agathopus?]. She asked for and received in cash in the house from the cash-box...

The above-mentioned HS...], in response to a question put by Titinia Basilis, Numerius Castricius Agathopus, has guaranteed (*fide iussit*) on behalf of Faecia Prima...

[Witnessed]:

Quintus Puteolanus Alacer
Gnaeus Pompeius Celer
Gaius Vestorius Felix
Publius Vedius Hermeros
Gnaeus Pollius Blastus
Marcus Popidius Optatus
Quintus Attius Icarus
Quintus Attius Primigenius
Numerius Castricius Agathopus

In this transaction Faecia's guarantor N. Castricius Agathopus, who is also listed among the witnesses, is very likely to have been her guardian. The lender Titinia Basilis has a Greek cognomen and may have connections with the overseas trading community. I assume that she is a depositor with the Sulpicii. She certainly appears to be a woman of some consequence since she has, or the Sulpicii have on her behalf, assembled a list of witnesses who have connections with two of Puteoli's leading families, the Vestorii and the Castricii.

From the tablets recording the borrowings of Euplia, we may reconstruct the procedure that was followed in a typical cash-box loan transaction. Witnesses were assembled (by the Sulpicii) in the lender's house. Euplia formally asked for and received her loan from the lender's cash-box. At some point in the proceedings she entered into a face-to-face stipulation on the terms and rate of interest, although no records of these stipulations have survived. We are told, however, that women did enter into stipulations – in the cash-box loan recorded in TPSulp. 63, where the author of the document states that Magia Pulchra has promised (*spopondit*) to make repayment by a certain date, and again in TPSulp. 99, where the author of the document states that Marcia Fausta has promised (*spopondit*) to make various stage payments.

Euplia presumably then withdrew, leaving her guardian Epichares to state that he authorised the transaction and also stood surety on her behalf. The final details of the transaction could then be entered by Epichares in the tablet (doubtless largely prepared in advance) which would then be sealed by the witnesses.

The cash-box loan was evidently a common procedure, as the jurist Gaius makes clear:[11]

> In the case of cash entries [in the lender's ledger] their validity depends on the money having been paid out and payment of money creates a real obligation.

There is no suggestion in Gaius' account that this type of loan, granted 'in the house from the cash-box' (*domo ex arcaria*), was limited to women borrowers, but on the evidence of the Murecine archive it was a type of transaction that was particularly favoured by women. Perhaps this was because they chose to avoid public appearances in the forum, where most banking business was carried out.

Did the women who took out cash-box loans do this to avoid taking out 'standard' loan contracts (*mutua*) (which involved writing out first-person statements) because they were illiterate? This seems unlikely and in any case it is impossible to prove. Against this it should be pointed out that there are examples elsewhere in the archive of male participants in financial transactions who actually admit to being illiterate and accordingly arrange for other people to write the requisite chirographs on their behalf. For instance in TPSulp. 78 Quintus Aelius Romanus wrote the formal guarantee for the loan made by Primus to the shipper Menelaus on behalf of the surety Marcus Barbatius Celer, 'because he says that he does not know how to write'. Similarly, in TPSulp. 46 Nardus, slave of Publius Annius Seleucus, warehouse manager, wrote a lease document on his master's behalf, 'because he says that he does not know how to read and write'. Evidently illiteracy per se did not disqualify a borrower from having his or her loan recorded in the form of a chirograph.

AN HEIRESS FROM POMPEII

To conclude this survey of the financial affairs of well-to-do women, we are going to move a few miles round the Bay of Naples to Pompeii. Two tablets (T. 23, 24) from the archive of L. Caecilius Jucundus record financial transactions carried out by a certain Umbricia Antiochis. She first appears in November 56:

T. 23
11 November 56

I, ..., slave of Umbricia Antiochis, have written that she has received HS645 from Lucius Caecilius Jucundus, on account of the auction (performed on her behalf) of fittings (*res imposiciae*)....Out of this sum she has [already] received HS200, with valuation costs (*arbitria*) of HS20, incidental expenses (*accessiones*) of HS13 and the [banker's] fee of HS51 [deducted from the proceeds]; today I received [the balance of] HS360.

In this tablet a slave of Umbricia Antiochis records on his mistress' behalf that she has received from Jucundus HS645 as the proceeds of an auction of 'fittings'. It is not entirely certain what is meant by fittings, but it is worth noting that under this heading the Roman jurists classified water pipes that fed fountains (*canthari, per quos aquae saliunt*).[12] The likelihood is that Umbricia Antiochis has inherited a house, which she has already sold, and she is now selling off separately some ornamental items. The *arbitria* and *accessiones* were sums advanced to Umbricia Antiochis by Jucundus to cover particular expenses. *Arbitria* usually means the expenses connected with a funeral, so-called because an assessor (*arbiter*) was employed to estimate them. It looks as if Umbricia Antiochis had been required to meet her benefactor's funeral expenses. *Accessiones* can mean additional amounts of tax.[13] It is known from T. 151 that there was a market tax (*mercatus*) at Pompeii and that Jucundus was involved in its administration. One possibility is that Umbricia Antiochis had sold in the market-place at Pompeii some items from her inherited house and now had arrears of tax to pay off.

The principal deduction of HS200 is presumably a repayment in connection with an outstanding loan made to Umbricia by Jucundus. The banker's fee of HS51 represents 8 per cent of the total realised by the auction – considerably higher than the 1 per cent that was considered standard in Roman Italy (see Chapter 4). All these deductions amount to HS284, leaving a balance due of HS361. Umbricia's slave states that he has actually received HS360, as the balance of the sum owed to his mistress by Jucundus: Jucundus has rounded the sum down, in his own favour.

But Umbricia had still more items to dispose of. A few days later, on 10 December, receipt is acknowledged of a further sum paid to Umbricia by Jucundus:

T. 24
10 December 56

I, M. Helvius Catullus, have written at the request (*rogatu*) of Umbricia Antiochis that she has received from L. Caecilius Jucundus HS6,252 less commission (*mercede minus*) on account of the auction of her slave Trophimus and this sum has been paid over (*persolutos*).

[Witnessed]

M. Helvius Catullus
Melissaeus Fuscus
Faber Proculus
Umbricia Antiochis
M. Helvius Catullus

On this occasion the statement that Umbricia has received the funds due to her is made by M. Helvius Catullus, who was presumably her guardian. Catullus writes at Umbricia's request that she has received from Jucundus HS6,252, less commission (*mercede minus*), for the sale at auction of the slave Trophimus. This was a good price for a single slave. To put it into perspective, the contemporary agricultural writer Columella expected to pay HS6,000 to HS8,000 for a skilled vine-dresser (*vinitor*); a farm bailiff (*vilicus*) would probably fetch a similar amount.[14]

It must be a strong presumption that Umbricia Antiochis was an heiress. She had inherited property and she took steps to sell the house and effects at three separate auctions. Jucundus arranged the auctions and advanced her various sums of money to provide her with cash for expenses (including the cost of the funeral). In the third auction she sold the slave Trophimus, who was surplus to her requirements; his high market value suggests that he was a skilled craftsman or even the bailiff (*vilicus*) of the property that she had inherited.

To sum up, the Murecine archive throws considerable light on the degree of freedom with which well-to-do women might engage in financial transactions during the first century. Women were free to sell goods at auction, to lease out property and to lend and borrow money. Women borrowers might choose to conduct their financial affairs through their slaves and freedmen or they might attend in person at the houses of lenders to take out cash-box loans. But they are not to be found in the forum entering into contracts of *mutuum*, which necessarily incorporated first person statements to the effect that a particular financial obligation had been undertaken by the borrower.

The presence of guardians at several transactions in the Murecine archive where women are borrowers indicates that time-honoured business procedures were still commonly observed. Take the loans to Euplia from Cinnamus and Titinia Anthracis. Epichares is recorded as having authorised all three transactions in his role as Euplia's guardian (*tutore auctore Epichare*). His authorisation was required, not because Euplia was necessarily a bad risk, but because a ward who borrowed money was putting her property under an obligation and it was a guardian's duty (and in his interest) to protect that property.[15] Epichares also acted as a guarantor. This duty was not required of a guardian, but if he was solvent it would be appropriate for him to stand as a surety. If he was not willing to do so, this would not give much confidence to the creditor.

The participation of women in financial affairs also differs markedly from that of men in as much as women hardly ever appear as witnesses to transactions. The absence of women from witness lists may simply be a reflection of an entrenched attitude – that women had no role to play in transactions between men – but it is less understandable when one or both of the principals is a woman. Acting as a witness to commercial and legal transactions was an important part of 'networking' in Roman society. Did women of independent means choose to stand apart from this networking? Or were they deliberately excluded? In the archives of Jucundus and the Sulpicii I have been able to find only one transaction, where a witness list has survived, in which a woman acts as a witness. This is T. 24, which records the payment to Umbricia Antiochis of the proceeds from the sale of her slave Trophimus. The receipt is drawn up by Helvius Catullus, her guardian, but Umbricia is allowed to sign as a witness. Perhaps the presence of Umbricia Antiochis among the witnesses means that she was especially wealthy or well-connected.

VIII

SLAVES

There were perhaps two million slaves in Roman Italy during the early Empire, amounting to a third of the total population.[1] Wealthy Romans first began to employ slaves on a large scale in the second century BC, when the legions were heavily engaged in warfare overseas and military commanders brought prisoners of war back to Italy as booty. Many slaves were taken directly to serve on the rural estates or urban households of the elite; some were distributed to the legionaries. Other prisoners were sold for profit in the slave markets. In addition, pirates took advantage of the upheavals in the Mediterranean world to capture tribesmen in the Greek-speaking east and sell them to professional slave dealers at trading centres such as the great emporium at Delos:[2]

> The export trade in slaves was the major cause of all this criminal activity [on the part of Cilician pirates], since it had become most profitable. For not only were the slaves easily captured, but the market, which was large and flush with cash, was not very far away – the island of Delos, where tens of thousands ('myriads') of slaves could be shipped in and despatched again [to Italy] on the same day. From this arose the saying, 'Merchant, sail in and unload your ship, your cargo is already sold'. The reason was that, after the destruction of Carthage and Corinth [in 146 BC], the Romans had become extremely rich and made use of large numbers of slaves; and since pirates could see how easy it was to make money in this way they sprang up all over the place and raided and traded in slaves themselves.

Slaves were also obtained from various sources within Italy – the offspring of existing slaves, infants exposed at birth or older children sold by their parents into slavery.

It was evidently common for Roman entrepreneurs to go into the slave dealing business:[3]

> We enter into a partnership either in respect of our entire fortunes or for some particular business (*unius alicuius negotii*), such as the buying and selling of slaves.

It was a business that was subject to the usual vicissitudes of trade:[4]

> Suppose...we form a partnership and buy slaves, and then you renounce at a time which is disadvantageous for selling slaves, you are liable to an action on partnership, because in this case you are altering my prospects for the worse.

Professional slave dealers were considered to be tricksters. Indeed the very term for a slave dealer – *mango* – stems from the Greek *manganon* (trickery). (A *mango* was also someone who polished up gemstones.) The sharp practices of the dealers led to action on the part of the government to regulate the slave markets to give consumers, i.e. the slave-owning classes, a measure of protection. The regulations were enshrined in an Edict promulgated by the Curule Aediles, the magistrates who were responsible for the good conduct of the public markets. The Edict was intended, as Ulpian said:[5]

> to check the wiles of vendors and to give relief to purchasers deceived by their vendors. It must, though, be recognised that the vendor is still liable, even though he be unaware of the defects which the aediles require to be declared...it is no concern of the purchaser whether his deception derives from the ignorance or the sharp practice of his vendor.

The majority of slaves in Roman Italy were to be found working in agriculture. Some thirty to forty rural jobs carried out by slaves can be identified from Columella's handbook *De Re Rustica* and the Digest. In the chapter of the Digest where the jurists discuss the legacy of a rural estate (*fundus*), it is made clear that the equipment (*instructum* or *instrumentum*) of the estate included not only tools and machinery but also the work force, which was provided 'for the producing, gathering, and preserving of the crops'.[6] Another sizeable group of slaves worked in the urban households of the wealthy, where as many as 50 different slave jobs have been identified (*16,17,18*).[7]

Children born to slave women took their status from their mother and were known as *vernae*. They seem to have been highly valued because they were easily trained and managed. The point is made by Cornelius Nepos in his description of the household of Atticus:[8]

> ...there were highly-educated slaves, excellent readers, and numerous copyists, so that there was not a single footman who could not both read and copy finely. Likewise, the other specialists required by domestic comfort were particularly good. Every one of them was born and trained in the household....

THE SLAVE MARKET

Slaves shipped in from overseas would usually arrive at Puteoli, Ostia or Brindisi. The elder Pliny brings the scene at the docks to life:[9]

There is another kind of chalk, which is called silversmith's, since it makes silver shiny, but it is very low grade and our ancestors decided to use it to mark the finishing line in the Circus, and to mark the feet of slaves brought from overseas to be sold. Among slaves of this kind there was Publilius from Antioch who was the first author of mimes, and his cousin Manilius the first astrologer, also from Antioch, and Staberius Eros the first grammarian – our great-grandfathers could see them all arrive on the same ship....This chalk marks the crowds of slaves up for sale.

From the docks the new arrivals would be taken to the forum, where the dealers exhibited their wares on a raised platform (*catasta*).[10] The chalk-mark on a slave's foot indicated that he was newly arrived and thus presumed to be easier to train than a veteran. Many dealers, however, said Ulpian,[11]

> are in the habit of selling as new slaves those who are not so, in order to get a better price; for it is assumed that the more recently he has been enslaved, the slave will be more malleable, more trainable to his function, more responsive to direction, and more adaptable to any service; on the other hand, it is difficult to re-train an experienced slave or one of long standing (*veterator*) and to mould his habits. And since slave dealers know that their customers will readily seek to purchase new slaves, they substitute those of long standing and sell them as new.

The practices of the slave dealers, the counter-measures taken by the authorities and the remedies at law available to aggrieved purchasers are set out in the chapter of the Digest that covers the Edict of the Curule Aediles (D. 21.1). To provide a guarantee against physical and mental defects, poor behaviour and any legal liabilities that the slave brought with him, a vendor was required to hang round the neck of the slave a bill of sale *(tabella emptionis)* providing detailed information:

> Those who sell slaves are to inform purchasers of any disease or defect in their wares and whether a given slave is a runaway, a loiterer on errands, or still subject to noxal liability [i.e. liable to being handed over to a third party as compensation for wrong-doing (*noxa*)]; all these matters they must declare in due manner when the slaves are sold.

One of the dealers' tricks was to dress slaves in fine clothes to disguise any defects. Potential purchasers might order that the slave be undressed to allow proper inspection. What would purchasers need to guard against? A slave has lost one or more fingers or toes: the issue is not how many he has lost, but whether he can still be put to use. A man who has lost a tooth is not diseased – but one with warts or polyps is to be regarded as such. It is not incumbent on the vendor to mention that a slave has one eye or jaw or arm bigger than the other, provided that he can perform his duties satisfactorily; but if one leg is shorter than the other, this can lead to imbalance and affect his performance and should be declared. Guttural speech or protruding eyes do not require that the slave be declared diseased, nor does left-handedness (unless he uses his left hand because of the weakness of his right hand). He has foul breath? This need only be declared if it stems from an ailment such as a liver or lung complaint. And so on.

If the vendor expressly excluded some disease and for the rest declared the slave to be healthy, the contract of sale might stand; and if a disease such as blindness, which was 'apparent to all' was not expressly excluded, there was no liability on that account:

> ...it has to be accepted that the Aediles' Edict is concerned with those defects which a purchaser might not detect or be able to detect.

All kinds of details had to be disclosed in the bill of sale. Was a female slave incapable of bearing children? Had a particular slave ever committed a capital offence, tried to commit suicide or been sent to fight beasts in the arena? Furthermore, those selling slaves,

> ...must state the country of origin (*natio*) of each at the sale; for a slave's place of origin frequently encourages or deters a buyer... since it is reasonable to suppose that some slaves are good because they originate from a race that has a good reputation, and others are thought bad because they come from a tribe that is notorious.

However the dealer's patter did not have to be taken too literally:

> Suppose that the vendor says that the slave is loyal or hardworking or diligent or vigilant or that through his thrift he has acquired a *peculium* and, on the contrary, he is fickle, wanton, slothful, sluggish, idle, tardy, or a wastrel. All these expressions of the vendor are not to be charged against the vendor with absolute literalism but should be reasonably interpreted. Hence, if he declares the slave to be loyal, one does not expect the absolute gravity and fidelity of a philosopher; if he declares him hardworking and watchful, he is not required to work all day and all night.

If a vendor sold a slave without complying fully with the regulations in the Edict, or contrary to what had been said at the time of the sale, the aediles would grant to the purchaser and to other interested parties an action for 'taking back' (*actio redhibitoria*) in respect of the slave. This action entitled the buyer to sue for recovery of the full purchase price, with interest, on returning the slave to the seller. The action was available only if serious defects were subsequently discovered, so serious as to undermine the usefulness of the slave. For less serious defects, the buyer was offered the action for diminution (*actio quanti minoris*); this allowed the buyer to recover the difference between what might be judged to be the slave's true value at the time of the sale and the price actually paid. If the slave turned out to have major faults, the buyer would be able to put forward his claim for return of the price within six months of the sale; for less serious defects there was a time-limit of a year.

In addition to a guarantee that there were no hidden faults in the slave being sold the vendor might also guarantee that the buyer would not be dispossessed by a person who turned out to be the true owner. It was the duty of the seller in Roman law to guarantee that the buyer would not be 'evicted' from ownership of the goods being sold:[12]

> ...the vendor must provide the object itself, that is deliver it. If the vendor was its owner, his act [of delivery] makes the buyer the owner also; if he was not, his act obligates the vendor only for an eviction, provided that the price was paid or security was given for it.

The guarantee could not prevent an eviction, since the rightful owner was entitled to recover his property by legal process, but it did entitle the buyer to sue the vendor for damages if he was evicted.

The seller gave his guarantee in the form of a stipulation to compensate the buyer in the case of eviction. This guarantee would often be for double the price (*stipulatio duplae pecuniae*). It was regarded as a breach of good faith for the seller to refuse to give a stipulation and he could be sued for his refusal to do so:[13]

> If the vendor does not give the undertaking for double the price and is sued on that ground, he must be condemned, as a defendant, for double the price.

SLAVES AS CHATTELS

Several transactions in the Murecine archive are concerned with slaves simply as chattels. TPSulp. 42, 43 and 44 are straightforward sales of slaves, under contract of purchase and sale (*emptio venditio*). In each of these transactions the buyer obtained under stipulation from the vendor a guarantee that he would receive double the price if he were subsequently to be evicted from ownership. In TPSulp 43, the most complete, both buyer and vendor have links with the Vestorius family; both may have been customers of the Sulpicii:

TPSulp. 43
21 August 38

> [The slave who is the subject of this sale is in good health and free from any charge of theft and crime]. He is not a runaway (*fugitivus*) or a loiterer (*erro*) and the other conditions which are written and included this year in the Edict of the Curule Aediles have been duly observed. Titus Vestorius Arpocra minor has stipulated, and Titus Vestorius

Phoenix has promised, that a double sum of money (*dupla pecunia*) according to the legal formula, as is the custom, be duly paid [in the event of eviction from ownership].

Some sales in the archive are concerned with slaves pledged as security by borrowers who had subsequently failed to repay their loans (see Chapter 4). Take for instance the three notices of sale TPSulp. 85-87 which relate to slaves pledged against a loan of HS26,000 made by Cinnamus to Marcus Egnatius Suavis. Up for auction were six slaves, all identified by name, whom Suavis was said to have given to Cinnamus as security (*fiducia*) for a loan of HS26,000. Similarly the notices of sale in TPSulp. 90-93 informed passers-by that the slave Fortunata was being sold by C. Sulpicius Onirus. Prospective purchasers were informed that Fortunata had been pledged by Marcia Aucta as security for a loan and could be bought for ready cash.

Notices of sale reveal how individual slaves were designated. Suavis' slaves are described as 'the man Felix' (*homo Felix*), 'the man Carus' (*homo Carus*), 'the man Januarius' (*homo Januarius*), 'the woman Primigenia' (*mulier Primigenia*), 'the woman Primigenia Junior' (*mulier Primigenia Junior*) and 'the boy Ampliatus' (*puer Ampliatus*). Marcia Aucta's slave is known as 'the woman Fortunata' (*mulier Fortunata*). The use of these blunt terms reminds us that in Roman eyes a slave had no ties of kinship. The very names that slaves bore were given them by slave dealers or by their owners. The law did take into account slave motherhood, because slave children belonged to their mother's owner; but under the law no slave, male or female, had a father and no male slave could be a father. Slave spouses (*contubernales*) were not legally recognised as husband or wife. The only familial relationship that slaves had under the law was with their owners, who had absolute power over them. This harsh reality was emphasised by the condescending term 'Boy' (*puer*) that masters used when they addressed male slaves.[14]

SLAVES ACTING UNDER DIRECT INSTRUCTIONS

As we have already seen, many slaves carried out business transactions for their masters. The most prominent of the slaves whose dealings are recorded in the archive is Hesychus, a member of the imperial household. In two loan transactions Hesychus appears to be acting under direct instructions from his master.

TPSulp. 51 (18 or 28 June 37) – The grain dealer Eunus states that he has been lent HS10,000 by the imperial freedman Evenus Primianus, but 'in the absence of Primianus' he has received the loan from Hesychus his slave. It is Hesychus who stipulates for repayment of the loan; but the emphasis that is put on the absence of Evenus Primianus suggests that Hesychus was acting under instructions from his master.

TPSulp. 52 (2 July 37) – Eunus states that he has been lent another HS3,000 by Hesychus, who again stipulates for repayment of the loan. This loan follows very soon after the first loan in the series. We may take it that Hesychus is still lending funds on the direct instructions of his master Evenus Primianus.

Similarly the slaves of two warehouse managers in the archive are clearly acting under direct instructions:

TPSulp. 45 – 'I Diognetus, slave of Gaius Novius Cypaerus, have written by order of my master Cypaerus and in his presence, that I have leased to Hesychus….'

TPSulp. 46 – 'I Nardus, slave of Publius Annius Seleucus, have written in the presence of and by order of my master Publius Annius Seleucus, because he says that he does not know how to write, that I have leased to Gaius Sulpicius Faustus….'

In several other transactions we may also infer that slaves are acting on their owner's instructions. For instance in TPSulp. 69 Cinnamus states on 2 May 51 that he owes to Phosphorus Lepidianus, slave of the emperor Claudius, the sum of HS94,000 and says that he has pledged to repay this debt on 13 June. As I argued earlier (Chapter 3), Phosphorus has made a short-term deposit of imperial funds; he was presumably acting on direct instructions from the imperial household.

Similarly in transactions where Caesia Priscilla is a borrower, she has instructed her slave Pyramus to act on her behalf. In TPSulp. 58 Pyramus promises Sulpicius Faustus that he will repay a loan of HS4,000; this loan is in addition to a loan of HS20,000 which has already been booked to the account (*ratio*) of Priscilla. And in TPSulp. 71 it is Pyramus who pays back to Amarantus a loan of HS3,000, which has been made to Priscilla. Again, in TPSulp. 73, the aristocratic Lollia Saturnina has arranged for her slave Gnostus, who is doubtless her cashier (*servus dispensator*), to handle the repayment of a loan made to her by Sulpicius Cinnamus.

However some slaves acted under instruction but with a considerable degree of independence. In Chapter 6 we met Primus, the slave of the merchant Attius Severus (TPSulp. 78). Primus is a business manager (*institor*) appointed as his master's agent in Puteoli; he has already drawn up a freight agreement with the shipper Menelaus. The subsequent loan of HS4,000 that he makes to Menelaus comes from his master's funds but the loan has been made on his own initiative.

TRADING THROUGH THE *PECULIUM*

As already noted (Chapter 2) a slave might trade through his *peculium*, the revocable fund of cash and other assets granted to him by his master or mistress; this allowed him a large degree of autonomy in his business dealings and provided his master (or mistress) with limited liability. Several transactions in the archive show slaves entering into contracts to lend and borrow funds. In any of these particular transactions is it possible to detect a slave trading through his *peculium*?

The strongest, albeit circumstantial, evidence for use of the *peculium* emerges from the proceedings of a court case involving Gaius Julius Prudens, a depositor with the Sulpicii:

TPSulp. 25
5 February 55

At a hearing before Lucius Clodius Rufus, the duumvir, Gaius Sulpicius Cinnamus formally asked Gaius Julius Prudens whether the men Hyginus and Hermes were his slaves and in his power (*servi eius et in potestate eius*).

Gaius Julius Prudens replied that the men Hyginus and Hermes, who were the subject of this matter, were his (*suos*) [and were in his power (*suaque im potestate*)]★.

And then and there, Gaius Sulpicius Cinnamus formally called on Gaius Julius Prudens to keep in his power Hyginus and Hermes, who were the subject of this matter, and exhibit them at Rome. He said this was relevant to the hearing (*cognitio*) by the judge who would hear the case between himself and Prudens concerning the money owed to him (*de credito suo*).

At the request of Gaius Julius Prudens these words have been recorded.

★ The words in square brackets have been struck out.

From this tablet we learn that Cinnamus (at a preliminary hearing before the Puteolan magistrate L. Clodius Rufus) put to the defendant Prudens, a double question. 'Were the slaves Hyginus and Hermes his and in his power?' Prudens apparently replied that the two slaves were 'his and in his power' (*suos suaque im (sic) potestate*). The phrase *suaque im potestate* has, however, been subsequently struck out of the record in the *scriptura interior*. This is an important point, as will emerge shortly. Cinnamus then formally called on Prudens to present the two slaves at Rome before the judge who was to hear the suit.

Much turns on the significance of the erasure of the phrase *suaque im potestate*. This was a formula that was used in 'noxal' actions – i.e. when a slave had committed some damage, and the owner might be liable bear liability.[15] The scribe presumably originally included the phrase in its entirety because that was what he was accustomed to write. But in this case the noxal formula was inappropriate: Prudens' slaves had not committed noxal damage. It is not clear what the precise case against Prudens was, but it looks as though his slaves had failed to pay back a loan made to them by Cinnamus (*de credito suo*). So the scribe altered the document at Prudens' request. The result of the alteration was that Prudens formally replied, on the record, only that the slaves Hyginus and Hermes were his – not that they were in his power. The significance of the alteration emerges from an opinion given by the jurist Ulpian:[16]

In an action on the *peculium*, the father or owner should not reply if asked whether he has the son or slave in his power, because the only question at issue is whether the *peculium* is in the defendant's possession.

By removing from the record that part of the formal reply which was required in a suit for 'noxal' damages – 'that the slaves were in his power' – Prudens hoped to ensure that the suit brought by Cinnamus concerning his loan (*de credito suo*) would be an *actio de peculio*.

Why was this so important to Prudens? The answer may lie in the terms of the original mandate (TPSulp. 48) that Prudens had given to Cinnamus seven years earlier (Chapter 3). In that mandate Prudens had promised to provide as much money as had been the subject of any deal (*quanti ea res erit, tantam pecuniam dari*) carried out by his freedman Suavis or his slave Hyginus 'or anyone else under their order'. It looks as if Prudens had failed to repay to Cinnamus a sum of money provided by the bank for a deal or deals carried out by Prudens' staff (which still included the slave Hyginus). (In present-day terms this could be said to be the equivalent of Prudens exceeding his overdraft limit.) Cinnamus now wanted to sue Primus to recover the funds. If, however, Prudens could be sued only for the recovery of debts under an *actio de peculio*, his liability would be limited to the extent of the funds in the *peculia* of these two slaves. This would leave the rest of his estate intact.

I believe that the third and fourth transactions carried out by Hesychus were made through his *peculium*. In TPSulp. 67, following the death of his master Evenus, Hesychus is now slave of the emperor Gaius and designated as Hesychus Evenianus (i.e. former slave of Evenus). On this occasion Eunus states unequivocally that he owes HS1,130 to Hesychus, who stipulates for repayment. The presence or absence of Hesychus' master is not an issue. It now seems unlikely that Hesychus is acting on direct instructions from his new master, the emperor, particularly when such a small amount is being lent: he is surely trading through his *peculium*.

Then in TPSulp. 68 Eunus states that he owes an outstanding balance of HS1,250 to Hesychus. On this occasion, in addition to the usual stipulation, Hesychus makes Eunus swear on oath to repay the money on a given date, at the risk of perjury and of paying a penal rate of interest on the sum outstanding. Hesychus is now very much in control. 'This is my *peculium*,' he seems to be saying, 'and I am the emperor's slave – I can do business in any way that I like.'

Was such high-handed behaviour frequent among members of the imperial household, the *Familia Caesaris*? Very probably. Slaves who worked for the emperor enjoyed high status and might be men of substance. Take for instance the grandest of imperial slaves, Musicus Scurranus, who held under Tiberius the post of superintendent of the imperial treasury in Gaul (*dispensator ad fiscum Gallicum*).[17] On a journey to Rome Musicus was accompanied by no fewer than 16 under-slaves (*vicarii*) including cooks, footmen and secretaries.

At least one other document (TPSulp. 56) seems to indicate that a slave is acting through his *peculium*. In this loan document Nicerus, treasury slave (*servus arcarius*) of the colony of Puteoli (*colonia Puteolana*) gives a pledge (*fide promissio*) to Cinnamus to repay a loan of HS1,000. Nicerus cannot be borrowing on behalf of the colony: to do so would require authorisation by a magistrate and no such authorisation is recorded for this transaction.[18] Nicerus is then trading through his *peculium*.

A significant feature to emerge from this group of documents is that there seems to have been no requirement for a slave to make a formal statement that he was trading through his *peculium*. This was an important piece of information, because anyone contemplating a business deal with a slave would need to know whether the slave's master or mistress had limited their liability to the amount that the slave held in his trading fund. It must be a strong presumption that this information was readily available to the bankers involved and that passing on this information was one of the services that they provided to any of their depositors who contemplated making a loan.

SLAVES AS WITNESSES

The Murecine archive shows that slaves might be called in to act as witnesses to business transactions; they would take their place alongside freeborn and freedman witnesses.

The lists of witnesses for the two warehouse leases, TPSulp. 45 and TPSulp. 46, are revealing. Take first the list in TPSulp. 45, the lease arranged in connection with the loans made by the slave Hesychus to the grain merchant Eunus:

Gaius Novius Cypaerus
Aulus Mevius Julius, son of Aulus, registered in the Falerna tribe
Diognetus, slave of Gaius Novius Cypaerus
Gaius Novius Eunus, freedman of Cypaerus
Irenaeus, slave of Gaius Julius Senecio
Diognetus, slave of Gaius Novius Cypaerus

Diognetus, the slave who actually drew up the contract, signs both in third and in sixth place. His master Cypaerus, the warehouse owner, signs first and thereby indicates that he is the principal in this transaction. In second place the signatory is the freeborn Aulus Mevius Julius of the Falerna voting tribe (the usual tribe in which Puteolans were registered). Mevius Julius has also acted as witness to one of the loans (TPSulp. 52) made by Hesychus to Eunus.

Eunus himself, who has arranged with his former master Cypaerus that Hesychus shall have the lease at a peppercorn rent (see Chapter 5), signs in fourth place. And the fifth place is taken by another slave, Irenaeus, slave of Gaius Julius Senecio. To sum up, the freeborn citizen Aulus Mevius Julius, the two freedmen Cypaerus and Eunus, and the two slaves Irenaeus and Diognetus join together as witnesses to this particular contract. Irenaeus' master, the freeborn Senecio, was later to stand as a witness for the sale of slaves in TPSulp. 43 (see above).

The boundaries of status are similarly blurred among the witnesses that sign another leasing contract, TPSulp. 46:

Publius Annius Seleucus
Gnaeus Pollius Rufus, son of Gnaeus
Gaius Julius Felix
Nardus, slave of Publius Annius Seleucus
Publius Annius Seleucus

In this transaction the freedman Publius Annius Seleucus, who is manager of the warehouse owned by Domitia Lepida, is the principal. He signs in first and last place. The free-born Gnaeus Pollius Rufus, signs in second place; the freedman Gaius Julius Felix signs in third place; and Nardus, slave of the warehouse manager, signs in fourth place.

It was an important part of a banker's service to depositors and borrowers to collect witnesses for their transactions. These witnesses might be drawn from the interested parties, from business associates, perhaps from neighbours and bystanders in the forum – and from slaves connected with the business in hand. One last point. The role played by slaves in the formalities that accompany business transactions is in striking contrast to the role played by women (Chapter 7). This reinforces the evidence of the Jucundus tablets from Pompeii: even someone as wealthy and well-connected as Umbricia Antiochis does not make first-person statements that she has received money from auctions of her property. (As we saw in the previous chapter, Umbricia does stand as a witness in one transaction (T. 24) where she is a principal, but this seems to be an exception to a general rule.) Although women feature as principals in several transactions recorded in the Murecine archive, and respond to stipulations they neither make first person statements nor stand as witnesses. Slaves, on the other hand, do both.

IX

DISPUTES

A third of the documents in the Murecine archive are concerned with litigation; they include promises to appear in a preliminary court, the appointment of a judge to try a case and an agreement to end a dispute. The Sulpicii appear both as claimants and as defendants; other cases involve third parties, doubtless customers of the bank.

THE PRELIMINARY HEARING

A civil suit began with a preliminary hearing in the court of a magistrate – the praetor in Rome, one of the *duumviri* in Puteoli.[1] The magistrate's role was to determine the essence of the dispute between the parties after hearing their claims and counter-claims in his court (*in iure*). He would then sum up his findings in a 'formula' and appoint a judge (*iudex*) to try the case at a specific time and place; the judge was required to make his judgment strictly in accordance with the issue as defined in the magistrate's formula.

For someone who wished to bring a civil suit the first requirement was to obtain a formula. To do this the claimant had to get the defendant to appear at the preliminary hearing in the magistrate's court:[2]

> Where anyone wishes to bring an action, he should give notice; for it seems most fair that one who is about to bring an action should give notice so that the defendant accordingly may know whether he ought to admit the claim or contest it further and so that if he thinks it should be contested, he may come prepared for the suit, knowing the action by which he is sued.

Details of procedure are given by Gaius in Book Four of the Institutes.[3] It was for the claimant to summon the defendant to come before the magistrate (*in ius vocatio*). The defendant had various options. He could go immediately before the magistrate; or he could provide a surety (*vindex*) as a guarantor of his future appearance; or he could give a formal undertaking, a bail promise (*vadimonium*), to appear before a magistrate.

DISPUTES

The *vadimonia* documented in the Murecine archive consist of two inter-connected sections. The first section records the promise given by the defendant to appear in a particular place on a particular day at a particular time for the case to be heard before the praetor or local magistrate. In the second section, the defendant pledges through stipulation to pay to the counterparty by way of penalty a fixed amount (*summa vadimonii*) in the event of his failure to appear. The document concludes with the place where and date when the *vadimonium* was enacted. The amount of bail required was regulated by the Praetor's Edict:[4]

> ...bail is taken for the amount sworn to by the claimant...subject to this, that bail is not taken for a sum exceeding half the amount of the claim or for more than HS100,000...If the matter in dispute is worth HS100,000, bail is not taken for more than HS50,000.

TPSulp. 4 provides an example of a *vadimonium*:

> 9 June 52
>
> Undertaking given by Zeno the Tyrian, freedman of Zenobius, [to appear] on 11 June next, at Puteoli in the forum before the Hordionian altar of Augustus at the third hour. Gaius Sulpicius Cinnamus stipulated and Zeno the Tyrian, freedman of Zenobius, promised that HS1,200 should be paid [by Zeno to Gaius Sulpicius Cinnamus in the event of Zeno's failure to appear].

In *vadimonia* where the dates have survived, the interval between making the promise to appear before the magistrate at Puteoli is two days (three by Roman inclusive reckoning) (TPSulp. 1b, 3, 4) and seven days (TPSulp. 1). In a *vadimonium* made at Puteoli for appearance at Rome (referred to in TPSulp. 27) the interval between the date of the bail promise and the date of the preliminary hearing is, not surprisingly, much longer – perhaps two months. A hearing at Rome was presumably required because the case arose out of business interests held in the capital either by Faustus the defendant or Eumenes the claimant. (More on this case below.)

Some of the bail promises in the Murecine archive may have stemmed from adjournments ordered by the magistrate at the preliminary hearing (*in iure*). Adjournments would be necessary in certain circumstances: for instance on their initial appearance the litigants might not have been able to agree on the appointment of a judge, or on a busy day the magistrate might simply have failed to reach their case.

Several tablets in the Murecine archive (TPSulp. 16-21) provide formal proof that a litigant had put in an appearance (*testatio sistendi*) at the magistrate's court on the agreed date:

> TPSulp. 16:
> 30 October 51.

...At Puteoli, in the forum before the Hordionian altar of Augustus, Gaius Sulpicius Cinnamus made an appearance (*stetit*) at the third hour.

The proceedings, mutatis mutandis, will have been similar to those described by Cicero in his speech for Quinctius:[5]

Naevius gave testimony: 'Publius Quinctius had not attended [the court hearing] and he Naevius had attended' (*P. Quinctium non stitisse et stitisse se*). The formal record (*tabulae*) was signed and sealed by the distinguished witnesses and the meeting broke up.

Preliminary hearings and full trials were held in public, in front of well-known landmarks – in Puteoli, at various altars in the forum. In Capua (TPSulp. 12) a preliminary hearing was to be 'in the Basilica before the Council House (*curia*)'. In Rome (TPSulp. 13-15, 19 and 27), various statues and altars in the Forum of Augustus were designated.

The majority of hearings in the magistrate's court at Puteoli were set for the third hour; this was normal practice in the courts at Rome – as indicated by Martial's comment, 'the third hour brings out the noisy pleaders' (*exercet raucos tertia causidicos*). (The third hour was from approximately 0700 to 0815 at midsummer and from 0900 to 0945 in midwinter.) But other times – the second hour (TPSulp. 18), the fourth (TPSulp. 15) and fifth (TPSulp. 13) – are also specified. Some appearances were even scheduled for the ninth hour in Puteoli (TPSulp. 10) and in Rome (TPSulp. 19). The gap between the fifth and ninth hour in the court's schedule confirms another of Martial's observations: all work ceased (for a siesta followed by exercise) during the sixth, seventh and eighth hours (1045 to 1430 at mid-summer and 1115 to 1330 in mid-winter). In Martial's scheme of things the ninth hour in Rome would be the time when people took their places for dinner.[6]

THE FORMULA

The formula issued by the magistrate at the preliminary hearing would be composed according to a set pattern, of which several examples are given by Gaius.[7] In Rome, the Praetor's Edict and standard formulae were displayed in the Forum Romanum so that they were available for inspection by anyone undertaking litigation.[8] Similarly copies of the Edict and the formulae will have been on display in the forum at Puteoli. In the magistrate's court the claimant, or his adviser, would present a draft formula containing the principal elements of his claim and ask for an action to be allowed on that basis. The formula was made up of a set of clauses of which the principal ones were:

- The appointment of the judge (*nominatio*).
- The plaintiff's statement of claim (*intentio*).

- A direction to the judge to condemn or absolve the defendant (*condemnatio*). This was expressed in monetary terms, stating that the defendant should, or should not, give a certain sum of money to the plaintiff.
- A statement of the facts from which the claim arose (*demonstratio*).

The defendant would put forward any amendments. The magistrate would then make any changes to the formula that he thought desirable, bearing in mind that the formula that he eventually issued to the judge who was to try the case must be in accordance with the Praetor's Edict.

As an example of a formula, let us take a hypothetical suit brought against a defendant for the repayment of a sum of money. In its simplest form the formula might be as follows:

> Let Titius be judge. If it appears that Numerius Negidius [the defendant] ought to give HS10,000 to Aulus Agerius [the claimant], let the judge condemn Numerius Negidius to Aulus Agerius for HS10,000; if it does not so appear, let him absolve.

In a case conducted in accordance with this formula, Negidius the defendant could only put forward one defence, that he did not owe the money. But what if, for instance, he wanted to admit that he did owe the money, but that the claimant had tricked him into entering the contract? In this case the formula could be modified to provide Negidius with a stronger defence:

> Let Titius be judge. If it appears that Numerius Negidius ought to give HS10,000 to Aulus Agerius, if in this matter nothing has been or is being done in bad faith by Aulus Agerius, let the judge condemn Numerius Negidius to Aulus Agerius for HS10,000; if it does not so appear, let him absolve.

Appointment (*nominatio*) of the judge who was to try the case was a key feature of the formula. The magistrate would make the appointment following consultation with the two parties.[9] The Murecine archive contains an agreement on the appointment of a judge:

> TPSulp. 22
> 14 January/13 February 35
>
> I Aulus Castricius Celer have written:
>
> I have come to an agreement with Gaius Sulpicius Faustus major concerning the matters, accounts, disputes, suits, petitions and actions between us, and the [matters at issue] between him and Aulus Castricius Isochrysus ...who is mentioned above, that Aulus Titinius Anthus major will be the judge between me and Gaius Sulpicius Faustus major before the Ides of April next.

But if that same Aulus Titinius Anthus major who is mentioned above, will not be appointed, because through me or my heir this does not happen, because through me or my heir through evil fraud (*dolo malo*) it does not happen that the same Aulus Titinius Anthus major who is mentioned above be appointed, then Gaius Sulpicius Faustus major has stipulated and I Aulus Castricius Celer have promised that HS100,000 be duly paid in good coin.

If the litigants could not agree on an appointee, the magistrate would either impose his choice or draw lots from a selection of candidates. In Rome judges would normally be chosen from the official list (*album iudicum*), made up of senators and equestrians. In Puteoli the *album* doubtless comprised members of the *ordo* and other freeborn citizens of good standing. But the judge might be chosen from a wider cross-section of society: Aulus Titinius Anthus major, the man chosen by the litigants in TPSulp. 22 as judge, was probably a freedman and therefore not included in the *album*.[10]

The Murecine archive contains two examples in the same document (TPSulp. 31) of formulae handed down at a preliminary hearing in Puteoli. The dispute is between Sulpicius Cinnamus, who is the claimant, and Gaius Marcius Saturninus. The magistrate at the preliminary hearing is the duumvir A. Cossinius Priscus.

The two formulae are interconnected:

TPSulp. 31
June/October 52.

This matter is concerned with a pledge (*sponsio*).

Let Gaius Blossius Celadus be the judge [at the full trial].

If it appears that Gaius Marcius Saturninus should give to Gaius Sulpicius Cinnamus HS6,000, which is the subject of the suit, let Gaius Blossius Celadus the judge condemn Gaius Marcius Saturninus [to pay] the HS6,000 to Gaius Sulpicius Cinnamus; if it does not so appear, let him absolve [Gaius Marcius Saturninus] from payment.

Let Gaius Blossius Celadus be the judge [at the full trial].

If it appears that Gaius Marcius Saturninus should give to Gaius Sulpicius Cinnamus HS18,000, which is the subject of the suit, let Gaius Blossius Celadus the judge condemn Gaius Marcius Saturninus to pay the HS18,000 to Gaius Sulpicius Cinnamus; if it does not so appear, let him absolve [Gaius Marcius Saturninus] from payment.
Aulus Cossinius Priscus, *Duumvir*, ordered the judgment to be made.

The first formula is explicitly concerned with a solemn promise in the form of a *sponsio*, the form of stipulation used between Roman citizens. What appears to have happened is this. Cinnamus is suing Saturninus for an outstanding debt of HS18,000 through an action for the return of a specific sum of money (*actio certae creditae pecuniae*). Saturninus thinks that he can win the case. If the case goes against him he promises to pay, besides the HS18,000, a third of this sum as a penalty. Consequently Cinnamus has put to Saturninus the question, 'Do you promise that HS6,000 will be given to me' (*mihi dari spondesne*)? Saturninus has replied, 'I promise' (*spondeo*). Cinnamus will have entered into a similar promise to pay HS6,000, if the judge finds against him. (The jurist Gaius explains that these penalties are intended to restrain rash litigation.)[11] We can see this procedure, known as the pledge of a third part (*sponsio tertiae partis*), being followed in the case where Cicero defended Roscius the comic actor:[12]

> A definite sum of money (*pecunia certa*) was owing to you, which you now claim before a judge, and there was also an engagement to pay a third part of it in addition, as appointed by law.

The second formula is concerned with the principal suit, through which Cinnamus hopes to recover the sum of HS18,000 which he claims is owing to him. We have no information on how the case turned out.

In some instances the parties would settle their dispute at the preliminary hearing. For instance the claimant might withdraw his case or the defendant might admit liability. Another route to settlement before a full trial was undertaken was the use of oaths:[13]

> Conscientious oath-taking is relied on as an important means of shortening litigation. Disputes are settled in this way through agreement between litigants or on the authority of the magistrate.

Typically a claimant would challenge the defendant to take an oath, which he would tender (*deferre*) to him in a particular form.[14] If the defendant accepted and took the oath, swearing that his case was just, he won; if he refused, he lost. Two complex and fragmentary tablets, TPSulp. 28 and TPSulp. 29, seem to be concerned with a charge of abusive language (*iniuria verbis*) brought against Cinnamus by Fortunatus. In the first tablet we find Cinnamus agreeing to swear an oath tendered to him by Fortunatus the claimant; in the second, which should presumably be dated some days later, Cinnamus is reported to have sworn the oath:

TPSulp. 28
1 February 49

> Concerning the bail promise which Gaius Sulpicius Cinnamus had given to Julius Fortunatus, Gaius Sulpicius Cinnamus said that he was ready to swear an oath, as agreed, if HS3,000 were paid to him, then Julius Fortunatus tendered the oath to him…money… at the statue of the Great Goddess….

TPSulp. 29
February (?) 49

Gaius Sulpicius Cinnamus swore the oath, when Julius Fortunatus tendered it to him, in accord with these words (*in ea verba*) which are written below:

In full awareness (*ex tui animi sententia*) ...

contrary to good behaviour [(*adversus bonos mores*)]...*

harm (*iniuriam*)...

if knowingly (*si sciens*)...

By Jupiter Best and Greatest and the Divinity of the Deified Augustus and the Genius of Tiberius Claudius Caesar Augustus

contrary to good behaviour [(*adversus bonos mores*)]...*

*The words in square brackets have been struck out.

These two tablets raise several questions: Why did Fortunatus agree to pay Cinammus HS3,000? What was the verbal abuse that Cinnamus was alleged to have uttered? Why has the phrase *adversus bonos mores* been struck through with a line in the two places where it appears? What if Cinnamus perjured himself and was subsequently discovered to have done so? The jurist Ulpian ruled that in money matters, which this seems to have been, the punishment for perjury was a flogging.[15] And no doubt this would have been the end of the Bank of the Sulpicii.

THE FULL TRIAL

If a lawsuit went to full trial, the parties were expected to attend the court in person; in special circumstances, however, a litigant could appoint a representative (procurator or *cognitor*) to take his place; if a representative did appear at the trial, his name would be substituted for that of the principal and he became the party to the action (see TPSulp. 27 below).

Each party might retain counsel to plead their case in court. The legal 'profession' was made up of jurists (*iurisprudentes*), who learned their trade through a form of pupillage, and advocates (*patroni, cognitores, causidici, advocati*), for the most part ambitious young members of the political elite, who had attended schools of rhetoric.[16] Jurists would advise clients – magistrates, judges and litigants – on points of law; they would also coach people in uttering the set formulae that were required in business and other transactions and advise them on the presentation of court cases. Advocates would argue a client's case in court. Fees were not supposed to be taken but frequently were; in the reign of Claudius advocates' fees were finally allowed as legitimate.

In a letter to his friend Maturus Arrianus, the younger Pliny, himself an experienced advocate, remembers his rival Marcus Regulus:[17]

> He used to be pale with anxiety, would write out his speeches though he could never learn them by heart, paint round one of his eyes (the right if he was appearing for the claimant and the left for the defendant), change a white patch from one eyebrow to the other, and never fail to consult the soothsayers on the result of his case.

The trial proceeded by means of alternate speeches from the advocates. The judge acted as 'umpire'. In another passage from the letter just quoted Pliny sets out how he thinks a judge should conduct a trial:

> Whenever I am hearing a case (which I do more often than I conduct one) I allow all the time anyone asks for, thinking it rash to predict the length of anything still unheard and to set a time-limit to a trial before its extent is known, especially when one of the first duties of a magistrate under oath is patience – an important element in justice itself.

Both written and oral testimony were allowed to be given in evidence but oral testimony was favoured because of its immediacy and because it gave the judge an opportunity to form an opinion as to the reliability of the witnesses. To reach his decision the judge might seek advice on points of law from jurists or from the magistrate who had appointed him. But on questions of fact he was expected to make up his own mind:[18]

> It is customary for [provincial] governors to answer the questions of judges on points of law, whereas, if they ask about points of fact, governors ought not to give advice but instruct them to give their decision in accordance with their oaths; for this [advising on questions of fact] sometimes brings disrepute and affords an opportunity for partiality and favouritism.

The duty of a scrupulous judge, said the jurist Papinian,[19]

> is to weigh the reliability (*fides*) even of the testimony given by a man of good standing (*integrae frontis homo*).

As we have already seen, in actions for the recovery of a specific sum of money (*actiones certae creditae poecuniae*), the judge was required simply to decide whether he should 'condemn' the defendant to pay or whether he should absolve him. This presumably reflected the fact that the judge was a citizen without any special authority; he had no officials to execute his judgment. A monetary judgment brought the matter to a straightforward conclusion. No reasons were given in the judgment nor, in the normal course of events, was an appeal possible.

All this sounds relatively straightforward. But a judge might be swayed by the status and character of the two parties to the suit. In the second century Aulus Gellius found himself appointed to act as a judge in a dispute over a loan. The claimant said that he had paid over the money but produced no documents or witnesses to substantiate his case. It was clear, however, continued Gellius,[20]

> that he was a thoroughly good man, of well-known and tested integrity and of blameless life....On the other hand the defendant was shown to be of no substance, of base and evil life, often convicted of lying and full of treachery and fraud. Yet he [the defendant] along with his numerous advocates (*patroni*) noisily protested that the payment of the money ought to be shown in the usual way, by a receipt for payment (*expensi latio*), by a book of accounts (*mensae rationes*), by producing a signature (*chirographi exhibitio*), by a sealed deed (*tabularum obsignatio*) or by the testimony of witnesses (*testium intercessio*). If nothing could be proved in any of these ways, he ought surely to be released at once and his opponent [the claimant] found guilty of false accusation (*calumnia*). He maintained that the testimony relating to the life and conduct of the two parties was irrelevant; for this was a case of claiming money before a private judge, not a question of morals to be settled before the censors.

Gellius took advice on how to proceed by consulting a panel (*consilium*) of leading advocates; they recommended judgment for the defendant. Still uncertain, he ordered an adjournment and consulted a friend, the philosopher Favorinus. Favorinus cited Marcus Cato who had said that if a case was evenly balanced, the judge should decide which of the two parties was the better man (*vir melior*), adding that this was a traditional Roman attitude. This would mean, in the present case, finding for the claimant. To his credit Gellius did not take his friend's advice. But he still could not make up his mind to absolve the defendant. Instead he stated on oath that the matter was not clear to him (*mihi non liquere*) and was released from sitting as judge in the case.

A defendant who lost his case had 30 days' grace in which to settle his debt. If, after this interval, the defendant had not complied with the judgment, the claimant would have to pursue before a magistrate an action on the judgment (*actio iudicati*). The debtor could then contest the validity of the judgment, whereupon another trial would follow. But this was a risky course of action for the debtor. He would have to provide security; he was also liable to double the sum originally sought if he was unsuccessful.

What happened if the defendant simply refused to co-operate in the *actio iudicati*? Under ancient law the claimant might take him off to custody to work off the debt. This might be impractical if the defendant was of superior status or could call on support from a gang of hired toughs. Furthermore imprisoning a debtor was of little comfort to the businessman seeking monetary recompense. Accordingly the claimant could seek an order from the magistrate for seizure of the debtor's entire estate (*missio in possessionem*). When the order was granted it would be publicised, to alert all those with an interest. The claimant would then take possession of the defendant's property and administer it on behalf of all the creditors. There would usually be an auction of the debtor's property (*venditio bonorum*):[21]

> Where the estate that is being sold belongs to a living person, the praetor orders that it be held in possession and advertised for 30 successive days….After that he orders the creditors to meet and appoint one of their number as manager (*magister*), to carry out the sale. And if the estate that is being sold is that of a living person, he orders this to be done in 10 days….

The estate would be sold to the bidder who offered the highest pay-out to the creditors. The debtor still remained liable for any unpaid part of the debt; if he still failed to pay, he was likely to suffer social disgrace. A black mark (*nota censoria*) would be entered against his name on the census lists and he would become a man of no reputation (*infamis*). This brought with it legal disabilities: an *infamis* could not hold office or a position of honour, bring criminal accusations, act as a representative or be represented in litigation or appear as an advocate. Furthermore it seems that he became unable to make a legal will or formal conveyance.[22]

The horrors of life for a man who was declared *infamis* are spelled out in highly coloured detail by Cicero in his speech for Quinctius:[23]

> If a man's goods are possessed under the [praetor's] edict his entire character (*fama*) and reputation (*existimatio*) are taken into possession along with his goods. If a man's name is posted up on placards in the most public of places, he is not even allowed the privilege of perishing in silence and obscurity; if a man has administrators (*magistri*) appointed and creditors (*domini*) put in [to sell his property], who will fix the rules and conditions of his ruin; if a man hears the voice of the auctioneer (*praeco*) calling out his name and setting the price of his goods, then alive and with his own eyes he attends his own most bitter funeral….

THE SULPICII AND THEIR ASSOCIATES IN COURT

Many of the documents in the Murecine archive which refer to court appearances and to litigation are fragmentary and isolated from their context. Nevertheless it is possible to construct brief case studies of several law suits involving the Sulpicii and their associates.

Sulpicius Faustus versus the Castricii

An early 'case file' in the archive consists of a set of three documents concerning a dispute in 35 between Sulpicius Faustus and various members of a well-known

Puteolan clan, the Castricii. As we saw above, in the first of these documents (TPSulp. 22) Castricius Celer, acting as spokesman for the Castricii, came to an agreement with Sulpicius Faustus at the preliminary hearing that the freedman Aulus Titinius Anthus major should be the judge in their case.

It will be remembered that a penalty, amounting to the large sum of HS100,000, was to be payable by Celer if the appointment of Titinius Anthus failed to materialise through some act of fault or dishonesty on his part or that of his heir. We must assume that Faustus, who is the claimant, was very keen that Titinius Anthus should try the case and was in a strong position vis-à-vis Celer.

The second and third documents relate to further preliminary hearings and are dated later than the Ides of April, when the full trial was originally scheduled to take place:

TPSulp. 23
19 April 35

At a hearing before Lucius Granius Probus, Duumvir, Gaius Sulpicius Faustus formally put to Aulus Castricius Onesimus the question whether he was heir to Aulus Castricius Isochrysus and what was his share in the estate.
    Aulus Castricius Onesimus replied that he was [heir] to Aulus Castricius Isochrysus and his portion was one twelfth plus one twenty-fourth of one fifth of the estate [i.e. less than one per cent].

TPSulp. 24
28 April 35

At a hearing before Quintus Puteolanus Aquila, Prefect, Gaius Sulpicius Faustus formally put to Aulus Castricius Eros Hordionianus the question whether he was heir to Aulus Castricius Isochrysus or was in possession of his goods and what was his share.
Aulus Castricius Eros Hordionianus replied that he was in possession of half the goods of Aulus Castricius Isochrysus.

Whether or not Titinius Anthus did try the original case, the situation has now changed: Isochrysus, one of the original defendants has died. As one of Isochrysus' creditors Faustus wants to ensure that he gets what is owed to him by the estate. The first of these new preliminary hearings is in front of a duumvir, Lucius Granius Probus; at the second hearing Probus is unable to attend and his place is taken by the prefect Quintus Puteolanus Aquila.

In these two documents Faustus is seeking to establish what share of the Isochrysus' estate is being taken by the heirs. Onesimus, the first respondent, has a tiny share. More significant is the response of Eros Hordionianus, who says that he is already in possession of half the estate. It looks very much as if Eros Hordionianus, himself a freedman, was patron of the deceased Isochrysus and had taken what was due to him under the Augustan *lex Papia*:[24]

> ...of the estate of a freedman who leaves a fortune of HS100,000 or more...where he leaves only one son or daughter as heir, half of his estate is due to his patron, just as if he had died childless.

Faenius Eumenes versus Sulpicius Faustus

The summer of 48 saw a dispute between Faustus and a certain Eumenes, in which Faustus was the defendant. The first document in the suit is a *vadimonium* in which Eumenes calls on Faustus to promise bail of HS50,000:

> TPSulp. 2
>
> Undertaking given by Gaius Sulpicius Faustus [to appear] on 24 June at Puteoli in the forum before the Hordionian altar [of Augustus] at the third hour.
>
> Lucius Faenius Eumenes, who is to bring an action for breach of a contract of sale (*acturus ex empto*), stipulated and Gaius Sulpicius Faustus pledged, that HS50,000 should be paid [by Faustus to Eumenes in the event of Faustus' failure to appear].

There was presumably a postponement, for a second *vadimonium* is given by Faustus after 24 June:

> TPSulp. 3
> 3 July 48
>
> Undertaking given by Gaius Sulpicius Faustus [to appear] on 5 July, at Puteoli in the forum before the Hordionian altar [of Augustus] at the third hour. Lucius Faenius Eumenes, who is to bring a suit for a sum greater than [the bail of] HS50,000 and has deposited a ring worth HS1,000 [with Faustus] as a token of good faith (*arrae nomine*), stipulated and Gaius Sulpicius Faustus pledged [that HS50,000 should be paid by Faustus to Eumenes in the event of Faustus' failure to appear].

These two documents refer to the same transaction or set of transactions, in which Eumenes has bought unspecified goods from Faustus. Eumenes has claimed that Faustus has failed to keep his side of the bargain. In the second *vadimonium*, Eumenes states that he is taking legal action to recover a sum greater than the bail of HS50,000 promised by Faustus. Eumenes also says that he has deposited with Faustus a ring worth HS1,000 as confirmation of having concluded a deed of sale. It was common practice for such deposits to be given:[25]

What is given by way of earnest (*arra*) is evidence that a contract of purchase and sale (*emptio venditio*) has been concluded.

We have no knowledge of what transpired on 5 July 48, the day fixed in the second *vadimonium* for the appearance of the two parties in the forum at Puteoli at the third hour. However in September the two parties came to an agreement:

TPSulp. 27
4 September 48

I, Lucius Faenius Eumenes, have written that I have agreed with Gaius Sulpicius Faustus to end the dispute between us, in which advocates (*cognitores*) have been appointed reciprocally (*ultro citro*) by us. I renounce my claim to the bail undertaking (*vadimonium… remittere*) to appear at Rome which the advocate of Sulpicius gave to my advocate. And I also formally release Gaius Sulpicius Faustus from the security that he gave in this affair.

Therefore [I have written that], if Tiberius Julius Sporus has deserted the bail of HS 50,000 which he promised to my representative Lucius Faenius Thallus for his appearance on 1 November in Rome, in the Forum of Augustus, before the triumphal statue of Gnaeus Sentius Saturninus, at the third hour, no one shall for this reason sue Tiberius Julius Sporus or his sponsor, or from either of them demand and exact it [i.e. the bail sum promised]; if contrary to this [declaration], any action will be taken, however much [the sum] may be, Gaius Sulpicius Faustus has stipulated that I will pay the amount [that is claimed] and I, Lucius Faenius Eumenes, have promised (*spopondi*) to do this. And in response to his formal question (*interrogante eo*) I have formally released Gaius Sulpicius Faustus from the pledge that he gave in this affair.

From this document it emerges that the litigants decided to make a direct approach to the praetor in Rome. Rather than attend in person at Rome, the two parties each nominated a *cognitor* to represent them. Faustus had appointed Tiberius Julius Sporus, Eumenes had appointed his freedman Lucius Faenius Thallus. The two advocates agreed between them a *vadimonium* for an appearance at Rome for the following 1 November; in this *vadimonium* a stipulation for HS 50,000 was promised by Sporus, acting for Faustus, in case he failed to appear. (It also emerges that the bail undertaking made by Sporus was guaranteed by a *sponsor*.) In the meantime, however, Faustus and Eumenes reached an agreement and decided to put an end to their dispute; and on 4 September, Eumenes the claimant sets out in this document the terms of the agreement.

The decision taken by the principals Eumenes and Faustus to settle the case out of court has, however, caused a problem. Their representatives, the two *cognitores*, had already agreed a *vadimonium* that required Sporus, Faustus' representative, to appear at Rome on 1 November. Under the terms of this agreement Sporus would forfeit

HS 50,000 if he did not make this appearance. Although the principals had come to an agreement and there was no need for anyone to go to trial at Rome, Sporus was still obliged in strict law to pay over the bail money under the promise he had made to Thallus, Eumenes' representative, if he failed to fulfil his undertaking to put in an appearance. This debt would be Faustus' to settle, since he was Sporus' principal, as the jurist Gaius makes clear:[26]

> From the defendant's side security (*satisdatio*) is due whenever a man appears on behalf of another, since without security one is never regarded as a suitable defender of someone else's case. The security, when the defence is conducted by a *cognitor*, is required from his principal....

The answer to the problem was for Eumenes to guarantee that Faustus would not suffer from any adverse financial consequences when his representative did not fulfil his bail undertaking; to ensure this Eumenes pledged by stipulation to compensate Faustus if necessary.

Sulpicius Cinnamus versus Julius Prudens

In the year 55, seven years after the original mandate given by Prudens to the Sulpicii (TPSulp 48, discussed in Chapter 3), relations between Prudens and his bankers had turned sour.

As we saw in Chapter 8, Cinnamus had brought a suit against Prudens concerning a loan (TPSulp. 25). Prudens hoped to ensure that the suit would be treated as an *actio de peculio*; in this way his liability would be limited to the extent of the combined funds in the *peculia* of his two slaves. The full trial was to take place in Rome, doubtless because this was where the business managed by the two slaves on Prudens' behalf was based.

Another six documents appear to bear on the dispute between Cinnamus and Prudens. The first of these documents reads:

TPSulp. 34

> ...in the contested law suit between you and me that is being heard by the judge... I am prepared to submit to the arbitration of Marcus Barbatius Epaphroditus in Puteoli or in Rome, and I shall agree to any requirements (*opera*) of the arbitrator and pay any [penalty] money that is due [in the event of my non-compliance]....

In this document the claimant declares that he is prepared to transfer a dispute, which is currently being heard before a judge, to the decision of an arbitrator (*arbiter*), Marcus Barbatius Epaphroditus. An arbitrator was a person appointed by the praetor (or local magistrate) to settle a dispute; the litigants agreed to meet the arbitrator's requirements and to pay a pre-arranged penalty in the case of non-compliance:[27]

> The penalty arising from a reference to arbitration is ...incurred...where the disobedience relates to the payment of money or the provision of a service.

The name of the claimant, the defendant and the date are missing. However there are two clues to suggest that this is a document from the suit between Cinnamus and Prudens that was due to be heard in Rome at some time during the year 55. First, it is expressly stated that the place of the new hearing can be in Puteoli or in Rome; this reminds us that the full trial of the suit between Cinnamus and Prudens was scheduled to take place in Rome. Second, a witness list has survived which includes Gaius Julius Prudens.

Several more documents (TPSulp. 35-39) are concerned with this case. The first is dated to 21 May 55 and the last is datable to some time in the following year. They all employ roughly the same form of words. The first (TPSulp. 35) may be reconstructed with the aid of other texts in the series and will serve as an exemplar:

TPSulp. 35
21/22 May 55

> Marcus Barbatius Epaphroditus the arbitrator, following the agreement between Gaius Sulpicius Cinnamus and Gaius Julius Prudens, in their presence appointed a day for the hearing and ordered them to attend on 4 June next at Puteoli in the Chalcidicum of Octavius from the third hour until the fifth hour.

This document tells us that the arbitrator Epaphroditus has fixed a day, place and hour for a hearing at Puteoli. The two parties have apparently broken off their lawsuit in Rome. Why did they do this? Presumably the two parties agreed to go before an arbitrator because they thought that they would get a more satisfactory outcome than if the final judgment was made by the judge. As Cicero said:[28]

> ...when people perceive that their cause is likely to fail before a judge, they have recourse to an arbitrator....

Two intriguing questions remain unanswered: why was the date for arbitration put off so frequently? And what was the outcome of the case?

DISPUTES BETWEEN THIRD PARTIES

Lucretius Firmus versus Aelius Valentinus

Two documents (TPSulp. 12 and 26), both enacted at Capua, refer to a dispute between a soldier, L. Lucretius Firmus, and a certain L. Aelius Valentinus. The first document in chronological order is a formal requirement (*denuntiatio*):

TPSulp. 26
27 August 40 or 43/4

Lucius Lucretius Firmus required (*denuntiavit*) Lucius Aelius Valentinus to keep the slave Felix in his power.

The second document is a *vadimonium*:

TPSulp. 12
29 August 40 or 43/4.

[Undertaking given] by Lucius Aelius Valentinus [to appear on...] at Capua, in the basilica before the council house at the first hour. Lucius Lucretius Firmus, a soldier of the 13th [urban] cohort in the century of Marcus Salvius Firmus, stipulated and Lucius Aelius Valentinus promised, that HS2,000 [should be paid by Valentinus to Firmus in the event of Valentinus' failure to appear].

The course of events seems be something like this. Firmus is suing Valentinus in connection with some misbehaviour on the part of Valentinus' slave Felix. Firmus wants to be sure that the slave Felix remains in the ownership of Valentinus and has not been set free or sold. To obtain the necessary assurance, Firmus put a formal question to Valentinus at the preliminary hearing before the duumvir; he asked Valentinus whether Felix was still in his possession and in his power (*potestas*). On Valentinus' reply that this was the case, Firmus then put it to him formally that he Valentinus was to retain Felix in his *potestas*. Two days later Firmus obtained a bail-promise from Valentinus that he would appear in court to defend a suit calling for damages resulting from his slave's wrongdoing. One (or both) of the two parties was evidently resident in Capua.

What has all this got to do with the Sulpicii? Perhaps the soldier Firmus was a depositor with the Sulpicii, who gave him legal advice. Alternatively, it may have been the defendant Valentinus who was the depositor with the Sulpicii; perhaps the bankers had undertaken, for a fee, to put up bail on his behalf.

Pactumeia Prima versus Aulus Attiolenus
In this dispute Faustus is playing one of a Roman banker's traditional roles, that of safe-keeper:

TPSulp. 40
? May 52

Gaius Sulpicius Faustus has testified that he produced publicly (*exhibuisse*) the woman Tyche (the subject of this affair, whom Pactumeia Prima and Aulus Attiolenus Atimetus had deposited with him) on 6 May at Puteoli in the forum before the Hordionian altar of Augustus at the third hour in the presence of both parties; and that, by the order of Aulus Attiolenus Atimetus, Pactumeia Prima had taken this woman.

Pactumeia and Atimetus have been involved in a dispute about the ownership of a slave, Tyche. Faustus has been acting as deposit holder (*sequester*); that is to say the two parties had deposited the slave with him after making arrangements for her to be kept safe, produced publicly when required, and then returned to the party in whose favour the dispute was settled.[29] It appears that the case was settled out of court and Atimetus admitted that the slave belonged to Pactumeia.

Two points are worth noting. First, it was not only deposits of money and valuables that were entrusted to bankers; slaves (who were regarded as chattels) might be placed in their charge. Slaves, of course, required food and accommodation, which the *sequester* would have to provide. No doubt the Sulpicii charged expenses and fees to the parties who were engaged in the dispute. Second, both parties to the dispute attended in person the formal handing over of the slave to Pactumeia. Neither Pactumeia nor Atimetus seem to have been sufficiently affluent to send a freedman or a slave to act as their proxy.

The case of the ship Notus

TPSulp. 106, a very mutilated document dated to 22 December 57 and drawn up at Puteoli, refers to a dispute concerning a cargo and a ship. The text mentions inter alia:

★ 'Gaius S...'
★ ...a missing name, 'son of Theodorus', and an indecipherable *origo*
★ 'the ship Notus'
★ a cargo of 'approximately 18,000 *modii*'
★ a missing name, 'son of...'
★ 'from Sidon'
★ the ship's 'emblem' (*parasemum*).

Other phrases in the text indicate the nature of the dispute:

★ 'under the auctioneer' (*sub praecone*)
★ 'on account of its cargo' (*ob honus*)
★ 'because he had diverted' (*quod...avertisset*)
★ 'to be legally due to' (*obligata esse*)
★ 'the exercise of first claim' (*protopraxia*)
★ 'according to law and custom' (*et iure ipso et consuetudine*)

Here we have a dispute concerning a cargo (*onus*) which is apparently up for auction (*sub praecone*); in other words, these are assets which are being sold off to meet

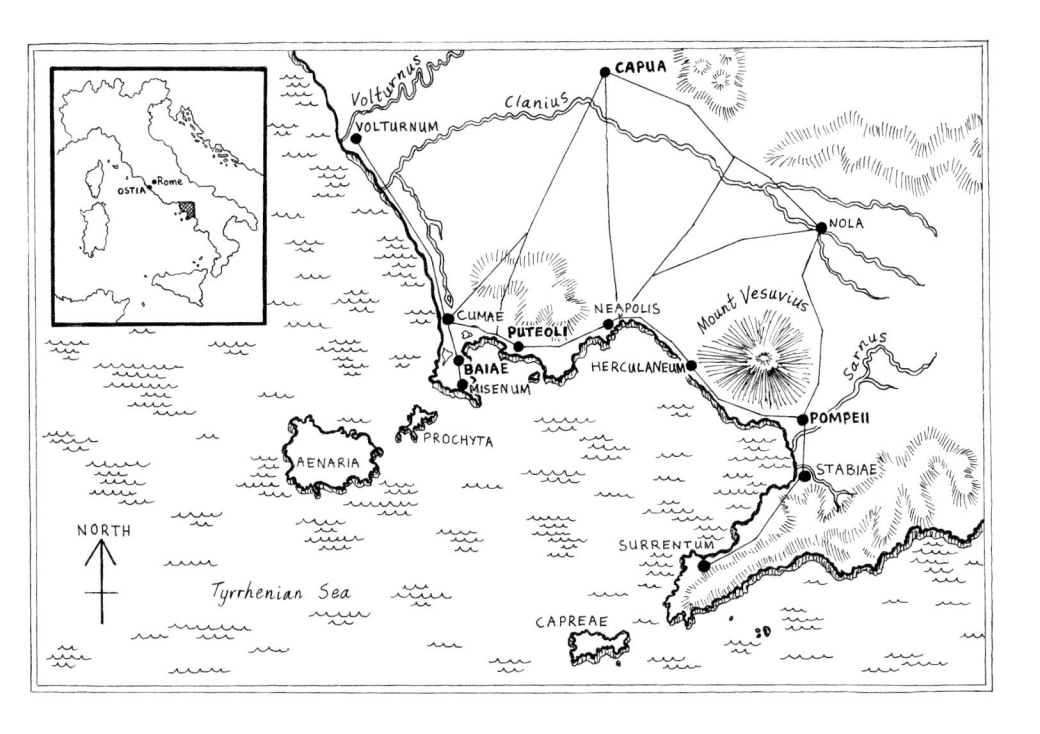

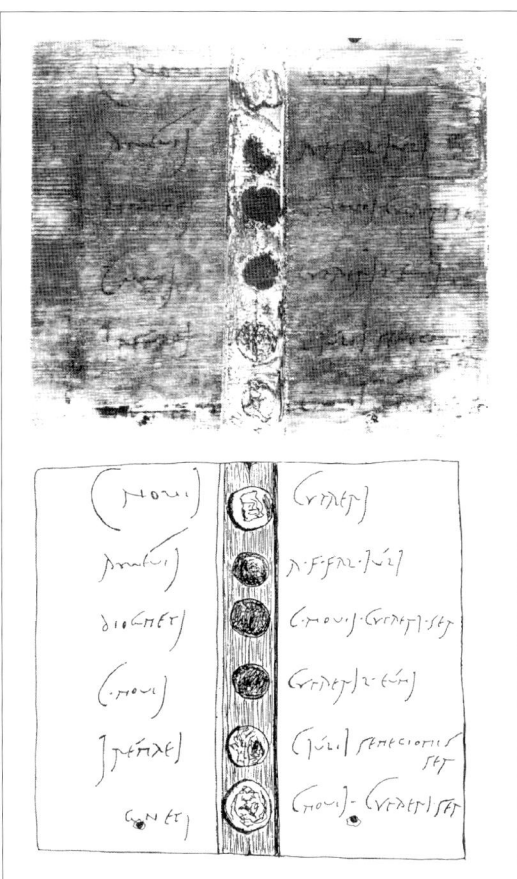

Above: 1 Map of the Bay of Naples

Left: 2 C. Novius Cypaerus is the first witness to sign and seal a lease for storing foodstuffs in the warehouse which he manages. Cypaerus' slave Diognetus signs in third and sixth place; his former slave, the freedman grain dealer C. Novius Eunus, signs in fourth place. (*TPSulp.* 45.)

3 A schematic view of the waterfront at Puteoli engraved on a fourth-century AD glass flask, which was sold to visitors as a souvenir. Among the sights depicted by the artist are the sea walls, the famous mole (*pilae*) and a fish pond; two triumphal arches; a stadium, an amphitheatre and a theatre; a temple (perhaps the Capitolium on Rione Terra); a *solarium* (possibly the site of a public sundial) and the Forum. (*From a flask in The World of Glass Museum, St Helens*)

4 Coastal vessels and lighters crowd the harbour at Puteoli, below the promontory of Rione Terra (*Reconstruction by Mevida Woodford*)

5 The river boat *Isis Giminiana* being loaded at Ostia with a cargo of grain for its journey up the Tiber to Rome. Porters carry sacks up the gang-plank while corn measurers check sample loads for quantity and quality. (*Original wall-painting in the Vatican Museum, Rome*)

6 A banker and his clerk reconcile the books. The banker is holding his ledger (*codex accepti et expensi*) in his left hand. On the table in front of him is a large bag of coins. The clerk reads out the transactions from the day-book (*adversaria*). (*Original in National Museum, Belgrade*)

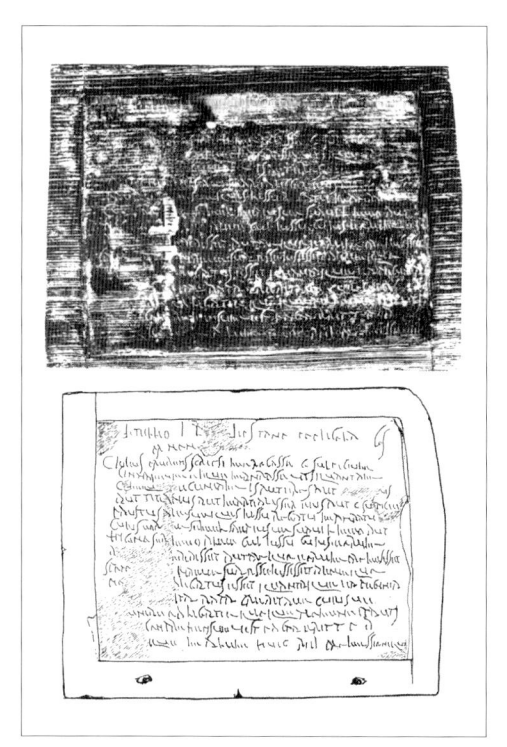

7 C. Julius Prudens, a deposit-holder with the Sulpicii, gives formal instructions to his bankers. The names of the consuls, indicating the year 48, and the day of the month (which has not survived in its entirety) appear in the first two lines of the tablet. Prudens' name appears at the beginning of the third line. (*TPSulp. 48*)

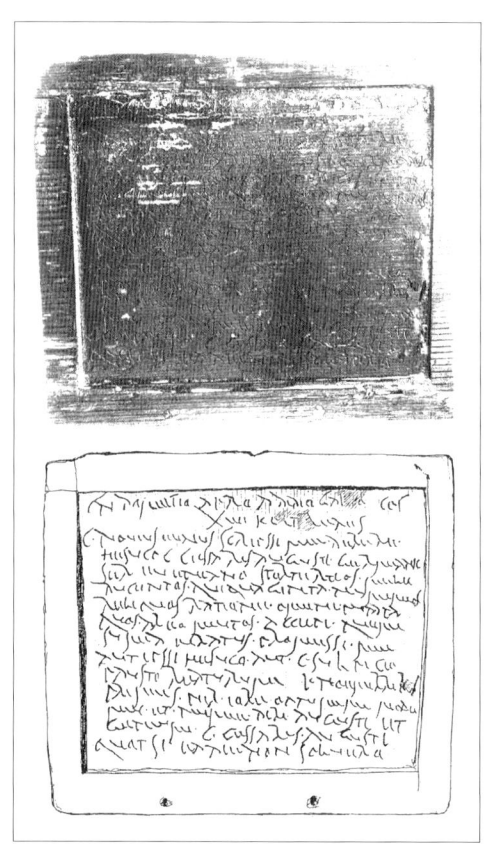

8 C. Novius Eunus borrows HS1,250 from the imperial slave Hesychus in this tablet dated to 15 September 39. (*TPSulp. 68*)

Right: 9 A receipt issued by the banker C. Sulpicius Cinnamus to Alcimus, slave of C. Eprius Valgus, for repayment of a loan. The date is 31 December 47. (*TPSulp. 72*)

Below: 10 A cloth merchant and his staff display goods to two seated customers. Stock pledged by a merchant as security for a loan was liable to be sold at auction in the event of his default. (*Original in Uffizi Museum, Florence*)

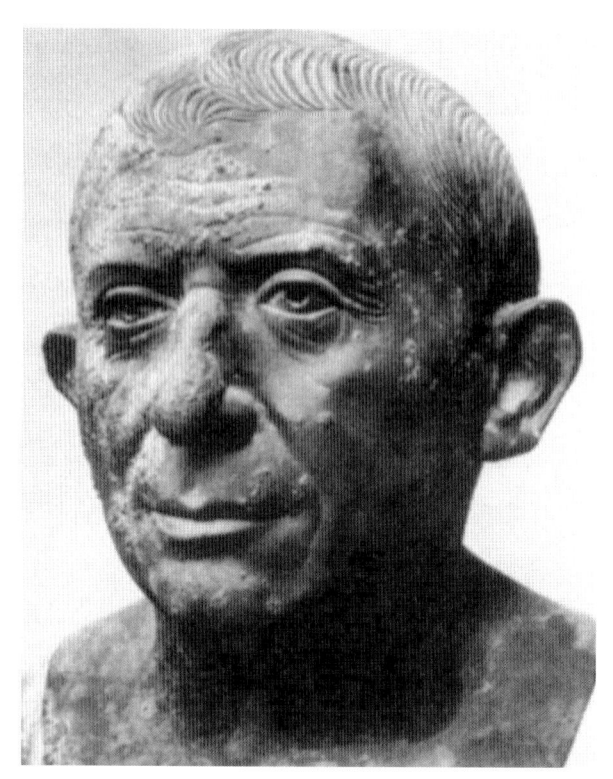

11 L. Caecilius Felix, probably the first proprietor of the bank of Jucundus in Pompeii. (*National Archaeological Museum, Naples*)

12 A grain measurer (*mensor frumentarius*) at work, with his measuring bucket (*modius*) and a rod to level off the grain. (*Original mosaic in the Piazza delle Corporazioni, Ostia*)

13 Warehouses at Ostia: the *Horrea Epagathiana et Epaphroditiana* – a business investment by two enterprising freedmen, originally built on three levels

14 Baling up a consignment at the dockside. (*Original in Musée d'Arles Antique*)

15 A Roman family. Freeborn women with three children (freedwomen with four) were privileged under Augustan legislation. (*Original in National Museum, Rome*)

16 Slaves tow a river boat. (*Original in Musée Calvet, Avignon*)

17 A slave waits at table. (*Original in Museum of Plovdiv*)

18 A slave keeps the furnace fired up for his master the blacksmith. (*Original in National Archaeological Museum, Aquileia*)

Left: 19 Mercury, god of shopkeepers and traders, was worshipped in the western provinces of the Roman Empire. (*Original in Circencester Museum*)

Below: 20 Daily shopping in the market. (*Original in Ostia Museum*)

Opposite above: 21 A wide range of implements and tools is on display at this stall in Rome. (*Original in Vatican Museum, Rome*)

Opposite below: 22 The trader Octavius writes to his contact in the garrison at Vindolanda: 'If you don't send me some cash, I shall be embarrassed.' (*Tab. Vindol. 2. 343*)

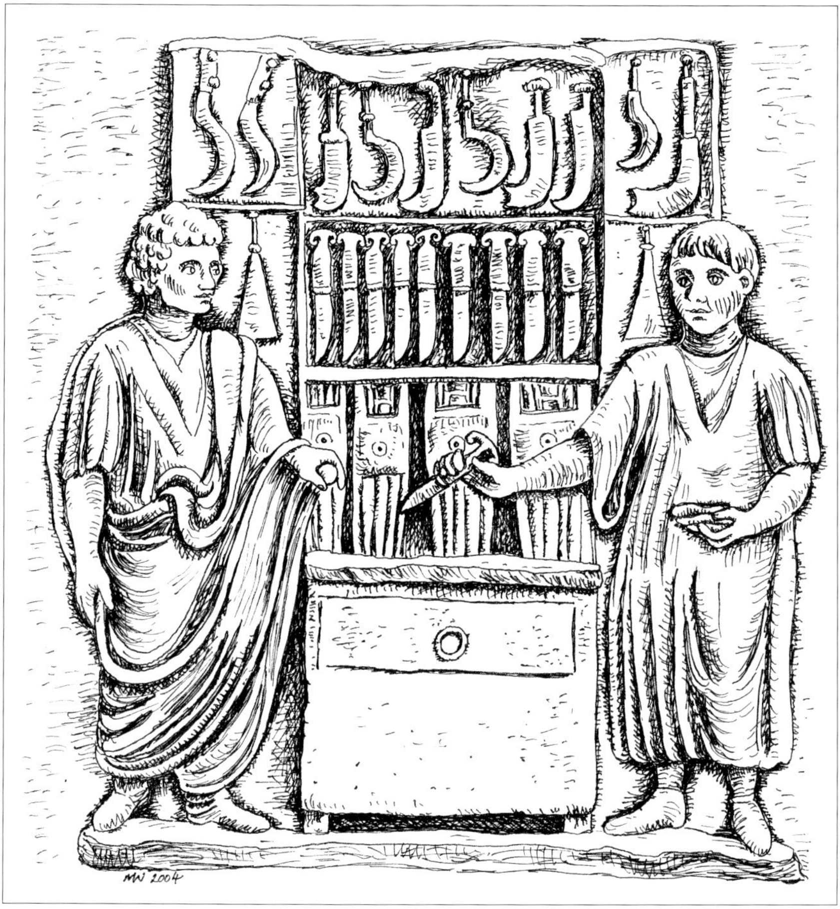
MW 2004

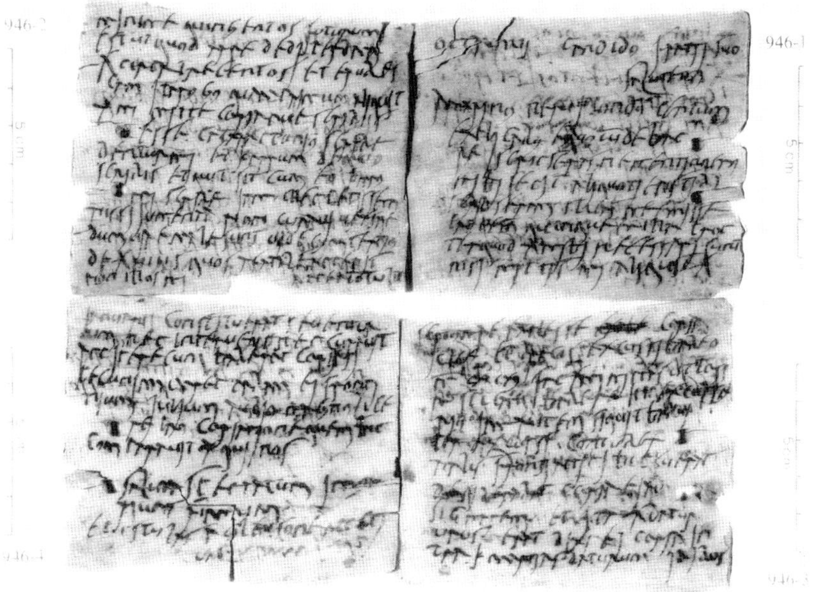
946-2
946-1
5 cm
946-4
946-3

23 Transshipping wine from a deep-sea freighter (indicated by the dolphin) to a river boat with a towing mast. (*Mosaic in the Piazza delle Corporazioni, Ostia*)

24 The shipbuilder Longidienus at work in his Ravenna shipyard. (*Original in National Museum, Ravenna*)

25 Slaves drive a treadmill to power a crane on one of the building projects of the contractor Q. Haterius Tychicus. (*Original in Vatican Museum, Rome*)

26 Tenant farmers pay their taxes. Landowners were required to act as tax collectors under the Empire. The man who scrutinises the coin so suspiciously is the bailiff (*vilicus*) or a government official. (*Original in Landesmuseum, Trier*)

27 The staff of the Secundinii make payments to out-workers, who watch the proceedings anxiously. (*The Igel Column, after L. Dahm*)

28 The butcher's wife keeps the books in this small family firm. (*Original in Dresden Museum*)

29 Sea-borne trade was the foundation of many family businesses – like that of the Pompeian *augustalis* C. Munatius Faustus. (*From the tomb built for Faustus by his wife, the freedwoman Naevoleia Tyche*)

30 A wealthy young Campanian couple (*National Archaeological Museum, Naples*)

the claims of creditors. The cargo had been carried by the Notus, a ship of 18,000 *modii*. We may speculate that the merchant (*negotiator*) was a freeborn peregrine, name unknown, son of Theodorus, and that he had appointed a shipper (*navicularius*) whose name has also disappeared, from Sidon.

The Notus ('South Wind') could be identified by its emblem (*parasemum*). A cargo capacity of 18,000 *modii* may be converted into an approximate burden of 120 tons. This was by the standards of the day a medium-sized ship (see Chapter 1).

The first person named in the text, Gaius S... may have been the principal creditor. However, the term 'diverted' (*avertisset*) suggests that there has been fraud of some sort; furthermore the expressions 'according to law and custom' (*iure et consuetudine*) and 'exercise of first claim' (*protopraxia*) suggest that tax collectors at Puteoli were exercising their right to stand at the front of the list of creditors.

A plausible interpretation of the events underlying this document is that, in addition to failing to pay other debts, the skipper of the Notus had attempted to evade the payment of harbour dues (*portorium*). He may have been stranded in Puteoli without funds, like the skipper whose ship was held in Cyrene for nine months (Chapter 6). The document belonged in the archive of the Sulpicii because they were the bankers arranging the auction of the Notus' cargo.

PART II

Looking beyond the Sulpicii

X

FINANCING TRADE AND INDUSTRY

The business of the Sulpicii was built around the provision of small, short-term secured loans. There is no evidence in the Murecine archive to suggest that the Sulpicii or their depositors made medium- or long-term loans for capital projects such as the construction of ships, buildings or workshops. Nor is there any sign that the Sulpicii or their depositors lent money for high-risk, high-reward maritime ventures. Furthermore the bank operated on a local basis. Apart from two tablets signed at Capua (TPSulp. 12 and 26) and one at Volturnum (TPSulp. 44) all the transactions where the place of signing is known were carried out in Puteoli. Yet some of the bank's customers operated in a Mediterranean-wide market and the bank took in deposits from, and lent cash to, members of the imperial household. The small scale of the loans and the restricted geographical area of operations were presumably self-imposed; the Sulpicii knew their market and stuck to it.

If you wanted to raise a loan for a business venture, and a small local bank like that of the Sulpicii was not going to meet your needs, you could go to the money market – in Republican Rome, this would have meant a visit to the Temple of Janus in the Forum.[1] Or perhaps to the Velabrum, to the docks and markets by the Tiber, where the Arcus Argentariorum can be seen to this day.

We catch a glimpse of the money-men at work in a letter that Seneca wrote to his friend Lucilius:[2]

> It will be necessary, however, for you to find a lender (*creditor*); in order to do business (*negotiari*) you must take on a debt (*aes alienum*). But I do not wish you to arrange the loan through a middleman (*intercessor*), nor do I wish the brokers (*proxenetae*) to be discussing your credit rating (*nomen tuum*). I will provide you with a lender, the one that Cato talks of when he says, 'You should borrow from yourself' (*a te mutuum sumes*). No matter how small it is, it will be sufficient if, whatever the deficit, we can supply it ourselves.

In this letter Seneca is encouraging Lucilius to adopt habits of self-reliance and he draws on business practice for a suitable metaphor. The metaphor is revealing. Loan finance is available through brokers and middlemen, but they will want to know too much about your financial affairs. Better to draw on your own resources – which in practice will mean the family's inherited wealth.

TRADE CREDIT

It was all very well for members of the elite such as Seneca to recommend the family fortune as a source of funds for a business enterprise, but most people engaged in business had no family fortune. The bulk of commercial transactions involved sales of foodstuffs, utensils and clothing through shopkeepers in towns, through stallholders at weekly markets, or through travelling pedlars (*circitores* or *institores*) at people's front doors.[3] The manufacture of artefacts was often carried out in the artisan's household or in small workshops (*tabernae* or *officinae*) attached to shops where the products were sold.[4] These enterprises were small family businesses and for most of the time cash earned from sales would keep the business afloat. Every now and then, however, there would be a need for short-term funds. The first step would be to seek trade credit; for instance a retailer would ask his supplier to allow him extra time in which to settle his bills. Doubtless Roman businessmen, like businessmen in any period, aimed at achieving 'positive' trade credit, which consists of an excess of debts owed to suppliers over debts owed by customers; logically, of course, not everyone in a given sector of business can achieve this simultaneously (*19,20,21*).

We may imagine how trade credit might have been used by Rufrius of Nola, whom the elder Cato recommended as a supplier of oil-milling equipment:[5]

> The best oil mills (*trapeti*) come from Pompeii and from Rufrius' yard (*maceria*) at Nola....
> Replacement mill-stones can be bought at Rufrius' yard for HS180 and fitted for HS30.
> The price is the same at Pompeii.

From time to time Rufrius must have needed credit from his supplier, the local quarry owner; this would allow him to defer payment until he had been paid in turn by his customers, the olive farmers.

The textile trade provides another example. We catch a glimpse of pack-loads of garments manufactured in Cisalpine Gaul being carried by mules across Alpine passes when we read the epitaph of the cloak merchant (*negotiator sagaricus*), Marcus Matutinius Maximus, a citizen of the Mediomatrici of Gallia Belgica; he was commemorated not in his own home territory but at Mediolanum, commercial centre, then as now, of Italy north of the Po.[6] I suspect that Maximus was given trade credit by his suppliers, the garment makers of Milan.

Trade credit does not always work to the advantage of the small businessman. In the early years of the second century a certain Octavius, supplier of foodstuffs and leatherware in northern Britain, complained about the unauthorised trade credit taken by his major customer, the Roman army. He wrote to his contact at the fort at Vindolanda:[7]

> Octavius to his brother Candidus, greetings.
> ...I have several times written to you that I have bought about five thousand *modii* of grain, on account of which I need cash (*denarii*). Unless you send me some cash, at least

five hundred *denarii*, the result will be that I will lose what I have laid out as a deposit (*arra*), about three hundred denarii, and I will be embarrassed (*erubescam*). So I ask you, send me some cash as soon as possible....

Octavius was caught in the classic dilemma of the small trader who lives between those who owe him money and those to whom he owes it. If he gets the balance right, he has positive cash flow; if he gets it wrong, disaster can follow (22).

Undoubtedly trade credit was, as it still is, an important source of short-term finance. But it is a fleeting and unreliable form of finance and it depends on informal arrangements between counter-parties which reflect their respective bargaining power.

CAPITAL IN KIND

In more complex business enterprises, capital in kind becomes an important form of finance. An example of this comes from an unexpected quarter, the business dealings of Verres, the corrupt magistrate prosecuted by Cicero. While Verres was governor of Sicily, he commissioned Lamia, a wealthy noblewoman of Segesta (*mulier Segestana perdives et nobilis*), to produce purple fabrics for him in a 'houseful of looms' (*plena domo telarum*). Lamia was not the only wealthy Sicilian to produce cloth for Verres on a mass production basis: Cicero lists in the same passage other notables who manufactured woven fabric (*stragula vestis*) for the governor. Cicero alleges that many of Verres' business activities in Sicily were criminal, but he concedes that Verres purchased (*emebat*) some of the goods that were produced for him. Freed from the cloud of abuse in which he was enveloped by Cicero, Verres might be plausibly described as an astute businessman: 'he supplied the cloth, his friends supplied the labour' (*ipse dabat purpuram, tantum operam amici*). In other words, Verres paid for the raw materials – thus providing capital in kind – and his friends, that is his business associates, used their workers (slave or free) to work at looms installed on their premises.[8]

LEASING

Businessmen who needed to have the use of premises, plant and equipment could avoid having to find cash by entering into leasing arrangements. Under the Roman contract for lease and hire of property (*locatio conductio rei*), the lessor (*locator*) would supply premises or equipment to the lessee (*conductor*) in return for rental payment (*merces*) in cash or kind. The lessor was entitled to his full rental only if he continued to provide the lessee with enjoyment of the asset's use throughout the term of the contract. If ownership of the premises changed hands, the new owner was required to continue to lease the premises and fittings to the original conductor.

Under these contracts it was the responsibility of the *locator* to make available to the *conductor* both the property and any equipment normally required for its use. Equipment provided under a farm lease, for instance, might include storage jars and an olive press and grinder with the appropriate tackle. With certain types of olive press might be supplied a press beam, winch, slats, press lids, the screws used for raising the beam and cauldrons for washing the olives. Storage jars for wine (to which the tenant was required to apply pitch) could also form part of a farm lease. A businessman renting manufacturing premises might expect to negotiate for an equivalent range of fixtures and fittings. A lessee might have to pledge security to obtain the lease in the first place and he would be required to keep the property in good condition. Leases could be renewed after the initial period of the lease; indeed if a man remained in the property after the term of hire was over he was deemed to have renewed the lease.[9]

Leased storerooms where people kept their valuables might be provided with slaves who acted as guards. But in commercial warehouses, where goods were stored by traders, the lessor was not responsible for providing guards unless special arrangements had been made. Surviving *leges horreorum* (the publicly displayed terms of leases) from Rome mention different types of storage facilities, the services of warehousemen (*cellararii*), requirements for security against payment of rent and opportunities for renewing leases. The *lex horrei* would serve as an advertisement, bringing to the attention of traders the storage facilities available as well as the terms and conditions of business. Since the surviving notices are carved in stone, the owners doubtless intended these facilities and conditions to be permanent.[10]

Three third-century papyri from Oxyrhynchus provide records of individual *locatio conductio* contracts in the pottery industry.[11] Under the contract recorded in the best preserved papyrus, two female landowners, Aurelia Leontarous and Aurelia Plousia, acting through their guardian (*epitropos*), leased a pottery for two years to a local potter, Aurelius Paesis. The landowners agreed to supply Paesis with store rooms, kiln and potter's wheel; Paesis undertook to produce a given number of finished wine jars for the two women. This part of the contract seems to embody *locatio conductio rei*: Paesis was the *conductor* and the landowners were the *locatores*, who supplied him with equipment and premises. However, the landowners were also to provide clay and firing material, water, and pitch for coating the jars, while Paesis was to supply potters, assistants and stokers. The landowners agreed to make payments of cash in instalments (and additional payments in wine) to the potter. The two Aureliae had first option on purchasing any extra output, over and above the number of jars that Paesis had contracted to make for them. This seems to embody another form of contract, the contract for carrying out a job (*locatio conductio operis faciendi*).

These arrangements illustrate how an independent potter might obtain working capital. Paesis not only leased premises and equipment, he was also supplied with raw materials; in return he had to produce a given quantity of finished pots, for which he would be paid. In addition, he was free to produce pots for sale on the open market. His requirement for working capital, to finance premises and stocks of raw materials and finished goods, was met by the two landowners, who were also his principal customers. It has been suggested that the two Aureliae were themselves in the business of selling wine, judging by the planned output of this pottery: some 64,000 gallons of wine would be needed to fill the 15,000 4-*choes* jars specified in the contract. Presumably the wine was destined in part for sale to the inhabitants of the town and *nome* of Oxyrhynchus, or even further afield.

Leases for other types of capital equipment, such as mills, oil presses and bakeries, appear in the Egyptian papyrus record. For instance, when a loom for 'Tarsian' weaving (a substantial piece of equipment, ten cubits long and six cubits broad) is sold, the vendor assigns all rights in the loom to the purchaser; he states that the new owner (and his descendants) will have the right 'to use it, or hire it out (*ekmisthoin*) or sell it'. The loom was evidently an important item of capital equipment that could be leased to other weavers.[12]

For many Roman businessmen the lease of premises and equipment, secured under a contract of *locatio conductio*, was undoubtedly a significant form of finance. These arrangements were not dissimilar to those in the Yorkshire wool trade in the late eighteenth and early nineteenth centuries:[13]

> ...The man with little capital need not sink *any* of it in plant. He could rent space – a single room, a floor or a whole mill; he could buy power from his landlord, and he might be able to rent the machinery as well.

PARTNERSHIPS

For capital-intensive or long-term enterprises a common means of obtaining external finance was through forming a partnership. Partners would enter into a formal contract of partnership (*societas*) through which they would agree on their respective contributions and on sharing profits and losses. Partnerships could be formed for a single piece of business, such as the purchase or construction of a property or an overseas trading voyage, or for a continuing business enterprise, such as keeping a shop, running a banking business, dealing in slaves or taking on a government contract to supply the army or to collect taxes. Partnerships involving free persons, freedmen and slaves were not unusual: Cicero explicitly refers to those who form partnerships with slaves, freedmen and clients (*cum servis, cum libertis, cum clientibus*).[14]

One feature above all made the partnership of great use to the entrepreneur looking for finance: this was the rule that a partner could contribute solely his expertise or hard work to the business while others contributed cash. Two instances quoted by the Roman jurists will illustrate the point. The first is a case concerning a stonemason's business:[15]

> Flavius Victor and Bellicus Asianus had agreed that monuments should be constructed: Victor was to purchase the land and Asianus was to provide the labour and expertise

(*opera et peritia*). The monuments would then be sold. Victor would recover his capital, with the addition of an agreed sum (*certa pecunia*), and Asianus would get the rest.

In this venture Victor contributed the capital in the form of a loan at an agreed rate of return. Asianus, who ran the workshop, provided labour and skill; he would make his profits through keeping costs down and selling the monuments at prices that brought in a good revenue.

In the same vein one of the partners in a business with trading interests might be appointed as overseas sales representative and be rewarded with a share of the profits:[16]

> Very often a partner works so hard for the partnership that his contribution is worth more to it than money, for example if he were to be the only partner to travel by sea or go abroad at all or expose himself to such dangers.

Partnership finance was particularly appropriate for capital-intensive business ventures. Take mining. Equipment used in the Spanish mines included 'large wooden water-wheels, bucket-chains, Archimedean screw-pumps and bronze piston-pumps'.[17] So it is not surprising to find partnerships recorded in stamps on lead ingots, a by-product of silver extraction, from Roman mine workings in southern Spain.[18]

Similarly partnership ventures are recorded in the great mass production industry of the Roman world, the manufacture of pottery. Manufacturers needed to finance capital equipment – kilns, lathes (for turning wooden blanks), moulds and pottery wheels – in addition to fuel and raw materials. Partnership was an effective means of raising the necessary finance.[19]

Livy records an early example of a business partnership, which was formed to bid for a contract in 215 during the war against Hannibal, to supply the armies in Spain, at a time when public funds had run very low:[20]

> It was resolved [by the Senate] that Fulvius the praetor should present himself to the public assembly of the people, point out the requirements of the state, and exhort those persons who had increased their patrimony through public contracts (*redempturae*) to furnish loans to the state (from which they derived their wealth) and to contract to supply what was needed for the army in Spain, on the condition of being first to be paid when there was money in the treasury. This the praetor laid before the Assembly, and fixed a day on which he would let the contract for furnishing the army in Spain with clothes and grain, and with such other things as were necessary for the crews.
>
> When the day arrived, three partnerships (*societates*) composed of 19 persons came forward to enter into the contract; but they made two requests: one was that they should be exempt from military service while employed in their public business, the second was that their shipments should be at the state's risk against attacks of the enemy or storms.

On obtaining both their requests, they entered into the contracts (*conduxerunt*), and the affairs of the state were conducted with private funds.

The episode, which might be described as an early example of a Public Private Partnership, had a sequel three years later. It was discovered that two of the nineteen traders involved in the contracts, Marcus Postumius of Pyrgi and Titus Pomponius of Veii, had fabricated false accounts of shipwrecks and even brought about real ones:[21]

Their practice was to put a few goods of little value into old, battered hulls, which they sank in the deep, taking off the sailors in boats prepared for the purpose, and then falsely to bill the cargo [for compensation] at many times its actual value.

A generation later, according to Plutarch, the elder Cato formed a maritime partnership:[22]

His method was as follows: he required his borrowers to form a partnership (*koinonia*) and when there were fifty partners, and as many ships, he took one share in the partnership himself and was represented by Quintio, one of his freedmen, who accompanied the borrowers in all of their ventures. In this way his entire investment was not put at risk, but only a small part of it, and his profits were large.

For the 50 or so partners – Plutarch writing three centuries later provides a suspiciously round number – the benefit of these arrangements lay in the opportunity to gain access to Cato's capital. For Cato the opportunity for profit lay in the return on the loans that he made to the partnership, whose policy and behaviour he was able to monitor by inserting his freedman Quintio into the fleet of ships. To put together a *societas* of so many ship-owners and merchants required considerable organisation and complex accounts. The contract of partnership was perhaps renewed annually for each sailing season. This would allow changes in membership; it would also allow the partners to make fresh arrangements among themselves, if they wished, to secure fresh finance.[23]

Partnerships might even be formed between farmers. A venture for cattle ranching in Gaul is described in Cicero's speech on behalf of Quinctius. In this case, things went wrong. Naevius, the partner who had contributed cash but not expertise, was not satisfied with the modest profits (*mediocris quaestus*). He withdrew funds from the partnership but was unable to render a satisfactory account (*commode rationem reddere*) of his business dealings.[24]

THE WEALTH OF THE ELITE

The banking operations of the Sulpicii, where the largest recorded sum is a loan of HS130,000, were on a small scale compared with the financial dealings of the Roman elite. Just two examples will provide a perspective. First, in March 45 BC Cicero had cash in hand of HS600,000 and a portfolio of loans which included another HS600,000 due to him from Clodius Hermogenes. He was also owed a substantial sum by Faberius, Julius Caesar's private secretary. Second, when the younger Pliny was contemplating the purchase of an estate adjoining his property at Tifernum, he did not see any difficulty in raising the HS3 million required, even if it meant calling in some loans and borrowing funds from his mother-in-law.[25]

For capital on a large scale, therefore, entrepreneurs could look to wealthy private investors, members of the small landowning elite that provided the state's political and military leaders. Elite families had built great fortunes during the years when Rome was building her Mediterranean empire - from booty, from the output of mines in conquered territory and from the annual tribute paid by Rome's provincial subjects.[26] To give a rough estimate of the numbers involved, the elite of Roman Italy in the early Empire consisted of the imperial family and court, 600 members of the senate, 5,000 or more members of the equestrian order (from whose ranks members of the senate were drawn) and some 20,000 local councillors (*decuriones* or *curiales*) in the municipalities.[27] These numbers need to be seen in the context of a total population that amounted to something like one million in Rome itself, one million in the other cities of Italy and four million in the Italian countryside.

In the absence of statistics any notion of the scale of elite wealth has to be based on anecdotal evidence. A by-word for wealth in the Republic was M. Crassus who had a fortune of HS200 million. Among members of the decurial class Sextus Roscius, who was 'by birth, descent and fortune' chief man (*primus*) in the municipality of Ameria, was said by Cicero to own farms which were valued at HS6 million. The list of recorded private fortunes in the early Empire is headed by Gnaeus Cornelius Lentulus and by Narcissus, the freedman of Claudius, each of whom was worth HS400 million. The younger Pliny, the senator about whose finances we are best informed, possessed a fortune in the order of HS20 million.[28]

A glimpse of more modest but still comfortable wealth comes from the welfare scheme introduced by Trajan at Veleia near Placentia (the modern Piacenza) in northern Italy. Landowners enrolled in the scheme were required to register the value of their local property holdings. At the upper end of the scale there were four landowning families who each declared property above, or just about level with, the HS1 million senatorial census qualification.[29] The average valuation of a landholding in this otherwise unremarkable corner of Roman Italy was between HS250,000 and HS300,000, well above the HS100,000 required to qualify for membership of the municipal council. (These figures probably underestimate the size of certain individual family fortunes, since some landowners registered at Veleia may well have owned property elsewhere in Italy and even in the provinces.) On the expected rate of return on agricultural land of 6 per cent, the landowners of Veleia received an average income of about HS17,000 a year. To put these incomes into perspective, a legionary soldier's pay (before stoppages) in the time of Trajan was 300 *denarii* (HS1,200) a year.

Wealthy men often affected to have qualms about lending money at interest. The elder Cato was reported to have approved with relish the view of 'our ancestors' that the moneylender was morally lower than a thief; on another occasion he declared that moneylending was as reprehensible as murder.[30] High-minded attitudes towards moneylending for profit continued into the late Republic and the early Empire. In the *De Officiis* Cicero quotes with approval the widely-held view (*haec fere accepimus*) that condemns usurers (along with a good many other 'base' occupations).[31] Augustus was no great friend to moneylenders: equestrians who had raised money at low rates of interest in order to lend it at higher rates (*quod pecunias levioribus usuris mutuati graviore fenore collacassent*) earned the emperor's particular displeasure.[32]

Nevertheless, whatever their publicly expressed views, the Roman elite were not averse to making a profit (*quaestus*) by lending out their surplus funds at interest. A revealing anecdote is told by Polybius. Two senators attended at the bank where Scipio Aemilianus had arranged for them to receive funds due to them; but they demurred at the amount that was being handed over to them. They said that they expected to receive only an instalment of the money due to them, not the whole amount; 'in Rome... nobody would pay one talent before the appointed day,' adds Polybius, 'so rigidly precise is everybody about sums of money, and conscious of time in their anxiety for profit.'[33]

Seneca had plenty to say on the nature and uses of wealth and made it clear that loans at interest played an important part in an elite investment portfolio. He described the characteristics of the 'fortunate man': a handsome family, a fine house, plenty of land under cultivation and plenty of money out on loan (*familiam formosam habet et domum pulchram, multum serit, multum fenerat*). Elsewhere he says that the rich man 'has gold furniture... a large book of loans (*magnus kalendarii liber*)...plenty of suburban property...'.[34] And it was land and money out on loan that made up Seneca's own wealth (*tantis agrorum spatiis, tam lato faenore*).[35]

The younger Pliny also invested in loans: 'my funds are almost totally tied up in land but I do have some money out on loan' (*sum quidem prope totius in praediis, aliquid tamen fenero*). And even though he was short of ready cash to buy an adjoining estate, he expected to be able to borrow (presumably free of interest in this case) from his mother-in-law.[36] In fiction, too, lending money at interest is a characteristic activity of the wealthy man. The freedman Trimalchio made his fortune in maritime commerce; as we have seen, he then invested in land and began to lend money to (or through) freedmen (*coepi libertos faenerare*). Another character in the Satyricon, Eumolpus, had HS30 million invested in Africa, in estates and loans (*fundis nominibusque*).[37]

On the face of it elite moneylending constituted a closed financial market which served the special requirements of very wealthy men. Under the Empire these requirements centred around conspicuous display – grand houses, large estates and the provision of finance for public buildings and benefactions ('euergetism'). Property was at the centre of the nexus of elite finance: loans were secured on property and loans were frequently invested in property. We may note Suetonius' comment on the arrival of the Egyptian treasure in Rome:[38]

> When [Octavian] brought the treasures of the Ptolemies to Rome at his Alexandrian triumph, so much cash passed into private hands that the interest rate on loans dropped sharply, while real estate values soared.

There is no suggestion that the acquisition of additional funds by the elite furthered, or could have furthered, the expansion of trade and industry. It was taken for granted by Roman commentators and their audiences that the Roman elite took no interest in commercial activities and did not consider investment in trade and industry as an appropriate use of their capital.

Nevertheless there are various indications that this aristocratic disdain for commerce was adopted more for show than as a guide for conduct. A few examples will suffice. Cato's views on usury, quoted above, did not stop him from lending money for shipping ventures; and he even recommended lending money (*fenerari*) along with trade (*mercatura*) and agriculture as a source of profit.[39]

Next, Cornelius Nepos, biographer of Cicero's friend and financial adviser the wealthy equestrian Atticus, felt it necessary to comment that Atticus never put up money for a public contract: 'for no enterprise did he become a surety (*praes*) or a contractor (*manceps*).' The implication is that many of Atticus' social equals were deeply involved in such activities.[40]

Lastly, Cicero claimed – in apparent contradiction to the views expressed in the *De Officiis* - that there were three means of earning money honestly (*honeste rem quarere*), by which I think he meant 'doing business in a way that was fitting for a Roman gentleman'. Cicero's approved occupations were: taking part in large-scale mercantile enterprises (*mercaturae faciendae*); undertaking public building contracts (*opera danda*); and collecting the government's taxes (*publica sumenda*).[41] In the next three chapters we shall explore these major sectors of the Roman economy. This will lead us in the final chapter to search for some of the rarely-glimpsed but vital players in the Roman economy – family businesses which carried on large-scale manufacturing and distribution over several generations. Behind the facade of upper class disdain for engagement in commerce we may well find that the Roman elite invested on a massive scale in trade and industry.

XI

MARITIME FINANCE

The roles of the various parties in a maritime enterprise are illustrated in a passage of the Digest:[1]

> The formal appointment [of a shipmaster (*magister navis*) by a shipper (*exercitor*)] provides third parties with a contractual position. If someone has appointed a shipmaster for the sole purpose of transporting people and goods for passage or freight money, and not for the purpose of leasing the ship (*ut vecturas exigat, non ut locet*)...the shipper will not be liable if the shipmaster has leased the ship out. And if the appointment is concerned only with leasing, and not with collecting fares and freight money, the same opinion applies. Again, if the appointment relates to the carriage of passengers, and not to loading the ship with goods, or vice versa, the shipper will not be liable for any obligation which results if the terms of the charter have been broken by the shipmaster.

This passage places the *exercitor* at the head of the enterprise; he is the person with the prime interest in the ship's operations. Ulpian provides the definition:[2]

> [The term *exercitor*] designates the person to whom all the income and revenues accrue, whether he is the owner (*dominus*) [of the ship] or whether he has leased it from the owner for a lump sum (*aversio*) or for a set period or for ever (*in perpetuum*).

Exercitor is not so much an occupational title as a legal term that corresponds to the French term *armateur*, the maritime entrepreneur, a term for which there is no precise equivalent in the English language. It was not necessary for an *exercitor* to travel on board the ship. He might appoint a shipmaster (*magister navis*), often a slave, who would be responsible for fitting out the ship, hiring a sailing master (*gubernator*), officers and crew, and supervising arrangements for cargoes and passengers. Under the shipmaster, an administrative officer (*toicharchos*) combined the roles of purser and cargo manager. Under the *toicharchos* might be a cargo clerk (*perineos*).[3]

The *exercitor* was liable for the transactions carried out by the shipmaster, provided that the shipmaster remained within the terms of his formal deed of appointment (*lex certa*). The jurist Ulpian praised the usefulness of the *actio exercitoria*, the law suit that was available to an aggrieved party; he pointed out that when business dealings needed to be carried out with a shipmaster, it was not usually practical to postpone a transaction to wait for verification of the master's status and standing.[4]

Where our sources are narrowly concerned with trading, that is the business conducted by a merchant, they often use the terms *negotiator* or *mercator*. It is difficult to be precise about the distinction between the two terms. As a rough rule, in the late Republic a man with a wide range of business interests (*negotia*) might be described as a *negotiator*, while a merchant who stuck to trading (*mercatura*) would be known as a *mercator*; *mercatura*, of course, might well be among the interests of a *negotiator*. Under the Empire, the term *negotiator* came to be the normal word for trader or merchant; and in legal texts the merchant (*negotiator*) is often bracketed with the shipper (*navicularius*).[5] The shipper may or may not be the legal owner of the ship. (It is worth repeating the point made in Chapter 6: in the Roman context, the 'shipper' is the man who carries goods by sea (*23*).)

A merchant might own and operate his own fleet of ships. Petronius suggests in the Satyricon that this is how Trimalchio ran his business:[6]

> I built some more [ships], bigger, better and luckier, so that no one could say I was not a brave man. You know, a great ship is a brave thing (*magna navis magnam fortitudinem habet*). I got another cargo….

FUNDING THE SHIP

Whatever the arrangements under which a particular enterprise was owned and managed, deep sea maritime ventures had special requirements for finance. A vessel that was capable of carrying heavy loads across several hundred miles of open sea had to be purchased or chartered; funds were required to meet operating costs – wages and food for the crew, repairs en route and harbour duties; above all, cash was needed to finance the purchase of outward and homeward cargoes. All these funds had to be raised many months before a merchant could sell his final cargo and take his profit on the entire venture.

First came the ship. Shipbuilding operations seem to have been on a small-scale. At one time the guild of shipbuilders (*corpus fabrum navalium*) at Ostia had nearly one hundred members; this looks like an industry made up of many small enterprises.[7] Typical may be the shipyard depicted in a tombstone from Ravenna.[8] As we saw earlier (Chapter 1), this seems to have been an enterprise where two freedmen, Publius Longidienus Rufio and Publius Longidienus Philadespotus, worked alongside their patron, the freeborn Publius Longidienus, as his assistants (*24*).[9]

Some merchant ships were built at shipyards in the countries that traded with Rome. Strabo noted that the large merchantmen carrying to Italy the exports of the Turdetanians of south-western Iberia were built in that region, using local timber.[10]

If large ships were built in regions such as Turdetania, which regularly sent cargoes to Rome, the question arises, how were these ships financed? Possibly by local producers of export goods or local merchants who traded regularly with Italy. Another possibility is that some ships built in the provinces were commissioned by *navicularii* based in Italy – just as a present-day oil company based in London or New York will commission an oil tanker to be built at a shipyard in Asia. Italian *navicularii* and *negotiatores* engaged in the grain trade certainly travelled overseas. The authorities recognised that this was a necessary part of their business:[11]

> [They are to be excused public duties (*munera*)] as compensation for the risks they run, and are indeed to be encouraged with incentives …so that men who undertake public duties abroad, involving risk and effort, may be freed from disruption and expense at home; indeed, it is not inappropriate to say that they are absent on public business when they are serving the grain supply of the city.

This passage could refer to merchants travelling with their cargoes; it is equally possible, however, that the jurist Callistratus was thinking of the wealthy Roman businessman who was visiting his suppliers, to explain his requirements, place orders and arrange finance. If he was an active or prospective ship-owner he might be visiting an overseas shipyard to commission a new vessel and to put up the working capital needed by the local shipbuilder for wages and materials.

What was the capital required for investment in a ship? A large ship with capacity to transport 300 tons of wheat might have cost somewhere in the region of HS250,000 to build.[12] This order of expenditure can be put into perspective. The commonly accepted annual rate of return on investment in agricultural land, through profits on farm produce or through rental incomes, was 6 per cent.[13] This meant that a senator holding the minimum census of HS1 million could expect to earn HS60,000 a year: for a senator, then, the cost of a large ship might work out at just over four years' earnings; similarly, for an equestrian, with a minimum census of HS400,000, the same ship would cost at least ten years' earnings, and for a municipal decurion, with a census of HS100,000, it would cost at least forty years' earnings. These figures are the roughest of approximations; nevertheless they give some inkling of the financial commitment required from wealthy Romans who invested in merchant ships.

Charter was a common alternative to outright purchase of a ship. An extant ship lease contract from Roman Egypt, described as a *misthosis*, is apparently for a fixed term.[14] The lessee is responsible for returning the ship to the owner in good condition and he must pay the cost of any damages, except those resulting from storms, fires in harbour or illegal seizure. It looks as if the 'rent' paid to the lessor was to be a share in the operating profits.

Another form of leasing, the 'lease-sale' (*misthoprasia*), also appears in Roman Egypt. In a third-century document Pbekis leases to Harmirumius a 'Hellenic' boat for a period of 60 years.[15] The boat comes fully equipped, with devices for handling, measuring and weighing cargoes of grain as well as the usual marine fittings. The rent (*phoros*) is to be one talent and 2,000 drachmas (the equivalent of HS8,000). This rent is to be paid in two instalments: the first payment, of one talent, has been received and is acknowledged in the contract. The remaining 2,000 drachmas are to be paid later, when Harmirumius visits Pbekis (at some unspecified date) to collect the boat-builder's receipt (showing that the builder had been paid by Pbekis, the original purchaser) together with other documents providing good title.

At the time of the contract Harmirumius has already taken possession of the boat and its fittings. It is now his to use as he wishes. The contract states that Harmirumius and anyone to whom he assigns the boat may sub-let it, or use it for freight transport; they may even break it up or rebuild it. The contract is signed by both parties.

The most distinctive feature of this contract is that it transferred uncontrolled use of the boat for 60 years. The lessee-purchaser might well die before the 60 years were up; but in that event the lease-sale contract could be continued through his heirs. The boat itself might rot, sink or be destroyed before the end of 60 years, or the lessee-purchaser might hand back the boat early. In either of these cases, the contract would come to an end.

OPERATING EXPENSES

Once he had purchased or chartered a ship, the shipper or merchant would have to ensure that funds were available for expenses on the voyage – principally to feed the crew, pay customs duties (*portoria*) and meet the cost of repairs. These payments would normally be handled by the *magister navis*, acting as his principal's agent under his letter of appointment – or by the shipper or merchant himself if he was travelling with his cargo.

As we saw in Chapter 6, customs duties were a significant item of cost, particularly since they might be levied on the same goods at several ports of call during a voyage.[16] Similarly, if the ship needed to put into a port for repairs, the agent or merchant would require to have at his disposal sufficient funds to meet the emergency. There were three options for funding expenses: to pay from cash carried on board; to obtain a loan from a local money-lender; or to draw on funds held at the home port, by using a letter of credit (*permutatio*).

Cash
To carry cash on board to make payments en route was the simplest course of action; in Chapter 6 we saw the Greek sea captain Menelaus taking out a loan in Puteoli. But carrying cash in large quantities was potentially hazardous. Coins and bullion were awkward to handle; because of their weight they required shipmasters to take as much care in stowage as they did for sacks of wheat or *amphorae* of wine. Next there was a constant danger from storms; coins and bullion might have to be jettisoned. Plutarch

records that when the younger Cato shipped nearly 7,000 talents from Cyprus to Rome (the proceeds of selling off the treasures of one of the Ptolemies) he attached cork marker-buoys to each of the chests of silver, to mark the spot in case the ship went down.[17] Piracy was also a recurrent hazard. A pirate vessel captured by Verres off Syracuse was said to be full of handsome young captives (presumably slaves), a cargo of woven textiles and silver plate and coins.[18]

Loans for repairs

The jurist Africanus graphically evokes the type of situation that could occur when a merchant vessel was far from its home port:[19]

> One may even have to ask whether the item to be purchased with the borrowed money was available in the place where the loan was made. Take the case where money is lent for the purchase of a sail and no sail is to be had in the whole island. In brief, the moneylender must act with some circumspection.

On Africanus' imaginary island a *magister navis* who wanted to take out a loan would have to persuade a local banker or moneylender that his principal was good for the repayment of a loan. He presumably established his credentials by presenting his letter of appointment; he would also have to give a warranty (*cautio*) to the effect that the loan was for a specific purpose. If the lender wanted to be sure that he could bring a suit against a shipmaster's principal under the *actio exercitoria* he would need to check that the ship needed repairs and that the sum borrowed did not exceed the estimated cost.[20]

Letters of credit

To pay for repairs in more cosmopolitan ports of call, a merchant might equip his *magister navis* with a *permutatio*. As we saw in Chapter 2, this was an advice from a banker or financier to his overseas agent (or a 'correspondent' banker) authorising payment of a sum of money to a person named in the letter. The *permutatio* was broadly similar to the modern-day letter of credit; it assured the recipient banker that the person named in the advice did in fact have access to funds up to a certain amount. The 'exchange' implied in the term *permutatio* refers to the fact that a letter of credit written in Rome and denominated in *denarii* or *sestertii* would need to be changed by the paying banker into local currency in a province such as Asia, where Roman currency was not legal tender. Provided that the financier who had drawn up the letter was known to the overseas agent or banker, a *permutatio* would be regarded as good for cash. Cicero quite frequently made use of letters of credit provided by Atticus; in his case the transactions were connected with personal or government business, not commerce, but his matter-of-fact references to this means of transferring funds indicates that the practice was well-established.[21]

FINANCING CARGOES

With the ship purchased or leased, and operating expenses arranged, the shipper or merchant was now faced with the crucial funding decision – how to finance the purchase of a cargo for the outward voyage. The purchase of a cargo could be the largest single element in shipping finance. A cargo of 50,000 *modii* of wheat might cost HS100,00 at the dockside in Alexandria (and would of course sell for considerably more in Rome).[22] Cargoes of luxury items could be even more valuable. It has already been noted that a medium-to-large ship of 300 tons burden might be purchased for HS250,000: some cargoes, then, might be worth more than the ships which carried them. In any event, merchants would often require external funds to finance a round-trip voyage. These funds would be supplied by investors in the form of a maritime loan (*nauticum foenus*).[23]

The special feature of the nautical loan, which was sometimes known as 'travelling money' (*pecunia traiecticia*) because the funds went overseas with the borrower, was that if the ship was sunk, or the cargo jettisoned, there was no obligation to repay the money borrowed. As a price for the risk being shouldered by the lender, the borrower whose ship returned safely had to repay the loan at a substantial rate of interest, which was not subject to the usual legal limit of 12 per cent a year.[24] When a lender advanced money in the form of a nautical loan, he took a mortgage over the cargo, normally the cargo bought for the return journey. If a merchant was also the shipowner (see the loan through an Egyptian bank discussed below) a mortgage might also be taken out on the ship. A time limit – less than a year, to reflect the sailing season – was set for the term of the loan; the risk was then on the creditor from the day on which it was agreed that the ship should sail. A lender might stipulate that a slave should travel with the cargo and that the borrower should pay the slave's expenses. There would be a stipulation as to the rate of interest; this might be implied in a loan agreement stating that a certain amount of capital and interest was payable if the ship returned safely.

A few instances of Roman maritime loans survive. Plutarch reports a loan (or series of loans) that the elder Cato made to a consortium (*societas*) of shippers. The jurist Scaevola discusses a loan concluded for a return voyage (of 200 days) from Beirut to Brindisi and back. An Alexandrian banker's advice informs four shipowners that loan funds are awaiting collection; and it is possible to detect in another papyrus document the terms of a loan that financed an immensely valuable cargo being carried from India to Alexandria.

The loans made by Cato

The shipping loans made by the elder Cato have already been discussed (Chapter 10) in the context of partnership finance.[25] In summary, Cato encouraged some fifty merchants to form a partnership (*societas*) and lent funds to them as a group, to finance their voyages. The partnership may have operated for several years, with a changing membership; new contracts and loans would have been arranged for each sailing season.

The 'Callimachus' loan

A case in the Digest describes the loan taken out by the merchant 'Callimachus':[26]

> Callimachus took a transmarine loan from Stichus, the slave of Seius, at Berytus [Beirut] in the province of Syria, for a [round-trip] voyage to Brentesium. The loan was for the full two hundred days of the voyage with security by way of *pignus* and *hypotheca* over the cargo bought at Berytus for transport to Brentesium and [over] that [cargo] which he would buy at Brentesium for transport by sea [back] to Berytus. It was agreed by the parties that when Callimachus reached Brentesium, he should, before 13 September next, himself take ship for Syria with other cargo purchased and put on board or, if by the said date he did not buy the cargo or set sail from that *civitas*, he would repay the whole amount at once, as if the voyage had ended, and pay all costs of those persons who recovered the money and took it to the city of Rome. Stichus, the slave of Lucius Titius, stipulated for the aforementioned payments and acts and Callimachus promised them. Pursuant to the agreement the [second] cargo was placed on board [at Brentesium], along with Eros, the fellow slave of Stichus, and the ship sailed for Syria before the thirteenth of September.

The stock names, including two for the lender's master (who is referred to initially as Seius and later as Lucius Titius) indicate that this was a hypothetical test-case; but it seems to have been adapted from a contract written in Greek (hence Brentesium for Brundisium). There is also another hint that this case is grounded in the real world, in the insistence in the contract that the borrower should set out on his return voyage from Brentesium to Berytus no later than 13 September. The contract in other words takes account of the hazards of winter sailing.

The transaction seems to be as follows. Stichus (who was based in Berytus) lent funds on behalf of his master (who was based in Rome) to Callimachus to purchase a cargo at Berytus for the outward leg of the journey; this cargo was to be sold at Brentesium, where another cargo would be purchased and carried back to Berytus. The cargoes were pledged to Stichus through *pignus*, which allowed the creditor to take immediate possession of the pledged cargo, and *hypotheca*, which allowed the creditor to take possession if the debt was not paid when it fell due.

Stichus sent a fellow-slave, Eros, to accompany Callimachus on the journey. If all went well, Callimachus would make a profit on the round-trip and be able to repay the loan (plus interest) out of his earnings, with money to spare. Eros' general responsibility would be to monitor Callimachus' dealings – to see that the loan money was only spent on the purchase of cargoes and that the specified dates and conditions of sailing were duly observed; in particular, if Callimachus failed to embark at Brentesium by the due date for the return journey to Berytus, Eros would be required to collect the funds due under the loan contract, and take the money to his master in Rome.

We may infer from this episode that merchants did not necessarily carry large sums of money on sea voyages. Callimachus borrowed money in Berytus to purchase his cargo. Money changed hands in Berytus when the loan was made and the first cargo was bought. But this money stayed in Berytus. Money next changed hands in Brentesium when the first cargo was sold and the return cargo was purchased. If Callimachus made a profit in Brentesium on selling the first cargo and buying the second, then he would have had a small surplus of coins. He might have carried this surplus back to Berytus. If, however, he expected to make enough money from selling his second cargo in Berytus to pay off the original loan and interest and make a sizeable profit for himself, then he might have left some or all of his surplus funds on deposit in Brentesium. It also emerges that it was common practice for wealthy men who financed maritime loans to send agents to accompany the cargoes that had been purchased with their money.

The jurist Scaevola was asked to rule whether Callimachus was liable to repay the money at Brentesium in two hypothetical cases. In the first case, Callimachus duly loaded the return cargo by 13 September, but he himself remained behind (i.e he did not travel with the cargo as promised). The ship sank. Was Callimachus bound to pay the money over at Brentesium ('as if the voyage had ended', to quote the terms of the loan agreement), if he could prove that he had the agreement of Eros, the lender's agent, that he need not sail with the ship? The jurist's answer was that Callimachus had no defence: Eros had no authority to vary the terms of the contract; he was only authorised to collect the money and take it to Rome. So Callimachus was liable to repay the money at Brentesium. In the second case, Callimachus did set sail in person with the cargo, but this time he missed the 13 September deadline for departure from Brentesium; again he had Eros' consent and again Scaevola ruled that Callimachus was liable to repay the money.[27] In both cases, Callimachus would have been released from his obligation only if Eros, the lender's agent, had been given discretion to vary the terms of the contract.

The loan made by Celer and Chares
The next example of a maritime loan comes from Roman Egypt:[28]

> 13 February 149
> From the [...? bank] of Marcus Claudius Sabinus, to Zoilos son of Zoigas and Kallimedes son of Diogenes, from [Aska]lon. By order of Gaius Longinus Celer and Tiberius Claudius Chares, to you with Sostratos and Sosos, both sons of Diopeithes, from Askalon, co-shipowners with you of the galley bearing the name 'Antinoos Philosarapis Sozon', joint sureties for discharge (of) a maritime loan according to a maritime contract of which the copy on land (is) with me the banker, on (the security of) your own (?) aforesaid ship and [all] its gear [and the] last cargo, so that the four of you have 7 tal. 5,160 dr. of silver, with the 7 tal. which you had by hand, the remaining [5,]160 dr., without diminution to the one of them, Gaius Longinus Celer, as regards the other [..dr.] which [Kallimedes] son of Diogenes owes him [--] inter[est--] tal.[--].

This document is the advice of a banker, Marcus Claudius Sabinus, informing four borrowers that funds forming the balance of a loan are ready for collection. The lenders are two Roman citizens, Gaius Longinus Celer and Tiberius Claudius Chares. They have made a loan of 47,160 drachmas (equivalent to HS47,160) to four shipowning merchants from Ascalon. Seven talents (42,000 drachmas) have already been paid in cash; the remaining 5,160 drachmas are now available. The banker Sabinus notes that this loan is in addition to a previous loan, not yet repaid, that has been made by Longinus Celer to Kallimedes, one of the borrowers.

Two questions arise. First, why was the loan for such an odd amount (7 talents and 5,160 drachmas, which is 47,160 drachmas)? Perhaps because the sum lent by the two private individuals was for a round 8 talents (i.e 48,000 drachmas). The difference between the sum owed under the formal agreement and the cash handed over comes to 840 drachmas. This would be 1.75 per cent of the sum originally requested, and may represent the banker's commission, charged to the borrowers, for handling the deal.

Second, how was the money paid? The document states that the first tranche of 7 talents was handed over in silver; was the payment made in Alexandrian tetradrachms? The Alexandrian tetradrachm had a face value equivalent to the denarius, but it had a lower silver content. Would tetradrachms have been of much use if the four shipowners wanted to make purchases of goods outside Egypt? It may be that the payment was made in silver bullion.

The 'Muziris' loan

My last example of a maritime loan is also from Roman Egypt. This was a transaction which financed a cargo worth almost HS7 million, an immense sum, which would have bought a good-sized estate in Italy during the second-century AD.[29] The cargo – which consisted principally of ivory and incense - is itemised on the verso of the 'Muziris' papyrus.[30] On the recto of this papyrus appear the terms of an agreement covering the transport of goods, presumably the goods listed on the verso, from a Red Sea port across the eastern desert to Koptos and then down the Nile to Alexandria.

The agreement on the recto refers to a maritime loan. Two parties, a lender and a borrower – who, we may assume, are a financier and a merchant – are mentioned. In the surviving text, the merchant outlines the procedures that he will follow for transshipment of the cargo. He will make the necessary arrangements and payments for the carriage of the cargo by camel from the coast through the desert to the tax officials' warehouse at Koptos; here the cargo will be held, under the financier's seal, until cleared for onward transit. The merchant will then arrange and pay for the cargo's river journey on the Nile to the tax warehouse at Alexandria, where again the cargo will be put under the financier's seal. The merchant then makes a declaration of his obligations under the loan agreement:

> ...on occurrence of the date for repayment specified in the contracts of lo[an] for (the trip to) Muziris, if I do not [then] duly discharge the aforesaid loan in my name, that then [you] and your administrators or managers are to have the option and comp[lete]

authority, if you so choose, to carry out execution without [notifica]tion or summons to judgement, to possess and own the afore[said] security and pay the quarter-tax, to convey the [three] parts which will be left where you choose and to sell or use them as security [and] to transfer them to another person, if you so choose, and to deal with the items of the security in whatsoever way you choose, and to buy them for yourself at the price current at the time, and to subtract and reckon in what falls due [on account of the aforesai]d loan, on terms that the responsibility for what falls due [lies] with you and your administrators and managers and we are free from accus[at]ion in every respect, and that the surplus or shortfall from the capital [goes] to me the borrower and giver of security.

In summary, this document reveals that the merchant has pledged goods purchased at Muziris (a port on the south-west coast of India) as security for finance provided for the venture. He will take the necessary steps to ensure that the cargo reaches Alexandria. If he does not repay the loan on time, the financier has the right to seize and sell the cargo, or to buy it from the merchant at the current price (i.e. the market price in Alexandria). The financier will deduct the interest and capital from the proceeds. If the financier cannot realise the amount of the debt by selling the goods, the shortfall will be made up by the merchant; but any surplus from the sale will go to the merchant. This statement seems to be an appendix to the loan contract itself. The loan contract will have been recorded in the normal way, that is to say in a document that stated the date of the agreement, the amount borrowed and the date when the sum borrowed fell due; the agreement will have been duly witnessed; and the rate of interest will have been agreed through a separate stipulation.

The two principals in this transaction, the merchant and the financier, had agreed the loan at Alexandria before the merchant set out to India. The merchant would probably have used the funds to purchase goods and bullion for export to India at Koptos, where he could also arrange the hire of the ship that would take him to India and back, camels for the outward and return desert journeys and a Nile boat for the journey back to Alexandria. Did he carry tons of tetradrachms from Alexandria to Koptos to finance his initial purchases? Unlikely, says Rathbone in his commentary. A financier with access to funds on this scale would have funds on deposit at local banks, provided perhaps by income from estates in Upper Egypt, on which the merchant could draw. The statement made by the merchant also reveals that the financier had managers or agents (*epitropai* and *phrontistai*) to monitor the passage of the cargo through Egypt. The financier evidently exercised control over the whole enterprise; he cannot be described as a passive investor.

THE INVESTORS

Under the Republic we hear of plenty of men from the Roman elite who invested, directly or indirectly, in overseas trade.[31] Cicero gives us a pen portrait of the equestrian Gaius Rabirius Postumus who 'was involved in many business deals, invested his money in many ventures, and made successful bids for many public contracts. He had business and banking enterprises in many provinces....'[32] In Chapter 1 we saw Postumus' ships landing cargoes of papyrus, linen and glass at the docks in Puteoli. In the great surge of overseas investment and trade during the late Republic Postumus cannot have been an isolated figure.

There are scattered indications in our sources that the senatorial elite invested in deep sea trade. This was despite the provisions of the *lex Claudia* of 218 BC (noted in the Preface) which restricted senators and their sons to owning vessels just large enough to carry the produce of an estate to market. A few examples of senatorial business enterprise can be cited. First, there are the maritime partnerships financed by the elder Cato. Plutarch commented that the stern Republican statesman demonstrated a sophisticated attitude to managing his affairs: 'in this way his entire investment was not put at risk, but only a small part of it, and his profits were large'.

Then we find the senator Verres owning a large and ornate cargo ship; when Cicero raised the issue in court in 70 BC his attack was based on the means that Verres had used to acquire the ship, not on the illegality of a senator owning such a vessel: 'those statutes [the *lex Claudia*] are ancient and dead (*antiquae sunt istae leges et mortuae*),' said Verres' counsel Hortensius, and Cicero did not contradict him.[33] This was evidently not an isolated incident, since Julius Caesar found it necessary to confirm the prohibition in his *lex Julia repetundarum*. And in the second century the jurist Scaevola still felt it necessary to point out that under this law senators were not allowed to own sea-going ships.[34]

Furthermore many Roman senators owned property overseas – we may remember Seneca waiting at Puteoli for news from his Egyptian estates. It must be a strong presumption that some of these wealthy landowners invested in ships to carry their own and other people's cargoes back to Italy.

I suspect, however, that much of the finance for maritime ventures came from wealthy merchants and shippers in ports such as Puteoli and Ostia – in other words from men who were members of the local elite, which included both freeborn citizens and also freedmen's sons (who were eligible to become magistrates). In Puteoli we have already encountered families such as the Avianii, Granii and Annii who had interests in shipping and trade and who supplied magistrates for the city over several generations. Ostia could produce businessmen of equal prestige, energy and wealth. Let us take three of them, whose names suggest that they are of freedman origin. First, there is the duumvir and five times financial officer of the town (*quaestor aerarii*) P. Aufidius Fortis. Among the several positions of power and influence that he held, Fortis was president (*patronus*) at Ostia of the guilds of corn measurers, corn merchants and river divers (who acted as salvage men); and he was also a member of the town council of Hippo Regius in Africa.[35] It looks as if Fortis regularly visited Hippo to negotiate the purchase and shipment of grain.

Second on our list of wealthy Ostians with interests in shipping is the grain merchant, M. Junius Faustus, also a duumvir, who was priest (*flamen*) of the cult of 'Rome and Augustus'. A patron of the guild of curators of sea shipping, Faustus was honoured with a statue by the merchants of Africa and Sardinia, both grain exporting provinces.[36]

Lastly we come to Gnaeus Sentius Felix. He was co-opted on to the council with the status of aedile; in the same year he was appointed quaestor of the treasury and designated duumvir for the following year.[37] During his career Felix became senior official, patron or co-opted member of a host of organisations in Ostia connected with maritime commerce or finance. These included the curators of sea-going ships; the shippers doing business in the Adriatic; the criers at auctions; the bankers; the wine dealers from the city of Rome; the grain measurers of Augustan Ceres; the rowers; the ferrymen at the Lucullus crossing; the hauliers; the citizens of the forum and the weighing house; the oil dealers; the fishermen; and the fish-merchants.

These three wealthy Ostian merchants are just the type of businessmen that we might expect to find investing in other people's maritime ventures. After all, the step from owning a ship and carrying one's own cargoes to lending money to someone else to build a ship and purchase cargoes, is not a very large one. We may take Trimalchio, a successful *negotiator* in his prime, as our model: 'I retired from day-to-day business and I began to lend money to or through freedmen (*sustuli me de negotiatione et coepi libertos faenerare*).'[38]

XII

PUBLIC WORKS

The Roman elite invested heavily in public works projects. Most notably they paid for buildings and other projects out of their own pockets, as a demonstration of their commitment to the glory and well-being of the community and as an enhancement of their personal power and prestige. Such benefactions brought no monetary return. This phenomenon, known as 'euergetism', is one of the most striking features of the Ancient World but it does not fall within the scope of the present book, which is concerned with the way in which the Romans conducted profit-making business.[1] Consequently this chapter is concerned principally with the partnerships formed by wealthy Romans to carry out construction projects commissioned and paid for by the government or by local municipalities. But we shall also be considering the operations and financing of builders and craftsmen who were involved as sub-contractors in every sort of work project, regardless of how any particular project was funded.

We have surprisingly few details of spending on individual public works projects.[2] We know the budget for one major state project in Rome: Frontinus tells us that in 144 BC the praetor Marcius was allotted HS180 million for rebuilding leaking water conduits and building a new aqueduct.[3] For expenditure on public works in Italy and the African provinces we have the evidence, most of it epigraphic, collected by Duncan-Jones.[4] Most expensive of the public works recorded in Italy are baths in Ostia (paid for by Antoninus Pius) which cost HS2 million. The most expensive African project on record is a temple at Lambaesis for which a private benefactor paid HS600,000.

In the eastern part of the empire higher expenditures are recorded. For instance a private donor contributed HS8 million towards the cost of an aqueduct at Aspendos in Pamphylia, while the father of Herodes Atticus contributed HS16 million towards an aqueduct at Alexandria Troas.[5] We also hear of public money wasted by mismanagement, as the younger Pliny reported back to Trajan:[6]

> The citizens of Nicomedia, Sir, have spent HS3,318,000 on an aqueduct which they abandoned before it was finished and finally demolished. Then they made a grant of HS200,000 towards another one, but this too was abandoned…

The theatre at Nicaea, Sir, is more than half built but it is still unfinished and has already cost more than HS10 million, or so I am told – I have not yet examined the accounts. I am afraid it may be money wasted.

THE CONTRACTORS

Building contractors at work were a common sight in Rome – and no doubt in other cities of the empire. In Rome, says Juvenal, you would do well to avoid the contractors' vehicles:[7]

> Here's the great trunk of a fir-tree
> Swaying along on its wagon, and look, another dray
> Behind it, stacked high with pine-logs, a nodding threat
> Over the heads of the crowd. If that axle snapped, and a
> Cartload of marble avalanched down on them, what
> Would be left of their bodies?

And Horace must have stopped to watch the work on a construction site:[8]

> The great crane swings up the stones and beams (*torquet nunc lapidem, nunc ingens machina tignum*).

First, the terminology: in inscriptions a man who undertook contracts is known as a *redemptor* or *manceps*; in the legal texts a public contractor is usually (but not invariably) known as a *redemptor*, a private contractor as a *conductor*. Contractors ranged from jobbing builders to rich businessmen who undertook the great projects of the Roman state. The small-time builder will have owned little more than one or two slaves and the tools of his trade; doubtless he aspired to earn a living wage for himself and his family and perhaps enough to pay a subscription to the builders' guild (*collegium fabrum tignariorum*). In a sample contract recommended to property-owners by Cato, the employer supplies the builder with all the materials and some of the tools.[9] This may have been common practice. What we can be sure of is that when any builder, large or small, entered into a formal agreement for a private project, relations between the two parties would be governed by a contract of *locatio conductio operis*. Under this type of contract, the client (*locator*) agreed with the contractor (*conductor* or *redemptor*) on the nature of the work to be done, provided a site and undertook to pay a certain fee (*merces*) for the job.[10]

A wealth of detail on building contracts is provided in Book 19 of the Digest, Chapter 2. A job could be let for a single lump sum (*aversio*), or priced by the day or by units of work completed - in feet or other measurements (*in pedes mensurasve*). When a contract specified that the payment should be made in a lump sum, the builder's obligation would be discharged following formal approval (*probatio*); it would be agreed in advance who would grant the approval, the client or his representative. When payments were made on a piece-work basis the builder's obligation would be discharged when the completed work met the required measurements.

In both private and public contracts it was not uncommon for payments to be made in two instalments, one at the beginning of the job, the other after final approval. For instance, the jurist Labeo discusses a case where someone who wanted a villa built had commissioned an estimate from a builder. On the basis of the estimate, the parties concluded a contract, at a price of '200'. The builder received half the *merces* in advance. (The builder later found that he could not complete the contract within budget; the total job was going to come to 300. The builder then stopped work, presumably hoping that the client would agree to pay the extra 100. The client refused to pay the extra cost.)

A builder was required to ensure that the work was completed within the agreed time. If no finishing date had been agreed, he was to ensure that the job was finished within a reasonable time. Inexperience was not a defence if things went wrong. However the client bore the risk of having to recompense the builder if the work could not be finished because of force majeure or accident. In such cases the client would have to pay the builder for the expense that the latter had incurred up to the time of the disruption. The client also had to recompense the builder if the work could not be finished due to defects in materials (*vitia materiae*) that he had provided. But unless there were such exceptional circumstances, a builder who did not produce the agreed result could not claim his fee (*merces*). The burden of proof was then on the builder to show that the overrun was due to a reason beyond his control. So much for the legal framework within which contractors, large and small, operated.

We meet small-time builders who worked on jobs for wealthy private clients in the person of various workmen employed by Quintus Cicero. During Quintus' absence on military service in Gaul, Marcus Cicero kept an eye on their work and reported on their progress:[11]

> I was at Arcanum on September 10. There I saw Mescidius and Philoxenus and the stream which they are channelling near the house…On the Manilius property I found Diphilus, slower than Diphilus…The columns placed by Diphilus are neither straight nor properly aligned. He will pull them down, of course. One day he may learn how to use a rule and plumb-line (*perpendiculum et linea*). All in all, I hope Diphilus' job will be finished in a few months. Caesius, who was with me at the time, is keeping a very watchful eye on it….
>
> [At another property, the 'Bobilius' place] I had Mescidius with me. He says he agreed with you on three *sestertii* per foot [for an aqueduct] and that he has measured the distance, by walking, as three thousand paces… I had sent for Cillo from Venafrum, but that very day at Venafrum a tunnel had fallen in, crushing four of his fellow slaves and pupils (*conservi et discipuli*)….

> Your bailiff Nicephorus impressed me very favourably. I asked him whether you had given him any instructions about that little bit of building at Laterium of which you had spoken to me. He answered that he had contracted to do the job himself for sixteen thousand *sestertii*, but that you had later made considerable additions to the work and none to the price, so he had done nothing about it....

In these reports, various different workmen can be identified. Mescidius seems to be an independent contractor, who has an assistant, Philoxenus. The incompetent Diphilus may also be an independent contractor. Cillo, whose tunnel at Venafrum collapsed, looks as if he was a slave running a building business, which he financed through his *peculium*, and in which he employed fellow-slaves (*conservi*). Caesius and Nicephorus are bailiffs (*vilici*), doubtless slaves, who form part of Quintus Cicero's *familia rustica*. Nicephorus, however, does paid building work for Quintus Cicero; he is confident enough to demand that he gets paid extra money when his master makes additions to the job after a contract has been agreed, and to do no work at all until the contract is suitably amended. It is also worth noting that Nicephorus is being paid a handsome sum for the work, HS16,000; he is, despite his servile status, to all intents and purposes a building contractor. In addition, under a contract for work on Quintus' house in Rome, mentioned in another letter, it emerges that Marcus Cicero has paid the (unnamed) contractor half the agreed price in advance.[12] Advance payments seem to have been standard practice, for both public and private building contracts, when a lump sum payment (*aversio*), rather than payment by piece-work, was agreed.

No doubt many public contracts were on a small scale and could be undertaken by contractors with modest resources: the several contractors who each paved a stretch of the *via Caecilia* were not necessarily wealthy men.[13] However the scale of operations required for large-scale public works – the construction of aqueducts, temples, forums, baths, theatres and amphitheatres – meant that only businessmen with substantial resources were likely to be successful in obtaining the principal contracts. A contractor on the grand scale was the *redemptor* Quintus Haterius Tychicus.[14] Tychicus and his wife are featured in the portraits that form part of the sculptural programme of the Tomb of the Haterii in Rome.[15] The tomb is carved with inscriptions defining its owners as freedmen and is decorated not only with portrait busts but also with three reliefs. One relief shows the lying-in-state of a female member of the family. For the purposes of the present enquiry, however, the chief interest lies in the two reliefs illustrating the business that underpinned the family's prosperity. Most of the second relief is occupied by a temple tomb that represents the actual Tomb of the Haterii. A large crane is positioned to the left of the tomb; it is powered by slaves working a treadmill. The third relief shows five buildings and parts of two others. Two of the buildings are labelled: the '*arcus in sacra via summa*' is presumably the Arch of Titus and the '*arcus ad Isis*' is the Arch of Isis. The Colosseum, unlabelled, is clearly recognisable. This relief seems to be a display of major Flavian building projects on which Quintus Haterius Tychicus worked as a principal contractor (*25*).

Another large-scale public contractor may have been L. Cocc…*redemptor*, from Cumae; he is probably to be identified with the Cocceius mentioned by Strabo, who built a tunnel between Lake Avernus and Cumae during the reign of Augustus.[16] Similarly, L. Paquedius Festus, *redemptor operum Caesar(is) et puplicorum* (sic), had contracts for building work on the Aqua Claudia.[17] Some contractors were specialists. Lucceius Peculiaris, who worked on the theatre at Capua, is described on his tomb as *redemptor proscaeni*; the crane depicted on Peculiaris' monument is similar to the one on the tomb of the Haterii.[18] Two freedmen, P. Turpilius A.l. Phronimus and P. Turpilius A.l. Niger, are jointly commemorated as *redemptores ab aerario*; it looks as if they had set up a partnership specialising in construction projects commissioned by the treasury.[19]

LETTING THE CONTRACT

It is possible to reconstruct the various stages of a large-scale public building project. An architect or a surveyor would be commissioned by the sponsor of the project – a magistrate under the Republic, an imperial appointee under the Empire or even the emperor himself – to draw up the plans and specifications. We catch a glimpse of a preliminary discussion between client and architect from an anecdote told by Cassius Dio: the young Hadrian, not yet emperor, interrupted a meeting between Trajan and the architect Apollodorus; he was curtly told by the architect to stick to his sketching.[20] On infrastructure projects a land survey would be required; Pliny asked Trajan to arrange for an architect or an engineer to be sent to Bithynia, to determine whether it would be practicable to dig a canal to connect the lake near Nicomedia to the sea.[21]

The next step was to let the contract. An architect might, presumably at the request of the appropriate magistrate or official, undertake the letting procedure: 'at the Julian colony of Fanum, I let for contract and superintended the building of a basilica,' says Vitruvius.[22] The usual procedure, however, was for the contract to be let by the magistrate or official who was sponsoring the project. The Greek historian Polybius, who wrote with an outsider's enthusiasm and curiosity about the Roman Republic in the mid-second century BC, describes the procedure:[23]

> Through the whole of Italy a vast number of contracts…are given out by the censors for the construction and repair of public buildings, and besides this there are many things which are put out to contract, such as navigable rivers, harbours, gardens, mines, lands, in fact everything that forms part of the Roman public domain. Now all these matters are undertaken by the people, and one may almost say that everyone is interested in these contracts and the work they involve. For certain people purchase the contracts from the censors, others are the partners (*koinonoi*) of these first, others stand surety (*enguetai*) for them, others pledge their own fortunes (*ousiae*) to the state for this purpose.

This account can be fleshed out from public documents and scattered literary references.[24] Under the Republic contracts to carry out public works in Rome were let at auction by a magistrate (censor, *consul*, praetor or aedile); in municipalities the contracts were let by the chief magistrates (*duumviri*); it was the responsibility of the magistrates awarding a contract, or their successors if the job lasted beyond their term of office, to certify that the work was done satisfactorily and on time and to exact penalties from the contractor if it was not. The contractor for his part had to provide sureties and real securities for the fulfilment of his obligations.[25] Polybius indicates that in addition to the contractor who was awarded the job several parties might be involved: the contractor's partners (Gk. *koinonoi*, Lat. *socii*); people who stood as personal sureties (Gk. *enguetai*, Lat. *praedes*); and other associates who pledged their wealth.

Under the Empire the contracts in Rome were commonly let by appointed officials, who would have had authority similar to that held by their Republican predecessors: Frontinus indicates that the water commissioners (*curatores aquarum*) had judicial powers equivalent to those of a praetor.[26] In the municipalities under the Empire there seems to have been no change to the Republican system. The municipal law of Malaga (*lex Malacitana*) refers to the councillors (*decuriones conscriptive*) letting contracts in the same way as the prefects of the treasury in Rome (*qui Romae aerario praeerunt*).[27]

A vivid description of the auction procedure in Republican Rome is contained in Cicero's speech against Verres.[28] (Here we need to bear one point in mind. Whereas Cicero's speeches in trials furnish valuable evidence for the practice and procedures of public and private business, they carry an advocate's bias and cannot be regarded as providing an entirely accurate account of the events they purport to describe.)

M. Junius, a freeborn contractor, was one of his young nephew's guardians. The boy's estate was threatened with having to pay for repairs to the temple of Castor and Pollux under the terms of a maintenance contract which had been held by the boy's late father. Junius wanted to obtain this subsidiary contract, to ensure that the cost was kept within reasonable bounds. Verres, the praetor responsible for administering the overall maintenance contract, had other ideas:

> Verres wasted no time; he proceeded with the tenders without any previous advertisement or announcement of the day for tendering, at a most unsuitable time, right in the middle of the Roman Games, when the Forum was covered in decorations.... The guardians hastened to the spot and Junius made his bid....

Verres, however, had no intention of letting the subsidiary contract to Junius and his associates, since he was in collusion with Habonius, another contractor: he intended to let the contract to Habonius at a higher price and then take a cut of the proceeds. Verres accordingly disallowed the bid from Junius. Cicero depicts Junius complaining bitterly against this injustice:

Here is a contract to be let for doing a repair for which I shall have to pay; and I undertake that I shall do it. You, who let the contract, will be able to see that the work is done properly; personal and real security is given to the state. (*Locatur opus id quod ex mea pecunia reficiatur; ego me refecturum dico; probatio futura est tua qui locas; praedibus et praediis populo cautum est.*)

Junius' point is that Verres, the magistrate letting the contract, has the authority to see that the work has been properly carried out; he adds that there is no danger of the state having to stand the cost of default, because two-fold security (*praedes et praedia*) will be given. (More on this contract later.)

A public building contract that has survived in its entirety is the *lex parieti faciendo Puteolana*, which (as we saw in Chapter 1) introduced us to several of Puteoli's leading families.[29] The text of the contract is datable to 105 BC, but the copy that has been preserved has been assigned to the early imperial period.[30] The contract is for the remodelling and reconstruction of a wall across the street from the temple of Serapis in Puteoli. The contract begins by specifying the site and then sets out the required financial arrangements: 'The contractor (*qui redemerit*) is to provide sureties (*praedes*) and shall register his properties as securities (*praedia*) at the discretion of the magistrates (*duumviri*).' The nature and dimensions of the work are then given, and the contract continues with detailed specifications for construction. The contractor in this case is to supply the materials.

The *lex* then sets out how the project is to be administered. The magistrates and council of ex-magistrates will be responsible for monitoring the work. A quorum of twenty members must be present when the matter is discussed and their decision on acceptance or rejection will be taken by majority under oath. Next come the details of timing and payment. The work is to begin on November 1 next. One half of the payment is to be made when the properties of the sureties have been registered. The other half is to be paid when the work has been completed and approved (*opere effecto probatoque*). Lastly appear five names and a price:

C. Blossius Q.f. / HS MD idem praes. Q. Fuficius Q.f. / Cn. Tetteius Q.f. C. Granius C.f. Ti. Crassicius.

Compared with the costs of public contracts already noted, HS1,500 is a very small amount; a plausible explanation is that this sum represents the sum of money that Blossius, the contractor, had personally underwritten (*idem praes*). Each of the other four signatories were probably personal guarantors for the same amount. This would make the total contract worth HS7,500, still a modest amount – but then the building of the wall was a modest project. The properties registered as pledges by Blossius provided the council with assurance that he could reimburse the city of Puteoli in case things went wrong; the other sureties were apparently not required to register their properties.

In line with the procedures that we know from the *lex Malacitana*, a record of the original contract would have been kept in the municipal archive. Why a copy of this particular contract was made at Puteoli long after the event, and exhibited in such a grandiose form, can only be a subject for speculation. Perhaps Blossius had undertaken the work for an especially modest fee, possibly below cost price. The later copy would then be a commemoration by the family, on some special occasion, of their ancestor's public-spirited generosity.

SUB-CONTRACTS

Contracts for public building works might be divided up into small parcels. For the paving of the *via Caecilia*, for example, we have a record of four sub-contracts, each of which was let to a different contractor (*manceps*).[31] On very large construction projects, however, it is unlikely that the government could supply the skilled staff to manage a large number of separate contracts. It looks as if at the Colosseum, for instance, where the work of different groups of craftsmen can be discerned, a few principal contractors were appointed to co-ordinate the work and manage the labour force.[32] Sub-contractors could then be hired by the principal contractors to undertake different parts of the project, such as laying foundations, transporting materials, carrying out basic building work and adding ornamentation.

The transport of columns formed a typical sub-contract. The jurist Gaius chose this job to illustrate the duty of care:[33]

> A man undertook to transport a column. If it broke while being raised or carried or repositioned, he is held responsible for the risk if this happens due to his own fault or that of those whose labour he employs; but there is no fault if all precautions were taken which a very careful person would have observed.

The transport of columns also provides the background to the curious episode of Vespasian and the engineer (*mechanicus*). The emperor had appointed the equestrian Lucius Vestinus to superintend the restoration of the Capitol.[34] Vespasian took a close interest in the project, which he personally inaugurated by carrying away the first basket-load of rubble.[35] During the project a proposal was put to him:[36]

> An engineer (*mechanicus*) offered to haul some huge columns up to the Capitol at moderate expense by using a mechanical device (*commentum*). Vespasian declined to use his services but nevertheless paid him a handsome fee. 'I must ensure that my poor people (*plebicula*) can feed themselves (*se pascere*),' the emperor said.

A plausible interpretation of this episode is that the *mechanicus* was a contractor with engineering skills who had tendered for a sub-contract at an exceptionally low price;

when asked how he proposed to make a profit on the contract, he explained that his device would enable him to economise on labour costs. Vespasian, however, had no wish to see contractors saving labour costs by introducing new technology; he preferred to see them providing plenty of paid work for the urban poor.[37]

We have very little specific information about the sub-contracts that formed part of public works projects; but they will have been governed by the same contracts of *locatio conductio operis* as were private building contracts. Indeed in one legal case we can see three parties involved – the lessor (in modern terminology, the client), the principal contractor and a sub-contractor:[38]

> A man had leased out the building of a house on the following terms: 'to the extent that stone is needed for this job, the owner will pay to the contractor seven [*sestertii*] for his stone and for his labour (*pro lapide et manupretio*).' The question asked is: should the job be measured [only] when it is finished or while still incomplete? He [the jurist Servius] replied: while it is still incomplete.

The principal contractor had apparently sub-contracted the stonework to a specialist mason. When the mason had finished his work, he asked for his payment. The principal contractor wanted the stonework to be measured by the client, even though the overall contract was by no means complete, because he wanted the client to approve this piece of work and provide funds to make the final payment to the mason. The jurist Servius said that the client should carry out the measurement, although the whole contract had not been completed. This meant that parts of the building would be measured, for the purposes of approval and payment, at least twice.[39] In this instance, the client would presumably pay off the sub-contractor.

GUARANTEES

When magistrates required a principal contractor to give guarantees, they were seeking to insure the state against the expense that would be incurred if he failed to complete the project or if he turned in unsatisfactory work. The size of most public contracts was so large that few individuals could contemplate providing on their own the necessary guarantees. This explains why contractors were frequently to be found working with so many associates – partners (*koinonoi*), sureties (*enguetai*) and others who pledged their own fortunes (*ousiae*) – as Polybius had noticed.[40] To win a large public contract, a contractor would need to assemble a group of associates with considerable financial resources – which meant members of the elite, senators and equestrians in Rome and municipal notables elsewhere.

Although, as already noted, senators and their sons were forbidden under the *lex Claudia* of 218 BC to engage in maritime commerce, there were no restrictions on their participation in public or private construction enterprises. Consequently under the Republic the wealthy senator M. Crassus was able quite openly to operate a large-scale property development business, while D. Brutus, a senator who was soon to be consul, stood as guarantor for the maintenance contract at the Temple of Castor and Pollux.[41]

And, of course, there were no legal impediments to prevent equestrians engaging in public works. As we saw earlier, Cornelius Nepos felt it necessary to comment that Atticus, one of Republican Rome's most wealthy equestrians, never took part in a public auction: 'for no enterprise did he become a surety (*praes*) or a contractor (*manceps*).'[42] The quid pro quo for standing as a surety for a construction project was usually a share in a partnership (and therefore in the profits); indeed guarantors, partners and their heirs (*praedes socii heredesque eorum*) were effectively treated as synonymous in the *lex Malacitana*.[43]

In practice, I imagine, the contractor and his partners usually stood as personal sureties and only gave pledges of real estate if specifically required. But a plausible suggestion is that the taking of two-fold security (personal pledges and pledges of real estate) from the same set of people would have given the sureties limited liability, i.e. they would not be liable beyond the value of their registered estates; and without registering their property with the treasury some sureties might not have had sufficient standing (*dignitas*) to provide guarantees.[44]

As the contract for building the wall at Puteoli indicates, sureties would be released from their obligations along with the main contractor after the project had received official approval (*probatio*).[45] If approval was not forthcoming, one or more sureties would be required to step forward and make good the sum of money required by the magistrates – which is what happened (as we shall see) in the case of the maintenance contract at the temple of Castor and Pollux. If very large sums were required, the magistrates could sell pledged *praedia* in order to raise the necessary funds.[46]

A hint of how these arrangements worked in practice emerges in an episode described by Tacitus.[47] A senior senator, Domitius Corbulo, complained bitterly about the state of many roads in Italy: numbers of roads were broken and impassable, owing to the fraud of the contractors (*mancipes*) and the lack of diligence (*incuria*) of the magistrates (presumably the *curatores viarum*). Corbulo then undertook to see that the back-log of maintenance was carried out. Among the results of his initiative were 'loss of property and reputation, due to ruthless condemnations and forced sales'. The government evidently foreclosed on the securities pledged by the contractors and their partners.

It was, then, no light matter to stand as a guarantor for a public contract. The only means of redress open to the sureties if things went wrong was to make claims in private law against the contractor. To put their arrangements on to a legally secure footing, it is probable that the sureties would enter into a series of separate partnership agreements with the contractor. If the worst happened and the contractor went bankrupt, the sureties would be called on to make good their pledges and would then have to take their place for recompense along with any other creditors.

WORKING CAPITAL

Building contracts in the Roman world, as at the present day, could take a long time to complete; for instance, in a private contract discussed in the Digest, the builder was asked under stipulation to promise that a block of flats (*insula*) would be completed by the end of two years.[48] The work on the Marcian aqueduct in Rome took a similar length of time; Marcius' term of office as praetor was extended for a second year to allow him to see the work through to completion. Although, as we have seen, a proportion of the contract fee was paid in advance, contractors nevertheless had to go out into the marketplace and purchase raw materials – timber, stone, bricks and tiles, metal fixings and nails and lead guttering are some of the more obvious items. They also needed to buy or hire plant and equipment for the site – for instance, treadmills, cranes, ladders and scaffolding. Along the whole chain of suppliers and sub-contractors on a major project there would be a constant need for working capital. Sooner or later someone at some point in the chain would be unable to meet his financial obligations. Take the case reported in the Digest of the marble dealer who could not pay his bills and was forced to part with his stock:[49]

> A loan was made to a marble dealer subject to a pledge of marble slabs, the sellers of which had been paid with the creditor's money. The debtor [i.e. the marble dealer] was also lessee of an imperial warehouse but had not paid his rent for a number of years. The imperial procurator claimed that he should be able to sell the slabs, under his duty to exact payment. The question put was whether the creditor could retain the slabs as his security. Scaevola replied that according to the facts stated he could.

We now come to what was probably the biggest item of all, the cost of labour. For basic navvying work, a contractor might be able to obtain cheap, or even free, labour from the ranks of convicts. For instance, Trajan told Pliny that elderly convicts who had served sentences of at least ten years might be set to work cleaning public baths and sewers or repairing streets and highways.[50] But for major building projects, skilled tradesmen – such as carpenters, bricklayers, masons and plasterers – would be needed. In forums all over the empire it was doubtless common to see contractors hiring day labourers (*mercennarii*) on verbal contracts, like the vineyard owner in Matthew's Gospel.[51] Otherwise a contractor might use his own slaves or hire them from someone else; the men on the treadmill that drives the crane on the Tomb of the Haterii were no doubt slaves. They may have belonged to the contractor Tychicus, or they may have been hired from other masters; in either event someone had to pay for their maintenance.

The task of approval was usually entrusted by the sponsor or client to a surveyor (*mensor*): when Pliny was investigating unexplained items in the accounts of the town of Prusa in his province, he wrote to Trajan and asked if a surveyor could be sent out:[52]

Substantial sums of money could, I think, be recovered from contractors of public works if we had dependable surveys made.

Final approval, however, could take a long time. To take an extreme example, in the case of the subsidiary contract for maintaining the temple of Castor and Pollux, Verres, the responsible magistrate, took more than three years to certify that the contractor L. Habonius had completed the job satisfactorily; but, as we shall see, Verres may have had criminal motives for his dilatoriness. In the general run of contracts, approval must have been much faster, but even so a contractor would still have bills to pay before he received his final payment.

Where, then, were contractors to find working capital? Guarantors – who were likely to be profit-sharing partners in a project – must have been the major source of finance. It was very much in the guarantors' interest to supply a contractor with adequate funds. There were two reasons for this. First, if all went well, investors in the contract stood to make a good deal of money. Second, as we have seen, heavy financial penalties faced guarantors if a public contract ran into difficulties and the contractor failed to meet his obligations.

Not all partners and guarantors will have found it easy to provide capital in the form of cash.[53] Once a notice had appeared in public that some or all of a surety's estates had been pledged to a contract, it could be difficult for him to raise further funds. There was, however, another way of providing working capital – albeit in a non-cash form – through the provision of labour, free of charge, to contractors. It was not uncommon for members of the elite to keep a pool of building workers in their town households (*familiae urbanae*). The best-known example is the millionaire senator M. Crassus, who was said to have built up a labour force of 500 slaves skilled in architecture and building. (Crassus bought up property cheaply during or after fires, and used his teams of skilled workmen to redevelop the sites so that they could be sold at a profit.)[54]

Similarly, when Agrippa became commissioner of the water supply he was able to bring with him a company of 240 slaves to carry out routine maintenance. On his death Agrippa left the company to Augustus, who in turn gave the whole team to the state; Claudius later added another 460 of his own slaves.[55] Construction workers are commemorated, too, in the *columbarium* of the Statilii Tauri, although not in large numbers – three *fabri*, three *fabri tignarii,* and a *structor parietarius*.[56] *Faber* denotes a general craftsman; a *faber tignarius* was a craftsman who worked with beams and the term came to be used for builders generally.[57] The *structor parietarius* (literally a wall builder) was probably a stonemason.

Teams of workers in great houses would have been available for employment on public works. When Augustus urged leading citizens to build or restore public monuments at their own expense, Agrippa and Statilius Taurus, both of whom retained building workers in their households, were among those who responded:[58]

Thus the Temple of Hercules and the Muses was raised by Marcius Philippus; that of Diana by Lucius Cornificius; the Hall of Liberty by Asinius Pollio; the temple of Saturn by Munatius Plancus; a theatre by Cornelius Balbus; an amphitheatre by Statilius Taurus; and a variety of magnificent buildings by Marcus Agrippa.

We have some circumstantial evidence to indicate that members of the elite provided labour to contractors. For instance a donor is recorded as giving 200 man–days (*operae*) of building labour for the amphitheatre at Tibur.[59] And particularly revealing is the passage where the jurist Ulpian mentions the provision of skilled slave craftsmen – under contracts of loan (*commodatum*) – and discusses the liabilities that could arise:[60]

> If I lend you (*commendavero*) a slave who is a builder (*tector*) and he falls from the scaffolding, Namusa holds the risk to be mine. But I think that is right only if I lent him to work on scaffolding. But if the loan was for him to work on the ground and you sent him up scaffolding, or else if the disaster happened because the scaffolding was defective having been lashed together, not by him, with too little care or with old ropes or poles, then I maintain that the risk which materialises from the fault of the borrower must be made good by him. In fact, it is also held in Mela's writings that, if a borrowed slave stonemason dies in a collapse of scaffolding, the contractor is liable in the action on loan-for-use (*commodatum*) for too negligently putting together the scaffolding.

Furthermore, wealthy backers who owned quarries, brickfields and timber yards may have contributed building materials free of charge to projects where they had invested risk capital. We may speculate that Agrippa provided marble for his projects: in the second century marble workshops belonging to the family are attested in Africa.[61] Similarly Statilius Taurus, who owned estates in Dyrrachium, presumably had access to large quantities of timber.[62]

In summary, although public works contracts often provided for half the estimated cost of a project to be provided up-front, contractors still faced heavy costs. It was in the interest of their guarantors and partners – often the same people playing a dual role – to provide them with working capital. As far as the contractors were concerned, labour was a major requirement; as far as their elite backers were concerned, skilled labour was a resource that they had in abundance. By supplying labour free of charge – and possibly building materials as well – members of the elite could provide non-cash working capital to contractors with whom they were in partnership.

THE CONTRACT FOR MAINTAINING THE TEMPLE OF CASTOR AND POLLUX

The most detailed description we have of the procedure for letting and approving public contracts occurs in Cicero's speech against Verres.[63] Cicero's attack is discursive and rhetorical, and no doubt biased, but it is possible to construct a reasonably coherent account of the events and personnel connected with the contract for maintaining the temple of Castor and Pollux in Rome.

From 80 BC the contract had been held by Publius Junius, a building contractor of sub-equestrian rank (*homo de plebe Romano*). The contract was guaranteed by the senator Decimus Brutus, who later became consul in 77 BC. On Junius' death (just before or during 75 BC), it emerged from his will that he had taken considerable care in the appointment of guardians (*tutores*) for his young son. Prominent among the guardians was Gaius Mustius, an equestrian who held shares in contracts for revenue collection (*eques Romanus, publicanus*); Mustius married Junius' widow and thus became the younger Junius' stepfather. The other guardians included Marcus Junius, the late contractor's brother, Publius Titius and Marcus Marcellus – all of whom Cicero suggests were models of probity – and Lucius Habonius, another building contractor, who had presumably been a business associate of Publius Junius. Habonius is described as unassuming and easy-going (*modestus et minime pertinax*) and it was partly from these character traits that the ensuing troubles stemmed.

Verres, who was praetor in 74 BC, had been instructed by the Senate to certify that various temple maintenance contracts had been properly carried out. Knowing that Publius Junius had recently died, Verres enquired as to who now held the contract. He was told that since the younger Junius was still a minor, the contract had been transferred to Habonius, one of the boy's guardians. Verres sent for Habonius and asked him for details of this arrangement. Habonius told the praetor that there had been no difficulty in transferring the contract, that no statues or offerings were missing from the temple and that the building was in good condition throughout.

Verres conducted an official inspection of the temple and, according to Cicero, found that it was in good condition. The praetor, however, was looking for an opportunity to make some money at the expense of Junius' estate. On the advice of a member of his staff, Verres called on the estate to have the temple's columns made plumb (*columnae ad perpendiculum exigantur*), a procedure which Cicero said was absurd; it was certainly not in the original contract. Verres nonetheless instructed Habonius to carry out these 'repairs' and to charge the cost of the work to Junius' estate. Verres' intention was to split with Habonius the profits from undertaking this unnecessary work. Habonius protested that the original maintenance contract merely gave an inventory of the number of pillars and said nothing about their being perpendicular. Privately, says Cicero, Habonius wanted to have nothing to do with accepting this job; from Habonius' point of view the problem was that if he did agree to carry out the work, and charge the cost to the estate of the original contractor, this would mean that when he eventually came to hand over the maintenance contract in his turn, he could be required to fulfil the same expensive obligation. Verres was not interested in Habonius' reservations. The praetor told the contractor that he was going to go ahead and demand that the pillars be made perpendicular; Habonius was to take on this subsidiary contract at a high price, which would be charged to Junius' estate. Habonius would then share with Verres the profits of this 'partnership' (*nonnulla spes societatis*).

The other guardians were horrified at being asked to pay for the columns to be made perpendicular, which they saw as a grave threat to Junius' estate. They made protests to Verres, and even approached Chelidon his mistress for help; Cicero says that Chelidon had great influence with Verres over the letting of maintenance contracts (*in his sartis tectisque dominata est*). The guardians achieved nothing. They eventually agreed to go ahead with the work and pay Habonius HS200,000 from Junius' estate to carry it out, even though they considered the true cost of the job to be worth only HS40,000. What did this new contract amount to? asked Cicero. In the event, scaffolding was erected, some of the pillars were dismantled, whitened and re-erected, a certain amount of marble (presumably facings for decorative purposes) was cut and brought to the site by a special transport wagon (*machina sua*). 'That was all: there was no stone and no timber brought there: all that the contract involved was paying some masons for a few days' work, plus the cost of scaffolding.'

Habonius reported to Verres that he would undertake the work and told him the terms that he had agreed with the other guardians. The praetor was not at all pleased: he wanted to make far more out of the contract than this. Verres accordingly decided to stage a public auction of the subsidiary contract; without any advertisement or announcement he staged it at a most inconvenient time, in the middle of the Roman Games. He also made Habonius cancel the agreement he had reached with his fellow-guardians, i.e. to do the work for HS200,000. The guardians, however, got to hear of what was going on and attended the auction in the Forum; Marcus Junius made a bid, on his nephew's behalf, to do the work for HS40,000. But Verres now arranged matters (quite how, Cicero does not make entirely clear) to exclude Marcus Junius from taking part as partner or shareholder or contractor in this particular contract (*socium ne admittito, neve partem dato, neve redimito*). The contract was let to Habonius, at a price of HS560,000; furthermore the terms of the contract (*lex*) stated that the cost of the work was to be paid to the contractor, up front, in cash (*pecunia praesens solvatur*). The money would have to come out of Junius' estate, since it was the estate that was, under the original maintenance contract, responsible for seeing that any repairs were carried out. However the person who now provided the cash for the payment of HS560,000 was Decimus Brutus, guarantor for the original contract. The unpalatable fact for this distinguished senator was that, despite the illegal way in which the subsidiary contract had been awarded, a magistrate had ordered that repairs were to be carried out, and under the maintenance contract the guarantor was liable to pay for them if the estate was unable, or unwilling, to do so. The money was paid over to Cornificius, Verres' clerk. Decimus Brutus was, naturally, not at all happy about any of this and exerted considerable pressure on Verres to return his money; the senator eventually received HS110,000 out of the HS560,000 he had paid as guarantor.

There is a final twist to the story. Habonius did not complete the 'repairs' to the columns by the due date. Verres saw this as an opportunity to withhold the certificate of approval (*opus in acceptum non rettulit*), presumably with the intention of extorting an even larger share of the spoils from his accomplice. Only when the prosecution of Verres was officially launched, more than three years later, did Verres capitulate and issue the certificate; he feared that if he refused to discharge Habonius from his contractual obligation, the contractor might become yet another hostile witness at his trial.

From all this, we may conclude, one major charge could be levelled against Verres, an elected magistrate of the Roman state: he had colluded with the contractor Habonius to defraud the estate of Publius Junius. Cicero presses home this charge with various allegations: first, the praetor had abused his position as inspecting magistrate to demand that the original contractor (in this case Junius' estate) should carry out unnecessary repairs to the temple fabric; second, although the representatives of Junius' estate agreed to carry out this work, Verres called a public auction to let this subsidiary contract; and third, at the auction he accepted Habonius' bid, although it was not the lowest, and added clauses to the terms of the contract which had the effect of specifically excluding the consortium led by Marcus Junius on behalf of the estate.

The administration of the contract for the maintenance of the Temple of Castor and Pollux cannot be regarded as typical, since it was (allegedly) marked by corruption on the part of a magistrate and a contractor. Nevertheless the episode illustrates two important points. First, to obtain a contract a builder had to obtain a guarantor or guarantors with substantial financial assets; this led to men of comparatively humble rank forming business relationships with senators and equestrians. Publius Junius, the original contractor at the Temple of Castor and Pollux, was described by Cicero as *homo de plebe Romano*; but the man whom Junius had obtained as his surety, Decimus Brutus, was a senior senator who became consul three years later. Perhaps Brutus was Junius' patron. Junius had also gathered support from other associates with sizeable financial resources: at least one of the guardians appointed in his will, Gaius Mustius, was of equestrian rank.

Second, guarantors were putting substantial sums at risk when they underwrote public works contracts: Decimus Brutus found himself required to pay out a very large sum of money in cash. Senators and equestrians in Rome, and wealthy men elsewhere, evidently believed that there were handsome profits to be earned through partnerships in public works contracts. Their contribution to these partnerships was primarily through the provision of financial guarantees; in some, perhaps many cases, they also provided working capital in the form of cash, loans of labour or supplies of building materials. We may conclude that the public works of the Roman world were largely financed with risk capital provided by the elite.

XIII

THE COMPANIES OF TAX COLLECTORS

With the spread of Roman influence across the Mediterranean, custom dues and harbour tolls (*portoria*) became a major source of income for the Republic's government. Goods travelling any significant distance might be required to pay duties and tolls at several points on the way.[1] Rome's tax revenues (*vectigalia*) increased considerably during the second century BC, when the state began to collect direct taxes (*tributum* or *stipendium*), in money or in kind, from conquered provinces. By the first century BC, Spain and most of Africa paid a fixed sum in taxes (*certum stipendium*); but in some provinces, notably Asia, direct taxes were levied on a percentage of the harvest, although some of the grain may have been sold on the local market for cash.[2] (Rome and Roman Italy were exempt from direct taxation.)

Republican Rome had almost no civil service and consequently the collection of taxes was contracted out to private citizens. In Sicily, following pre-Roman practice, the collection of direct taxes was leased by the governor to locally-based businessmen (*decumani*), who seem to have been responsible for collecting the tithes of corn and transporting the grain as far as the ports.[3] Tribute from the majority of provinces, however, was collected by Roman businessmen who undertook contracts to 'farm' the public revenues. These businessmen were known as *publicani*.[4] The contracts for tax collection in the various provinces were let at auction by magistrates, usually the censors, to the highest bidders, '*vectigalia summis pretiis…locaverunt*'.[5]

Although a tax collection contract was let to an individual (*manceps*), he would invariably be the front man for a partnership (*societas*). The principal purpose of a partnership was to assemble a group of wealthy men who would pledge property to the value of the contract; this was to assure the government that it would receive its tax revenues – or the equivalent in real estate, if the company failed to meet its obligations. And, as in the case of public works contracts (Chapter 12), the partners (*socii*) most probably contributed working capital. This capital would be required by the company to enable it to maintain premises overseas, together with large numbers of staff, slave and free; finance would also be needed to enable the tax collectors to enter into and fulfil a host of sub-contracts with shippers, grain dealers and so on. In their heyday, that is in the late Republic, massive sums of money were invested by the Roman elite in the *societates publicanorum*. These companies were engaged in a wide range of activities – tax collection, shipping, grain trading and banking. They were the corporate conglomerates of the Roman world.

TAX COLLECTION CONTRACTS

Public documents and references in Cicero's letters and speeches indicate that the contracts for the collection of taxes were auctioned in much the same way as the public works contracts described by Polybius.[6] A partnership of tax collectors (*societas publicanorum*) would put in its bid through a representative, the *manceps*; on being awarded a contract a successful *manceps* was required to produce associates (*socii*) who would stand as guarantors (*praedes*) and put up securities in the form of land (*praedia*). The *manceps* might himself be a guarantor. Furthermore the titles of the properties to be mortgaged as security for public contracts were put under a seal at the treasury (*praedia subsignare*).[7] The successful bidder for a tax collection contract was bound by a law (*lex censoria*) laid down by the censors who had let the concession. Evidence for the scope of a *lex censoria* comes from the *lex portorii Asiae*. Inscribed in the reign of Nero, this is a revised version of a law regulating the collection of taxes for the province of Asia, which was initially issued in the first century BC. The Asian tax law contains information about the boundaries of the tax district, the location of the customs offices and the rights and duties of the tax farmers, as well as regulations about procedures and the level of taxation. The law also specifies procedures for letting contracts and the obligations of the *manceps*.[8]

References to *leges censoriae* can also be found in the legal sources. For instance, the Augustan jurist Alfenus Varus quotes the *lex* that governed the payment of customs dues in the ports of Sicily; this specified inter alia that dues were not payable on slaves brought home for the personal use of the owner.[9] And the powers of the tax farmers under a typical *lex censoria* are discussed by the jurist Gaius:[10]

> By the censors' law, farmers of public taxes of the Roman people were allowed to seize the pledged property of those who owed taxes under some statute.

SHAREHOLDERS

The *publicani* who took a share in the large-scale tax contracts of the Roman Republic were drawn from the ranks of the *equites*. Cicero described the *publicani*, whom he regarded as his political allies, as 'the fine flower of the equestrian order, the ornament and bulwark of the Roman State' (*flos enim equitum Romanorum, ornamentum civitatis, firmamentum rei publicae publicanorum ordine continetur*).[11] The equites continued to play a role in tax collection during the early Empire: Tacitus describes Roman administration of the system during the reign of Tiberius:[12]

Levies of grain, cash and other state revenues were handled by companies of equestrians.

Tax collection, as well as participation in maritime commerce, was an occupation from which senators were barred.[13] This prohibition was presumably intended to avert conflicts of interest. It was part of a provincial governor's duty to monitor and control the activities of the *publicani*; if the governor and his senatorial staff were *socii* in a tax collection company active in their province, they could hardly carry out their responsibilities conscientiously. This is the assumption behind one of Cicero's allegations in his speech for the prosecution during Verres' trial: the former governor of Sicily had virtually been a partner (*socios habuisse decumanos*) in the Sicilian tax collection companies which, as governor, he was duty-bound to supervise.[14] Cicero put the case for the prosecution very eloquently; however, as we shall see shortly, he was quite prepared to use personal influence with the provincial authorities to benefit the tax collection companies when it suited him or his friends. He cannot have been the only member of the elite to do so.

Despite the prohibition on active participation in the tax collection business, it appears that senators did invest in tax collection companies. Senatorial shareholdings seem to have been a contributory factor in the controversy over the Asian tax contract in 61–59 BC (which will be discussed below). Because of the legal prohibition on direct senatorial involvement in the tax collection companies, it is highly likely that senators held some sort of loan stock. This would mean that they held shares which guaranteed them a fixed return at regular intervals - rather than holding partnership shares, which entitled their holders to a share in the profits.

It is not clear whether the equestrian partners in a tax collection company would normally be required to provide security for one year's revenue, on a roll-over basis, or whether they and their guarantors would have to give pledges to cover the entirety of the taxes due over the five-year term (*lustrum*) of the contract. On balance it seems likely that the pledges were provided on a roll-over basis.

The problem with a system whereby security was pledged for the full five years would be the magnitude of the sums required. Some rough and ready figures will give an idea. It has been estimated that the Asian tribute under the Republic amounted to 15 million *denarii* a year; meanwhile Plutarch indicates that the annual tribute from Bithynia, Cilicia and Syria came to 35 million *denarii*.[15] These figures give a combined annual total of direct tax collected from just these four provinces amounting to 50 million *denarii*, or HS200 million. If the real estate pledged was intended to cover the tax due over the entire five-year term of the contracts, then the properties required to be pledged for these four companies alone amounted to a total of HS1 billion. This would amount to the minimum property qualification of 1,000 men of senatorial rank or of 2,500 equestrians. It seems unlikely that the Roman elite would have committed capital on this scale over a period of five years.[16]

The Roman elite in the first century BC sought shares in tax collection companies with similar eagerness to that shown by their predecessors in the second century BC for shares in public works contracts.[17] An idea of the scale of this enthusiasm emerges from the episode of the Asian tax contract. In 61 BC, the Asian company of *publicani* asked the Senate for part-remission of the taxes that they had contracted to raise. A century earlier, according to Polybius, the Senate had been prepared to make readjustments of contracts for public building works.[18] This was presumably because cost overruns were frequent and sometimes outside the contractor's control. But when it came to contracts for the collection of taxes, as a general rule the authorities were not prepared to make concessions to companies which had overbid:[19]

> Where the heat of competition has led a bidder to offer a contract for tax collection (*vectigal*) above the usual level, this contract should still be allowed, provided the victorious bidder is prepared to offer satisfactory verbal guarantors and a pledge (*cautio*)....No one is to be compelled against his will to farm the collection of *vectigal*; hence, when the time limit on a contract has expired, the *vectigal* must be leased out afresh. Tax farmers who have failed to produce all the *vectigal* they have contracted for are not to be permitted to make a fresh contract until they have fulfilled the existing one.

In 61 BC, however, Marcus Crassus, with Cicero's backing, gave the Asian tax company full support in the Senate. Cicero may also have been financially involved, although he said that he gave the company his support because he wished to preserve harmony between the *equites* and the Senate.[20] The affair of the Asian taxes rumbled on at Rome for some two years, during which a group of senators led by the younger Cato succeeded in obstructing the demands of the *publicani*. But eventually Caesar, now consul, gave way to the publicans' request:[21]

> When the tax farmers asked for relief, he cancelled one-third of their obligations, but gave them frank warning not to bid too high for their contracts in future.

Caesar's leniency was probably due to the fact that he too held shares in the Asian company. This would explain Cicero's accusation in the same year that a certain Vatinius had sought to 'extort' shares in the company from Caesar. The shares would have been particularly attractive in 59 BC, because the company had just secured a partial remission of the Asian contract and was consequently back on a sound financial footing.

The men of wealth and power in Rome who invested in the companies of tax collectors expected to earn a handsome return on their investment. It would not be surprising, therefore, to find that they used their influence and connections to ensure, to the best of their ability, that the company was highly profitable. For instance, when a member of the elite took up a post as a provincial governor or member of the governor's staff, he might be asked by investors in Rome to smooth the company's path in negotiations with the local communities and local trading counterparties and in any disputes which might come before the governor's court. The provincial official could expect to be rewarded for his compliance on his return to Rome.

The two-way flow of favours and rewards is well illustrated in a letter written at some time in the 50s by Cicero from Rome to Furius Crassipes, who was serving in Bithynia as quaestor:[22]

From Cicero to Crassipes greetings.

I have already recommended the Company of Bithynia to you in person as strongly as I could, and it was evident to me that of your own free will as well as in consequence of my recommendation you were anxious to accommodate the Company in any way that you were able. However, since those concerned consider it very much to their advantage that I should also declare to you by letter my friendly disposition towards them, I have not hesitated to write this letter.

I have always been very ready to study the interests of the tax-farmers as a class, which is only right in view of the important services they have rendered me. But I should like it to be clear to you that I have a special regard for this Company of Bithynia. The quality of the membership in itself makes the Company an important section of the community (it is a consortium of all the other companies) and, as it happens, it contains a great many very good friends of mine. I would mention one of them in particular who has a special responsibility at the present time, namely the Chairman, P. Rupilius, son of Publius, of the Tribe Menenia.

In view of the above, let me particularly request you to give your most generous support to the Company's agent, Gnaeus Pupius, assisting him in every way that you are able. I hope you will ensure, as you easily can, that his employers are thoroughly satisfied with his services, and will be good enough to protect and further their business interests as far as possible – and I am not unaware how much a quaestor can do in that direction. I shall be much obliged. I can also promise and guarantee from experience that if you oblige the Company of Bithynia you will find that its members have long and grateful memories.

THE LEGAL POSITION

Like the partners in any Roman *societas*, the *publicani* undertook to contribute finance or services, or both, to the enterprise and to share in gains, or losses, in an agreed proportion. However, a passage in the Digest indicates that there were special rules for *societates vectigalium*:[23]

The partnership continues even after the death of a partner, provided that the share of the deceased has been assigned to the person of the heir, so that the partnership [stake] must pass to him...For the deceased may be the man chiefly responsible for forming the partnership or without whom the partnership cannot be run.

This indicates that a *societas vectigalis* was not dissolved by the death of a member and that, subject to certain rules, the heir succeeded to the share of the deceased, including any liabilities. It was in the public interest that the companies could not be dissolved at will, since they were responsible for managing large sums of public money.

A company whose official representative (*manceps*) had successfully won a tax collection contract might well seek to renew the contract at the end of the first and subsequent five year periods. If a new partnership won a contract, however, it would presumably need to purchase the assets of its predecessor. These assets would consist principally of slaves and property, which could cost the purchasers dear since they would be buying in a seller's market. A simpler option for new investors would be to buy shares in the existing company. Certainly some sort of continuity is implied by the passage in Tacitus, where Nero's advisers remind the emperor (in 58) that 'very many [contemporary] companies for collecting [indirect] taxes had been established (*constitutae*) by consuls and tribunes in the freest times of the Republic'.[24]

Indeed it appears that at some time the *societas vectigalis* was granted a form of corporate entity.[25] The principal evidence is provided in the second century by the jurist Gaius:[26]

> Partners in tax farming, gold mines, silver mines, and saltworks are allowed to form corporations (*vectigalium publicorum sociis permissum est corpus habere vel aurifodinarum vel argentifodinarum et salinarum*)....Those permitted to form a corporate body consisting of a *collegium* or partnership...have the right, on the pattern of the state (*ad exemplum rei publicae*), to have common property, a common treasury and an attorney or legal counsel through whom, as in a state, what should be transacted and done in common is transacted and done.

In other words, a tax collection partnership could sue and be sued and be represented in court as a legal entity. Furthermore, it appears that a person wronged by a slave belonging to the *familia publicanorum* could sue any of the *socii*, and if successful he could obtain compensation from any of them:[27]

> [In a law suit] the words against 'the owners' [of slaves working for tax collectors], should be interpreted as meaning 'against the partners in tax (*vectigal*) transactions', even if they are not owners [of the slaves].

The special claims of the tax collectors to corporate status seem to have been recognized as early as the first century BC. This emerges from the distinction, noticed by Nicolet, between the ad hoc partnerships formed to undertake public works projects and the longer-lasting partnerships set up to collect the state's taxes and rents.[28] Nicolet pointed out that while public works partnerships were usually designated by the name of the principal contractor, the tax collection companies were typically described by their business objectives or by a title that embodied their geographical location. An example of a company which was described by its business objective is the *societas* in Sicily that held several franchises, chief among them the collection of rents for public grazing land:[29]

> Vettius wrote a letter to Carpinatius in Sicily, as a director of the company farming the pasture tax and six other imposts (*[Vettius] misit in Siciliam litteras ad Carpinatium, cum esset magister scripturae et sex publicorum*).

For a 'geographical' title we can look to the tax collectors of Bithynia: their company was described by Cicero both as the *Bithynica societas* and as the *socii Bithyniae* in the letter to Crassipes quoted above.[30]

ORGANISATION

It is possible to sketch out, from Cicero's second speech against Verres, the organisation of the *societas scripturae et sex publicorum* in Sicily, which was run on a day-to-day basis by the managing director (*promagister*), Lucius Carpinatius. At the head of the company were the directors (*magistri*), who were based in Rome. We know the names of several of these men, Publius Vettius Chilo, Publius Servilius, Gaius Antistius and Lucius Tullius. Cicero states that Chilo was an equestrian and most probably the others were, too.[31] One of these men was presumably the *manceps* who had formally put in the bid which won the contract. The directors' principal role – which, as will emerge shortly, they were accused of failing to discharge adequately – was to ensure that the funds of the shareholders were being properly managed.

A general meeting of the company had been called to express the shareholders' thanks to Verres, the returning governor of Sicily, for the favours (*officia*) that Verres had done for Carpinatius, the managing director.[32] (Once again a caveat is necessary: Cicero's account of the general procedures and practices of the company's business provide invaluable information, but he may well be misrepresenting particular events in the interests of his case.) It appears from Cicero's somewhat confusing account that Verres and Carpinatius had colluded in defrauding the shareholders.[33] By a decree of the senate Verres had been empowered to make official purchases of grain over and above the regular tithes. He was authorised to use funds which were owed to the state treasury (*aerarium*) but were kept on deposit in Sicily with the local offices of the tax collection companies. One of these was the company managed by Carpinatius. Verres drew down the funds but instead of paying them over to the farmers for grain, he lent the money back to the tax companies and actually charged them interest – at a rate of 24 per cent, double the usual maximum – and then kept the interest for himself. At the shareholders' meeting, Verres replied to the vote of thanks:

He said that it had been a pleasure to perform these services, and he spoke in glowing terms of the work (*operae*) done by Carpinatius. He then instructed one of his friends, who was at the time Chairman of the company, to take great care and precaution to see that the company's records (*litterae sociorum*) should contain nothing that could stand against his (Verres') position (*caput*) or reputation (*existimatio*). Accordingly the Chairman, after the main body of the shareholders (*multitudo sociorum*) had dispersed, called a meeting of the tithe-collectors (*decumani*) and put this matter before them. They passed a resolution that those records which might damage the reputation of Gaius Verres should be removed and that care should be taken that this course of action should not expose Verres to a charge of fraud.

The presence of the *decumani*, Sicily-based collectors of tithes, at the meeting in Rome and the role that they played on this occasion suggest that they were active *socii* in the company and furthermore that their agreement was necessary for major decisions to be taken – even when these decisions went against the interests of the shareholders as a whole. Sicily, however, was a special case. It was more usual for the *promagister* in a province to make agreements (*pacta*) directly with the local communities for tax, in cash or kind, to be delivered to the company's representatives.

To support the actual tax collectors, the company's staff in the province was organised very much along the lines of the slave household (*familia*) of an elite family. Senior slaves were appointed as *vilici* to manage operations and supervise staff, just as senior slaves were employed as bailiffs on farms. Other members of the *familia* worked as labourers in the company's warehouses, as clerks in the counting houses where cash payments were received and as despatch-bearers (*tabellarii*) carrying messages on the company's behalf to and from the *promagister* in the province and the *magistri* in Rome.[34]

SOURCES OF INCOME

Under a tax farming contract the successful bidder undertook to produce in each year of a five-year cycle a given amount of revenue. For provinces where tribute was levied in grain, at a rate of one-tenth of the crop, the companies had to base their bids on forward estimates of acreage under cultivation and likely crop yields. Furthermore, in provinces such as Asia where tribute delivered in the form of grain would often be sold by the *publicani* for cash, they needed to be able to make an informed estimate of the future trend of wheat prices. To modern eyes, this appears to be an uncertain business which required well-founded local information if reasonably reliable forecasts of revenue were to be made. Nevertheless, as has already been indicated, investment in a tax collection company was considered to be lucrative, partnerships were eagerly sought by the elite and the contracts were keenly contested. Presumably over long periods of time crop yields were relatively constant and prices were relatively stable.

The *publicani* must have been confident that in each year of their contract they could deliver to the treasury in Rome the grain, or the cash, for which they had contracted.

There was another factor, however, which made investment in tax collection companies such an attractive business. The companies of *publicani* enjoyed several revenue streams – income from commissions and fees connected with the core business of collecting the government's taxes; profits from banking, shipping and trading; and opportunities to make money from activities that can only be described as criminal.

Commissions and fees

In the first place, the companies of *publicani* earned commission on the taxes they collected. Cicero mentions a commission (in kind) of 6 per cent of the total crop assessed in a district of Sicily; but this figure may have been exaggerated to discredit Verres. Elsewhere Cicero suggests that the normal rate of commission was 10 per cent of the tithe collected, i.e. 1 per cent of the total crop. The commission was, in any event, charged to the taxpayers, not to the government.[35]

The *publicani* also charged the taxpayers various fees when they could get away with it. Cicero accused Verres of levying certain charges when he was purchasing grain on the open market in Sicily on behalf of the government. These fees were for such spurious items as 'inspection' (*spectatio*), currency exchange (*collybus*), 'wax money' (*cerarium*), presumably for sealing official receipts, and a clerk's fee (*scribae nomen*) of 4 per cent ; again we should assume that these charges were levied on the total tax collected.[36] Other so-called fees were exacted from time to time by the tax collectors. For instance, when Nero was under pressure to abolish indirect taxation, notably the customs dues (*portoria*), he side-stepped the issue by introducing various reforms. One reform was that the regulations with regard to each tax, previously kept secret, should be posted for public inspection. Another was that the 'fortieth' (2.5 per cent) and 'fiftieth' (2 per cent) and other illicit exactions for which the *publicani* had invented titles should be abolished.[37]

The tax collectors were also empowered to seize the goods of taxpayers who were in default.[38] Presumably they were often able to make a profit, after remitting the due proceeds to the government, when they sold these goods at auction.

Banking

Banking provided another source of income for the tax collection companies. The deposit base of their banks was built on inflows of cash at different times. The principal source of deposits was, of course, cash paid directly as tribute or resulting from local sales of tax grain. A portion of these funds would not be sent to Rome, but held by the tax companies until they were required for disbursement in the province - for instance when a new governor or army commander arrived to take up his duties. So when Pompey was given his special command in 67 BC to drive pirates out of the Mediterranean, he was empowered to take from the provincial treasuries 'and the tax companies' whatever funds he needed.[39] Conversely, an outgoing governor might deposit surplus funds of his own with the *publicani*: Cicero deposited his unspent 'expenses', HS2.2 million worth of local *cistophori*, with the Asiatic tax company's office in Ephesus, at the conclusion of his governorship of Cilicia.[40]

The *publicani* in some provinces would negotiate agreements with local communities on the amount of tax that would be delivered each year. They would frequently work in concert with the governor. Two letters from Cicero reveal the system in operation:[41]

> When I reached my province...there were great gatherings of people at these towns and I relieved many communities of savage imposts and cruel usury and fraudulent debts (*acerbissimis tributis et gravissimis usuris et falso aere alieno*).

> The reputation of Terentius Hispo, local manager of the grazing rents company...depends very largely on his concluding agreements (*pactiones*) with the remaining communities. I do not forget that I tried my own hand at the business in Ephesus and was quite unable to get the Ephesians to oblige.

Cicero's experience on arriving in his province reveals not only that a Roman governor was expected to negotiate tax agreements with the local communities but also that the *publicani* were entitled to lend funds to the very taxpayers from whom they demanded revenues. Any lateness in payment was penalised by the imposition of interest at a rate fixed in the *pactio*. Some governors might be persuaded to set a high rate. For his governorship of Cilicia Cicero set a rate of 12 per cent, the maximum permitted in Italy.[42]

Banking was an essential part of the business of the *publicani*. It was in its capacity as a bank that the company managed by Carpinatius held the public funds which Verres was held to have misused during his governorship. The crime could not have been committed without the active participation of at least one official on the spot, who 'borrowed' the funds back from Verres, paid him interest out of the company's funds and then destroyed most of the evidence.[43] And in another twist to the story of Verres' relationship with Carpinatius' company, Cicero alleged that the governor kept an account with the tax collectors' banking arm under the clumsy pseudonym Verrucius. The company lent various Sicilians money to pay bribes to Verres, no doubt at a healthy rate of interest; on receiving the bribes, Verres immediately deposited the funds with the bank in the 'Verrucius' account.[44]

Shipping and trading

Lastly, a substantial part of the business of the *publicani* consisted of shipping and trading. It is likely that many of the collectors of indirect taxes under the Republic were in fact merchants with overseas trading interests. Such men had staff and agents in position at ports and frontier posts and consequently collection of customs duties and trading could be regarded as complementary businesses. The sea-going traders who undertook the contract to supply the state with military equipment and supplies in 215 BC were probably tax collectors as well as merchants: they are described by Livy as persons who had increased their patrimony through public contracts (*qui redempturis auxissent patrimonia*).[45]

Sea-going traders had several roles to play in the long chain that led from the collection of taxes at the farm gate in the provinces to the delivery of grain (or cash in lieu) to the appropriate authorities in Italy. First, they were required to transport tribute from the provincial port to Italy: when taxes were collected in money, part at least of the receipts would have to be remitted to Rome; this required ships that could carry bullion or coins.[46] Second, they might be required to trade on behalf of the *societas* – to go into the local market to buy grain. This would be the case in years when the farmers failed to deliver their quota of tax grain, or if the government in Rome authorised the *publicani* to buy grain over and above the tithe that was normally due. Third, even if tribute was collected in cash (as it seems to have been in Asia after 46 BC) the *societas* would still need the services of merchants. This was because farmers in inland areas were unlikely to have much cash; if they continued to pay their tax in kind, this tax grain would subsequently be traded for cash at ports in the province – which would require the trading skills of professional merchants.[47]

A proportion of tax grain would also be made available for sale to grain merchants operating in the open market in Rome, Ostia and Puteoli. The proceeds from these sales could represent handsome additional profits for the *societas*; the people best placed to handle these transactions on their behalf were, of course, merchant-shippers who worked for the partnership; some of these merchant-shippers may have been partners themselves. And, in addition to tax grain, substantial shipments of non-tax grain were also imported for sale on the open market: as Tacitus said, 'the people of Rome were accustomed to buy their food on a daily basis'.[48] Here there were further opportunities for profit.

Under the Republic, the authorities would from time to time intervene in the open market, in the interests of ensuring continuity of supply and stability of price. In 57 BC, for instance, Pompey was given a special command (*cura annonae*) with authority to buy up grain wherever he could and arrange its shipment to Rome.[49] (It was later made a criminal offence under the *lex Julia de annona*, to impede the flow of grain to Rome or to enter into a cartel to force up the price.)[50] The net effect of these arrangements meant that merchants who worked with the *publicani* had opportunities to trade profitably in both surplus tax-grain and grain that they had bought from overseas suppliers. Furthermore, as yet another perquisite, merchants working with the *publicani* could carry non-grain cargoes on board grain freighters sailing on government contracts.

Under the Republic, then, merchants and equestrian *publicani* worked in close partnership to ship grain, cash or bullion – or even goods totally unconnected with the service of the *annona* – from the provinces to Rome. Opportunities for profit, over and above the earnings derived from the government contracts let to the *publicani*, became self-sustaining. Once again, the activities of the equestrian Gaius Rabirius Postumus, 'who had large shareholdings in tax companies', are instructive.[51] Postumus, says Cicero, lent not only his own money to Ptolemy, exiled king of Egypt, but that of his friends. After the king's restoration Postumus was appointed royal treasurer in Alexandria. But things did not go well in Egypt. After various misadventures Postumus fled from Alexandria, but he managed to make money in fresh trading ventures.

PROFIT AND LOSS

We can now draw up a pro-forma profit and loss account for a typical Roman tax company at the end of each year of its five year contract. On the income side of the account will be the total amount of tax revenue (in cash or kind), commissions and fees that had been collected from the taxpayers; to this can be added the revenues from banking, shipping and trading. On the expenditure side of the account, the principal item will be the amount of tax (in cash or kind) that the company paid to the government under its contract. To this must be added the costs of premises, labour and the operational costs of shipping and trading.

But this is by no means all. A present-day accountant's view of the business of the *publicani* omits two major elements – extortion on the income side and bribery on the expenditure side. We just do not know how frequently the shareholders in Rome turned a blind eye to extortion on the part of tax collectors in the provinces. Nor do we know how easy it was for victims of extortion to go to law and win a case.

If governments were aware of the problem, the widespread participation of the elite as shareholders must have inhibited action to put an end to abuses. Tacitus tells us, characteristically, that when Nero brought in his new rules to curb the excesses of the companies of *publicani* (see above) these rules were soon evaded.[52]

The Digest indicates that regulations were introduced to exercise some control over the tax collectors' activities:[53]

> Any illegal exaction, private or public, is paid back to the victims with as much again; but where the extortion was made by force, the restitution is threefold; those responsible are in addition liable to extraordinary criminal punishment.

As a famous passage in Luke's gospel shows, *publicani* were synonymous with sinners in the first century; and at many times throughout our period they appear to have extracted from the taxpayers more than was officially due to them.[54] The point has been put succinctly: 'there is no good way of quantifying the illegal extras collected; therefore, no saying if they constituted a more serious abuse in AD 250 than, say, under Augustus.'[55] On the expenditure side of the account, it is also necessary to add in a host of items – fees, commissions, kick-backs and straight bribes – that the tax collectors on the ground paid as 'sweeteners' to local officials from the governor downwards.

Once the income from extortion and the expenditure on 'sweeteners' had been added to the respective sides of the account, the company's profit (or loss) at the end of each year of its contract could be calculated. When there was a profit, this was available for distribution – in the form of dividends to the equestrian partners and as interest on the 'loan stock' held by senators. Judged by the enthusiasm of the Roman elite for investing in the tax collection companies, the profits were usually extremely high.

THE DECLINE OF THE *PUBLICANI*

Equestrians who were equity shareholders in a tax collection company will have been invited to join the venture on the strength of the funds that they undertook to contribute; the provision of finance for ships must have been one of the first calls made on their resources. Similar calls will have been made on the funds provided to the venture by senators in return for loan stock. It is fair to say that, through their participation in the tax collection companies under the Republic, the senatorial and equestrian elite financed a significant portion of Rome's merchant shipping fleet.

By the end of the Republic, however, links between tax collectors and shippers began to be loosened. One factor was the weakening of the position of the tax companies. The civil wars ravaged the companies' funds, since their funds in the provinces were pillaged by opposing commanders. Next, Julius Caesar took measures to change the system for collecting Asia's direct taxes. Our sources differ in the details: Cassius Dio says that Caesar abolished tax farming and introduced a combined payment (*phorou synteleia*) to replace existing taxes; Plutarch says that he reduced taxes in Asia by one-third; Appian says that he remitted one-third of the amounts then being collected and transferred the collection from the *publicani* to the provincial communities.[56] The account given by Appian, who served as a financial official (*procurator Augusti*) under the Antonines and no doubt had a grasp of financial matters, may be considered the most reliable.

The measures taken by Caesar began a long process whereby the government shifted the burden of tax collection in the provinces on to members of the local community councils (*curiae*). Under the Republic the *publicani* had guaranteed to the state the tax revenues that they were bound to pay under their contracts; under the system that evolved under the Empire the state looked to each community to make up any deficit in the taxes for which it had been assessed. As far as direct taxes were concerned, the *curiales* were required to take on the burden of tax collection; although there were still some *publicani* at work in the second century AD, and individual tax farmers (*conductores*) are also attested, these men were hardly the buccaneering entrepreneurs of the late Republic and seem to have come under the control of imperial procurators (*26*).[57]

A second structural change was the appointment by Augustus of the *praefectus annonae*, whose task was to coordinate corn supplies and to plan ahead to avoid shortages (see Chapter 1). Tax collection contracts were still being let in Tiberius' reign to companies of equestrians;[58] but in Nero's reign, Columella reported that there were regular auctions of state contracts simply for the transport of grain from the provinces to Rome.[59] This shift was surely the practical consequence of the appointment of the *praefectus annonae*: it emerges from the inscription set up at Hispalis in Baetica in honour of Sextus Julius Possessor in the second century, that Possessor was, at one point in his career, aide to the *praefectus annonae* 'with responsibility for keeping account of African and Spanish oil, transporting supplies and paying the shippers (*vecturas naviculariis exsolvendas*)'.[60] It looks as if the shipping of tax grain had become uncoupled from its collection. Many members of the elite who had an eye to increasing their fortunes presumably reverted to more traditional ways of making money, such as agriculture and money-lending: *multum serit, multum faenerat*, is how Seneca characterised the rich man of his day.[61] And for ambitious members of the equestrian order new opportunities for personal enrichment began to appear, in the shape of procuratorships in the imperial civil service.

These changes probably contributed to difficulties that arose under the Empire in recruiting shippers to work for the *annona*. As noted in Chapter 1, a stream of incentives was offered to merchants (*navicularii et negotiatores*) who undertook to ship grain (and other staples) to Rome. But there were unintended consequences: the new measures created tax loopholes, which proved so attractive that the wealthy began to abuse them. Hadrian found it necessary to state that immunity from public duties (*munera*) was available only to those owners of vessels who devoted a significant portion of their wealth to maritime trade.[62] It was also necessary to make it clear that membership of the corporation of shippers was not of itself sufficient to win privileges. Marcus Aurelius and Lucius Verus restated the official position:[63]

> There were also other people who claimed to escape *munera* on the same grounds as shipowners and people supplying the market of the Roman people with corn and oil, who are immune, although they were not making voyages and did not have the greater part of their capital invested in maritime and mercantile business; such people are to be deprived of immunity.

It is time to summarise. The tax collection companies raised their finance in two forms: through pledges of property made by the equestrian *publicani* to the government, as guarantees for fulfilment of the state contracts, and through the provision of working capital by both equestrians and senators. It seems likely that the equestrian partners subscribed their funds on an equity (i.e. risk) basis while senators held a form of loan stock. The profits of these companies, which included net gains from what would today be called criminal conduct, constituted a substantial source of elite income during the late Republic and early Empire.

A significant portion of the funds contributed to the tax collection companies by elite investors was invested in Rome's merchant shipping fleet. Furthermore, the ships that carried tribute in cash or kind to Italy from the tax-paying provinces were able to carry export goods on the return journey; this provided shippers working on tax collection contracts with a subsidy. This, in turn, enabled shippers to offer low-cost freight rates to the general run of manufacturers and commodity producers. The impact that this had on the growth in Roman trade, particularly in the late Republic, is unquantifiable, but it must have been significant.

During their heyday the companies of *publicani*, with their directors and shareholders in Rome and large staffs in the provinces, were substantial corporations with widespread interests, legal and not so legal. They demonstrated that rapacious private enterprise might be harnessed to the service of the state. But over time the role of the great tax collection companies was diminished. Beginning with the measures taken by Julius Caesar the government passed much of the responsibility for tax collection to the local councillors (*curiales*) in the provinces. The link between tax collection and shipping was broken.

This brought about a profound change. Uncoupled from tax collection and all its associated opportunities for making money, shipping tribute grain for the *annona* was not a very attractive proposition. Shippers and merchants holding contracts to serve the *annona* found themselves competing on price to provide an unprofitable bulk freight operation and in the first and second centuries they had to be given special incentives to invest in grain carriers. Consequently many of them looked outside government contracts for business opportunities, or even quit the shipping business altogether.

XIV

THE FAMILY FIRM

Although maritime ventures and public works contracts enterprises were often conducted on a large scale and involved considerable sums of money, they were characterised by their impermanence. Even the great tax collection companies had a predetermined lifespan, since they operated on five-year contracts. Yet not all Roman trade and industry was conducted on a short-term, opportunistic basis. A proportion, unquantifiable, of Roman business was conducted by sizeable organisations that may be described as family firms. By family firm I mean a business enterprise financed from a family's inherited wealth (*patrimonium*) that was engaged in trade and manufacturing, employed a substantial workforce and lasted over more than one generation. This chapter is principally concerned with three family firms drawn from different periods and engaged in very different types of business. Other family firms are treated more briefly in Appendix 4.

ESTATE-BASED ENTERPRISES

The place to begin has to be the landed estate, where it was common for the elite paterfamilias to invest in mining, quarrying and manufacturing enterprises. An early example of estate-based enterprise is provided by the elder Cato, exponent of traditional Roman values but nonetheless a hard-nosed businessman:[1]

> When he began to apply himself more energetically to making money, he came to regard agriculture as a pastime (*diagoge*) rather than as a source of income (*prosodos*), and he invested his capital in solid enterprises which involved the minimum of risk. He bought ponds, hot springs, land devoted to producing fuller's earth, pitch factories, and estates which were rich in pasture land or forest. All these undertakings brought in large revenues (*polla chremata*) and could not, to use his own phrase, be ruined by Jupiter [i.e. by the vicissitudes of the weather].

It was Cato who had advised the would-be entrepreneur, 'You must borrow from yourself' (*a te mutuum sumes*).[2] In other words, a new business venture should ideally be financed from the *patrimonium*, which has been passed down through the generations, rather than by taking out a loan from a third party. If Cato had his way, Plutarch commented, a man would be honoured 'almost as a god' if when he died he was found to have added to his patrimony more than he had inherited.[3]

Writing in the late first century BC, Varro positively encouraged his readers to invest family funds in business. He suggested activities that might be carried out for profit on an estate: spinning, weaving and other crafts; the exploitation of clay pits (*figlinae*), mines (*fodinae*), stone quarries (*lapicidinae*) and sandpits (*harenariae*); and running an inn (*tabernae deversoriae*).[4]

Examples of similar enterprises are discussed in the Digest:[5]

> May the farmer [with a life interest in a property] open stone quarries (*lapidicinae*) or chalk pits (*cretifodinae*) or sand pits (*harenifodinae*)? My opinion is that he is entitled to do so, providing he does not appropriate for this purpose land that is required for something else. Accordingly he can search for sites suitable for quarries and other similar mining operations; therefore he can either work such mines of gold, silver, sulphur, copper, iron or other minerals as were opened up by the owner, or he can open such mines himself, providing this does not harm the cultivation of the land.

After mining and quarrying, the manufacture of clay bricks, tiles and pottery containers was an obvious avenue of diversification. The manufacture of jars (*amphorae*) or storage vats (*dolia*) is specifically mentioned by the jurist Paul.[6] Were the slave potters (*figuli*) who worked in the pottery yards (*figlinae*) to be considered as part of the equipment (*instrumentum*) of the farm if they worked on agricultural tasks for most of the year?[7] And among the members of an estate owner's household (*familia rustica*) there might be a whole squad of craftsmen – builders (*fabri*), fullers (*fullones*), spinners (*lanificae*) and weavers (*textores*) – all or any of whom could doubtless be set to working for profit.[8] An estate might also include a *taberna* – a workshop, a shop or an inn – which could serve the general public.[9] We may conclude that on some, perhaps many, rural estates a proportion of the workforce produced goods and services for the open market.

Similarly in Rome a great man's household (*familia urbana*) might include a large labour force over and above the staff employed purely on domestic duties. As we saw in Chapter 12, craftsmen (*fabri*) and builders (*fabri tignarii*) were commemorated in the family tomb (*columbarium*) of the Statilii Tauri; and both Agrippa, Augustus' chief lieutenant, and the emperor Claudius supplied skilled slaves for the maintenance of Rome's aqueducts.[10]

Even, or perhaps especially, the imperial household might be engaged in moneymaking activity. We have already come across several instances in the Murecine archive of imperial slaves and freedmen actively involved in commerce. Similarly a tailor (*vestifex*) or an engraver (*caelator*) working for the emperor might well sell products and services to other wealthy customers.[11] In the second century the particular commercial interest of emperors was in the production of lead pipes and bricks, where imperial freedmen were employed as workshop managers (*officinatores*). The output of these factories is marked in the archaeological record by such products as the tile stamped 'made on the estate of Domitia Lucilla at the Lesser Domitian claypits by Aelius Alexander'.[12] Domitia Lucilla is to be identified as the mother of the emperor Marcus Aurelius; Aelius Alexander will have been her workshop manager (*officinator*).

THE SESTII OF COSA

And now for our three elite family firms. The first and best documented is the manufacturing and shipping enterprise of the Sestii, a senatorial family with estates at Cosa in Etruria. The family of the Sestii originated at Fregellae (*Fabrateria Nova*), north of Naples, and Sestii are attested among the Roman traders on Delos in the second century BC. The particular Sestii with whom we are concerned are three generations from the first century BC.[13] First there is the equestrian Lucius Sestius, whom Cicero described as wise, pious and earnest (*sapiens, sanctus, severus*); he was a man 'who did not so much wish to hold [senatorial] offices as to appear worthy to hold them' (*reliquis honoribus non tam uti voluit quam dignus videri*).[14] He sounds rather like Atticus, another wealthy equestrian, who rejected politics in favour of 'honest leisure' (*honestum otium*).[15] Atticus devoted himself in part to making money on his own account and in part to handling the affairs of his wealthy friends (see Appendix 8). Lucius Sestius most probably devoted most of his time and attention to running the family business.

In the next two generations the Sestii produced senators who became involved in the hectic politics of the late Republic.[16] Publius Sestius, son of the equestrian Lucius, was quaestor at Rome in 63 BC, the momentous year of Cicero's consulship. He played his part in quelling the Catilinarian conspiracy and later worked hard for Cicero's recall from exile. When Publius Sestius was prosecuted for public disorder (*vis*) in 56 BC, he was defended by a team of talented lawyers, Crassus, Hortensius and Cicero, and acquitted. He was prosecuted later for corruption (*ambitus*), was again defended by Cicero and again acquitted. After serving as propraetor in Cilicia in 49 BC, Publius Sestius joined the Caesarian party. However Publius' son, Lucius Sestius Quirinalis, the third of our Sestii, joined the opposition party, the tyrannicides, in 44 BC. We shall return to this Lucius Sestius shortly.

Light is thrown on the business interests of the first-century Sestii from traces in the archaeological record, from chance references in Cicero's letters and from an unusual quarter, an ode dedicated by Horace to Lucius Sestius the younger. First, the archaeological record.[17] Worldwide attention was focused on the products of the Sestius family firm in 1952, when the French underwater diver and photographer Jacques Cousteau explored an ancient shipwreck on the rocks of the Grand Congloué, an island off the French coast at Marseilles. In the wreck he discovered thousands of *amphorae* bearing on their rims the letters SES, SETS or SEST which together with accompanying symbols (anchors, tridents and other devices) were evidently trademarks of the house of the Sestii. On the basis of finds of similar *amphorae* in precisely dated contexts at the Athenian Agora, it was established, after several years of scholarly dispute, that the Grand Congloué *amphorae* bearing the Sestius trademarks are to be dated to the late second or early first centuries BC.

Meanwhile excavations over many years at the town and harbour of Cosa in Etruria uncovered several thousand *amphorae*; analysis of the finds was completed in 1979. This analysis revealed a preponderance of Sestius stamps among *amphorae* found on both the town and the harbour sites. In a seminal article published in 1979 Will stated, 'since Cosa was apparently not an entrepôt, and since the figures [of Sestius *amphorae*] for Cosa, and especially for the Portus Cosanus, are so high, we have strong circumstantial evidence that a factory for the manufacture of Sestius *amphorae* existed near Cosa, quite probably in the area of the port'.

Will has also considered the ownership, in different generations, of the Sestius factory. At this point we move to the literary record. Various allusions in Cicero's letters indicate that Publius Sestius owned property at Cosa; Cicero even described him in a letter to Atticus as 'our man from Cosa' (*noster Cosanus*).[18] Publius Sestius was wealthy, too. The poet Catullus referred to the costly dinners (*sumptuosae cenae*) that he provided for his guests.[19] In 62 BC Cicero sent Publius Sestius an obliquely worded plea for financial assistance; almost two decades later, towards the end of his life, Cicero told another correspondent that he owed Publius Sestius a great debt (*ego illi uni plurimum debeo*).[20]

As already noted, Lucius Sestius, son of Publius, chose the losing side in the political manoeuvres that surrounded Caesar's assassination. He served as proquaestor under Marcus Brutus in Macedonia, was prosecuted on Brutus' defeat at Philippi and deprived of his citizenship. He was later pardoned by Augustus but continued to display images of his defeated leader in his house. His forthrightness appealed to Augustus who praised him and chose him to become suffect consul in 23 BC.[21]

It is this Sestius who has come down to posterity as the dedicatee of Horace Ode 1.4, *Solvitur acris hiems*. The Latin text is given in Appendix 10; this translation is by the Victorian scholar J. Conington:[22]

> The touch of Zephyr and of Spring has loosen'd Winter's thrall;
> The well-dried keels are wheel'd again to sea:
> The ploughman cares not for his fire, nor cattle for their stall,
> And frost no more is whitening all the lea.
> Now Cytherea leads the dance, the bright moon overhead;
> The Graces and the Nymphs, together knit,
> With rhythmic feet the meadow beat, while Vulcan, fiery red,
> Heats the Cyclopian forge in Aetna's pit.

'Tis now the time to wreathe the brow with branch of myrtle green,
Or flowers, just opening to the vernal breeze;
Now Faunus claims his sacrifice among the shady treen,
Lambkin or kidling, which soe'er he please.
Pale Death, impartial, walks his round; he knocks at cottage-gate
And palace-portal. Sestius, child of bliss!
How should a mortal's hopes be long, when short his being's date?
Lo here! the fabulous ghosts, the dark abyss,
The void of the Plutonian hall, where soon as e'er you go,
No more for you shall leap the auspicious die
To seat you on the throne of wine; no more your breast shall glow
For Lycidas, the star of every eye.

In this ode Horace is ostensibly celebrating the return of spring and calling on Sestius to make the most of the time that is left to him. The seasons come and go; we mortals die once and for all; let us enjoy our lives while we can. But in this poem the generalities of the familiar theme of *carpe diem* are personalised by an undercurrent of allusion. Lucius Sestius has been pardoned by Augustus for his support of the tyrannicides; his return to the circle of the ruling elite is being celebrated. In line 2, the ships with their dry keels (*siccae carinae*), which have been pulled well clear of the water for the winter, are being hauled down to the sea by winches (*machinae*). It was common knowledge that the Sestii had contributed fine ships (*navigia luculenta*) to Brutus' cause.[23] While he was away at war and afterwards, while he was in disgrace, Lucius had neglected the family shipping business. For some years the family's merchant fleet has been out of commission; now the ships can be put to work again. In line 7 Vulcan, god of the smithy fire, visits the workshops (*officinae*) of the Cyclops: the furnaces of the Sestii's pottery kilns can be lit again.

It may not be too far-fetched to see in the 'palace-portal' (*regum turris*) of line 14 the turreted villas of the ager Cosanus.[24] Certainly 'O beate Sesti' in the same line suggests a man blessed with worldly wealth. And lastly, what are we to make of the warning in lines 17-19 that once he is in Pluto's grim house Sestius will no longer cast lots to be Ruler of the Wine (*nec regna vini sortiere talis*)? Horace is warning Lucius Sestius that in the underworld there are no ceremonial banqueting rituals; but perhaps he is also alluding to the vineyards owned by the Sestii in Etruria, which, along with their ships and their potteries, their arable land and their pastures, contributed to the family's prosperity.

The earliest Sestius trademarks do not reveal the identity of the member of the family responsible for the manufacture of the *amphorae*. However several stamps on Dressel 1 vessels provide us with the name of L. Sestius and can be dated to the latter part of the second quarter of the first century BC. Thus Lucius Sestius the younger, immortalised by Horace, is the first Sestius who can be positively identified as a manufacturer of *amphorae* found at Cosa.

The firm's history may be summarised. The Sestius enterprise achieved great prosperity over a period of a hundred years or so, beginning in the second half of the second century BC. *Amphorae* bearing Sestius trademarks from this period have been discovered along the coasts and the principal rivers of France and as far north as the Celtic *oppidum* of Manching on the Danube. Diversification during the years of the firm's heyday is indicated by finds of other Sestius containers that seem to have been designed to carry fish sauce (*garum*).[25] Production of *amphorae* seems to have ceased in the second half of the first century BC, possibly as the result of the proscription of L. Sestius and the confiscation of his property. After his pardon, the family firm diversified into brick manufacture both at Cosa and, interestingly, at Rome, where the Augustan building boom created a market for fired *tegulae*, a new form of bricks.[26]

Settefinestre

It is tempting to associate with the business enterprise of the Sestii the extensively excavated villa of Settefinestre in the ager Cosanus. The excavations at Settefinestre revealed that the villa was fronted by a miniature 'town wall' with turrets; it possessed spacious accommodation for the family, *cellae* identified as slave quarters, a walled orchard and three gardens. There were several presses for wine and oil production and the site has yielded large quantities of Dressel 1 and Dressel 2-4 *amphorae*.[27] The building of Settefinestre, however, has been dated to 40 BC, when the fortunes of the Sestii had taken a turn for the worse and no direct connection with the family has been established. What we can say is that Settefinestre was the site of large-scale wine production. The villa fits into a pattern of economic activity in northern Etruria that has been further illuminated by a field survey of three *coloniae* – Cosa, Saturnia and Heba.[28] This study concluded that wine was produced for the Mediterranean market, beginning in the second century BC, at large 'rationally managed' villas.

The core business

So much for the broad picture. It is time to fill in some details about the way the Sestii conducted their business during the years of their greatest prosperity. It is legitimate, I believe, to construct a model of the firm's operations; when there is no direct evidence I have drawn on relevant material about Roman trading practice which is in keeping with what we do know about the firm's activities.

As I see it, the core business was built on three mutually supportive elements – wine production for export, pottery manufacture and shipping. The connections were straightforward: in their role as wine exporters the Sestii needed containers and on their estates they had access to clay and wood for *amphora* manufacture; the port of Cosa gave them facilities for shipbuilding and for running a sea-freight business. Furthermore the ownership and operation of freight vessels dovetailed nicely with the production of *amphorae*; this was because *amphorae* destined for overseas markets had to meet the specifications, as far as shape and size were concerned, that were laid down by the shippers. Since the Sestii owned the ships that carried cargoes of wine to Gaul, it made good business sense for them to produce the containers for those cargoes.

Customers and suppliers

I rule out the assumption that the enterprise was devoted to shipping wine grown only on estates owned by the family – on the grounds that the large number of Sestian *amphorae* which made up a single cargo is out of proportion to the wine production of a single estate or even a group of family-owned estates.[29] By the late second century BC the Sestii were evidently selling surplus capacity - both *amphorae* and cargo space – to outside customers. The Sestii could regard the wine growers of Etruria - including their own vineyards – either as their customers or as their suppliers. In practice, both ways of operating could have been adopted, consecutively or even simultaneously. The business was long-lived and evolved over time. Different heads of the family in different generations doubtless had different ideas about the best way to run the business.

Wine growers could be viewed as customers when the firm was principally concerned with selling the *amphorae* produced in the Sestii's kilns and selling cargo space on its sea-going freighters. In this phase of the business, *amphorae* would be supplied to the Sestii's own vineyards, to other Etrurian wine growers and to wine merchants who bought the crop at auction.[30] The vineyards owned by the Sestii may have paid a transfer price to the potteries for their containers, or they may have obtained the *amphorae* free of any direct charge. Third party growers and merchants, on the other hand, will have bought *amphorae* on commercial terms. The wine remained the property of the grower or the merchant; the Sestii made their profit from supplying empty containers and shipping them overseas when they had been filled.

The other way of running the business was for the Sestii to view Etrurian wine growers as their suppliers; their customers were then the wine buyers of Gaul. When the business was run on these lines, the Sestii would purchase wine from the growers or merchants, ship it in their own containers and market it overseas under their own brand name. Through running the business in this way, the Sestii could profit from adding value to the basic product.

Regardless of how the business might have begun, I suggest that this second method of operation was how the Sestii operated at the height of their commercial success. This would explain the importance and ubiquity of their trademarks: it was not the bulk container that had to appeal to overseas customers – the merchants, retailers and consumers of Gaul – but the wine that was being carried in the container. The brand name of the Sestii, built up over several generations, provided a guarantee of quality. This last point is of considerable importance. It suggests that the Sestii were prepared to bear any liability if an *amphora* of wine was found to have gone off when it was opened at its final destination. Much of the jurists' discussion of this issue is based on the premise that the vendor is the original wine producer and the purchaser is the end-consumer.[31] But Gaius does recognise that transactions may involve a merchant who regularly buys and sells wine (*mercator qui emere vina et vendere solet*).[32] Contracts of sale between the Sestii and their distributors in Gaul would be drawn up in accordance with local practice:[33]

The measures and prices with which merchants (*negotiatores*) deal in wine are a matter for the contracting parties; no one is obliged to sell, if dissatisfied with the price or the measures, especially when nothing is done contrary to the custom of the region.

Logistics

The wine destined for overseas markets had first to be transported from the vineyards to the docks. Some light on this stage of the process is provided by a passage in the Digest:[34]

> We draw off wine into jars (*amphorae*) and containers (*cadi*) with the intention that it remain in them until it is poured out for use, and we certainly sell it along with these jars and containers. We place it in vats (*dolia*), however, with a different intention, namely that we may subsequently either draw it off from these vats into *amphorae* and *cadi* or that it may be sold without the vats themselves.

This indicates that it was usual for wine to be stored initially by the growers in large vats and later drawn off by them into smaller containers – presumably for sale to shops, bars, inns and even affluent private houses. Wine might also be sold for carrying away in wineskins (*utres*) or leather bottles (*cullei*).[35] Wine merchants in the inland trade could bring their own containers – *amphorae*, wineskins or leather bottles – to the vineyard for filling. Businessmen in the export business, however, might make other arrangements: Varro noted that in the region of Brundisium and in Apulia, merchants (*mercatores*) employed trains of donkeys with panniers (*greges asellis dossuariis*) to carry oil, wine, grain and other products to the coast.[36] At Cosa this method of working would have enabled growers or merchants to send the wine down to the coast in skins so that it could be poured into the *amphorae* (produced, as noted above, in potteries near the docks) for shipment overseas. This would have been more economic than sending the empty *amphorae* inland and then carrying them back again to the coast when filled.

Direct labour, contractors and agents

A complex business is now beginning to emerge from this analysis. The Sestii were involved in a series of interconnected operations. These included: the manufacture of *amphorae* in potteries at Cosa, potteries which were supplied with clay and fuel from their estates; the transportation of wine from inland vineyards to the coast; filling the *amphorae* with wine for overseas shipment; marshalling freight vessels at the docks; assembling porters to load these vessels and seamen to crew them; and then the sea voyage itself. At the port of destination, cargoes had to be unloaded at the docks and shipped inland by road or river to inland markets.

Although these various activities were coordinated by the Sestii, the family did not necessarily own all the business units involved. It must be a strong presumption that the Sestii owned potteries at Cosa and the freighters that carried cargoes of wine overseas. They owned some of the vineyards that produced the wine for export. However, other links in the long supply chain that led to the markets of Gaul may well have been supplied by outside contractors and by agents. Take – purely for illustration – the transportation of wine from inland vineyards to the docks at Cosa. Did the Sestii really get involved in all this? It was, after all, seasonal work – just as the grape harvest itself was seasonal work – and it was easier and more economical to let out the work to sub-contractors. Even so, the Sestii had to exercise control over this phase of the operation. Tenders for bids had to be issued to muleteers and wagoners, contracts had to be negotiated and agreed, the contractors' performance had to be monitored and, when necessary, contracts had to be enforced at law.

The operation of the firm's sea-going freighters was, I imagine, entrusted to shipmasters, usually slaves from the *familia* who had been given specific appointments and who therefore held the legal status of *institores*. Agents, also *institores* drawn from the *familia*, will have handled incoming cargoes at the port of destination in southern Gaul, made the necessary payments to customs, agreed contracts with local merchants for the cargoes of wine and entered into other contracts for the purchase of goods to be carried back to Cosa on the return run. These agents had to be chosen from among the most able and trustworthy slaves and freedmen, given formal appointments, equipped with funds and provided with accommodation. Probably the performance of agents was monitored through periodic visits by senior management. We happen to know that Publius Sestius visited Marseilles, at some time in the early 50s BC, with his second wife Cornelia.[37] The visit was ostensibly to meet his new father-in-law, L. Cornelius Scipio Asiaticus, who was living in exile in Gaul; no doubt the visit provided an opportunity for Publius Sestius to check up on the firm's overseas staff – and to make or refresh business contacts.

To set in motion and keep running all this activity, the Sestii had to deploy and manage a substantial labour force of slaves and freedmen; in addition, they and their agents had to negotiate commercial terms with trading partners who could have included, at different times, any or all of a host of contractors – shipbuilders, wagoners, shippers, and merchants in Gaul. The firm was engaged in a logistical exercise that matched in complexity the supplying and deployment of a legion. The comparison is apposite. Members of the Sestii family, in different generations, will have had opportunities to observe how professional soldiers managed the logistics of military supply since - like most members of the Roman aristocracy – they will have served for limited periods as officers in the army.

THE UMBRICII SCAURI OF POMPEII

The Umbricii Scauri of Pompeii, our second family firm, ran a very different type of business from the Sestii – they supplied branded foodstuffs to the Italian market.[38] The Umbricii were a *gens* of Etruscan origin; they are attested among the Italian traders on Delos in about 100 BC.[39] Umbricii occur at Pompeii as participants in, or witnesses to, transactions carried out by the auctioneer/banker L. Caecilius Jucundus. Umbricia Antiochis was a vendor at two, possibly three, of Jucundus' auction sales (Chapter 7), Umbricia Januaria was a vendor at another and A. Umbricius Modestus was a witness on two occasions.[40]

The member of the *gens* with whom we are now concerned is the elder Aulus Umbricius Scaurus, producer in Pompeii of the fish-based products *garum* and *liquamen*. His son, also Aulus Umbricius Scaurus, was a magistrate of Pompeii. Their relationship and other details are recorded in the sepulchral inscription on the family tomb outside the Herculaneum Gate:[41]

> To Aulus Umbricius Scaurus, the son of Aulus, of the tribe Menenia; duumvir with judicial authority. The decurions decreed to this man the site for a monument and HS2,000 towards his funeral and an equestrian statue to be placed in the Forum. Scaurus the father to his son.

This inscription tells us that the younger Scaurus had attained high office in Pompeii, that of duumvir; the grant of money towards his funeral costs suggests that he died in office. In fact Scaurus was especially honoured. The award of an equestrian statue (which has not survived) in the forum puts him in the company of the only other Pompeian we know to have to been so honoured, Quintus Sallustius.[42] Sallustius was also a senior magistrate; in his case he held the prestigious office of Fifth Year Magistrate, whose chief responsibility was the revision of the register of local property owners (*album*). In addition Sallustius was honoured by his fellow Pompeians as patron of the town (*patronus coloniae*). For the younger Scaurus to be honoured on a par with such a distinguished citizen suggests that he was highly regarded by his fellow citizens.

The elder Scaurus imported his raw material from Spain, a noted centre of the fish processing industry: his name in the genitive case appears on an *amphora* from southern Spain along with that of the shipper Marcus Valerius Euphemus.[43] But Scaurus senior produced his fish sauces in Pompeii. We may even hazard a guess that the house at 1.12.8, where six large *dolia* in the peristyle were used as processing vats, was his workshop; formerly a residential property, the building was converted to commercial use, probably after the earthquake of 62.[44]

The name of A. Umbricius Scaurus appears in painted labels (*tituli picti*) on more than fifty fish sauce containers, the long-necked jars known as *urcei*. From the labels we can see (a) that Scaurus produced fish sauce in his own workshop, (b) that production was carried out in workshops managed by members of his *familia* and (c) that some manufacture was carried out by franchisees:[45]

> (a) The flower of *garum* made from mackerel by Scaurus, from the workshop of Scaurus (*gari flos scombri Scauri ex officina Scauri*).

> (b) The flower of *garum* made from mackerel, the highest quality, from the workshop of Abascantus, [slave] of A. Umbricius (*gari flos scombri optimum ex officina A. Umbrici Abascanti*).

(c) The flower of *garum* made from mackerel by Scaurus, from the workshop of Agathopus, [slave] of Scaurus (*gari flos scombri Scauri ex officina Agathopi*).

Furthermore, it is possible to detect – through the preposition *ab* (which seems to indicate 'distributed by') – the names of retailers, some who were members of the *familia* and some who were not, who handled products originating in the Scaurus workshops. For instance, among names preceded by '*ab*' on containers of Scaurus' fish sauce there occur the names of (d) Eutyches, a slave of Scaurus and (e) Martialis, an imperial freedman:[46]

(d) The flower of *garum* made from mackerel by Scaurus, [distributed] by Eutyches, slave of Scaurus (*gari flos scombri Scauri ab Eutyche Scauri*).

(e) The flower of *garum* made from mackerel by Scaurus, from the workshop of Scaurus [distributed] by Martialis, freedman of the emperor (*gari flos scombri Scauri ex officina Scauri ab Martiale Augusti liberto*).

In summary, Umbricius Scaurus was a member of an old-established Pompeian family. He invested family money in a business where there were handsome profits to be made – as we saw in Chapter 6, *garum* could be sold at high prices – and he was proud of the increased wealth that this brought him. His family was not socially disadvantaged by his decision to pursue a business career: his son was elected to the office of duumvir and on his early death was granted the rare honour of having an equestrian statue erected to him.

The integration of firm and family is displayed in the large town house of the Umbricii Scauri (VII Ins. Occ. 12-15), which is built on two levels. The main entrance, No. 13, has been dated to the second century BC. Entrance 15, however, which is constructed in *opus reticulatum* framed in brick, does not predate the Augustan period. This entrance leads into an atrium with a floor decorated in white and black *opus tessellatum*. At each corner of the *impluvium* is a representation of an *urceus*, carrying the *titulus pictus* that would appear on many real-life sauce jars. Two of these labels record that the jar contained *garum* and two *liquamen*; and three of the four mention *Scaurus*. Visitors to the house of the Scauri, whether for business or social purposes, could have been left in no doubt that the family was wealthy and that their wealth derived from trade.

THE SECUNDINII OF TRIER

My third case study, that of the Secundinii of Trier, is drawn from Gallia Belgica in the third century AD. This takes us beyond the parameters of geography and time that provide the framework of this book, but I include it because it provides a unique window into the textile industry, which was probably the largest employer of people and resources in the Roman empire.[47]

A traveller approaching Trier (Augusta Treverorum) along the Mosel valley would have come to a tower-tomb some five miles to the south-west of the city.[48] The roads leading to a Roman city were often lined with burial monuments since, by ancient law, the interment of bodies or ashes was forbidden within city boundaries.[49] The number and size of these tombs might stand as an advertisement of the city's wealth and prosperity; at Aquileia for instance six of the roads that radiated from the city were lined with funerary monuments, which in places appear to have stood 5ft deep.[50] However this particular tomb in the Mosel valley (located in the village of Igel and generally known as the Igel Column) was an isolated monument located presumably on land belonging to a family estate. The (now fragmentary) inscription on the south face, the first to be seen by passers-by, indicated that the brothers Lucius Secundinius Aventinus and Lucius Secundinius Securus had commissioned the tomb in honour of their deceased relatives and themselves (*parentibus defunctis et sibi*).[51]

The brothers have commemorated six deceased persons. First they mention their father Publius Aelius Secundinus; he is described as *evocatus Augusti*, that is to say he had served for at least sixteen years in the imperial praetorian guard and was then, most likely, promoted to officer rank.[52] Then come two sons of Secundinius Securus, whose names have not survived, followed by Publia Pacata, wife of Secundinius Aventinus, and two other people, Lucius Saccius Modestus and his son Modestius Macedo. Above the inscription is a tall vertical panel; this depicts the two brothers and a very young man, one of Securus' sons, whose death and departure to the next world are the focus of this commemoration. Father and son clasp hands in a scene of leave taking. Portraits of three other family members (one of them a woman) appear in medallions above the brothers' heads. One of the males commemorated in the medallions is presumably the brothers' father, Publius Aelius Secundinus, the paterfamilias to whom the monument is principally dedicated; the woman is probably Publia Pacata. The third portrait, that of another very young man, may be the other son of Securus, who had predeceased his brother. The remaining two dedicatees, Lucius Saccius Modestus and his son Modestius Macedo, are not portrayed. Their names suggest that they were not immediate members of the family; who they were is a question to which I shall return later.

When our traveller had read and digested this information he would no doubt inspect the remainder of the scenes portrayed on the south side. If his attention was sufficiently engaged, he could then progress round the other three sides of the monument and view the rest of the extensive programme of reliefs commissioned by the Secundinii brothers to proclaim the ideals and achievements of their family.

THE SCULPTURAL PROGRAMME OF THE IGEL COLUMN

	SOUTH SIDE	EAST SIDE	NORTH SIDE	WEST SIDE
STEPS	[Damaged]	[Damaged]	River transport	River transport
BASE	Sale of cloth	Weaver's workshop (?)	Trussing the bale	Wagon
MAIN PANEL	Family portraits and inscription	Achilles and Thetis	Apotheosis of Hercules	Perseus and Andromeda
FRIEZE	Family meal	Kitchen	Transport over the mountains.	Payment of rent in kind
ATTIC	Examination of cloth	Counting house	Eros and Griffins	Travelling into town
PEDIMENT	Hylas and nymphs	Moon	Sun	Mars and Rhea-Silvia

This programme not only encompasses both the sacred and the profane but it also blends scenes from everyday family life with scenes of commercial transactions. The traveller is left in no doubt that commerce is the source of the family's prosperity. Two scenes that establish the nature of the family business are shown on the south side of the column, in close proximity to the portraits of past and present members of the Secundinii family. One is the sale of cloth (portrayed on the base); the other is the examination of cloth (on the attic storey).

The sale of cloth
The setting is a room with a shelf running just above head height along the back wall; the shelf can be closed off from view with curtains, which at present are tied back to display its contents. In the middle of the shelf is a display case. A bolt of cloth hangs open over the case; more bolts of cloth hang over the curtain rail. Lengths of folded cloth are stacked on smaller shelves. In front of and below the main shelf two transactions are taking place. On the left of the panel a man in Gallic sleeved costume sits at a table on which is a pile of coins. He holds a waxed tablet. Behind the man with the ledger are two more men, while behind the table four men are concerned with counting the coins. Another man stands in the background, almost in the middle of the relief; he is watching the coins being counted.

The right-hand scene shows a group of six men also in Gallic costume standing by a table where a length of cloth is being displayed. The man on the left lifts up the cloth, which others are examining. The two men on the right seem to be bystanders, although one is carrying another bolt of cloth over his shoulder.

The quantities of cloth on display, the number of people who are working there and the amount of money changing hands suggest that this is a warehouse where bolts of cloth are sold to garment manufacturers, rather than a shop where goods are sold to the general public.

The examination of cloth

The scene is a room with doorways at either end. Through the door on the left a man enters carrying a long bolt of cloth on his shoulder. A second man offers to take the bolt from him and a third man standing in the background is also looking towards the new arrival. In the middle of the room is a large pile of folded lengths of cloth. Two men are examining a length of cloth that has just arrived. On the right a clerk records the result of the examination on a waxed tablet. Two men are standing in the background, watching the examination; one of them, who looks anxious, may be the person whose cloth is being inspected at this very moment. This looks like another scene from the warehouse: weavers are bringing in their finished products and the warehouse staff are carrying out a detailed examination, to ensure that the firm's quality requirements are being met. These two scenes of commercial life, the first to be seen by passers-by, convey a direct message. They indicate that the business of the Secundinii is the supply of cloth to the garment trade and that the cloth they sell is subject to rigorous examination before it reaches the customer. These scenes amount, in effect, to an advertisement for the family business.

If the traveller followed round the column in a clockwise direction he would come across other scenes depicting the commercial activities of the Secundinii and reinforcing the initial message on the south side of the monument. On the east side the base of the column is badly damaged, but the relief appears to show a man sitting in a room, his arms outstretched; it has been conjectured that he may be a weaver working at his loom. The Secundinii, therefore, may have had interests in the weaving trade.

Paying suppliers and outworkers

The relief on the attic storey of the east side of the column is in better condition. It depicts a room with doorways at either end. In the middle of the room is a large table. A clerk in a sleeved tunic stands behind the table counting coins; at the end of the table another clerk in a tunic sits in a carved chair; he is checking a ledger inscribed on a wax tablet. In addition to the two clerks, the relief shows four men wearing the hooded cloaks of Gallic tribesmen. One is entering the room from the left; he carries a sack over his shoulder from which he pours coins on to the table. The other three Treverans are watching the clerk who is counting the coins. One of them is holding up the fingers of his right hand and tapping his neighbour on the shoulder, apparently to draw his attention; the neighbour seems to be counting on his fingers (*27*).

This scene is usually interpreted as the payment of rent by tenants in the estate counting house. It has been suggested, however, that the scene depicts not the payment of rent by tenants, but payments made to local people who have undertaken work for the Secundinii.[53] I find this suggestion entirely plausible, not least because the payment of rent (in kind but not in cash) is depicted in another scene from the Igel Column – on the frieze on the west side, where a line of countrymen holding country produce walk in file towards a single figure standing in a doorway.[54]

I take it that in this scene from the east side of the column the Treveran who is pouring out the coins from a sack is a member of the counting house staff; and I suggest that the men who are making calculations on their fingers, and watching the counting of the coins so carefully, are people who are being paid by the Secundinii. Some will be suppliers, some will be craftsmen. The suppliers will be sheep farmers who provide the Secundinii with fleeces - the starting point of the whole wool textile production process. The craftsmen are outworkers, carrying out the various textile processes in their homes. In addition to spinners and weavers many specialist craftsmen and women were employed in the manufacture of woollen cloth: in Cisalpine Gaul, for instance, we encounter woolcombers (*pectinatores, lanari pectinarii, lanari coactores* and *carminatores*), dyers (*infectores* and *purpurarii*) and fullers (*lotores*).[55]

The narrative of the Igel Column indicates, then, that the Secundinii were cloth merchants who controlled a complex chain of production. The starting point was the purchase of fleeces from sheep farmers; the raw wool was then transferred along the links in the chain of outworkers – the woolcombers, the spinners, the weavers, the dyers and the finishers. At each stage the Secundinii paid fees to the craftsmen involved; at the end of the chain they took delivery of the bales of finished cloth. In and around Trier they could draw on a pool of skilled labour. The city was building a reputation as an important centre of the textile trade: woollen cloaks produced by the Treveri were to be capped at a maximum price of 8,000 *denarii* in the Prices Edict of the emperor Diocletian.[56] Later, in the fourth century, the city was a prime supplier of clothing, provisions and weapons to the imperial armies stationed along the Rhine frontier (*imperii vires…alit…vestit et armat*).[57]

Markets
Other scenes from the Igel Column depict mules carrying packs across a range of hills surmounted by a building which may be a customs post and bales being transported by road and by water (presumably up the Mosel). Overland portage from the higher reaches of the Mosel to the Saône and then by river again to the Rhone at Lyon is likely: inscriptions recording *nautae* and *negotiatores* are clustered around the Rhone-Saône axis and suggest heavy traffic. All this suggests that the Secundinii did not extend their interests as far as the production of finished garments. Their business was the supply of fine grade woollen cloth to far-flung markets; only good quality cloth could command high prices and thus repay the costs of long-distance carriage. We may take it then that among the customers of the Secundinii were the garment makers of northern Italy.

The Secundinii may be seen as the forerunners of the great wool merchants of the Middle Ages, who had their raw material processed by outworkers whom they paid by the piece. This business process was familiar to the Roman jurists: 'if you dye my wool, the now purple wool remains mine…'[58] The expertise of the merchant lay in purchasing the best wools, in selecting the most skilled sub-contractors, in maintaining consistent standards and in marketing finished fabrics. And at the end of the chain it was the wool merchant who sold the finished cloth and took the profits.[59]

We may now speculate about the role of the two men commemorated on the Igel Column who do not appear to be members of the immediate family. I suggest that Lucius Saccius Modestus and his son Modestius Macedo may have been senior managers (freedmen procurators perhaps) who supervised outworkers in the long production chain that linked woolcombers, spinners, weavers, dyers and finishers; alternatively they may have been agents who travelled to centres of textile production – among them Padua (Patavium) and Modena (Mutina) – to act as the firm's representatives.[60]

GENERAL MANAGEMENT

In the discussion that follows I shall take the Sestii of Cosa as a typical family firm but, mutatis mutandis, similar observations may be made about other family enterprises. Business undertakings of this size and complexity required trained personnel. They had to employ line managers for vineyards, potteries and shipping operations; they required commercial managers to negotiate and oversee contracts with trading partners in Italy; and they needed agents to represent them overseas. Family firms were able to stay in business and flourish only because they were well organised and competently managed. Where could a paterfamilias find managers of the appropriate calibre?

The most detailed information on business organisation in the Roman world comes from the companies of tax collectors (*societates publicanorum*). As we saw in the last chapter, the company that farmed a group of taxes in Sicily was controlled by directors (*magistri*) and shareholders (*socii*) based in Rome; in the province its business was carried out by a locally-based managing director (*promagister*) whose staff, in addition to the tax collectors themselves, included clerks, porters and messengers. The company's officers, while not senators, were equestrian members of the elite: for instance in the Asian tax company of the late 60s BC Gnaeus Plancius was *magister* in Rome and P. Terentius Hispo was *promagister* in the province.[61]

It is hardly surprising that a *societas publicanorum*, which had a contractual responsibility to the government and was required to account for its activities to outside shareholders, was organised in this formal way and drew its management from the Roman elite. However the firm of the Sestii at Cosa was family-owned; it had to draw its managers from members of the household, the *familia*. This can be put another way. Only the head of a large *familia* would have the resources of personnel to run a manufacturing and trading firm of this size and complexity.

If the paterfamilias wanted advice on important issues he could convene a family council made up of relatives and friends (*consilium propinquorum et amicorum*) to advise him. Generally summoned to deal with issues touching on the honour of the family, such as the allegedly improper behaviour of a son or wife, the *consilium* might be convened for other matters, for instance to ratify the manumission of slaves.[62] Advice was not necessarily sought or proffered on a formal basis: 'as usual, I am including you among my advisers (*adsumo te in consilium rei familiaris, ut soleo*),' Pliny wrote to his friend Calvisius Rufus, when he was considering the purchase of an estate adjoining his property in Tifernum.[63] Over the years, doubtless, heads of the Sestii family turned to their relatives and friends to discuss major issues of business strategy: expansion into a new overseas market; the launching of a new product line at Cosa; or investment in brick and tile manufacture near Rome.

The procurator

One of the first decisions to be taken by any paterfamilias who wished to launch a business was the selection of a procurator, to act as general manager. This should not have been too difficult. Men of property were accustomed to employ a procurator to head up their household and to look after their affairs. The procurator was usually a freedman and might have been manumitted specially to take up the appointment.[64] Originally a mandate to act on someone's behalf was gratuitous.[65] But by the early Empire it seems to have become common for a procurator to receive a salary.[66]

A procurator was, strictly speaking, the representative of someone who was absent:[67]

> Someone is rightly (*legitime*) called a procurator who administers all the property of someone who is away from Italy or is absent [from his property] on public business (*rei publicae causa*), who is almost the owner (*paene dominus*), that is who acts as the legal representative of someone else (*alieni iuris vicarius*). He may be your tenant (*colonus*), your neighbour (*vicinus*), your client, your freedman or anyone who exercises power, including the act of expulsion, for you at your request or in your name.

During the late Republic or early Empire the ancient Roman laws governing possession and ownership were amended to enable a procurator to act as his principal's agent. This presumably reflected the increasing use of independent persons, i.e. people other than the principal's slaves or children, to enter into commercial contracts on a principal's behalf. The jurist Neratius stated in the late first century:[68]

> If my procurator buys something for me on my instruction, and it is delivered to him in my name, ownership...in it is acquired by me although I am unaware of the delivery.

Gaius ruled half a century later:[69]

> If someone has been given free administration of the affairs of the owner, who is going on a journey, and he sells and delivers something, he makes it the property of the recipient.

And in the early third century Ulpian summed up the procurator's role as the business agent of his principal:[70]

> Payment [in settlement of a debt] is validly made to a genuine procurator. Now we accept as a genuine procurator one who has either been given a special mandate or has been entrusted with the administration of affairs generally (*omnium negotiorum administratio*).

For a wealthy Roman with business interests the procurator was an essential member of the household; indeed a man with many interests might employ several procurators. For instance, Cicero's wealthy friend L. Aelius Lamia managed his *negotia* in Africa through *procuratores, liberti, familia*.[71]

Keeping accounts for the *familia* was usually part of the procurator's job. Indeed the first person that Trimalchio's guests saw after they had entered his house was the procurator, sitting in the dining room, where he was working on the books.[72] Seneca said that the master who becomes obsessed by his business interests is acting like a procurator:[73]

> He checks accounts, he wears out the pavement in the forum, he works at his ledger: he is no longer the master but the manager.

The other part of the procurator's job was to supervise the bailiff (*vilicus*) (or line manager in the case of a manufacturing unit) who was responsible for the day-to-day work of the farm or business. Acting on his patron's behalf a procurator even had the power to appoint a manager.[74] Columella describes the procurator's role on a country estate:[75]

> The bailiff (*vilicus*) should have his living quarters by the gate, so that he can keep an eye on people coming in and going out; the general manager (procurator) should have his quarters above the gate, for the same reason, and also so that he can keep a close watch on the bailiff.

The general managers of great men could become wealthy. One of the success stories of the early Empire was the career of M. Aurelius Zosimus, the freedman of M. Aurelius Cotta, consul in AD 20:[76]

> Marcus Aurelius Zosimus, freedman of Marcus Aurelius Cotta Maximus and official attendant (*accensus*) of his patron. I was a freedman, I confess; but in death I have been honoured by my patron Cotta. He generously gave me the equivalent of an equestrian's fortune (*census equestris*). He ordered me to raise my children, he helped support them, and he always entrusted his wealth to me (*suas commisit opes mihi semper*). He provided dowries for my daughters, as if he were their father. He obtained for my son Cottianus the rank of military tribune, which he proudly (*fortis*) held in the imperial army. What did Cotta not give us? And now he has with sadness paid for this message which can be read on my tombstone.

The vilicus

By contrast with the freedman procurator, the *vilicus* was usually a slave who had been specifically appointed as his master's bailiff or agent – that is to say he held the legal status of *institor* (see Chapters 2 and 6). He would run the business on an everyday basis; the *vilicus* would not necessarily be paid, but he may have made a good income on the side.

The role of bailiff on an agricultural estate set the pattern for the system of line management adopted in manufacturing or trading enterprises.[77] In addition to organising the work of the farm and supervising the labour force, the *vilicus* was expected to carry out a variety of managerial tasks, ranging from keeping detailed records and accounts to negotiating contracts. The bailiff's terms of reference would usually be spelled out in a formal letter, the *certa lex praepositionis*.[78] Contracts negotiated by an *institor* were binding on his master, provided that the bailiff stayed within his terms of appointment:[79]

> ...full liability attaches to the person who appoints another to lend money or to run a farm or to be a trader or a public contractor. And he will be liable on account of a slave whom he appoints to run a bank.

What was expected of the bailiff is laid down by Cato in his manual of farm management:[80]

> When the master arrives at the farm...let him go over the whole estate, if possible on the same day; if not at least on the next. When he has found out how work on the fields has progressed, what has been completed and what still remains to be done, let him summon his bailiff (*vilicus*) the next day, and ask him what work has been completed and what work remains to be done...whether he can finish the remainder within the stipulated time and what were the figures for wine, wheat and other products. Having obtained this information, he must calculate the time and labour consumed. If the amount of work done seems inadequate, but the bailiff...gives many excuses...you must recall him to your estimate of the work done and the labour employed. If it has been a rainy period, remind him of the work that could have been done on wet days....
>
> After all this has been done calmly (*aequo animo*), give orders for the completion of what work remains: run over each account....
>
> Give orders that any shortfall in the current year's supplies should be made up and any surpluses be sold; contracts should be let for whatever work needs to be put out to contract. Give directions as to what work you want done on the place and what you want let out, and leave the directions in writing.

More details are given by the other agricultural writers. Varro, for instance, says that bailiffs are expected to stay on the farm, except when travelling on business, and then not to be away for more than a day.[81] The ideal bailiff, according to Columella, was middle-aged, fit and knowledgeable about agriculture. A first-class memory was required and might be preferable to literacy: if a man could read and write he was more likely to cook the books.[82]

The job specification for a *vilicus* appointed to run a manufacturing unit was similar to that for the bailiff on a farm. His principal task, like that of the bailiff, was to supervise the labour force, the bulk of which was made up of slaves. The conditions under which slaves worked could be appalling: witness Diodorus Siculus' description of slave labour in the Spanish mines during the late Republic and Apuleius' grim picture of slaves at work in a flour mill in the second century AD.[83] It is difficult to believe, however, that similarly harsh conditions prevailed in potteries producing clay artefacts, where craftsmanship and technical skill were at a premium. Furthermore freeborn labourers (*mercennarii*) were employed in seasonal work on farms (at harvest time, for instance), in portering at the docks or on building sites.[84] It is quite likely that the Sestii employed *mercennarii* in industrial production. They would then have come under the direct control of a slave *vilicus*.

Vilici are widely attested both in agriculture and in industrial and commercial occupations. Inscriptions that are industry-specific provide instances of *vilici* acting as business managers in the perfume trade, the shoe trade and in shopkeeping; in warehouse management; in quarrying; in moneylending; and in tile and metal manufacture.[85] However we rarely hear of individual *institores*; one reason for this is presumably that *institor* is a legal category, rather than a job description. When *institores* do appear in the literary record, they are usually mentioned in derogatory terms, for instance as travelling salesmen. Indeed it is not possible to deduce from literary references that *institores* worked as agents for principals; as Aubert points out in his study of business managers, to make this connection would be to admit that the elite had an association with a disreputable class of people.[86] Similarly, the term *institor* appears infrequently in the epigraphic record: Aubert was able to find only five Latin inscriptions that mention the term.

The officinator

A multi-faceted business such as that of the Sestii would be composed of separate industrial units – potteries, shipyards and so on. The general term for such an establishment is an *officina*, which may be translated as a workshop; this would be managed by an *officinator*, the Roman equivalent of a foreman. But, as with *institores*, the literary sources hardly mention *officinatores*: one exception is Vitruvius, who says that it is the *officinator* who should receive the praise for fine workmanship on a building.[87] The term is used in a handful of inscriptions: Aubert lists just six business managers in Italy and Sicily who have been designated in this way.

In his attack on Verres, Cicero provides a caricature of an *officinator*. Cicero alleged that Verres had confiscated silver ornaments (*emblemata*) from the people of Syracuse and then set up a workshop where these ornaments were attached to gold cups and basins (which were presumably also stolen):[88]

[Verres] set up a workshop (*officina*) – a large one – in the palace at Syracuse [the governor's official residence, formerly the palace of the Syracusan kings]. He gave orders that all skilled workmen – engravers, metal workers and so on - should assemble there, in addition to the considerable number that he had in his own service. He penned the whole crowd in there. He gave them enough work to keep them busy for eight months without a break, and every vessel they produced was made of gold....The governor, himself, who tells us that peace was kept in Sicily because of his watchful attention, used to sit in this workshop for most of the day, dressed in a grey tunic and a Greek cloak (*cum tunica pulla et pallio*).

Cicero did not have to spell out to his audience that this was not the conduct or the dress expected of a Roman senator.

We may now summarise the management structure of a family firm such as that of the Sestii. The paterfamilias would probably appoint a freedman from his household to act as his general manager; the procurator was expected to keep a watchful eye on the various line managers (*vilici*) and to monitor the accounts. The principal task of the *vilici*, who were likely to be slaves, was to superintend the workforce, but they might also be empowered to enter into contracts with third parties; these contracts, provided that they fell within the terms of their appointment, would be backed with the full resources of the paterfamilias. Under the *vilici* would be various foremen (*officinatores*) in charge of particular workshops or construction yards.

FINANCIAL MANAGEMENT

The accounts kept by a Roman paterfamilias have already been touched upon in connection with the books kept by Roman bankers (Chapter 2). To recapitulate briefly, a paterfamilias would keep two principal records – the rough record of transactions as they occurred (*adversaria*) and the cash book (*codex accepti et expensi*). These books were kept in narrative form with items of every sort entered in the same ledger in date order. Outgoings would include payments for purchases of equipment and loans to debtors and among receipts might be listed income from sales of finished products and interest on loans. Roman bookkeeping made no distinction between capital and income; nor was there was any system of interlocking accounts ('double entry').

However it would be a mistake to dismiss Roman accountancy methods out of hand as primitive. The keeping of individual accounts for the different activities on the farm was recommended by the elder Cato.[89] In addition to the cash account (*ratio argentaria*), the *vilicus* was to keep accounts for grain (*ratio frumentaria*), fodder (*pabulum*), wine (*ratio vinaria*) and oil (*ratio olearia*). He was to look at what had been sold, what payments had been collected, the balance of debts due and what was left that was still saleable. Satisfactory guarantees of payment should be accepted, outstanding balances were to be chased up.

Furthermore the third century AD Heroninos archive from Eqypt, which relates to the large estate of a wealthy Alexandrian, Aurelius Appianus, illustrates considerable sophistication in accounting practice. Rathbone has reconstructed the estate's accounting system.[90] Each manager (*phrontistes*) submitted monthly accounts to the central administration for the unit (*phrontis*) for which he was responsible. At the end of the year the monthly returns were consolidated with transactions carried out by the central administration. This system could be used to monitor the performance of individual business units as well as the performance of the business as a whole. Rathbone argues that the accounts of the Appianus estate may have been to some extent influenced by the system of accounts used by the Roman army; he also points out that the senatorial and equestrian elite and the upper classes of Egypt had mutual knowledge of each other's agricultural systems. 'If sophisticated accounting and economically rational estate management were practised in Roman Egypt, the probability must be that they were practised in Roman Italy too and at a much earlier date.'[91]

In a brief cameo Petronius satirises Trimalchio checking on his accounts. The cashier (*actuarius*) is reading out the latest entries in the *adversaria*:[92]

> *July 26: On Trimalchio's estate at Cumae*
>
> Slaves born: Thirty boys and forty girls.
> Taken from the threshing floor into the barn: five hundred thousand *modii* of wheat.
> Oxen broken in: five hundred.
>
> *On the same date*
> Mithridates the slave was crucified for having spoken ill of the spirit of our lord Gaius.
>
> *On the same date*
> Returned to the strongbox (*arca*) ten million sesterces which could not be invested (*collocari*).
>
> *On the same date*
> A fire broke out in the gardens at Pompeii, which started in the house of Nasta the bailiff.
>
> 'What's this?' said Trimalchio. 'When did I buy any gardens at Pompeii?'
>
> 'Last year,' said the cashier, 'and so they have not yet been entered in the accounts (*in rationem nondum venerunt*).'
> Trimalchio was incandescent with rage. 'When property of any sort,' he said, 'has been bought for me, unless I know about it within six months, I forbid it to be entered in the accounts….'

Both in fiction and in life the weakness of Roman accounts was that they made no distinction between capital and income and so were not suited for measuring the true profitability of a business venture. But this did not seem to matter very much. Wealthy Romans frequently worried that their slaves were deceiving them: in his prosecution of Verres, for instance, Cicero plays on the jury's anxieties by likening the governor of Sicily to a *vilicus* who sells part of the estate, pockets part of the proceeds and then tells his master that the remaining cash represents an increase in the estate's revenue.[93] The principal purpose of accounting in many Roman households was to keep a check on the honesty of the staff (*28*).

THE EMBEDDED FIRM

Did the paterfamilias require that a sharp division should be drawn between his personal finances and the finances of his business? I can find no evidence that he treated commercial activities as a separate category. I take it as the norm that in a substantial Roman manufacturing or trading firm, funds were provided from the master's *patrimonium*. Industrial and commercial businesses owned by the paterfamilias were run in parallel with his other moneymaking activities – managed farms, tenanted farms, moneylending through the *kalendarium*; when it came to funding, all these activities were inextricably intertwined. Support for this assertion comes from an unexpected source – the accounts documented in the early second century writing tablets which have been discovered at the fort of Vindolanda in northern Britain. In his analysis of the accounting procedures at the fort, Bowman comments:[94]

> We should not draw too clear a line of demarcation between accounts and transactions in the fort as a whole and those in the *praetorium* as if the former were official and the latter were private in the sense that they stood outside the military establishment as a whole. In fact, it is precisely the variety of the documentation which evokes a picture of a military community in which the *familia* of the commanding officer was central and integral.

The phraseology of Cicero's letter (see Chapter 2) commending L. Aelius Lamia to the governor of Africa is also revealing:[95]

> ...I would only ask you to believe that if you protect Lamia's interests (*negotia*) and assist his agents, freedmen and household as occasion may require, I shall be more beholden to you than if your generosity had to do with my own business (*rem familiarem meam*).

The intimate connection that Cicero makes between family and business affairs could hardly be more clearly spelled out. I believe that, mutatis mutandis, an enterprise such as the firm of the Sestii stood in a similar relationship to the *familia* of the Sestii as did the garrison of Vindolanda to their commanding officer's *familia*, or the slaves and freedmen engaged in business on behalf of Cicero and Lamia to the *familiae* of their respective masters (*29*).

The central and integral role played by the household in business affairs throws light on the frequently quoted passage from Columella, where he is recommending investment in a vineyard:[96]

> Assuming the heaviest expenses for vineyards, seven *iugera* do not require more than the labour of one vintner,...if he is bought for HS8,000 and the seven *iugera* for HS7,000 and the vineyards with their allotment of stakes and willows [to provide support for the vines] are planted for HS2,000 per *iugerum*, then the price of all this amounts to HS29,000. Add to this the annual interest at 6 per cent for two years when the young vineyard bears no fruit, which amounts to HS3,480. The whole expense of capital and interest amounts to HS32,480.

In his calculations Columella makes no mention of such items as the cost of buildings, of maintenance for slaves and of depreciation – and he has been roundly criticised by some modern commentators for these omissions.[97] These criticisms are not, in my opinion, justified. I agree with those who reply in Columella's defence that the Roman elite saw themselves operating within two interlocking economic structures – a self-sufficient natural economy and a market-based monetary economy.[98] The natural economy of the self-sufficient villa formed a given, costless structure that underpinned activities in the market sector. Columella's audience of landed proprietors was already well-provided with buildings and slaves; there was no need to take the cost of these resources into account. Columella assumes that personal finance and business finance are inextricably intertwined: financing and managing a business enterprise is no different from financing and managing any other activity undertaken by the paterfamilias.

The intermingling of personal affairs and business life is also illustrated by a passage from the Augustan jurist Alfenus Varus.[99] Alfenus is discussing the law (*lex censoria*) governing the harbour tax of Sicily. The law stated that no one was obliged to pay the tax on slaves that he was taking home for his own use. Was someone who sent slaves from Sicily to Rome in order to staff an estate (*fundus*) due to pay the tax? Alfenus sees two questions here, What is meant by 'to take home' (*domum ducere*)? What is meant by 'to take for his own use'? His definition of 'home' is that it is the place where each person has his residence and keeps his accounts and organises his affairs (*ubi quisque sedes et tabulas haberet suarumque rerum constitutionem fecisset*). And as far as the slaves were concerned, 'for his own use' clearly meant those who were charged with looking after his personal needs – masseurs, bedroom attendants, cooks and domestic servants. The status of other slaves – cashiers (*dispensatores*), men in charge of apartment blocks (*insularii*), bailiffs (*vilici*), doorkeepers (*atrienses*), weavers (*textores*) and rural labourers (*operarii rustici*) – was more ambiguous; Alfenus is not sure how they should be treated for tax purposes. Perhaps the acid test should be whether the owner had bought the slaves to possess them himself and use them for some purpose, whether domestic or business, as opposed to buying them simply in order to sell them at a profit. The whole passage suggests that the Roman elite drew no hard and fast distinction between the domestic and the business environments.

Lastly, the integration of the elite household and the family firm is reflected in the design of the upper class house. Cicero makes the point that the house will be required to accommodate many visitors:[100]

> High status (*dignitas*) may be increased by a house, but should not be sought entirely from a house. It is not the house which does honour to the master, but the reverse. And, as in other matters, account has to be taken not only of oneself but of others, so in the house of a prominent man in which many guests must be received and a large number of all types of people admitted, attention must be paid to a certain spaciousness.

Vitruvius sets out the principles that should govern the layout of an upper-class town house:[101]

> The private rooms (*propria loca patribus familiarum*) are those into which nobody has the right to enter without an invitation, such as bedrooms, dining rooms, bathrooms, and all others used for similar purposes. The common areas are those which any people have a right to enter, even without an invitation: that is entrance courts, *cava aedium*, peristyles and so on. This means that men who have an everyday sort of fortune (*communis fortuna*) do not need entrance halls, counting houses (*tablina*) or atriums built in the grand style – since they discharge their obligations (*officia*) by going round to other people's houses rather than have other people coming round to them...
>
> For moneylenders (*feneratores*) and tax farmers (*publicani*) more comfortable and showy apartments must be constructed, which are secure against robbery... for men of rank (*nobiles*) who hold offices and magistracies (*honores* and *magistratus*) and so have obligations (*officia*) to their fellow citizens, lofty entrance halls in regal style, and very spacious atriums and peristyles, with shrubberies (*silvae*) and broad walks, must be built. They also need libraries, picture galleries and halls (*basilicae*), finished in a style not dissimilar to that of great public buildings, since public councils as well as private law suits and hearings before arbitrators are very often held in the houses of such men.

It has been well observed that the layout of the great house – *vestibulum-atrium-tablinum* – reflects the progress of the most important visitors at the morning *salutatio* from the entrance lobby through the atrium to an audience with the master in his counting house.[102] The house was the centre of a great man's public life as well as his private life. It was the centre of all his networks - political, business and private. A wealthy man's residence was not, as for so many in present-day society, the home to which people return each day to get away from work; it *was* the place of work. This is, of course, very much the underlying theme of the Igel Column where scenes from the everyday family life of the Secundinii are intermingled with scenes of commercial transactions.

We may conclude, then, that the wealthy Roman *familia*, a central institution of Roman society, was capable of providing the resources to finance and operate a substantial business enterprise over several generations. Headed by the paterfamilias, financed out of funds held in the *patrimonium* and staffed by the household's freedmen and slaves, the Roman firm was embedded in the structure of the Roman family.

EPILOGUE

The principal conclusion of this enquiry is that investment in the industrial and commercial infrastructure of the Roman world was funded by the landed elite, who possessed the overwhelming share of the empire's wealth. The elite *patrimonium* was the source of capital for marine ventures, for public works contracts, for companies set up to collect taxes and for the 'family firm'.

This conclusion does not require us to suppose that senators, equestrians and municipal notables took part in the everyday business of manufacturing or trading overseas, any more than did their counterparts in medieval Florence or Genoa. There was, and of course still is, an important distinction to be made between those who control a business enterprise (*qui negotia habent*) and the people of lower status who are engaged full-time in business (*qui negotiantur*). This distinction was often blurred by Roman writers but it was in fact widely appreciated: I suspect that it was in Cicero's mind when he described mercantile trade (*mercatura*) as despicable (*sordida putanda*) if it was conducted on a small scale (*tenuis*), but not so very discreditable (*non est admodum vituperanda*) when it was undertaken on a grand scale (*magna et copiosa*).[1] It seems to me undeniable that many members of the Roman elite did control business enterprises and did actively pursue profit (*quaestus*) during the late Republic and early Empire.

But why, we may well ask, did the Roman elite go to so much trouble to disguise their interest in trade and industry? Answers that cite 'the innate conservatism of the Roman elite', or 'aristocratic disdain for commerce' only lead to an antecedent question: why were non-economic values such a potent factor in the Roman social system? And in practice, as D'Arms points out in a perceptive discussion, aristocratic codes of behaviour generally provide feeble defences against the temptations of making serious amounts of money.[2]

A more fruitful approach to this issue is, I suggest, to concentrate on the readiness of time-honoured institutions within the system, in particular the *familia*, to adapt to the mercantile world of the late Republic and early Empire. And this leads us to the role of freedmen. Through making over their *peculium* to ex-slaves, elite families provided start-up capital to the freedmen who were some of Rome's most successful entrepreneurs. But even among freedmen, non-economic values held sway. It is noteworthy that enterprises run by freedmen, although numerous and often successful, did not produce a 'middle class' of businessmen. For wealthy freedmen, membership of the order of *augustales* was the route to achieving status (*dignitas*). Successful freedmen did not necessarily withdraw entirely from participation in trade and industry; we may imagine that many of them, like their fictional archetype Trimalchio, made a seamless transition from trading in mixed cargoes ('wine, bacon, beans, perfumes and slaves') to settling down on a country estate and providing finance for another generation of ex-slave entrepreneurs. There was, however, no impediment to prevent the descendants of freedmen moving into the ranks of the elite. The family of the freedman M. Licinius Privatus from Ostia provides an informative example.[3] Privatus became president of the guild of builders, made a gift to the town of HS 50,000 and was rewarded with a special seat in the theatre and honorary membership of the council. But what is significant in the present context is that after his statue had been set up, additional lines were added to his inscription, to the effect that among his children and grandchildren were town councillors and Roman knights (*patri et avo decurionum, patri equitum Romanorum*). The descendants of men such as Privatus formed a cadre of new recruits to the elite class, which would thus be constantly renewed and would continue to hold the greater part of Rome's wealth.

We shall end where we began, with the bankers of Puteoli, a group of ex-slaves. Why did Roman banking remain a low-status activity, in the hands of slaves and freedmen? Why did Roman banks confine their activities to bridging loans and the provision of working capital? Why did they operate on the margins of trade and industry? The immediate answer is that deposit-taking bankers such as the Sulpicii were professionals – they had to be – and status-conscious wealthy Romans did not wish to commit themselves to such demanding, but in their eyes mundane, activities.

But there is another way of approaching this issue – by looking at the structure of the elite Roman household. The elite *familia* was a flexible institution capable of accommodating complex business processes. A wealthy Roman paterfamilias might run a lending business through his *kalendarium*; he would take in cash from his tenants and lend it out to a range of borrowers. He had managers and agents, slave and free, to run his trading and manufacturing interests - managers who could enter into contracts, within the limits of their *peculium* or of their specific appointment. Further, when the paterfamilias had cargoes to ship he would station agents in foreign ports to look after his interests and manage his cash balances. Reciprocal arrangements with his peers, cemented by the bonds of *amicitia*, would ensure that both at home and abroad his creditworthiness was recognised. The tight-knit circle of the Roman elite performed for its members many functions that medieval merchants sought from banks or set up their own banks to provide. In summary, during the late Republic and early Empire the elite controlled, through the institution of the *familia*, such a great part of the commercial sector as well as of the nation's wealth, that they felt no great need for bankers or for banking instruments such as negotiable bills of exchange.

Is the reluctance of the Roman elite to engage directly in banking a matter of some significance? It may well be. Strong and profitable banks can stimulate consumption and investment and would seem to be a necessary condition of a vigorous economy. But the creation of such banks requires the engagement of wealthy and powerful men. Such engagement was not forthcoming from the Roman elite. This was, I suggest, a major factor that limited long-term growth in the Roman economy.

APPENDICES

I FREEBORN PERSONS IN THE ARCHIVE

Name	Status	Roman voting tribe★	Role	Tablet
Trupho Potamonis f. Alexandrinus	Peregrine	-	Defendant in lawsuit	TPSulp. 13, 14
C. Julius C. f. Fal. Senecio	Roman citizen	Falerna	Witness	TPSulp. 43
C. Munnius C. f. Rufus	Roman citizen	N/K	Witness	TPSulp. 43
[?] Modius L. f. Fal. Rusticus	Roman citizen	Falerna	Witness	TPSulp. 44
A. Mevius A. f. Fal. Iulius	Roman citizen	Falerna	Witness	TPSulp. 45, 52
Cn. Pollius Cn. f. Rufus	Roman citizen	N/K	Witness	TPSulp. 46
Purgias Alexandri f. [---]	Peregrine	-	Depositor	TPSulp. 49
M. Antonius M. f. Col. Maximus	Roman citizen	Collina	Borrower	TPSulp. 50
Epichares Aphrodisi f. Atheniensis	Peregrine	-	Guarantor	TPSulp. 60, 61, 62.
Euplia Theodori f. Meliaca	Peregrine	-	Borrower	TPSulp. 60, 61, 62.
Magia L. f. Pulchra	Roman citizen	-	Borrower	TPSulp. 63

Name	Status	Roman voting tribe*	Role	Tablet
Menelaus Irenaei f. Ceramieta	Peregrine	–	Borrower	TPSulp. 78.
? Theodori. f.	Peregrine	–	Shipper	TPSulp. 106

*The tribe *Collina*, in which M. Antonius M. f. Col. Maximus was enrolled, was one of the four 'urban' tribes whose members originated from Rome itself. Citizens of Puteoli were enrolled in the tribe *Falerna*.

2 FREEDMEN FORMALLY IDENTIFIED IN THE ARCHIVE

Freedmen from private households with status identifier
- Zenon (*Zenon Zenobi l. Tyrius*) (TPSulp. 4)
- Eunus (*C. Novius Cypaeri l. Eunus*) (TPSulp. 45)
- Jucundus (*L. Marius Didae l. Iucundus*) (TPSulp. 53, 79)
- Blastus (*Cn. Pompeius Epiri l. Blastus*)(TPSulp. 70)
- Primogenes (*P. Bennius Corinthi l. Primogenes*) (TPSulp. 103)
- Cinnamus (*…Cinnami liberti*) (TPSulp. 111).*

*This is not necessarily C. Sulpicius Cinnamus, freedman of Faustus.

Imperial freedmen with status identifier
- Evenus (*Ti. Iulius Augusti l. Euenus Primianus*) (TPSulp. 45, 51, 52)
- Celadus (*Ti. Claudius Augusti l. Celadus*) (TPSulp. 89)
- Myrtilus (*Ti. Iulius Augusti l. Myrtilus*) (TPSulp 101)
- Num (?) …*Caesaris Augusti l. Num*… (TPSulp. 119)

Other indications of status
In a handful of transactions, the freedman status of a participant emerges from internal evidence provided in the text:
- Primus gives instructions to the Sulpicii to make payments to 'my freedman Suavis or my slave Hyginus' (*Suavi liberto meo aut Hygino servo*) (TPSulp. 48).
- Cinnamus twice reveals that he is handling payments on account of 'my patron Faustus' (*in debitum Fausti patroni mei* and *ex debito Fausti patroni mei*) (TPSulp. 72, 74).
- L. Patulcius Epaphroditus produces a receipt on behalf of his freedwoman Patulcia Erotis (*rogatu et mandatu libertaes* (sic) *meae*) (TPSulp. 82).

In addition, two of the Sulpicii describe themselves as procurator, the title given to someone, often a freedman, who held the position of manager or agent appointed under a mandate:

- Gaius Sulpicius Eutychus declares that he is manager for Sulpicius Cinnamus (*qui se procuratorem esse dicebat C. Sulpicii Cinnami*) (TPSulp. 87).
- Gaius Sulpicius Cinnamus declares that he is agent for Gavia (?) Primigenia (*qui se procuratorem G[…]ae Primigeniae esse dicebat*) (TPSulp. 105).

3 PUTEOLI'S OTHER BANKERS

The Sulpicii were of course not the only bankers doing business in Puteoli during the mid-first century.[1] As we saw in Chapter 4, the *argentarius* (or *coactor argentarius*) Aulus Castricius, acted for the Sulpicii at an auction sale (TPSulp. 81). Other bankers must have acted for the Sulpicii when they put pledged goods up for auction. We also catch a fleeting glimpse of Messius, a money-changer (*nummularius*) who practised his trade in the *vicus Tyanianus*, where merchants from Cilicia and Cappadocia congregated.

We know that Messius had connections in at least one other city on the Bay of Naples. A graffito from Herculaneum provides a glimpse of his business:

> Hermeros, under-slave of Phoebus, invites the Lady Primigenia to come to Puteoli in the vicus Tyanianus and find him at the office of the banker Messius (*Hermeros Primigeniae dominae: veni Puteolos in vico Tyaniano et quaere a Messio numulario Hermerotem Phoebi*).

Messius evidently employed at least two slaves, Phoebus and his under-slave Hermeros, at his office in the *vicus Tyanianus*. A plausible interpretation of this message is that Messius had a customer, Primigenia, in Herculaneum and had sent Hermeros to visit her on the firm's business. Unable to find her, Hermeros had left a message asking her to come over to Puteoli where she would find him in Messius' office.

4 MORE FAMILY FIRMS

The House of Ateius

Tableware bearing the stamp of Cn. Ateius has been found on many sites in Italy and the western provinces. A plausible account of Ateius' career is that he started manufacture in a workshop at Arezzo towards the end of the first century BC; he later opened a branch workshop in Pisa, presumably to be near the coast for his growing export business; and then opened a third branch at Lyon, probably to supply the markets of Gaul and the legions in Germany. But it is not clear whether these workshops were all operating simultaneously; and there is no agreement among scholars about Ateius' relationship with the various craftsmen, slave and freed, whose names appear joined with his in stamps on *terra sigillata* products.[2]

The House of Fortis

Lamps bearing the name of Fortis were produced at between 20 and 30 workshops – in northern and central Italy, Gaul, Germany, Pannonia, Dalmatia and Dacia. There is no consensus of opinion on the relationship between Fortis and the workshops that produced lamps stamped with his name. Some, perhaps many, of these workshops may have been managed by appointees of Fortis, in which case he was master of a very large-scale enterprise. Or local workshops may have paid a fee to use the Fortis name or may have even pirated his trademark. The evidence does not permit any definite conclusion.[3]

The Laecanii Bassi

In the late first century BC the senatorial family of the Laecanii Bassi began to export olive oil from Istria in *amphorae* of their own manufacture. A kiln site at Fazana, a few miles north of Pola, was evidently engaged in production on a large scale over many years: *amphorae* manufactured at Fazana have been discovered at more than fifty sites in Cisalpine Gaul, Noricum, Pannonia and Raetia, and it is possible to detect from the pottery stamps three phases of ownership. During the first phase, from the end of the first century BC to the Flavian period, the workshop was the property of the Laecanii. The family then disappears from the record. In the second phase, from the Flavian period to the reign of Hadrian, *amphorae* produced at Fazana bore the stamps of emperors; presumably the property of the Laecanii and the business conducted there had been taken into the imperial *res privata*. In the third phase, the second half of the second century AD, *amphorae* carrying the stamp of M. Aurelius Justus, perhaps an imperial freedman, were produced on the site.[4]

The Sexti Fadii

The Sexti Fadii of Narbonne are known to us from sherds found in Rome's Monte Testaccio. Two names can be identified with confidence, those of Sextus Fadius Anicetus and Sextus Fadius Musa. The names of Spanish cities, among them Corduba and Hispalis, have been found on many of the Sexti Fadii fragments in the Monte Testaccio. This might suggest that the contents of the *amphorae* (usually oil) were shipped to Rome from Baetica. However, an inscription from a statue base in Narbonne, datable to 149, records that Sextus Fadius Pap. Secundus Musa, was patron of the guild of builders (*fabri subaediani*) in the city, chief city of the province of Gallia Narbonenis.[5] Musa had held all the official posts in the city (*omnibus honoribus in colonia Narbonensi functus*) and was senior priest of the imperial cult (*flamen primus Augusti*); he contributed to the guild of builders the sum of HS16,000; the annual interest on this sum was to be used in perpetuity by the guild to celebrate his birthday with a feast. Musa's membership of the tribe Papiria indicates that he was a Roman citizen and his cognomen suggests he was of freedman stock. Sexti Fadii are also attested at Ostia, Italian port of arrival for cargoes despatched from Gaul and Spain; they may be descended from freedmen stationed there as agents on behalf of the family firm.[6]

It is possible to construct a plausible account of the business of the Fadii. They were shippers based in Narbonne. They bought consignments of oil from Spanish producers, packed them in *amphorae* made in Baetica and then shipped the full containers to Italy; the Fadii may even have controlled the manufacture of these containers and they are very likely to have owned the freighters in which their cargoes were shipped. They stationed agents (probably freedmen) in Spain to handle the outgoing cargoes as they went through the port and in Ostia to see the incoming cargoes through customs. Their agents based in Spain will have negotiated contracts with local growers for consignments of oil, made the appropriate payments and paid duty to the customs authorities in Spain on the outgoing cargoes. Their agents based in Italy handled the incoming cargoes, paid import duties and collected payments from the Italian merchants who were their customers.

5 MONEY AND CREDIT

Money
Money in the form of coins was used for both small and large transactions. In the early Empire everyday items were priced in copper *asses* (four *asses* to the *sestertius*) – witness this fragment of a conversation between a farmer visiting the weekly market (*nundinae*) and his landlady:[7]

> Innkeeper, let's settle the bill.
> For the wine and bread, one *as*. For the porridge, two *asses*.
> Agreed.
> For the girl, eight *asses*.
> Agreed.
> Fodder for the mule, two *asses*.
> That mule will get me back to work.

For larger transactions the alloyed *sestertius* and silver *denarius* (four *sestertii* to the *denarius*) were widely used. In 46 BC gold coins, aurei, were introduced at an exchange rate of one aureus to 25 *denarii* or 100 *sestertii*. When people discuss loans, property prices, the value of legacies and so on, they usually do so in *sestertii*; the majority of the transactions in the Murecine archive and in the archive of L. Caeciliius Jucundus at Pompeii are denominated in *sestertii*. However Julius Alexander, who ran a money-lending business in Dacia (the modern Romania), made loans denominated in *denarii*.[8] People became accustomed to use the gold and silver currencies in whatever way they found most convenient: at Pompeii a 'typical' find of coins consisted of 1 *aureus*, 6 *denarii* and 10 assorted bronzes.[9]

Credit

The Roman money supply consisted of bullion and coins in circulation (i.e. not hoarded) and bullion and coins deposited with bankers. Roman banks did not 'create' money by issuing banknotes; nor, as far as we know, did banks in Italy provide accounts which could be drawn on through some form of cheque.

Although the money supply was limited to bullion and coins, it was supplemented by the widespread use of credit. Credit enabled coins and bullion to work harder since it increased the velocity of money in circulation. Credit might take the form of trade credit from suppliers, advance payments by bankers to vendors at auctions and arrears of rent allowed to tenants (*reliqua colonorum*). And the Sulpicii effectively opened an overdraft account for Primus (TPSulp. 48). The 'letter of credit' (*permutatio*) was an order form a banker to another banker, usually overseas, authorising payment, to a person named in the letter, of a sum of money.

In Republican Rome there was a flourishing market in IOUs, debt claims on named individuals (*nomina*). On one occasion, says Cicero, the house of Chelidon, Verres' mistress, was full of people paying her cash (*nummi*), while others were signing IOUs (*tabellae*); they hoped that she would put in a good word for them with the praetor.[10] *Nomina* were negotiable and might be sold at a discount: this emerges from the financial manoeuvres that Cicero and Atticus discussed in 45 BC, when Cicero was trying to raise funds for a memorial to his daughter.[11] Evidence for the use of the debt-claim as a negotiable payment instrument is limited to transactions amongst the elite in Rome: what was acceptable in the closed networks of the elite *familiae* and a man's close associates (*amici*) does not seem, as far as we know, to have been used as a negotiable instrument between business counterparties. It is of course possible that the IOUs of the local elite circulated in ports and other major commercial centres.

6 MOVING CASH

How were large sums in cash, such as those required for the property transactions of the aristocracy, physically transferred between counterparties? I suspect that under the early Empire, *aurei* (the commonly used gold coins of the period) were widely used as a means of transporting funds. For instance, while he was a private citizen, the future emperor Galba was said to have regularly travelled with a carriage (*vehiculum*) containing 10,000 *aureus* coins, the equivalent of HS1 million *sestertii*.[12] This suggests how Pliny, for instance, might have handled the payment for the estate adjoining his property at Tifernum, if he had decided to go through with the transaction.[13] The asking price was HS3 million: Pliny, or a member of his staff, could have transported the purchase funds to the vendor in two or three carriages containing bags of gold coins. The sacks of coins would have been sealed and their contents certified by a banker – usually a moneychanger (*nummularius*) – to be of a certain amount and of good metal.[14]

Bands of disaffected slaves and gangs of armed robbers compounded the logistical difficulties of transporting large sums of money on land. Most notorious of Roman brigands was Bulla Felix, who ran a gang of 600 men in Italy for two years in the early third century. Bulla's spies kept him informed 'about everybody that was setting out from Rome and everybody that was putting into port at Brundisium, who and how many there were and what and how much they had with them'.[15] Augustus found it necessary to station armed police in bandit-ridden districts; Tiberius stiffened up this police force by decreasing the distance between their guard posts.[16] But security on journeys was essentially a private matter; a wealthy man would recruit his own entourage to provide an escort for himself, his *familia* and his possessions.[17] We may imagine that convoys of carriages packed with sacks of coins and guarded by armed outriders were a common sight on the roads of Roman Italy. (The special problems of transporting cash by sea were outlined in Chapter 11.)

7 INTEREST RATES

Interest rates in Rome fluctuated with the ebb and flow of political events. For instance in July 54 BC Cicero wrote to Atticus that the amount of bribery in the elections had pushed up the demand for money so much that interest rates had risen from 4 per cent to 8 per cent.[18] Conversely interest rates fell steeply following Octavian's distribution of the wealth of Egypt.[19]

Although an annual rate of 12 per cent was a maximum, it was frequently regarded as a norm.[20] Pliny, for instance, demanded 12 per cent interest from his friend Voconius Romanus.[21] And writing to Trajan from Bithynia about the proper use of municipal funds lying idle, Pliny says that people could not be found to borrow public funds, especially at the rate of 12 per cent, 'the same rate as for private loans'.[22]

Although lenders charged 12 per cent on loans when they could, the long-term rate of return on investment tended to be lower. The commonest home for elite capital was investment in agricultural land; this produced an income from rents paid by tenant farmers and from the sale of livestock and crops. It was generally assumed that the annual rate of return on long-term funds invested in land would be in the region of 5 to 6 per cent. A return of 6 per cent was assumed by Columella to be the norm for conventional mixed farming enterprises.[23] That 5 to 6 per cent was a standard return on agricultural investment can be also be deduced from the arrangements made under various welfare schemes to invest in land and secure an income for the beneficiaries. For instance when Trajan set up a scheme at Veleia to provide an income for local children, local landowners were required to take out cash loans from the government; the landowners and their successors were to hold the loaned funds in perpetuity, paying annual interest for the benefit of the children at 5 per cent.[24] Similarly when Pliny set up a private foundation at Comum, he handed over land to the municipality and then leased it back at an annual rate of 6 per cent of the land's nominal value; this rate was to be payable in perpetuity by successive owners.[25] It would have been difficult if not impossible to persuade estate owners to take up loans and leases on this basis if the annual interest payments were out of line with prevailing rates.

Variations in interest rates were, not surprisingly, to be found between regions within Italy and between Italy and various provinces. The jurist Gaius commented on the effect on interest rates of local variations in supply and demand for money:[26]

> The price of things varies from one city and region to another, especially of wine, oil and corn; even in the case of money, though it is supposed to have the same purchasing power everywhere, yet it can be quite easily raised and at low interest in some places, and with difficulty and at steep interest in others.

Potentially the most profitable lending opportunities of all were available in the shipping business (see Chapter 11). The risks were considerable, because of the many opportunities for fraud and the high incidence of losses due to piracy and storms at sea. Consequently, interest rates on maritime loans were exempted from the maximum of 12 per cent per annum.

8 ELITE FINANCIERS

Cicero and his circle in Rome made frequent use of financiers, usually equestrians and therefore their social equals, to handle their financial affairs (*rem gerere*) and to look after their business interests (*negotia procurare*). Titus Pomponius Atticus, friend, confidant and advisor of Marcus Cicero and of Quintus Cicero, who married Atticus' sister, is the best known of these financiers. Atticus was an equestrian with substantial business interests, who owned estates in Greece and property in Rome.[27]

The services that Atticus provided for his associates were described by his biographer Cornelius Nepos as mandates (*mandata*).[28] When carried out for friends these services would be free of charge. Mandates, as we know from Cicero's letters, included providing cash and credit for Cicero at various crises in his life, collecting debts, supervising the quality of coin in payments, witnessing and executing wills, attending or conducting sales, making purchases or investments, placing loans with other bankers and providing letters of credit (*permutationes*).[29] Marcus and Quintus Cicero, Q. Hortensius, A. Torquatus and 'many Roman knights' were among those who made use of Atticus' services.

Although he did not earn fees an elite financier was able to profit indirectly from his activities. He offered his clients introductions to a wide range of associates; and by continually exploiting his network of contacts he was able to create fresh business opportunities for himself. Atticus, for instance, earned interest from lending his own money – as well as earning money for his associates by placing loans on their behalf. On occasion he lent his own money to his brother-in-law Quintus Cicero, whom he then pressed hard for repayment.[30]

An elite financier could also expect to receive favours in return for services rendered. 'Do not keep on mentioning your *(officia)* acts of service to your peers; the recipient should remember them,' said Cicero.[31] So when Atticus was finding it difficult to obtain repayment of a loan from the people of Sicyon, he asked Cicero to intercede on his behalf with the senate in Rome; on this occasion the senate was not helpful.[32] Cicero then wrote letters advancing Atticus' case to two successive governors of Macedonia, Gaius Antonius Hybrida and Gaius Octavius.[33] Furthermore, in addition to assistance from the living, a financier could hope for tangible rewards from the dead: Atticus was said to have received many inheritances.[34]

9 ROME'S IMPORTS OF GRAIN

Modern estimates of the total annual amount of grain required by Rome vary widely – from 60 million *modii* to 30 million *modii*.[35]

One way of approaching the problem is to look at what a Roman landowner regarded as a subsistence diet: the elder Cato regarded three to four *modii* of wheat per month, or say 40 *modii* per year, as an average individual requirement.[36] At the time of Augustus a plausible estimate puts the population of Rome (free citizens, children and slaves) at approximately one million; this gives an average wheat requirement in the capital of 40 million *modii* per year.

At this time the bulk of Rome's grain was shipped in from overseas. How much of the 40 million *modii* was shipped through Puteoli? The principal sources of grain, states Josephus, a contemporary witness, were Africa, which provided wheat for Rome for eight months in the year, and Egypt, which provided four months' supply.[37]

Given this ratio, and staying with conveniently round numbers, we might assume that of the required imports of 40 million *modii* of grain per year, Africa provided some 25 million *modii* and Egypt some 15 million *modii*; this suggests that something in the order of 100,000 tons passed through Puteoli in a year. These figures merely serve to give an idea of the quantities of grain involved, the logistical problems that had to be solved by the *praefectus annonae* and the business opportunities that were available to shipowners, shippers and merchants and local traders.

10 HORACE ODES 1.4

Solvitur acris hiemps grata vice veris et Favoni,
　trahuntque siccas machinae carinas;
ac neque iam stabulis gaudet pecus aut arator igni,

nec prata canis albicant pruinis.
iam Cytherea choros ducit Venus imminente Luna,
    iunctaeque Nymphis Gratiae decentes
alterno terram quatiunt pede, dum graves Cyclopum
    Vulcanus ardens urit officinas.
nunc decet aut viridi nitidum caput impedire myrto
    aut flore, terrae quem ferunt solutae.
nunc et in umbrosis Fauno decet immolare lucis,
    seu poscat agna sive malit haedo.
pallida Mors aequo pulsat pede pauperum tabernas
    regumque turres. O beate Sesti,
vitae summa brevis spem nos vetat incohare longam.
    iam te premet nox fabulaeque Manes
et domus exilis Plutonia: quo simul mearis,
    nec regna vini sortiere talis
nec tenerum Lycidan mirabere, quo calet iuventus
    nunc omnis et mox virgines tepebunt.

NOTES

English versions of Greek and Latin literary texts are based principally on the Penguin Classics and Loeb editions; quotations from the legal sources are based on Watson (1998) and de Zulueta (1946). Where appropriate the original versions have been modified to take account of the commercial or financial setting.

PREFACE
1. The ancient economy has been the subject of vigorous debate since Finley's publication in 1973 of *The Ancient Economy*. (A second edition, incorporating 'Further Thoughts', appeared in 1985 and an updated, posthumous, edition in 1999.) More recently, several articles collected in Scheidel, W. and von Reden, S. (2002) review many of the issues first raised by Finley. For Roman banking, Andreau (1974, 1987 and 1999) and Camodeca (1992 and 1999) are fundamental. Other recommended reading: D'Arms (1981)(attitudes of the Roman elite towards commerce, and the key role played by freedmen) and Aubert (1994)(Roman business managers).
2. Cic. *Off.* 2.87.
3. Cic. *Off.* 1.150-51.
4. Livy 21.63.4.
5. Johnston (1999) 24-29.
6. For the value and relevance of Graeco-Roman material, see Rathbone (2002).

INTRODUCTION: THE MURECINE ARCHIVE
1. Camodeca (1999) 11-13.
2. Camodeca (1999) 20-21.
3. TPSulp. 12, 26; 44.
4. For full list and comprehensive analysis, see Camodeca (1999) 27-28 and Index III.
5. Sen. *Ep.* 15; Plin. *NH* 16.16.27; Suet. *Aug.* 39.
6. Suet. *Nero.* 17; Paul. *Sent.* 5.25.6.
7. The Latin word is *stilus*, but 'stylus' has become common English usage.
8. For a description of the writing tablets and instruments found at Vindolanda, see Birley (2002) 31-35.
9. For the use of *C.* and *Cn.*, see Quint. *Inst.* 1.7.28.
10. D. 22.4.4.
11. For acts based on good faith, see Meyer (2004) 148-158; for the Praetor's Edict, see Johnston (1999) 3-4.
12. Cic. *Off.* 3.70.
13. Gai. *Inst.* 3. 92-93.
14. Varro. *Rust.* 2.2.5-6
15. D. 19.5.24.
16. D. 17.2.71pr.

17. The Augustan jurist Ateius Capito, quoted in Macrob. *Sat.* 7.13.12.
18. Cic. *Q.fr.* 1.1.13.
19. Plin. *NH* 33.21
20. D. 22.5.3.5. For further discussion of the role of witnesses, see Gardner (1993) 118-123, 179-186; Meyer (2004) 158-163.
21. D. 22.5.1pr.
22. D. 22.5.3pr. For the calling of witnesses in civil law suits, see D. 22.5.1.1.
23. Plin. *NH* 33.28.
24. For rankings among witnesses to the transactions of the Pompeian banker L. Caecilius Iucundus, see Jongman (1988) 224-238.
25. Camodeca (1999) 106.
26. Sen. *Ben.* 3.15.2.
27. For criteria for selection of witnesses, see Andreau (1974) 179 and Jongman (1988) 272.
28. Meyer (2004) 161-163.
29. Duff (1957) 55.

I A PORT AND ITS PEOPLE
1. Suet. *Aug.* 98.
2. For the measures taken by Augustus to organise the grain supply, see Rickman (1980) 61-64. For the history, government and economic development of Puteoli, see D'Arms (1974), Frederiksen (ed.Purcell) (1984), Camodeca (1994) and Camodeca (1996).
3. Livy 34.45.
4. Plut. *Sulla* 37.
5. For urban businesses, see Wallace-Hadrill (1994) 118-42.
6. Diod. Sic. 5.13.1-2.
7. Vitr. *De Arch.* 7.11.1.
8. For a survey of the Puteoli flasks, see Painter (1975).
9. Vitr. *De Arch.* 2.6.
10. Strab. 5.4.6.
11. Petron. *Sat.* 101.
12. For ancient merchant ships and their mode of operation, see Rickman (1980) 123-27, Houston (1988), and Horden and Purcell (2000) 140-43.
13. Livy 32.7.
14. For the history of Delos as a trading centre, see Rauh (2003), 53-65.
15. Strab. 14.5.2.
16. Lucilius fr. 123.
17. Cic. *Rab. Post.* 2.4.
18. For elite wealth, see Chapter 10.
19. Plin. *NH* 36.70.
20. Strab. 2.5.12; 17.1.13; Plin. *NH* 6.104-6.
21. Strab. 17.1.7.
22. Plin. *NH* 6.101; 12.84.
23. For the role of the *praefectus annonae*, see Rickman (1980) 79-93.
24. Sen. *De Brev. Vit.* 18.3.
25. Garnsey (1983) 119-21.
26. Tac. *Ann.* 12.43.
27. Meiggs (1973) 298-301; Rickman (1980) 222-3.
28. CIL 10.7580.
29. CIL 14.2045.
30. CIL 10.1562; CIL 10.1729.
31. Sen *Ep.* 77.1-3.
32. Meiggs (1973) 323.

33. CIL 11.139.
34. Fabre (1981) 339.
35. For the terms *navicularii* and *negotiatores*, see Garnsey (1983) 124-126.
36. Hunt and Edgar 113.
37. Plin. *NH* 19.3.
38. Philo *In. Flacc.* 26.
39. For details of St. Paul's voyage, see Acts 27-28.
40. Yeo (1946) 238-240.
41. The wrecks that have been investigated are mostly those of vessels carrying cargoes of wine outward from Italy. For an account of the issues involved, see Pomey and Tchernia (1978) 233-5.
42. Dion. Hal. 3.44. However Casson (1965) n.8 argues that 'fair-size freighters very likely of 200 tons burden' were towed up to Rome.
43. For the proportions of grain that came from Africa and Egypt respectively, see Appendix 9.
44. Plin. *NH.* 15.74.
45. Strab. 5.35.
46. Varro *Rust.* 2.6.5.
47. Yeo (1946) 225.
48. Suet. *Claud.* 19.
49. Gai. *Inst.* 1.32c
50. Tac. *Ann.* 13.51.
51. D. 50.5.3.
52. Rickman (1980) 123.
53. Meiggs (1973) 159.
54. Tac. *Ann.* 15.18.3.
55. Tac. *Ann.* 15.42, *Suet.* Nero 31.
56. For Neronian date for the breakwater, see Camodeca (1994) 111.
57. For prices at Rome, see Duncan-Jones (1974) 345.
58. For ports and shipping in the pre-industrial period, see Stevens Cox (1999).
59. Cic. *Att.* 5.2.
60. For development along the coast to the west of the city, see Camodeca (1994) 111-13.
61. IG 14. 830.
62. NAM inv. 3231 (Serapis); NAM inv. 2425 (The Holy God); NAM inv. 3248 (Dusares). The first of these inscriptions (NAM inv. 3231) provides details of a building contract and is reproduced as FIRA 3. 153 (see n. 75 below).
63. NAM inv. 3274 (merchants).
64. NAM inv. 6780 (statue base); Tac. *Ann.* 2.47 (earthquake).
65. For full list, see Camodeca (2000) 281-88.
66. For the aqueduct, see D'Arms (2002) 84-85; for the buildings and artefacts revealed by the excavations on the Rione Terra, see de Caro (2002) 54-59.
67. CIL 10. 1614. For the employment of Cocceius by Agrippa, see Strab. 5.4.5.
68. CIL 1782-3.
69. For a detailed account of this building programme, see Camodeca (1996) 94-95.
70. For euergetism, see Veyne (1990).
71. TPSulp. 46.
72. Gardner (1999) 13.
73. Suet. *Aug.* 44.
74. The *macellum* was once thought to be a temple of Serapis, following the discovery of a statue of the Egyptian god on the site.
75. FIRA 3.153. Consular names provide the date of 105 BC. The inscription in the National Archaeological Museum in Naples has been dated to the first century AD by letter-forms and the use of Luna marble, see Bodel (2001) 53-55.

76. Security pledged for a building contract might be seized by the municipal council (*curia*) if the consortium failed to complete the contract on time or did not meet the agreed specifications.
77. Plut. *Sulla* 37.
78. Cic. *2 Verr.* 5.154.
79. Caes. BC 3.71.1.
80. TPSulp. 23.
81. CIL 10. 1782, 1783.
82. Cic. *2 Verr.* 5.74.
83. Meredith (1953) 38-40.
84. Plin. *NH* 22. 84-85.
85. D'Arms (1974) 107-08.
86. Bantia, FIRA 1.16; Tarentum, CIL 1. 590; Heraclea, CIL 1. 593.
87. CIL 10. 202; 581; 710; 3775.
88. FIRA 3. 153.
89. For text and commentary, see D'Arms (2002) 321-29.
90. TPSulp. 56.
91. T. 141-44.
92. Tac. *Ann.* 13.48.
93. Tac. *Ann.* 14.27.
94. For the aftermath of the riot in Pompeii, which saw the replacement of the duumvirs of 59/60 before the end of their term of office, see Cooley and Cooley (2004) 61.
95. For visitors from the last years of the Republic to the year 69, see D'Arms (2002) 49-101.
96. Cic. *Att.* 2.8.2.
97. Strab. 5.4.5.
98. Cic. *Cael.* 35.
99. D'Arms (2002) 55-57.
100. Cic. *Att.* 14.13.1.
101. Cic. *Planc.* 65.
102. Cic. *Leg. Agr.* 2.14.36.
103. D'Arms (2002) 62n.3.
104. Cic. *Fam.* 13.75.
105. Cic. *Acad. Pr.* 2.80.
106. Cic. *Fam.* 13.79.
107. For the distinction between *gens* and *familia*, see Saller (1994) 78-9.
108. CIL 10.1792; 1793.
109. Cic. *Fam.* 13.56.
110. Cic. *Att.* 5.2.
111. Cic. *Att.* 14.12.3.
112. Cic. *Att.* 14.9.1; 14.10.3; 14.11.2
113. Suet. *Gai.* 19.
114. Cass. Dio 59.17.1-11
115. CIL 5. 5050.
116. Suet. *Claud.* 25.2.
117. Tac. *Ann.* 14.3.5-10.5; Suet. *Nero* 27.
118. Plin. *NH* 8.6.
119. Philostratus, *Vit. Apoll.* 7.10-11.
120. Philostratus, *Vit. Apoll.* 8.8-10.
121. *Eph. Ep.* 8.369.
122. For the sons of freedmen, see Gordon (1931).
123. For *augustales* and *seviri augustales* see Duthoy (1974) and (1978) and Hope (2001) 29-36.

124. Text, translation and analysis in D'Arms (2000) 126-44.
125. D'Arms (1981) 147.
126. For Petronius' career, see Tac. *Ann.* 16. 18-19. For the date, authorship and setting of the *Satyricon*, see Rose (1971).
127. Petron. *Sat.* 29.
128. Petron. *Sat.* 76.
129. Petron. *Sat.* 71.
130. Petron. *Sat.* 38.
131. Petron. *Sat.* 46.
132. Petron. *Sat.* 57.

2 THE BANK OF THE SULPICII
1. Andreau (1999) 30-31.
2. D. 2.13.12 ; D. 2.10.13.6.3.
3. D. 2.13.4-11.
4. Suet. *Div.Aug.* 2, 4.
5. Suet. *Vesp.* 1.2.
6. Hor. *Sat.* 1.6.85-87.
7. Schol. ad. *Sat.* 1.6.86.
8. D. 2.13.4.3.
9. D. 14.5.8.
10. Hippol. *Haer.* 9.12.1.
11. D. 14.3.20.
12. CIL 6. 9182; CIL 6. 9181 ; CIL 6. 9179.
13. CIL 4. 4528; CIL 4. 8204 ; CIL 4.8203.
14. D. 16.3.7.2.
15. Dem. 36.11.
16. D. 2.13.4pr.
17. D. 2.13.4.1.
18. D. 2.13.10.1.
19. D. 2.13.9pr.
20. Cic. *Q.Rosc.* 1-9. See also De Ste Croix (1956).
21. Gai. *Inst.* 3. 131.
22. Gai. *Inst.* 3. 128-130.
23. Rostovtzeff (1957) pl. xliii 1 (6).
24. D. 16.3.24.
25. D. 2.14.47.1.
26. Polyb. 31.27.1-11.
27. Cic. *Att.* 5.13.2.
28. Cic. *Att.* 11.1.2.
29. Cic. *Att.* 12.24.1
30. Cic. *Att.* 12.27.2.
31. *Eph.Ep.* 8.451
32. For *familia* and *domus*, see Saller (1994) 74-101.
33. Treggiari (1975).
34. Petron. *Sat.* 75.
35. ILS 7382; 7380; 7378 ; 7376.
36. Cic. *Rep.* 5.5.
37. Champlin (1991) 140.
38. For the *kalendarium*, see Giliberti (1999) 165-78.
39. Petron. *Sat.* 53.

40. D. 32.91pr.
41. D. 15.1.58.
42. D. 40.7.40.4.
43. D. 14.3.18.
44. D. 14.5.8.
45. Aubert (1994) 9-16
46. D. 14.3.18 (Paul); D. 14.3.3, D. 14.3.7.1 (Ulpian).
47. For the *peculium* and its use in commercial life, see Kirschenbaum (1987) 31-88.
48. D. 15.1.7.4-5; D. 33.8.6pr; D.33.8.25.
49. D. 14.3.5.3; D. 2.13.4.3.
50. For the legal position of freedmen, see Gardner (1993) 7-51.
51. For independent freedmen, see Garnsey (1981).
52. Gai. *Inst.* 3.40-42.
53. Gai. *Inst.* 1.32c, 33, 34.
54. Juv. 1.102-6.
55. Petron. *Sat.* 76.
56. Joshel (1992) 61.
57. Varro. *Rust.* 2.10.5.
58. D. 15.1.53.
59. D. 33.8.8.2; D. 33.8.14; D. 33.8.23.1.
60. Petron. *Sat.* 76.
61. Cic. *Parad. Stoic.* 6.46.
62. Petron. *Sat.* 76.
63. For *operae*, see Gardner (1993) 20-21; 29-32.
64. *Rhet.Her.* 2.13.19.
65. D. 2.14.25pr.
66. FIRA 3.157.
67. FIRA 3.122.

3 THE BUSINESS OF THE SULPICII
1. Cic. *Font.* 11.
2. D. 12.2.13.6.
3. Camodeca (1999) 134.
4. For Cicero's finances in 45 BC, see Rauh (1989) 60-69.
5. Plin. *Ep.* 3.19.
6. For the size of private fortunes, see Duncan-Jones (1982) 343-44.

4 SALES AT AUCTION
1. For markets and market days, see MacMullen (1970) 333-341.
2. CIL 4.8863.
3. D. 46.3.88.
4. CIL 4. Suppl. 1, 3340.
5. Gai. *Inst.* 3.79.
6. CIL 4.3340. 154-5. Translated and discussed in Cooley and Cooley (2004) 169-70.
7. Schol. ad *Sat.* 1.6.86.
8. CIL 6. 9183.
9. Sen. *Controv.* 1 pr.19.
10. Cic. *Clu.* 180.
11. Gai. *Inst.* 4.126 a.
12. Cato *Agr.* 146; Cic. *Rab.Post.* 11.30.
13. D. 5.3.18 pr.

14. See Introduction.
15. *Purpuras laconicas reliquas* should be in the nominative, since these items are the subject of the verb *venibunt* ('will come up for auction').
16. Ovid *Ars. Am.* 3.169-172.
17. Hor. *Od.* 2.18.7-8.
18. *Ed. Diocl.* 26, 27, 28.
19. NAM inv. 3274.
20. Dinah Prentice, *pers. comm.*
21. Cato *Agr.* 59.
22. CIL 7861, 7863-64.
23. Petron. *Sat.* 46.
24. Gai. *Inst.* 3.78-79.
25. Andreau (1974).
26. CIL 4.138; CIL 4.1179; CIL 4.1180. Details of Mains' career in Cooley and Cooley (2004) 52-54.
27. Jongman (1988) 338-364.

5 GRAIN DEALERS
1. For the transport, storage and distribution of grain in Rome, see Rickman (1980) 120-155.
2. Tac. *Hist.* 4.38.
3. Camodeca (1994) 107. For discussion of the price of grain in Egypt and Rome see Rickman (1980) 148-155.
4. Camodeca (1994) 104-106.
5. D. 12.2.13.6.
6. For Domitia Lepida, see Gardner (1999) 13.

6 THE MERCHANT, THE AGENT AND THE SHIPPER
1. CIL 15. 3642-5, 4748-9.
2. Strabo 3.2.6.
3. Cic. 2 *Verr.* 5. 154.
4. D. 40.9.10.
5. Cicero's letters of recommendation are formulaic, which indicates that they were established commercial practice. For similar use of formulae, see the letters of recommendation written by present-day bankers.
6. Cic. *Fam.* 12.29.2.
7. For the role of sons, slaves and freedmen in Roman commerce, see Kirschenbaum (1987).
8. The remedies are summarised in Gai. *Inst.* 4. 69-74a.
9. D. 14.1.1.22.
10. Johnston (1999) 100-105.
11. For the use of the *peculium* in commerce, see Watson (1987) 90-101.
12. D. 14.3.5.2.
13. D. 14.3.5.7.
14. Cic. *Off.* 3.50.
15. Cato. *Agr.* pr.
16. D. 14.2.2. 2-3.
17. Petron. *Sat.* 76.
18. For the basic principles of identifying the participants in the supply chain, see Tenney Frank (1937) 72-79.
19. Aubert (1994) 265-267.
20. CIL 15 (ii) 4366.
21. The names of Spanish cities, among them Corduba and Hispalis, have been found on many

of the fragments in the Monte Testaccio.
22. CIL 12.4393.
23. CIL 14. S 4708.
24. For customs duty, see Duncan-Jones (1990) 194-95.
25. For shippers, agents and offices at Ostia, see Meiggs (1973) 283-289.
26. IG 14. 830. The sum involved is not entirely clear.
27. Cic. Rosc. Amer. 132.
28. Cic. Fam. 14.5.1; 16.21.1.
29. For speed of communications, see Duncan-Jones (1990) (7-29).
30. Cic. Fam. 16.5.2.
31. Rauh (2003) 83.
32. Petron. Sat. 101.
33. D. 4.9.3.1.
34. For details of the different contracts and legal remedies, see Thomas (1976) 299.
35. D. 14.2.10.2.
36. D. 14.2.10.1.
37. D. 4.9.3.1.
38. D. 14.2.1-2pr.
39. D. 14.2.10.1.
40. D. 19.2.13.1.
41. D. 22.2.1.
42. Camodeca (1999) 178-9.
43. Rathbone (2003) 207
44. Livy 23.48.10-49.3; Livy 25.3.10.
45. Suet. Claud. 18.
46. D. 19.2.15.6.
47. D. 19.2.61.1.
48. Livy 32.7.3.
49. Duncan-Jones (1990) 194-95.
50. Suet. Rhet. 1.16.
51. Curtis (1991) 172-73.
52. Plin. NH 6.101.

7 WELL-TO-DO WOMEN
1. For the legal and financial position of Roman women, see Gardner (1986).
2. Dixon (1986) 93-120.
3. Gai. Inst. 1.190.
4. Gai. Inst. 1. 18-19.
5. Treggiari (1969) 96-97.
6. D. 40.5.19.
7. Camodeca (1999) 211.
8. Gai. Inst. 3.124.
9. Camodeca (1999) 172.
10. Gai. Inst. 1. 193.
11. Gai. Inst. 3.131.
12. D. 30.1.41.11.
13. Cic. 2 Verr. 3.32.76.
14. Columella Rust. 3.3.
15. Gai. Inst. 1.192.

8 – SLAVES
1. There is a vast literature on the subject; good introductions are Watson (1987), and Bradley

(1994).
2. Strab. 14.5.2. For Delos and the slave trade, see Rauh (2003) 53-65.
3. Gai. *Inst.* 3.148.
4. D. 17.2.65.5.
5. D. 21.1.1.2.
6. D. 33.7.8. See also Bradley (1994) 57-80.
7. Treggiari (1973 and 1975).
8. Nep. *Att.* 13.3.
9. Plin. *NH* 35.199-201.
10. Tib. 2.3. 63-64.
11. D. 21.1.37.
12. D. 19.1.11.2.
13. D. 21.2.2.
14. D. 50.16.204.
15. Camodeca (1999) 86.
16. D. 11.1.9.8.
17. ILS 1514.
18. Camodeca (1999) 147.

9 DISPUTES
1. For a succinct account of civil procedure, see Johnston (1999) 112-132.
2. D. 2.13.1pr.
3. Gai. *Inst.* 4.183-187.
4. Gai. *Inst.* 4.186.
5. Cic. *Quinct.* 6.25.
6. For the Roman day, see Martial 4.8 and Balsdon (1969) 16-55.
7. Gai. *Inst.* 4.39-68. See also Crook (1967) 77 and Johnston (1999) 113-15.
8. D. 2.13.1.1.
9. D. 5.1.80.
10. Camodeca (1999) 78.
11. Gai. *Inst.* 4.171.
12. Cic. *Rosc. Com.* 4.10.
13. D. 12.2.1
14. D. 12.2.3pr.
15. D. 12.2.13.6.
16. For details, see Crook (1967) 89-92.
17. Plin. *Ep.* 6.2.
18. D. 5.1.79.1.
19. D. 22.5.13.
20. Gellius *Noct. Att.* 14.2.
21. Gai. *Inst.* 3.79.
22. For *infamia*, see Crook (1967) 83-85.
23. Cic. *Quinct.* 15.50.
24. Gai. *Inst.* 3.42.
25. Gai. *Inst.* 3.139.
26. Gai. *Inst.* 4.101.
27. D. 4.8.39pr.
28. Cic. *Rosc. Com.* 4.13.
29. The rules governing deposits are set out in D. 16.3.

10 FINANCING TRADE AND INDUSTRY
1. Cic. *Off.* 2.87.

2. Sen. *Ep.* 119.1-2.
3. For *institores* as small-time traders, see Aubert (1994) 18-24.
4. For rural workshops, see Aubert (1994) 201-11; for urban businesses, see Wallace-Hadrill (1994) 118-42.
5. Cato *Agr.* 135.2; 22.4.
6. CIL 5.5929.
7. Tab.Vindol. 2.343.
8. Cic. 2 *Verr.* 4.59-60.
9. For the contract of lease and hire, see Borkowski (1997). Examples of leasing contracts can be found in D. 19.2.
10. For warehouse leases, see Rickman (1980) 139-40.
11. P.Oxy. L 3595-7. Cockle (1981) provides translation and commentary.
12. For Egyptian leases, see Johnson (1938) 357-88; for the Tarsian loom, see Hunt and Edgar 1.36.
13. Heaton (1937) 3.
14. Cic. *Parad. Stoic.* 6.46.
15. D. 17.2.52.7.
16. D. 17.2.29.1.
17. For an overview of the mining industry, see Greene (2000) 747-50.
18. Domergue (1990) 254-57 (Table : *Lingots de plomb romains d'Espagne,* nos. 1046, 1042, 1041, 1002).
19. For co-operation between potters, see Aubert (1994) 209-11.
20. Livy 23.48.10 - 49.3.
21. Livy 25.3.10.
22. Plut. *Cat. mai.* 21.6.
23. For Cato's venture, see Rathbone (2003) 213-14.
24. Cic. *Quinct.* 4. 11-14.
25. For Cicero's finances, see Rauh (1989) 60-69; for Pliny, see *Ep.* 3.19.
26. For the supply of precious metal resulting from conquest and for the use of coinage and bullion as a means of exchange, see Howgego (1992).
27. Jongman (1988) 193-94.
28. For the size of private fortunes, see Duncan-Jones (1982) 343-44.
29. Duncan-Jones (1982) 304.
30. Cic. *Off.* 2.89.
31. Cic. *Off.* 1.150.
32. Suet. *Aug.* 39.
33. Polyb. 31.27.1-11.
34. Sen. *Ep.* 41.7; 87.7.
35. Tac. *Ann.* 14.53.6.
36. Plin. *Ep.* 3.19.
37. Petron. *Sat.* 76; 117.
38. Suet. *Aug.* 41.1.
39. Cato *Agr.* pr.
40. Nep. *Att.* 6.3.
41. Cic. *Parad. Stoic.* 6. 46.

11 MARITIME FINANCE
1. D. 14.1.1.12.
2. D. 14.1.1.15.
3. For the hierarchy on a sea-going merchant ship, see Casson (1995). 314-21.

4. D. 14.1.1pr.
5. D. 50.6.6.3.
6. Petron. *Sat*. 76.
7. Meiggs (1973) 323.
8. CIL 11.139.
9. Fabre (1981) 339.
10. Strab. 3.2.6.
11. D. 50.6.6.3.
12. For a detailed account of the financing of maritime commerce, see Rathbone (2003).
13. For a return of 6 per cent on agricultural investment, see Duncan-Jones (1982) 33.
14. Llewellyn & Kearsley (1992) 6.12.
15. Hunt and Edgar 1.38.
16. Duncan-Jones (1990) 194-95.
17. Plut. *Cat. min*. 38.1.
18. Cic. 2Verr. 5.63.
19. D. 14.1.7.1.
20. D. 14.1.7pr.
21. The term *permutatio* is also used to denote barter, as at Gai. *Inst*. 3. 141.
22. Rickman (1980) 148-155.
23. For details of the maritime loan, see D. 22.2.
24. For interest rates, see Appendix 7.
25. Plut. *Cat. mai*. 21.5-6.
26. D. 45.1.122.1.
27. The second case stretches the bounds of probability, in as much as Callimachus was very likely to have gone down with his ship. Presumably his heirs would then have been liable.
28. SB 14. 11850. For translation and commentary, see Rathbone (2003) 217-220.
29. See for instance Plin. *Ep*. 3.19, where Pliny considers buying for HS3 million an estate at Tifernum which was originally valued at HS5 million.
30. SB 18. 13167. For translation and commentary, see Rathbone (2000) 39-50.
31. The business interests of leading Republican families are listed in Wiseman (1971) 197-202. See also D'Arms (1981) 48-71.
32. Cic. *Rab. Post*. 2.4.
33. Cic. 2Verr. 5.45.
34. D. 50.5.3.
35. CIL 14. S 4620; 4621.
36. CIL 14.4142.
37. CIL 14.409.
38. Petron. *Sat*. 76.

12 PUBLIC WORKS
1. For euergetism, see Veyne (1990).
2. For public works administration in the city of Rome, see Strong (1968) 97-109.
3. Frontin. *Aq*. 7.4.
4. Duncan-Jones (1982) 156-62 (Italy), 89-93 (African provinces).
5. Duncan-Jones (1982) 31-2.
6. Plin. *Ep*. 10.37.1; 10.39.1.
7. Juv. 3.254-261, tr. Green (1974).
8. Hor. *Epist*. 2.2.73.
9. Cato *Agr*. 14.
10. For the contract of *locatio conductio*, see Gai. *Inst*. 3.142-47 and Martin (1989) passim.
11. Cic. *Qfr*. 3.1.1-3,5.

12. Cic. *Qfr.* 2.4.2.
13. CIL 6.31603.
14. CIL 6.607.
15. For the tomb of the Haterii, see Kleiner (1992) 196-97.
16. CIL 10.3707. Strab. 5.4.5.
17. CIL 14.3530. Martin (1989) 58.
18. CIL 10.3821.
19. CIL 6. 9852a and b.
20. Cass. Dio 69.4.2. For Hadrian's own building programme and aspirations to competence in architecture, see Birley (1997) 110-112.
21. Plin. *Ep.* 10.41.
22. Vitr. *De Arch.* 5.1.6.
23. Polyb. 6.17.1-4.
24. Key sources are the *lex Malacitana* (FIRA 1.24.cc.63.64.65) and Cic. 2 *Verr.* 1.141-42.
25. For summaries of the procedures, see Brunt (1980) 84-88 and Martin (1989) 21, 131-132.
26. Frontin. *Aq.* 129.
27. FIRA 1.24.cc.63,64,65.
28. Cic. 2 *Verr.* 1.141-42.
29. FIRA 3.153.
30. Consular names provide the date of 105 BC; for dating of the copy to the later period by letter-forms and use of Luna marble, see Bodel (2001) 53-55.
31. CIL 6.31603. See also Brunt (1980) 85.
32. For different contractors working on the Colosseum, see Boethius and Ward Perkins (1979) 233 and Martin (1989) 60-61.
33. D. 19.2.25.7.
34. Tac. *Hist.* 4.53.
35. Suet. *Vesp.* 8.
36. Suet. *Vesp.* 18.
37. For discussion of this episode, see Brunt (1980) 81-3.
38. D. 19.2.30.3.
39. Martin (1989) 115-16.
40. Polyb. 6.17.4.
41. Plut. Crass. 2.4-5; Cic. 2 Verr. 1. 130-50.
42. Nep. Att. 6.3
43. FIRA 1.24.65.
44. Lintott (1990) 210, n.99.
45. FIRA 3. 153.3.
46. FIRA 1.24.64-65.
47. Tac. *Ann.* 3.31.7.
48. D. 45.1.124.
49. D. 20.4.21.1.
50. Plin. *Ep.* 10.32.2.
51. Matt. 20. 1-16. For freeborn labour in Rome, see Brunt (1980) and Treggiari (1980).
52. Plin. *Ep.* 10.17b.2.
53. D. 17.2.29.1.
54. Plut. *Crass* 2.4-5.
55. Frontin. *Aq.* 116.3.
56. CIL 6. 6283,6284,6285,6363,6364,6365,6354.
57. D. 50.16.235.1.
58. Suet. *Aug.* 29.5.
59. Duncan-Jones (1990) 175.

60. D. 13.6.5.7.
61. CIL 8. 14580-2.
62. For elite ownership of raw materials in Italy and the provinces, see Whittaker (1985) 9-20.
63. Cic. 2 *Verr.* 1. 130-150.

13 THE COMPANIES OF TAX COLLECTORS
1. For a review of *portoria* and other indirect taxes, see
Cottier (2003) 398-99.
2. Rickman (1980) 36-45. See also Brunt (1981) 161 and Duncan Jones (1990) 187-98.
3. Rickman (1980) 40-41.
4. D. 50.16.16.
5. Livy 39.44.5-8. For the contract system, see Brunt (1981) 161-72 and (1990) 354-432, Lintott (1993) 86-91 and Aubert (1994) 325-30.
6. Polyb. 6.17.1-4.
7. FIRA 1.24.63-65.
8. Lintott (1993) 85.
9. D. 50.16.203.
10. Gai. *Inst.* 4.28.
11. Cic. *Planc.* 23.
12. Tac. *Ann.* 4.6.3.
13. D'Arms (1981) 36 and n.80; see also Badian (1972) 50.
14. Cic. 2Verr. 3.130.
15. For the size of the Asian revenues, see Brunt (1969) 123 [89]; for Bithynia, Cilicia and Syria, see Plut. *Pomp.* 45.3. 15.
16. For the contrary view, that the *publicani* only became liable at the end of the *lustrum* for the sums they owed, see Lintott (1993) 89.
17. See Chapter 12.
18. Polyb. 6.17.5.
19. D. 39.4.9pr., 1-2.
20. Cic. *Att.*1.17.9.
21. Suet. *Iul.* 20.
22. Cic. *Fam.* 13.9.
23. D. 17.2.59pr.
24. Tac. *Ann.* 13. 50-1.
25. Crook (1967) 233, Badian (1972) 70, Nicolet (1979) 69-95, Brunt (1990) 372-76 and Aubert (1994) 326 all claim, with differing degrees of certainty, that the *societates publicanorum* enjoyed a form of 'corporate' status.
26. D. 3.4.1pr; D. 3.4.1.1.
27. D. 39.4.3.1.
28. Nicolet (1979) 69-95.
29. Sicily, Cic. 2 *Verr.* 3.167.
30. Cic. *Fam.* 13.9.
31. Cic. 2 *Verr.* 2.169 (Carpinatius); 2 *Verr.* 3.166-67 (other directors). See also Balsdon (1962) 134-41.
32. Cic. 2 *Verr.* 2.172-73.
33. Cic. 2 *Verr.* 3.163-169.
34. Aubert (1994) 345-347.
35. Cic. 2 *Verr.* 3.116 (6 per cent of total crop in Sicily); *pro Rab. Post.* 30 (10 per cent of tax assessed).
36. Cic. 2 *Verr.* 3.181.
37. Tac. *Ann.* 13.50-51.

38. Gai. *Inst.* 4.28.
39. Plut. *Pomp.* 25.
40. Cic. *Att.* 11.1.2.
41. Cic. *Fam.* 13.65.1; Cic. *Fam.* 15.4.2.
42. Cic. *Att.* 5.21.11.
43. Cic. 2 *Verr.* 3.165-66.
44. Cic. 2 *Verr.* 2.186-91.
45. Livy 23.48.4.
46. Duncan-Jones (1990) 187-98 lists and discusses provinces where tax was collected in kind, in money and possibly in both forms of payment.
47. Duncan-Jones (1990) 193-94.
48. Tac. *Hist.* 4.38.
49. For a detailed account, see Rickman (1980) 55-58.
50. D. 48.12.2.
51. Cic. *Rab.Post.* 2.4.
52. Tac. *Ann.* 13. 50-1.
53. D. 39.4.9.5.
54. Luke 15.1-2.
55. MacMullen (1988) 130.
56. Cass. Dio 42.6.3; Plut. *Caes.* 48.1; App. *B.C.* 5.4.
57. Brunt (1990) 377-386.
58. Tac. *Ann.* 4.6.3.
59. Columella *Rust.* 1pr. 20.
60. CIL 2. 1180.
61. Sen. *Ep.* 41.7.
62. D. 50.6.6.8.
63. D. 50.6.6.6.

14 THE FAMILY FIRM
1. Plut. *Cat. mai.* 21.5.
2. Sen. *Ep.* 119.1-2.
3. Plut. *Cat. mai.* 21.8.
4. Varro *Rust.* 1.2.21-23.
5. D. 7.1.13.5.
6. D. 8.3.6 pr.
7. D. 33.7.25.1
8. D. 33.7.12.4-6; 50.16.203.
9. D. 32.35.2; 32.38.5.
10. Craftsmen and builders: CIL 6. 6283-5; 6363-5; slaves posted to service on aqueducts: Frontin. *Aq.* 116.
11. Weaver (1972) 8.
12. CIL 15.171.
13. Castren (1983) 220.
14. Cic. *Sest.* 3.6.
15. Cic. *Att.* 1.17.5.
16. For the careers of Publius Sestius and his son Lucius Sestius, see Richardson (2001) 49-55.
17. Will (2001) 35-47 tells the story and brings up to date her article of 1979.
18. Cic. *Att.* 15.29.1.
19. Catull. 44.
20. Cic. *Fam.* 5.6.2; *Fam.* 13.8.3.
21. Cass. Dio. 53.32.4; App. BC 4.51.

22. My interpretation is based on that of Will (2001).
23. Cic. *Att.* 16.4.4.
24. The best known of these is the villa at Settefinestre.
25. For the manufacture and export of fish-based products from Cosa, see McCann (2002).
26. Will (2001) 43.
27. For a review of the excavation report by Carandini *et al*, see Purcell (1988). For other aspects of the *ager Cosanus*, see Manacorda (1978) (commercial production in villas); Rathbone (1983) (free peasant labour working alongside slaves); and Aubert (1994) 162-7 (diversification at Settefinestre).
28. Attolini *et al.* (1991).
29. Richardson (2001) 49-55.
30. For buying grapes in advance of the harvest, see Plin. *Ep.* 8.2.
31. D. 18.6.1-6. For discussion of the legal issues and the role of traders, see Paterson (1998).
32. D. 18.6.2pr.
33. D. 18.1.71.
34. D.33.6.15.
35. D.33.6.3.1.
36. Varro *Rust.* 2.6.5.
37. Cic. *Sest.* 7.
38. For a full case study, see Curtis (1988).
39. Castren (1983) 232.
40. Antiochis: T.23, T.24; Ianuaria: T.25; Modestus: T.104; T.113.
41. CIL 10.1024.
42. CIL 10.792.
43. Curtis (1988) 31.
44. Curtis (1988) 29-30.
45. CIL 4.5694; 4.5689; 4.5690
46. CIL 4.2576; 4.9406.
47. For the structure of the industry, see Jones (1974) 50-364.
48. The tomb is by the roadside in the village of Igel.
49. Toynbee (1971) 48-49. Tombs can be seen lining the approaches to many Roman cities, including Puteoli. The Via dei Sepolcri at Pompeii and the Via Aureliana at Arles provide particularly good examples.
50. Hope (2001) 9.
51. For detailed description of the Igel Column, see Zahn (1968).
52. For *evocati Augusti*, see Watson (1969) 18.
53. Drinkwater (1982).
54. The payment of rent was a common sculptural theme at this time: see reliefs in the Rheinisches Landesmuseum at Trier.
55. Chilver (1941) 165-66. For wool processing and marketing in Roman Italy, see Frayn (1984) 142-172.
56. The Edict, promulgated in 301, fixed maximum prices (and wages). It does not indicate whether the prices specified are wholesale or retail nor is it clear whether these are current prices which were to be pegged, or previous prices to which the government required people to return. The wool textile industry is covered in Chapters 19 and 25 of the Edict, see Frank (1933-40) vol. 5.
57. Auson. *Ordo.Nob.Urb.* 6.4.
58. D. 41.1.26.2
59. For the manufacture and marketing of woollen cloth in medieval Europe, see Spufford (2002). (241-248).
60. For manufacturing centres, see Strabo 5.1.12.

61. Nicolet (1979) 75.
62. Sen. Clem. 1.15.1-7 (son); Tac. Ann. 13.32 (wife); Cic. Cael. 68 (slaves).
63. Plin. Ep. 3.19.1
64. Gai. Inst. 1.19.
65. D. 17.1.1.4.
66. D. 17.1.7.
67. Cic. Caecin. 20.57.
68. D. 41.1.13pr.
69. D. 41.1.9.4.
70. D. 46.3.12pr.
71. Cic. Fam. 12.29.2.
72. Petron. Sat. 30.
73. Sen. Ep. 2.18.
74. D. 14.3.5.18.
75. Col. Rust. 1.6.7.
76. CIL 14.2298
77. For studies of the *vilicus*, see Aubert (1994) 146-75; Carlsen (1995).
78. D. 14.1.1.12.
79. D.14.3.5.2.
80. Cato Agr. 2.1-6.
81. Varro Rust. 1.16.5.
82. Columella Rust. 1.8.3-4.
83. Diod. Sic. 5.38.1; Apul. Met. 9.12.
84. Treggiari (1980) 48-52. For building sites, see Chapter 12.
85. For business managers in Latin inscriptions, see Aubert (1994) 442-476.
86. Aubert (1994) 16-30.
87. Vitr. De Arch. 6.9.
88. Cic. 2 Verr.4.54.
89. Cato Agr. 2.1-6.
90. Rathbone (1991) 376, Table 18.
91. Rathbone (2002) 166-67.
92. Petron. Sat. 53.
93. Cic. 2 Verr. 3.119. See also Wiedemann (1981) 150-52.
94. Bowman (1994) 40.
95. Cic. Fam. 12.29.2.
96. Columella Rust. 3.3.8.
97. For criticism of Columella, see Finley (1999) 117 and Duncan Jones (1982) 39-59.
98. For support for Columella, see Carandini (1983) 177-203; Nicolet (1988) 138-39.
99. D. 50.16.203.
100. Cic. Off. 1.139.
101. Vitr. De Arch. 6.5.2.
102. Wallace-Hadrill (1994) 10-12.

EPILOGUE
1. Cic. Off. 1. 151.
2. D'Arms (1981) 45-47.
3. CIL 14.374.

APPENDICES
1. For other bankers known to have practised their trade in Puteoli, see Camodeca (2000)

281-88.
2. For networks in the *terra sigillata* industry, see Aubert (1994) 276-302.
3. For a wide-ranging study of the lamp industry, see Harris (1980).
4. Bezeczky (1998) 1-4.
5. CIL 12.4393.
6. Meiggs (1973) 289.
7. CIL 9.2689.
8. FIRA 3. 122.
9. Crawford (1970) 42.
10. Cic. 2 *Verr.* 1.137.
11. For Cicero's finances in 45 BC, see Rauh (1989) 60-69.
12. Suet. *Galba* 8.1; for the introduction and use of *aurei*, cf. Howgego (1992) 11.
13. Plin. *Ep.* 3.19.
14. For certificates of value attached to sacks of coins (*tesserae nummulariae*), see Andreau 1999 (80-89).
15. Cassius Dio 76. 10. 1-5.
16. Suet. *Aug.* 32.1: armed police; Suet. *Tib.* 37: police posts.
17. Nippel (1995) 38-39.
18. Cic. *Att.* 4.15.7.
19. Suet. *Aug.* 41.1.
20. D. 22.2.4.1.
21. Plin. *Ep.* 9.28.5.
22. Plin. *Ep.* 10.54.
23. Columella *Rust.* 3.3.9-10. See also Duncan-Jones (1982) 33.
24. CIL 11.1147. See also Duncan-Jones (1982) 288-319.
25. Plin. *Ep.* 7.18.
26. D. 13.4.3
27. Nep. *Att.* 14.3.
28. Nep. *Att.* 15.2.
29. Horsfall (1989) 94.
30. Cic. *Att.* 7.18.4.
31. Cic. *Amic.* 71.
32. Cic. *Att.* 1.13.1; 1.19.9; 1.20.4.
33. Cic. *Fam.* 5.5.3; *Att.* 2.1.12.
34. Nep. *Att.* 21.1.
35. Casson (1980): 60 million *modii*; Rickman (1980): 40 million; Garnsey (1983): 30 million. Garnsey also summarises and assesses the ancient evidence.
36. Cato *Agr.* 56-8.
37. Josephus *B.J.* 2.383, 386.

BIBLIOGRAPHY

Andreau, J. (1974) *Les affaires de Monsieur Jucundus*, Rome, Collections de l'École française de Rome, 19.
Andreau, J. (1999) *Banking and business in the Roman world*, Cambridge, Cambridge University Press.
Attolini I. et al. (1991) 'Political geography and productive geography between the valleys of the Albegna and the Fiora in northern Etruria', in Barker, G. and Lloyd, J. (eds) *Roman Landscapes: Archaeological Survey in the Mediterranean Region*, London, British School at Rome, 142-52.
Aubert, J-J (1994) *Business Managers in Ancient Rome: a social and economic study of institores, 200 BC.-AD. 250*, Leiden, Brill.
Aubert, J-J (1999) 'Les *institores* et le commerce maritime dans l'Empire romain,' *Topoi*, 9, 145-64.
Badian, E. (1972) *Publicans and Sinners: Private Enterprise in the Service of the Roman Republic*, Oxford, Blackwell.
Balsdon, J.P.V.D. (1962) 'Roman history, 65-50 BC Five problems', *Journal of Roman Studies*, 52, 134-41.
Beard, M., North J. and Price, S. (1998) *Religions of Rome*, Cambridge, Cambridge University Press.
Bezeczky, T. (1998) *The Laecanius amphora stamps and villas of Brijuni*, Vienna, Verlag der österreichische Akademie der Wissenschaften.
Birley, A.R. (1997) *Hadrian: The Restless Emperor*, London, Routledge.
Birley, A.R. (2002) *Garrison life at Vindolanda: A Band of Brothers*, Tempus Publishing, Stroud and Charleston.
Bodel, J. (ed.) (2001) *Epigraphic Evidence: Ancient History from Inscriptions*, London, Routledge.
Boethius A. and Ward Perkins J.B. (1979) *Etruscan and Roman Architecture*, Harmondsworth, Penguin.
Borkowski A. (1992) *Textbook on Roman Law* (2nd ed.), London, Blackstone Press.
Borriello, M. and Giove, T. (2001) (eds) *The Epigraphic Collection of the National Archaeological Museum of Naples*, Naples, Electa Napoli/Soprintendenza Archeologica di Napoli e Caserta.
Bowman, A. (1994) *Life and Letters on the Roman Frontier*, London, British Museum Press.
Bowman, A. and Thomas J. (1994) *The Vindolanda Writing Tablets (Tabulae Vindolandenses II)*, London, British Museum Press.
Bradley, K.R. (1994) *Slavery and Society at Rome*, Cambridge, Cambridge University Press.
Braudel F. (1982) (Reynolds, S. tr.) *Civilization and Capitalism, 15th-18th Century, Vol. 2: The Wheels of Commerce*, London, Collins.
Brunt, P.A. (1965) 'The *equites* in the late Republic', in *Second International Conference of Economic History: Aix 1962*; repr. in Seager, R. (ed.) *The Crisis of the Roman Republic,* Cambridge, Heffer.

Brunt, P.A. (1980) 'Free labour and public works in Rome', *Journal of Roman Studies*, 70, 81-100.
Brunt, P.A. (1981) 'The revenues of Rome,' *Journal of Roman Studies*, 71, 161-72.
Brunt, P.A. (1990) 'Publicans in the Principate,' in *Roman Imperial Themes*, Oxford, Clarendon Press.
Camodeca, G. (1992) *L'archivio puteolano dei Sulpicii*, I, Naples.
Camodeca, G. (1994) 'Puteoli porto annonario et il commercio del grano in età imperiale', in *Le ravitaillement en blé de Rome et des centres urbains des débuts de la République jusqu'au Haut Empire: actes du colloque international organisé par le Centre Jean Bérard et l'URA 994 du CNRS, Naples, 14-16 février 1991*, Rome, École Française de Rome.
Camodeca, G. (1996) 'L'élite municipale di Puteoli fra la tarda repubblica e Nerone', in *Les élites municipales de l'Italie péninsulaire des Gracques à Néron: actes de la table ronde de Clermont Ferrand (28-30 novembre 1991)*, Rome, École Française de Rome.
Camodeca, G. (1999) *Tabulae Pompeianae Sulpiciorum: Edizione critica dell'archivio puteolano dei Sulpicii*, 2 vols., Rome, Edizioni Quasar.
Camodeca, G. (2000) 'Un *vicus Tyanianus* e i mestieri bancari a Puteoli: rilettura del graffito ercolanese CIL iv. 10676', *Ostraka*, 9, 281-88.
Carandini, A. (1983) 'Columella's vineyard and the rationality of the Roman economy', *Opus* 2,1, 177-204.
Carandini A. et.al. (1985) *Settefinestre. Una villa schiavistica nell'Etruria romana*, 3 vols., Modena, Panini.
Carlsen, J. (1995) *Vilici and Roman Estate Managers until AD 284*, Rome, Series Analecta Romana Instituti Danici, Suppl. 24, Rome, 'L'Erma' di Bretschneider.
Casson, L. (1965) 'Harbour and river boats of ancient Rome', in *Journal of Roman Studies*, 55, 31-39.
Casson, L. (1980) 'The role of the state in Rome's grain trade', in D'Arms J.H. and Kopff, E.C. (eds) *Roman Seaborne Commerce: Studies in Archaeology and History*, Rome, Memoirs of the American Academy at Rome, 36, 21-33.
Casson L. (1995) *Ships and Seamanship in the Ancient World*, Baltimore, Johns Hopkins University Press.
Castren, P. (1983) *Ordo Populusque Pompeianus: Polity and Society in Roman Pompeii* (2nd edn.), Rome, Bardi.
Champlin, E. (1991) *Final Judgments: Duty and Emotion in Roman Wills, 200 BC-AD 250*, Berkeley, University of California Press.
Chilver G.E.F. (1941) *Cisalpine Gaul: Social and Economic History from 49 BC to the Death of Trajan*, Oxford, Clarendon Press.
Cimma, M. (1981) *Ricerche sulle società di publicani*, Milan, Giuffrè.
Cockle, H. (1981) 'Pottery manufacture in Roman Egypt: a new papyrus', *Journal of Roman Studies*, 71, 87-97.
Cohen, E.E. (1992) *Athenian Economy and Society: A Banking Perspective*, Princeton, Princeton University Press.
Cooley, A.E. and Cooley M.G.L. (2004) *Pompeii: A Sourcebook*, London and New York, Routledge.
Cottier, M. (2003) '*Quadragesima Galliarum*: l'organisation douanière des provinces alpestres, gauloises et germaniques de l'Empire romain', *Journal of Roman Studies*, 93, 398-99.
Crawford, M. (1970) 'Money and exchange in the Roman world,' *Journal of Roman Studies*, 60, 40-48.
Crook, J.A. (1967) *Law and Life of Rome*, London, Thames and Hudson.
Curtis, R.I. (1988) 'A. Umbricius Scaurus of Pompeii', in Curtis, R.I. (ed.) Studia Pompeiana e Classica in Honor of Wilhelmina F. Jashemski, New York, Caratzas, 19-50.
Curtis, R.I. (1991) *Garum and salsamenta: Production and Commerce in Materia Medica*, Leiden, Brill.
D'Arms, J.H. (1975) 'Tacitus, *Annals* 13.48, and a new inscription from Puteoli', reprinted in

Zevi, F. (2003) (ed.) *Romans on the Bay of Naples and other essays on Roman Campania by John H. D'Arms*, 321-29.

D'Arms, J.H. (1974) 'Puteoli in the second century of the Roman Empire: a social and economic study', *Journal of Roman Studies*, 64, 104-24.

D'Arms, J.H. (1981) *Commerce and Social Standing in Ancient Rome*, Cambridge, Harvard University Press.

D'Arms, J.H. (2000) 'Memory, money and status at Misenum: three new inscriptions from the *collegium* of the Augustales', *Journal of Roman Studies*, 90, 126-44.

D'Arms, J.H. (2002) Romans on the Bay of Naples, reprinted in Zevi, F. (ed.) *Romans on the Bay of Naples and other essays on Roman Campania by John H. D'Arms*, Bari, Edipuglia.

De Caro, S. (2002) *I Campi Flegrei, Ischia, Vivara: Storia e Archeologia*, Naples, Electa Napoli/Soprintendenza per i Beni Archeologici di Napoli e Caserta.

De Neeve, P.W. (1990) 'A Roman landowner and his estates: Pliny the Younger', *Athenaeum*, 78, 363-402.

De Ste Croix, G.E.M. (1956) 'Greek and Roman accounting', in Littleton, A.C. and Yamey, B.S. (eds) *Studies in the History of Accounting*, London, Sweet and Maxwell, 14-74.

Dixon, S. (1986) 'Family Finances: Terentia and Tullia,' in Rawson, E. (1986) (ed.) *The Family in Ancient Rome*, London, Routledge.

Domergue, C. (1990) *Les mines de la Peninsula Iberique dans l'antiquité romaine*, Rome, Collection de l'École française de Rome, 127.

Drinkwater, J.F. (1982) 'The wool textile industry in Gallia Belgica and the Secundinii of Igel,' *Textile History*, 13.1, 111-28.

Duff, A.M. (1928) *Freedmen in the early Roman Empire*, Oxford, Oxford University Press.

Duncan-Jones, R.P. (1982) *The Economy of the Roman Empire: Quantitative Studies*, Cambridge, Cambridge University Press.

Duncan-Jones, R.P. (1990) *Structure and Scale in the Roman Economy*, Cambridge, Cambridge University Press.

Duthoy R. (1974) 'La fonction sociale de l'augustalité', *Epigraphica*, 36, 134-54.

Duthoy R. (1978) 'Les Augustales,' in *Aufstieg und Niedergang der Römischen Welt II*, 1254-1309.

Fabre, G. (1981) *Libertus: Recherches sur les rapports patron-affranchi de la république romaine*, Rome, Collection de l'École française de Rome, 50.

Finley, M. (1999) *The ancient economy*, (2nd edn. updated w. foreword by Morris, I.), Berkeley, California University Press.

Frank, T. (ed.) (1933-40) *An Economic Survey of Ancient Rome*, (5 vols), Baltimore, Johns Hopkins University Press.

Frank, T. (1937) 'Notes on Roman commerce', *Journal of Roman Studies*, 27, 72-79.

Frayn, J.M. (1984) *Sheep-Rearing and the Wool Trade in Italy during the Roman Period*, Liverpool, Cairns.

Frederiksen, M.W. (1966) 'Caesar, Cicero and the problem of debt', *Journal of Roman Studies*, 56, 128-41.

Frederiksen, M.W. (1975) 'Theory, evidence and the ancient economy', *Journal of Roman Studies*, 65, 164-71.

Frederiksen, M.W. (1984) *Campania* (ed. w. addns by Purcell, N.), London, British School at Rome.

Frier, B.W. (1977) 'The rental market in early imperial Rome', *Journal of Roman Studies*, 67, 27-37.

Fülle, G. (1997) 'The internal organization of the Arretine *terra sigillata* industry: problems of evidence and interpretation', *Journal of Roman Studies*, 87, 110-55.

Gardner, J. (1986) *Women in Roman Law and Society*, London, Croom Helm.

Gardner, J. (1993) *Being a Roman Citizen*, London, Routledge.

Gardner, J. (1999) 'Women in business life: some evidence from Puteoli', in *Acta Instituti Romani Finlandiae*, 22, 11-27.

Garnsey, P.D.A. (1981) 'Independent freedmen and the economy of Roman Italy under the Principate', *Klio*, 63, 359-71.
Garnsey, P.D.A. (1983) 'Grain for Rome', in Garnsey P.D.A., Hopkins, K. and Whittaker, C.R. (eds) *Trade in the Ancient Economy,* London, Chatto and Windus, 118-130.
Garnsey, P.D.A. and Saller, R.P. (1987) *The Roman Empire: Economy, Society and Culture*, London, Duckworth.
Giliberti, G. (1999) 'De la rente agricole à l'investissement financier: le rôle de l'esclave *kalendario praepositus*', *Topoi*, 9, 165-78.
Gordon, M.L. (1931) 'The freedman's son in municipal life', *Journal of Roman Studies*, 21, 65-77.
Green P. (tr.) (1974) *Juvenal: The Sixteen Satires*, Harmondsworth, Penguin.
Greene, K. (1986) *The Archaeology of the Roman Economy*, London, Batsford.
Greene, K. (2000) *Industry and Technology* = Chap.25, *Cambridge Ancient History* (2nd edn.) Vol XI, Cambridge, Cambridge University Press.
Hardy, E.G. (1912) *Roman Laws and Charters: Translated with Introduction and Notes*, Oxford, Clarendon Press.
Harris, W.V. (1980) 'Roman terracotta lamps: the organisation of an industry', *Journal of Roman Studies*, 70, 126-45.
Harris, W.V. (1993) 'Between archaic and modern: some current problems in the history of the Roman economy', in *The Inscribed Economy: Production and Distribution in the Roman Empire in the light of instrumentum domesticum', Journal of Roman Archaeology,* Suppl. Series No 6, 11-29.
Harris, W.V. (2000) *Trade* = Chap.24, *Cambridge Ancient History* (2nd edn.) Vol XI, Cambridge, Cambridge University Press.
Heaton H. (1937) 'Financing the industrial revolution', *Bulletin of the Business Historical Society*, 11, 1-10.
Hope, V. (2001) *Constructing Identity: The Roman Funerary Monuments of Aquileia, Mainz and Nîmes*, British Archaeological Reports, BAR International Series 24, Oxford, Hedges.
Hopkins, K. (1978) *Conquerors and Slaves: Sociological Studies in Roman History*, Cambridge, Cambridge University Press.
Hopkins, K. (1980) 'Taxation and trade in the Roman empire (200 BC - AD 400)', *Journal of Roman Studies*, 70, 101-28.
Hopkins, K. (1983a) Introduction to Garnsey, P.D.A., Hopkins, K. and Whittaker, C.R. (eds) *Trade in the Ancient Economy,* London, Chatto and Windus, ix-xxv.
Hopkins, K. (1983b) 'Models, ships and staples', in Garnsey P.D.A. and Whittaker C.R. (eds) *Trade and Famine in Classical antiquity*, Cambridge, Cambridge Philological Society, 84-109.
Hopkins, K. (2002) 'Rome, taxes, rents and trade', in *Kodai: Journal of Ancient History*, VI/VII (1995/6), 41-75; repr. in Scheidel W. and von Reden, S. (eds) *The Ancient Economy*, Edinburgh, Edinburgh University Press, 190-230.
Horden, P. and Purcell, N. (2000) *The Corrupting sea: A Study of Mediterranean History*, Oxford, Blackwell.
Horsfall, N. (tr.) (1989) *Cornelius Nepos: A Selection, Including the Lives of Cato and Atticus*, Oxford, Clarendon Press.
Houston G.W. (1988) 'Ports in perspective: some comparative materials on Roman merchant ships and ports', *American Journal of Archaeology*, 92, 553-564.
Howgego, C. (1992) 'The supply and use of money in the Roman world, 200 B.C. to A.D. 300', *Journal of Roman Studies*, 82, 1-31.
Hunt A.S. and Edgar C.C. (1932) *Select Papyri (vol. 1): Non-literary Papyri (Private Affairs)*, Cambridge, Mass, and London, Harvard University Press and William Heinemann (Loeb Classical Library).
Johnson A.C. (1938) *Roman Egypt to the Reign of Diocletian* = Frank, T. (ed.) (1933-40) *An economic survey of ancient Rome*, Vol. 2, Baltimore, Johns Hopkins University Press.
Johnston, D. (1999) *Roman Law in Context*, Cambridge, Cambridge University Press.

Jones, A,H.M. (1974) (ed. Brunt, P.A.) *The Roman economy: Studies in Ancient Economic and Administrative History*, Oxford.
Jongman, W. (1988) *The Economy and Society of Pompeii*, Amsterdam, Gieben.
Joshel, S. (1992) *Work, Identity, and Legal Status at Rome: A Study of the Occupational Inscriptions*, Norman, University of Oklahoma Press.
Kehoe, D. (1997) *Investment, Profit, and Tenancy: The Jurists and the Roman Agrarian Economy*, Ann Arbor, University of Michigan Press.
Kenrick, P.M. (1997), 'Cn. Ateius – the inside story', *Rei Cretariae Romanae Fautorum Acta*, 35, 179-90.
Kirschenbaum, A. (1987) *Sons, Slaves and Freedmen in Roman Commerce*, Jerusalem, Hebrew University Press.
Kleiner, D.E.E. (1992) *Roman Sculpture*, New Haven, Yale University Press.
Levi, P. (1997) *Horace: A Life*, London, Duckworth.
Llewellyn, S.R. and Kearsley, R.A. (1992) *New Documents Illustrating Early Christianity* (vol. 6): *A Review of the Greek Inscriptions and Papyri Published in 1980-81*, Macquarie University, Ancient History Documentary Research Centre.
Lewis N. (1983) *Life in Egypt under Roman Rule*, Oxford, Clarendon Press.
Lewis N. and Reinhold M. (tr.) (1990) *Roman Civilisation: Selected Readings* (2 vols.), (3rd edn.), New York, Columbia University Press.
Lintott A, (1993) *Imperium Romanum: Politics and Administration*, London, Routledge.
Loane, H.J. (1938) *Industry and Commerce of the City of Rome, 50 BC - AD 200*, Baltimore, Johns Hopkins University Press.
MacMullen, R. (1970) 'Market days in the Roman Empire', *Phoenix*, 24, 333-41.
MacMullen, R. (1988) *Corruption and the Decline of Rome*, New Haven, Yale University Press.
Manacorda, D. (1978) 'The Ager Cosanus and the production of the *amphorae* of Sestius: new evidence and a reassessment', *Journal of Roman Studies*, 68, 122-31.
Martin, S.D. (1989) *The Roman Jurists and the Organisation of Private Building in the Late Republic and Early Empire*, Brussels, Latomus.
McCann, A.M. (2002) *The Roman Port and Fishery of Cosa: A Short Guide*, Rome, American Academy in Rome.
Meiggs, R. (1973) *Roman Ostia*, (2nd. edn.), Oxford, Clarendon Press.
Meredith, D. (1953) 'Annius Plocamus: two inscriptions from the Berenice road', *Journal of Roman Studies*, 43, 38-40.
Metzger, E. (2000) 'The current view of the extra-judicial *vadimonium*, '*Zeitschrift der Savigny-Stiftung für Rechtsgeschichte (Romanistische Abteilung)*, 117, 132-178.
Meyer, E. (2004) *Legitimacy and Law in the Roman World:* Tabulae *in Roman Belief and Practice*, Cambridge, Cambridge University Press.
Mickwitz, G. (1937) 'Economic rationalism in Graeco-Roman agriculture', *English Historical Review*, 52, 577-89.
Miniero, P. (2000) (ed.) *The* Sacellum *of the* Augustales *at Miseno*, Naples, Electa Napoli/Soprintendenza Archeologica di Napoli e Caserta.
Morley, N. (2004) *Theories, Models and Concepts in ancient History*, Routledge, London and New York.
Mouritsen H. (2001) 'Roman freedmen and the urban economy: Pompeii in the first century AD', in *Pompeii tra Sorrento e Sarno, Atti del terzo e quarto ciclo di conferenze di geologia, storia e archeologia Pompeii, gennaio 1999 – maggio 2000*, Rome, Bardi, 1-27.
Nicolet, C. (1966-74) *L'ordre equestre à l'époque républicaine, 312-43 av. J.C* (2 vols.) Paris, Bibliothèque des écoles françaises d'Athènes et de Rome, 207.
Nicolet, C. (1979) 'Deux remarques sur l'organisation des sociétés de publicains à la fin de la république romaine', in van Effenterre H. (ed.) *Points de vue sur la fiscalité à Rome*, Paris, Université de Paris, 69-95.
Nicolet, C. (1988) *Rendre à César: Économie et société dans la Rome antique*, Paris, Gallimard.
Nippel, W. (1995) *Public Order in Ancient Rome*, Cambridge, Cambridge University Press.

Painter, K. S. (1975) 'Roman flasks with scenes of Baiae and Puteoli', *Journal of Glass Studies*, 17, 54-67.
Paterson, J. (1982) 'Salvation from the sea: *amphorae* and trade in the Roman west', *Journal of Roman Studies*, 72, 146-57.
Paterson, J. (1998) 'Trade and traders in the Roman world: scale, structure and organisation', in Parkins, H. and Smith, C. (eds) *Trade, Traders and the Ancient City*, London, Routledge, 149-67.
Pavis d'Escurac, H. (1977) 'Aristocratie senatoriale et profits commerciaux', *Ktema*, 2, 339-55.
Pavis d'Escurac, H. (1978) 'Pline le Jeune et la transmission des patrimoines', *Ktema*, 3, 275-88.
Pleket, H.W. (1983) 'Urban elites and business in the Greek part of the Roman empire', in Garnsey, P.D.A., Hopkins, K., Whittaker, C.R. (eds). *Trade in the Ancient Economy*, London, Chatto and Windus, 131-44.
Pomey, P. and Tchernia, A. (1978) 'Le tonnage maximum des navires de commerce romains', *Archaeonautica*, 2, 233-251.
Purcell, N. (1988) (Review articles) 'Le vin de l'Italie romaine: essai d'histoire économique d'après les amphores' ; 'Settefinestre: una villa schiavistica nell'Etruria romana', *Journal of Roman Studies*, 78, 194-98.
Radice B. (1963) (tr.) *The Letters of the Younger Pliny*, Harmondsworth, Penguin.
Rathbone, D.W. (1981) 'The development of agriculture in the Ager Cosanus during the Roman Republic: problems of evidence and interpretation', *Journal of Roman Studies*, 71, 10-23.
Rathbone, D.W. (1991) *Economic Rationalism and Rural Society in Third Century A.D. Egypt: The Heroninos Archive and the Appianus Estate,* Cambridge, Cambridge University Press.
Rathbone, D.W. (2000) 'The "Muziris" papyrus (SB XVIII 13167): financing Roman trade with India', in *Alexandrian Studies II in Honour of Mostafa el Abbadi, Bulletin de la Société Archéologique d'Alexandrie*, 46, 39-50.
Rathbone, D.W. (2002) 'The ancient economy and Graeco-Roman Egypt,' in Criscuolo, L. and Geraci, G., (eds) (1989) *Egitto e storia antica dall'ellenismo all'età araba*, Bologna, Cooperativa Libraria Universitaria Editrice Bologna, 159-76; repr. in Scheidel W. and von Reden, S. (eds.) *The Ancient Economy*, Edinburgh, Edinburgh University Press, 155-69.
Rathbone D.W. (2003) 'The financing of maritime commerce in the Roman empire I-II AD', in Lo Cascio, E. (ed.) *Credito e moneta nel mondo romano, Atti degli Incontri capresi di storia dell'economica antica, (Capri 12-14 ottobre 2000)*, Bari, Edipuglia, 197-229.
Rauh, N. K. (1986), 'Cicero's business friendships: economics and politics in the late Roman Republic', *Aevum*, 60, 3-30.
Rauh, N.K. (1989) 'Finance and estate sales in republican Rome', *Aevum* , 63, 45-76.
Rauh, N.K. (2003) *Merchants, Sailors and Pirates in the Roman world*, Tempus Publishing, Stroud and Charleston.
Rawson, E. (1976) 'The Ciceronian aristocracy and its properties', in Finley M. (ed.) (1976) *Studies in Roman property*, Cambridge, Cambridge University Press, 85-102.
Rawson, E. (1986) (ed.) *The Family in Ancient Rome*, London, Routledge.
Richardson, L. (2001) '*Sestius noster*', in Goldman N. (ed.) (2001) *New Light from Ancient Cosa: Classical Mediterranean Studies in Honor of Cleo Rickman*, New York, Lang, 49-55.
Rickman, G.E. (1980) *The Corn Supply of Ancient Rome*, Oxford, Clarendon Press.
Rose, K.F.C. (1962) 'Trimalchio's accountant', *Classical Philology*, 62, 258-59.
Rose, K.F.C. (1971) *The date and author of the Satyricon,* Leiden.
Rostovzeff, M. (1957), (2nd edn., rev. by Fraser, P.M.), *The social and economic history of the Roman Empire,* (2 vols), Oxford, Clarendon Press.
Rowe, G. (2001) 'Trimalchio's world', *Scripta Classica Israelica*, 20, 25-45.
Saller, R. (1984) '*Familia, domus,* and the Roman conception of the family', *Phoenix*, 38, 336–55.
Saller, R. (1994) *Patriarchy, property and death in the Roman family*, Cambridge, Cambridge University Press.

Scheidel, W. and von Reden, S. (2002) (eds) *The Ancient Economy*, Edinburgh, Edinburgh University Press.
Shackleton Bailey, D.R. (1978) (tr.) *Cicero's Letters to Atticus*, Harmondsworth, Penguin.
Shackleton Bailey, D.R. (1978) (tr.) *Cicero's Letters to His Friends (2 vols.)* Harmondsworth, Penguin.
Shatzman, I. (1975) *Senatorial Wealth and Roman Politics*, Brussels, Latomus.
Sherwin-White, A.N. (1966) *The Letters of Pliny: A Historical and Social Commentary*, Oxford, Clarendon Press.
Sherwin-White, A.N. (1973) *The Roman Citizenship*, (2nd edn.) Oxford, Clarendon Press.
Spufford, P. (2002) *Power and Profit: The Merchant in Medieval Europe*, London, Thames and Hudson.
Stevens Cox, G. (1999) *St. Peter Port 1680-1830: The History of An International Entrepôt*, Woodbridge and Rochester, Boydell Press.
Strong D.E. (1968) 'The administration of public building in Rome during the late Republic and early Empire', *Bulletin of the Institute of Classical Studies*, 15, 97-109.
Talamanca, M. (1954) 'Contributo allo studio delle vendite all'asta nel mondo antico,' in *Memorie dell'Academia dei Lincei*, ser. 8, v.6.
Tchernia, A. (1986) *Le vin de l'Italie romaine: Essai d'histoire économique d'après les amphores*, Rome, Bibliothèque des écoles françaises d'Athènes et de Rome, 265.
Temin, P. (2001) 'A market economy in the early Roman Empire', *Journal of Roman Studies*, 91, 169-81.
Thomas, J.A.C. (1976) *Textbook of Roman Law*, Amsterdam, New York, Oxford, North-Holland Publishing Company.
Toynbee, J.M.C. (1971) *Death and Burial in the Roman World*, Baltimore, Johns Hopkins University Press.
Treggiari, S.M. (1969) *Roman Freedmen during the Late Republic*, Oxford, Clarendon Press.
Treggiari, S.M. (1975) 'Jobs in the household of Livia', *Papers of the British School at Rome*, 43, 48-77.
Treggiari, S.M. (1980) 'Urban labour in Rome: *mercennarii* and *tabernarii*', in Garnsey, P.D.A. (ed.) (1980) *Non-Slave Labour in the Greco-Roman World*, Cambridge, Cambridge Philological Society, 48-64.
Treggiari, S.M. (1991) *Roman Marriage: Iusti Coniuges from the Time of Cicero to the Time of Ulpian*, Oxford, Clarendon Press.
Veyne, P. (1961) 'Vie de Trimalchio', *Annales:economiques-sociétés-civilisations*, 16, 213-47.
Veyne, P. (1990) (Pearce, B. tr.) *Bread and Circuses: Historical Sociology and Political Pluralism*, London, Penguin.
Wallace-Hadrill, A. (1994) *Houses and Society in Pompeii and Herculaneum*, Princeton, Princeton University Press.
Watson, A. (1987) *Roman Slave Law*, Baltimore, Johns Hopkins University Press.
Watson, A. (ed. and tr.) (1998) *The Digest of Justinian* (2 vols.), Philadelphia, University of Pennsylvania Press.
Watson, G.R. (1969) *The Roman Soldier*, London, Thames and Hudson.
Weaver, P.R.C. (1972) *Familia Caesaris: A Social study of the Emperor's Freedmen and Slaves*, Cambridge, Cambridge University Press.
White, K.D. (1970) *Roman Farming*, London, Thames and Hudson.
Whittaker, C.R. (1985) 'Trade and the aristocracy in the Roman Empire', *Opus*, 4, 1-27.
Wiedemann, T. (1985) 'The regularity of manumission at Rome', *Classical Quarterly*, 35, 162-75.
Wiedemann, T. (1988) 'The duties of freedmen', *Classical Review*, 38, 331-33.
Wiedemann, T.E.J. (1981) *Greek and Roman Slavery*, London, Croom Helm.
Wiegand T. (1894) 'Die puteolanische Bauinschrift,' *Jahrbücher für Klassische Philologie*, Suppl. 20, 660-778.

Will, E.L. (1979) 'The Sestius Amphoras: A Reappraisal,' *Journal of Field Archaeology*, 6, 339-50.

Will, E.L. (2001) 'Defining the *regna vini* of the Sestii', in Goldman N. (ed.) *New Light from Ancient Cosa: Classical Mediterranean Studies in Honor of Cleo Rickman*, New York, Lang, 35-47.

Wiseman, T.P. (1971) *New Men in the Roman Senate 139 BC - AD14*, Oxford, Oxford University Press.

Yeo, C.A. (1946) 'Land and sea transportation in Imperial Italy', *Transactions and Proceedings of the American Philological Association*, 77, 221-244.

Zahn, E. (1968) (rev'd 1976) *Die Igeler Säule bei Trier*, Neuss, Rheinische Kunststätten.

INDEX

PEOPLE

Free and freed male Romans are listed under family name (*nomen*), free and freed women under first name, slaves under their single name.

Emperors are listed under names in present-day common use. Resident aliens are identified by their place of origin. Ancient authors are referenced when they are discussing commercial or financial matters in which they are directly involved or have special competence. **Sulpicius Cinnamus, C.** and **Sulpicius Faustus, C.** appear throughout Chapters 2-9.

Aelius Lamia, L., Roman businessman 235, 240

Aelius Secundinus, P., Gallic cloth merchant 229

Annaeus Seneca, L., ('the younger Seneca'), senator, author and businessman 26-8, 165, 173, 216, 235

Annius Plocamus, P., Puteolan merchant 36

Annius Plocamus, tax farmer 36

Annius Seleucus, P., Puteolan warehouse manager 99-101, 130, 139, 143

Annius, M., Puteolan merchant 36

Ateius, Cn., pottery manufacturer 249

Attius Severus, P., fish oil importer 69, 103-17

Aufidius Fortis, P., Ostian magistrate and merchant 185

Augustus, emperor 13, 23, 25-6, 33-5, 38-41, 48, 57-8, 119-20, 173, 191, 198, 216, 219, 221, 253

Aurelius Appianus, wealthy Alexandrian 239

Aurelius Paesis, Egyptian potter 168

Avianius Flaccus, C. (1), Puteolan merchant 39

Avianius Flaccus, C. (2), Puteolan magistrate 39

Barbatius Epaphroditus, M., Puteolan arbitrator 157-8

Blossius Celadus, C., Puteolan judge 148

Blossius, C., Puteolan businessman 35, 193, 194

Bulla Felix, bandit chief 253

Caecilius Felix, L., founder of Bank of Jucundus 88

Caecilius Jucundus, L., Pompeian banker 37, 80, 83, 88-90, 130-1, 226

Callimachus, deep-sea merchant 181-2

Callistus, banker and Pope 48

Calpurnius Capitolinus, L., Puteolan magistrate 33

Calpurnius Daphnus, L., Roman banker 82

Cassius Cerealis, L., Puteolan magistrate 37

Cassius Frontinus, Dacian banker 62-3

Castricius [---], A., Puteolan banker 80, 249

Chelidon, mistress of Verres 201, 252

Claudius Sabinus, M., Egyptian banker 182-3
Claudius, emperor 14, 30-2, 35-6, 41, 43, 47, 58, 65, 104, 114, 120, 139, 151, 198, 219
Clodia Metelli, Roman socialite 38
Clodius Rufus, L., Puteolan magistrate 140
Cluvius, M., Puteolan financier 39-40
Cocceius Auctus, L., architect 34, 191
Cominius Abascantus, Q., trader at Misenum 42
Cornelius Scipio Aemilianus, P., senator 52, 173
Cornificius, Verres' clerk 201
Cossinius Priscus, A., Puteolan magistrate 148

Dicidia Margaris, Pompeian moneylender 81
Diognetus, slave of Cypaerus 95-6, 139, 142
Diphilus, building contractor 189-90
Domitia Lepida, aristocratic warehouse owner 35, 101, 121, 143
Domitia Lucilla, aristocratic brickfield owner 220
Domitian, emperor 41

Epichares of Athens 74, 125-7, 129, 132, 247
Euplia of Melos 69, 71-2, 125-7, 129, 132, 247
Evenus Primianus, freedman of the emperor Gaius 68, 93, 138-9

Fabius Agathinus, M., Pompeian businessman 89
Fadii, Narbonese merchants 109-10, 250-1
Faenius Thallus, L., Roman advocate 156
Faustilla, Pompeian moneylender 49
Flavius Petro, T., banker (grandfather of Vespasian) 48
Fortis, lamp manufacturer 250

Gaius ('Caligula'), emperor 28, 40, 93, 97, 141
Galba, emperor 252

Granius Probus, L., Puteolan magistrate 36, 154
Granius, P., Puteolan merchant 36

Habonius, L., Roman building contractor 192, 198, 199-202
Hadrian, emperor 191, 216, 250
Haterius Tychicus, Q., Roman building contractor 190
Hesychus, slave-agent of (1) Evenus Primianus, (2) the emperor Gaius, 68, 93-99, 138-9, 141
Hordionius, T., wealthy Puteolan 40
Hortensius Hortalus, Q., senator and advocate 39, 82, 185, 220, 254

Julius Alexander, Dacian banker 62-3, 251
Julius Caesar, C., dictator 13, 40, 115, 172, 185, 215, 217
Julius Prudens, C., wealthy depositor 61, 66, 140-1
Julius Sporus, Ti., Roman advocate 156
Junius Brutus, D., senator 200-02
Junius Faustus, M., Ostian magistrate and merchant 185
Junius Moderatus Columella, L., agronomist 131, 134, 235, 237, 241, 253
Junius, P., Roman building contractor 200, 202

Laecanii Bassi, Istrian landowners and merchants 250
Lichas of Tarentum (fictional), sea captain 24, 111
Licinius Crassus, M., senator and property developer 172, 196, 198, 206, 220
Licinius Privatus, M., Ostian businessman 245
Longidienus, P., Ravenna shipbuilder 27, 176
Lucceius Peculiaris, building contractor 191

Marcus Aurelius, emperor 216
Marius Agathemer, L., Puteolan textile merchant 84-6
Marius Jucundus, L., Puteolan grain dealer 70-1, 99-102
Matutinius Maximus, M., Gallic textile merchant 166
Menelaus of Ceramos, Puteoli-based shipper 69, 103-17
Mescidius, building contractor 189-90
Messius, Puteolan money-changer 249
Modestius Macedo, manager in cloth trade 229, 233

Naevius, S., partner in cattle-ranching enterprise 146, 171
Nero, emperor 11, 31-2, 35, 37-8, 41, 43, 58, 204, 208, 211, 214, 216,
Nicephorus, bailiff and building contractor 190
Novius Cypaerus, C., Puteolan warehouse manager 95, 139, 142
Novius Eunus, C., Puteolan grain dealer 68-9, 73-5, 77, 92-99, 128, 138, 141-2, 248

Octavius C., (grandfather of Augustus), banker 48
Octavius, trader in northern Britain 166-7

Paquedius Festus, L., Roman building contractor 191
Philogenes, Atticus' agent in Ephesus 53
Plancius Cn., chairman of Asian tax farming company 233
Plinius Caecilius Secundus, C., ('the younger Pliny'), senator, advocate and landowner 77, 151, 172-3, 187, 191, 197, 234, 252-3
Plinius Secundus, C., ('the elder Pliny'), senator and polymath 17-18, 25, 28, 36, 115, 134
Pompeius Magnus, Cn. ('Pompey'), senator 39, 211, 213
Pompeius Paulinus, prefect of the grain supply 26
Pomponius Atticus, T., elite financier 39, 47, 53, 134, 174, 179, 196, 220, 252-5
Pomponius, T., merchant and government contractor 171
Porcius Cato, M., ('the elder Cato'), senator and businessman 83, 85, 107, 152, 165-6, 171, 173-4, 180, 185, 188, 218-9, 238, 255
Postumius, M., merchant and government contractor 171
Primus, slave-agent of Attius Severus 69, 103-17, 139
Ptolemy of Alexandria, Pompeian textile trader 90
Puteolanus Aquila, Q., Puteolan magistrate 154

Quinctius, P., partner in cattle-ranching enterprise 146, 153, 171
Quintio, Cato's agent in maritime ventures 171

Rabirius Postumus, C., merchant and tax farmer 25, 185, 214
Roscius, S., Italian landowner 172
Rufrius, supplier of oil-milling equipment 166

Saccius Modestus, L., manager in cloth trade 229, 233
Secundinius Aventinus, L., cloth merchant 229
Secundinius Securus, L., cloth merchant 229
Sentius Felix, Cn., Ostian magistrate and merchant 186
Sestius, L., (1), businessman 220-26
Sestius, L., (2), son of Sestius P., senator and businessman 220-26
Sestius, P., senator and businessman 220-26

Sulpicius Eutychus, C., procurator of Sulpicius Cinnamus 56, 60-2, 87, 249
Sulpicius Onirus, C., successor to Sulpicius Cinnamus 54-5, 61-2, 81, 138

Terentia, Cicero's wife 119-20
Terentius Hispo, P., managing director of Asian tax farming company 212, 233
Terentius Varro, M., antiquarian and agronomist 16, 59, 219, 225, 236
Tiberius, emperor 34, 40, 141, 204, 216, 253
Titinius Anthus, A., Puteolan judge 147-8, 154
Trajan, emperor 32, 58, 172, 187, 191, 197, 253
Trimalchio (fictional) 43-46, 56, 58-59, 85, 108, 173, 176, 186, 235, 239, 245
Trimalchio's guests (fictional) 43-46
Tullius Cicero, M., (1) senator, advocate and author 38-41, 53-54, 110-11, 189-90, 206-7, 212, 254-5
Tullius Cicero, M., (2), son of Cicero (1) 53-54
Tullius Cicero, Q., brother of Cicero (1) 189-90
Turpilius Niger, P., building contractor 191
Turpilius Phronimus, P., building contractor 191

Umbricia Antiochis, Pompeian heiress 130-2, 143, 226
Umbricius Scaurus, A. (1), Pompeian producer of fish sauces 227-8
Umbricius Scaurus, A. (2), Pompeian magistrate 227

Verres C., senator and businessman 167, 185, 192-3, 199-202, 205, 209-12, 237-8
Vespasian, emperor 48, 194-5
Vestinus, L., supervisor of building works on Capitol 194
Vestorius, C., Puteolan businessman 24, 40

Vipsanius Agrippa, M., senator 34, 198-9, 219
Vitruvius Pollio, M., architect and engineer 191, 237, 242

PLACES

Africa 26, 29, 110, 185, 187, 255
Alexandria Troas 187
Alexandria 23, 25-32, 34, 35, 85, 90, 93-96, 100, 101, 107, 180, 183, 184, 214, 239
Apulia 225
Aquileia 115
Arabia 25, 33, 36
Asia 34, 53, 111, 179, 203-6, 210, 212, 213, 215, 233
Aspendos 187

Baetica 109, 216, 250, 251
Baiae 24, 34, 38-41, 43, 123
Bithynia 127, 191, 205, 207, 209, 253
Brundisium 181, 225, 253

Capri 23, 26, 40
Capua 25, 43, 77, 146, 158, 159, 165, 191
Carthage 29, 133
China 25
Cilicia 34, 39, 53, 133, 205, 212, 220, 249
Comum 253
Cosa 220-6, 233, 234
Cumae 34, 39, 43, 54, 79, 191, 239

Dacia 62, 63, 250, 251
Delos 25, 133, 220, 226

Egypt 13, 17, 23-26, 28, 29, 31-33, 35, 36, 92, 108, 173, 177, 180, 182-5, 214, 239, 253, 255
Elba 24
Ephesus 53, 212

Fanum 191

Gaul 64, 110, 115, 141, 166, 171, 189, 223, 224, 226, 232, 249, 250
Grand Congloué 220, 221

Herculaneum 25, 249

Igel 229-33
India 25, 108, 115, 180, 184

Lake Avernus 31, 191
Lake Lucrinus 31, 33, 34
Lambaesis 187

Malaga 192
Milan 166
Misenum 33, 34, 42
Mutina 233
Muziris 183, 184

Nicaea 188
Nicomedia 187, 191
Nola 25, 34, 166
Nuceria 38

Ostia 187
Ostia/Portus
  harbour trades 27, 185
  rivalry with Puteoli 29-33
  wealthy investors 185-6, 245
Oxyrhynchus 168-9

Padua 233
Piraeus 31
Pompeii 7, 9-11, 25, 34, 36-39, 49, 54, 79, 81, 88, 90, 91, 130, 131, 143, 166, 226, 227, 239, 251
Portus Julius 33, 34
Puteoli
  amphitheatre 35, 37
  an entrepôt 23
  annona staff 26

augustales 41
Augustan city 33-35
contract for rebuilding wall 193-4
fish and meat markets 35
harbour works 31-32
leading families 34-37, 185
manufacture and trade 23-28
merchants 33-34
mise en scène for *Cena Trimalchionis* 43
pivotal role in Rome's grain supply 29-33
projected canal to Tiber 31-32
public building contract 35, 37
public disorder 38
role of freedmen 41-46
served by aqueduct 34
slave trade 24-25
Temple of Serapis 35
visitors 38-41
worship of foreign gods 33

Ravenna 27, 176
Red Sea 25, 36, 108, 183
Rome
  building work on the Colosseum 194
  elite demand for goods 25
  government interest in Puteoli 23, 38
  headquarters of *annona* 26
  high prices 33
  imports of wheat 26, 29-33
  sea routes via Puteoli 28
  money markets 165
  public works Chapter 12 passim
  restoration of Temple of Castor and Pollux 192-193, 199-202

Settefinestre 223
Sicily 209-11, 233, 237-8, 240, 241
Sicyon 255
Spain 104, 109-10, 114, 115, 116, 170, 203, 227, 250-1

Syria 28, 34, 181, 205

Tifernum 77, 172, 234, 252
Trier 228-9, 232
Turdetania 104, 176-7

Veleia 172, 253
Venafrum 189-90
Vindolanda 13, 166, 240-1
Volturnum 77, 165

GENERAL TOPICS

Accounting 50-52, 56, 238-40
Annona 26-33
Augustales 41-42

Capital in kind 167, 198-9

Elite households 55-60
Elite wealth 171-4
Estate-based enterprises 218-20
Euergetism 173, 187
Exercitores 175-6

Finance for shipping 176-86
Financial guarantees 195-6
Freedmen 41-46, 57-60
Freedwomen 120-1

Garum trade 115-6, 226-8
Grain trade 26-33, 92-102

Harbour and port trades 27

Institores 56-57, 65, 93, 106-7, 125, 139, 166, 226, 236-7

Junian Latins 58-59

Kalendarium 56, 240, 245

Leasing 167-9
lex Claudia 8, 115, 185, 195

Mancipes 89, 174, 188, 194, 196, 203-4, 208-9
Maritime loans 180-6
Mercatores 27, 34, 36, 85, 92, 107-9, 176, 224-5
Mining 170, 218-9
Money market 165
Moneylending 49, 62, 173, 237, 240

Naval bases 33
Navicularii 27, 109-11, 113, 161, 176-7, 216
Negotiatores 26-27, 30, 42, 109, 114-5, 161, 166, 176-7, 186, 216, 225, 232

Officinatores 220, 237-8

Partnerships 15-17, 45-46, 51, 59-63, 89-90, 96, 133-4, 169-71, 180, 185, 187, 191, 196, 199-200, 202, 203-14
Peculium 57, 59, 60, 98-99, 105-7, 136, 139-42, 190, 244-5
Postal service 110-11
Praedes 192-3, 196, 204
Procurators 56, 60-62, 67, 71, 87, 105, 114, 121, 123, 150, 197, 215-6, 233-6, 238, 240, 248-9
Public disorder 38, 220
Public slaves 37, 71, 141

Redemptores 188, 190-1

Sailing season and journey times 28, 30, 76-7, 116, 171, 180
Shipwrecks 29, 32, 108, 112, 171, 220
Shipyards 27, 176-7, 237
Stonemasons 169, 198-9
Sub-contracts 187, 194-5, 197, 203, 226, 232

Textile trade 74, 85, 120, 228-33

Trade credit 166-7, 252

Underwater archaeology 220

Vilici 56, 131-2, 190, 210, 235-41

Welfare scheme 172, 253

If you are interested in purchasing other books published by Tempus,
or in case you have difficulty finding any Tempus books in your local bookshop,
you can also place orders directly through our website

www.tempus-publishing.com